Ezra Pound:
The Last Rower

Ezra Pound, Venice, 1960s. (*Copyright by Horst Tappe.*)

Ezra Pound: The Last Rower

A Political Profile by

C. David Heymann

A Citadel Press Book
Published by Carol Publishing Group

ACKNOWLEDGMENTS:

Chicago Sun-Times: From "Pound, Accused of Treason, Calls Hitler Saint, Martyr," by Edd Johnson. May 9, 1945.

City Lights: From *Encounters with Ezra Pound* by Allen Ginsberg. Copyright © 1974 by City Lights Books. Reprinted by permission of City Lights Books.

The John Day Co., Publishers: From *The Trial of Ezra Pound* by Julien Cornell. Copyright © 1966 by Julien Cornell. Reprinted by permission of The John Day Co., Publishers.

Mary de Rachewiltz: From *Discretions*.

Holt, Rinehart and Winston, Inc.: From *Selected Letters of Robert Frost* edited by Lawrance Thompson. Copyright © 1964 by Lawrance Thompson and Holt, Rinehart and Winston, Inc. Reprinted by permission of Holt, Rinehart and Winston, Publishers, and the Estate of Robert Frost.

Macmillan Publishing Co. Inc., M. B. Yeats, Miss Anne Yeats, and Hart-Davis Macgibbon Limited: From *The Letters of W. B. Yeats*, Allan Wade, Ed. Copyright © 1953, 1954 by Anne Butler Yeats. Reprinted by permission.

Sheri Martinelli: From a letter to Ezra Pound.

Eustace Mullins: From *This Difficult Individual, Ezra Pound*, (Fleet, 1961).

New Directions Publishing Corp.: Ezra Pound, from *The Cantos*, Copyright 1934, 1937, 1940, 1948, © 1956, © 1959, © 1962, © 1963, © 1965, © 1966, © 1968, © 1969, © 1970, © 1972 by Ezra Pound. From *Gaudier-Brzeska*, Copyright © 1970 by Ezra Pound; all rights reserved. From *Guide to Kulchur*, Copyright © 1970 by Ezra Pound. From *The Literary Essays*, Copyright 1918, 1920, 1935 by Ezra Pound. From *The Selected Letters (1907-1941)*, D. D. Paige, Ed., Copyright 1950 by Ezra Pound. From *Selected Poems*, Copyright 1949 by Ezra Pound. From *Selected Prose 1909-1965*, William Cookson, Ed., Copyright © 1950 by Ralph Fletcher Seymour, Copyright © 1955 by Ezra Pound, Copyright © 1973 by the Estate of Ezra Pound. From *Pavannes and Divagations*, Copyright © 1958 by Ezra Pound.

From *Make It New*, Copyright 1935, © 1963 by Ezra Pound. Henry Miller, from *Stand Still Like the Hummingbird*, Copyright © 1962 by Henry Miller. Hilda Doolittle, from *Collected Poems of H. D.*, Copyright 1925, 1953 by Norman Holmes Pearson. William Carlos Williams, from *Autobiography*, Copyright 1948, 1949, 1951 by William Carlos
(*Continued on next page*)

To the Memory of My Father
Ernest Frederic Heymann
1887–1965

If an artist falsifies his report as to the nature of man, as to his own nature, as to the nature of his ideal of the perfect, as to the nature of his ideal of this, that or the other, of god, if god exist, of the life force, of the nature of good and evil, if good and evil exist, of the force with which he believes or disbelieves this, that or the other, of the degree in which he suffers or is made glad; if the artist falsifies his reports on these matters or on any other matter in order that he may conform to the taste of his time, to the proprieties of a sovereign, to the conveniences of a preconceived code of ethics, then that artist lies. If he lies out of deliberate will to lie, if he lies out of carelessness, out of laziness, out of cowardice, out of any sort of negligence whatsoever, he nevertheless lies and he should be punished or despised in proportion to the seriousness of his offence.

—"The Serious Artist," 1913

Tard, très tard je t'ai connue, la Tristesse,
I have been hard as youth sixty years.

(Canto LXXX)

Contents

*Illustrations appear on pages 41–47, 127–31,
203–204, 279–92*

Preface

Ezra Pound, with his unencumbered sensibility[1]*—a sensibility that would not waver or compromise—was so steeped in controversy for most of his career that there is a danger that his genuine abilities and his considerable contribution to literature will be forever tarnished. Certainly his embracing of anti-Semitism, his turning to Fascism and, to a lesser extent, Nazism, his prewar and postwar flirting with fanatics on the political fringe, have done little to help his reputation.

But there was another side to Pound: the discerning mentor, the astute critic, the persevering guide. An editorial in *The New York Times* on November 5, 1972, a few days after his death, hailed Pound as the great midwife of twentieth-century English letters, a man who had a hand in bringing out the work of some of the most illustrious writers of the modern era. He considered the art of poetry a sacred trust and "could not have been more devoted to that cause than a religious to his faith." As much as anyone, Pound turned the course of English and American writing from the Victorian to the modern. Both by his own practice and by persuasion he helped his fellow laborers to carry out their ideas and taught them to be stubborn, as a poet must be who intends to do good work, in spite of editors and publishers and scornful friends. Above all, he left in *Personae* and in parts of *The Cantos* a body of work that will not die.

The problem, then, for reader and critic alike is how best to reconcile such disparate elements as a man's work and his life. Can a work of

* The figures refer to the Notes, which begin on page 343.

art stand outside the life of the man who created it? The case of Ezra Pound evokes additional problems as well, critical problems, the question of genius and sanity, the artist's relation to society, the relation of poetics and aesthetics to political ideology. At what point, if any, should man-made and tyrannically enforced law take precedence over what an individual conceives in his heart to be divine law? This is the unresolved dilemma at the core of Sophocles' *Antigone*; and there is no age (including Pound's), in the two thousand years since the play was written, that hasn't seen itself mirrored in this conflict.

Pound will no doubt always be regarded as a hugely problematic figure. His supporters have tended in the past to depict him in terms most favorable to him—to emphasize the power of his poetry—but have ignored some of the paramount concerns—economic and political—that plagued him during a major portion of his life. Conversely, there are those more interested in the fact that he was an anti-Semite, a drumbeater for Hitler and Mussolini, than they are in coming to terms with his poetry. The poetry, let us not forget, is difficult and often obscure; it is much easier to think of Pound as a political fanatic and to dismiss his verse as the work of a madman.

The task, as I perceived it, was to present a multidimensional perspective of the poet, an objective and documented study of Pound's case for treason against the United States during World War II. I felt strongly that his political and economic attitudes were integral to his achievement and as such merited a more detailed treatment than had previously been rendered. In this endeavor I was greatly aided by the timely intervention of Attorney General Elliot Richardson. It was Richardson, acting in the wake of Watergate, who made available to me, under the Freedom of Information Act, the massive FBI files on Pound. Clarence M. Kelley, director of the FBI, was helpful in carrying out the Attorney General's directives. And Special Agent Allen H. McCreight, of the Washington bureau, was responsible for sifting through the files and culling out the appropriate material.

Other acknowledgments are also due. First of all, Ezra Pound and Olga Rudge: their hospitality during my two brief visits to Venice in 1971 and 1972 provided me with all the inspiration I would ever need to complete this study.

I am grateful to Mary de Rachewiltz, James Laughlin, Omar Pound, and the trustees of the Ezra Pound estate for reading an early version of this book and offering many helpful suggestions. This is not to say that they approved of the way I treated some of the poet's views, but I did have the advantage of their guidance and judgment.

I wish to thank the following U.S. government agencies and bureaus for their assistance in securing certain documents and records: The Adjutant General's Office, Department of the Army; The Bureau of Intelligence and Research, Department of State; Foreign Affairs Document and Reference Center, Department of State; General Services Administration, National Archives and Records Service; Training and Research Services, Saint Elizabeths Hospital, Department of Health, Education, and Welfare; World War II Records Division, National Archives and Records Service.

In addition to those libraries and special collections which appear in the Notes section of this book I am indebted to the respective staffs of The Paterno Library, Casa Italiana, Columbia University; The Library of the State University of New York at Stony Brook; and The Wabash College Library.

I am especially grateful to those who provided me with data and information by which I could corroborate my own point of view of what was vital and important in the formation of Pound's thought: Sherman Adams, Carlos Baker, Ronald Bayes, Julian Beck, Marcella Spann Booth, Basil Bunting, Stephan Chodorov, Robert Connolly, Julien Cornell, Guy Davenport, Valerie Eliot, David Farmer, Abe Fortas, R. Buckminster Fuller, Donald Gallup, Carl Gatter, Allen Ginsberg, Giovanni Giovannini, Roger Guedalla, Gabriel Hauge, Mary Hemingway, Eva Hesse, T. David Horton, Harry Levin, Archibald MacLeish, Jackson Mac Low, Harold Mantell (Films for the Humanities), Sheri Martinelli, Harry M. Meacham, Martha Miller, Eustace Mullins, Isamu Noguchi, Norman Holmes Pearson, Camillo Pellizzi, Henry E. Petersen, William D. Rogers (Arnold and Porter), William P. Rogers, Aditi Nath Sarkar, Catherine Seelye, Frances Steloff, Noel Stock, Henry Swabey, Aldo Tagliaferri, José Vázquez-Amaral, John Voss (American Academy of Arts and Sciences), Francis O. Wilcox, Louis Zukofsky.

I was supported in part by a grant from the American P.E.N. Center in New York. I should like to record a special note of thanks to my friend, Leah Shatavsky; her patience and unfailing encouragement helped me through the most trying days. Also to my editor, Richard Seaver, whose boundless energy I greatly admire. And to Georgette

Felix, for whose careful reading I am indebted. Finally, I must mention my mother, Renée Heymann, and my wife, Jeanne: their love was steadfast and true.

C.D.H.

Settings

(1885–1939)

1

In 1969, early June, Ezra Pound—elegant in old age, the voice silenced
—came back to the United States on what was to be his final visit.
Among other things, he had in mind an expedition to his birthplace. He
wanted to make the voyage over again, to return, as he had once put it,
to the frontier.

His father, Homer Loomis Pound, had moved to Hailey, Territory
of Idaho, in 1884, with his bride, to open a U.S. government land office
for registering mining claims. Miners came from as far away as two
hundred miles to file their claims and have their ore assayed. Intending
to stay, Homer built the settlement's first plaster residence, a large frame
building, with three bedrooms, living room, music room, dining room,
kitchen, and pantry. There was a good-sized lawn to the south and west
of the house, a stone wall separating the property from the one adjacent
to it. All through the years, the structure remained intact, the outside
unchanged except for a bay window, off the living room, which had been
eliminated by recent occupants. Ezra Pound was born in this house on
October 30, 1885, and he longed to see it again, and the distant Saw-
tooth Mountains, the Big Wood River, and the Salmon River to the
north, "the River of No Return." In the end, when it was discovered how
wearing a journey it would be, the idea was abandoned, and the poet
returned to Italy. There, in the Hidden Nest, the tiny three-room apartment on a shaded side street in the section of Venice called San Gregorio,
not far from where the Giudecca and the Grand Canal come together,
he set out to reread his own earlier accounts of how the odyssey began,
fragments of a nearly forgotten past. To retrace the Homeric "periplum,"
to strike at Dantescan roots: it was his way perhaps of redeeming time,
of consolidating events—in short, of making his life cohere.

What thou lovest well remains,
the rest is dross
What thou lov'st well shall not be reft from thee
What thou lov'st well is thy true heritage
(Canto LXXXI)

A scene and setting: New York City, 1887. "The infant Gargantua," as Pound dubbed himself in his 1923 "experiment" in autobiography ("Indiscretions, or *Une Revue de Deux Mondes*"), was less than two years of age when his family left Idaho. Isabel Weston Pound, the child's mother, had been unable to adjust to the high altitude of Hailey, approximately one mile above sea level. According to record, the trip cross-country was made during the Great Blizzard of 1887, behind the first rotary snowplow, the inventor of which was on board the train. As voyage out, this journey therefore "provided one of those incidents—an idea into action—which had a particular significance for the poet":[1]

> . . . First connection with vorticist movement during the Great Blizzard of '87 when I came East, having decided that the position of Hailey was not sufficiently central for my activities—came East behind the first rotary snow-plough, the inventor of which vortex saved me from croup by feeding me with lumps of sugar saturated with kerosene.
> —Letter to Kate Buss, March 1916[2]

In New York, the family—father, mother, son—stayed with the parents of Isabel Pound, at their brownstone on East Forty-seventh Street: "And the infant Gargantua lay in his parambulator or baby carriage (*anglicé*: pram) in the back-yard (*anglicé*: garden) of 24 E. 47th St., by the cellar doorway, and above the cellar was the basement, and above the basement was the first floor." Probing his own childhood, Pound came to sense the awakening of consciousness as a series of spaced flashes of light—moments and instances of sudden illumination —with the intervals between them gradually diminishing until bright blocks of perception were formed and seized by the mind. Among his truncated autobiographical reveries we have, for example, a picture of the infant lying in his carriage in the back-yard while from a window his uncle dangled a strawberry on a piece of cotton to teach him to look about, "to look up and be ready for the benefits of the gods, whether so whither they might come upon him."

A process was taking hold. With great voracity the young child began to absorb the sights and sounds of his new environment. Coupled with remembrances of subsequent visits to New York, made as a school-boy, a historiographical landscape presented itself, which in its turn was sketched:

> The New York "wharves," as heaped with watermelons and bushel-baskets of peaches, must have been not too unlike the old fruit market and other seemingly endless "Covent Gardens" on the west side "down town," to which I was taken. . . . I remember a man throwing a large jack-knife some fifty feet áfter a fleeing male figure. The incident was unique so far as I was concerned, but seemed to arouse no curiosity among the bystanders. . . .

> And at the end of the street jingled the small horse bells of the Madison Avenue horse-cars, bobbing down towards the white-washed tunnel, and beyond the car line was the Express Company, and beyond that the tracks from the "Grand Central," invisible because of the wall and the Express Company; and beyond that was 596, Lexington Avenue—with the cable cars.
>
> —*Indiscretions*, 1923

At quite another juncture—amidst the loneliness and uncertainty of the Detention Training Center outside Pisa, 1945—this same New York would come back to him, the inspiration or spirit of the moment a welling up of memory or emotion, the voice detached but personal, "perfectly suited to the mood of quiet regret for something once known, that is now gone, and yet somehow seems to live on":[3]

> and the remains of the old South
> tidewashed to Manhattan and brown-stone
> or (later) the outer front stair
> leading to Mouquin's
> or old Train (Francis) on the pavement in his plain wooden chair
> or a fellow throwing a knife in the market
> past baskets and bushels of peaches
> at $1. the bushel
> and the cool of the 42nd St. tunnel   (periplum)
> white-wash and horse cars, the Lexington Avenue cable
> refinement, pride of tradition . . .
>
> (Canto LXXIV)

I don't have to try to be American. Merrymount, Brain-tree, Quincy, all I believe in or by, what had been "a

plantation named Weston's." Vide also the host in Longfellow's "Wayside Inn." Wall ornament there mentioned
still at my parents'.

—Letter to Hubert Creekmore,
February 1939[4]

There were factoidal rumors of family ancestors having landed on
the American shore aboard the *Lion*, at an appropriately short interval
after the *Mayflower*.[5] The Westons, forebears of the aforementioned
New York City clan, had owned a large farm in early New England.
Quakers and whalers by the name of Pound had settled in New Jersey
and had later moved to Pennsylvania. Ezra was distantly related on his
mother's side to Captain Joseph Wadsworth "who in 1687 stole the
Connecticut charter and hid it in Charter Oak, to protect it, apparently,
from the designs of the Governor-general";[6] he was also related to the
poet Henry Wadsworth Longfellow, a fact, claimed D. H. Lawrence, he
was constantly trying to live down.

Other family ties can be linked to his choice of middle names. To fit
the occasion and period of his life, he went through a number of alterna-
tives, variously signing himself Ezra Weston Pound, Ezra Weston
Loomis Pound, and, what seems to be his first choice, Ezra Loomis
Pound. That choice is probably due to admiration for his Loomis ascen-
dants, some of whom had fought in the Revolution, and some of whom
became notorious in upstate New York as "the Loomis Gang." They
were horse thieves but, Pound assures us, "very good horse-thieves,
never . . . brought to book." Investigated by the state legislature, they
were finally rounded up by a posse, with shootings, hangings, and
barn burnings, but the Loomis women, Charles Norman insists, were
not harmed. Two of them eventually married into the Pound family.

Thaddeus Coleman Pound, Ezra Pound's grandfather on his father's side, married one of the Loomis daughters, Susan Angevine, and it
was from her that the writer inherited his middle name. A lumberman
and railroad baron, "T.C.P."—as he appears in *The Cantos*—was also a
party politician, serving as lieutenant-governor of Wisconsin and for
three terms as a member of Congress. A contemporary credits him with
"merchandising in about all of its branches, agriculture in all its forms."
His lumbering concern issued its own scrip, good as money in the company mills and stores:

STATE OF WISCONSIN
Union Lumbering Company
Chippewa Falls
Will pay to the bearer on demand
FIFTY CENTS
IN MERCHANDISE OR LUMBER

In Canto 103, among the thrones, Thaddeus is described as trying in the 1880s "to keep some of the/non interest-/bearing etc./in circulation/as currency." Pound also recollects that "It was only when my father brought some old newspaper clippings to Rapallo . . . that I discovered that T.C.P. had already in 1878 been writing about, or urging among his fellow congressmen, the same essentials of monetary and statal economics that I am writing about today" (*A Visiting Card*, 1942). To be sure, Thaddeus Pound's agreement with Greenback party platforms supporting government control of an adequate supply of money was similar to his grandson's adoption and support of Social Credit fiscal policy. The mixture of agrarian and labor groups that composed the Greenback party constituency corresponded to the poet's ideal of an agrarian-guild craftsman economy. In this sense, Ezra Pound had never abandoned the frontier.

He was eight years old and living at 166 Fernbrook Avenue in Wyncote, Pennsylvania, on the outskirts of Philadelphia, when Grover Cleveland was elected to his second term as President. It was 1893. Pound Senior was assistant assayer at the Philadelphia Mint, the inner workings of which fascinated his son. "The principle of gold assaying can be grasped by the normal mind," Ezra wrote in 1920. It is true: the process of assaying gold is more or less mechanistic in design. It is weighed, then refined and weighed again. The refining fire floats the "dross" to the top; the grade of the ore is determined by the relative weights, by what remains. What counts is the incredibly delicate machinery of the scales:

> The gold balance lives in its own glass house; the gold and the weights are lifted by longish forceps. The balances have tantrums in thundery weather. They will weigh you an eyelash; they will weigh you a bit of hair an eyelash long, but which weighs considerably less than an eyelash. I have known Homer to weigh a man's name on his visiting card. Very simple. You weigh the card, then you have the man write his name on it

in pencil; then you weigh the card with the signature. This is, however, rather a stunt.

—*Indiscretions*, 1923

Silver is an entirely different matter. The procedure of assaying silver, like the process of placing one musical note in juxtaposition to another or of gauging the stroke of a paint brush against canvas, is an almost indefinable art. Words alone can not describe it. "You just look at some stuff in a bottle,"[7] was one explanation Pound offered. At another point he put it in similar though somewhat more explicit terms: "The test for silver is a cloudy solution; the accuracy of the eye in measuring the thickness of the cloud is an aesthetic perception, like the critical sense."[8] In the soundproof rooms of the Jupiter and Chestnut Street Mint the future versifier was already interested in exact detail: "I like the idea of the fineness of the metal, and it moves by analogy to the habit of testing verbal manifestations." Seen in a different light, and in a suitably altered context, this might have been Aristophanes speaking.

Eighteen ninety-three was also the year the Administration called for a recount of the silver coinage. Ra, as he then spelled his name (pronounced "Ray"), watched as workmen in the Mint vaults shoveled the coins into immense binlike counting machines: "All the bags had rotted in these enormous vaults, and they were heaving it into the counting machines with shovels bigger than coal shovels. This spectacle of coin being shoveled around like it was litter—these fellows naked to the waist shoveling it around in the gas flares—things like that strike your imagination."[9] This image, once implanted, remained with him. In Canto 97, in the volume *Thrones de los Cantares*, composed some sixty years later during his incarceration at St. Elizabeths, there is mention of these same silver dollars, 37¼ grains silver, the language toned down, the sense of the setting transmogrified into declarative, matter-of-fact verse: "And I have seen them by shovels full/lit by gas flares." And as part of this same book, in Canto 105, the full impact of the subject is, irrevocably and in a single cutting phrase, driven home: "Coin is the symbol of equity."

At age twelve, during the summer of 1898, he was taken on a three-month long European vacation by his Great Aunt "Frank" from New York, set forth in *Indiscretions* as an adventurous dowager who "believed that travel broadened the mind" and was apt to use, as she did, only one adjective to sum up all the sights seen: "Beautiful"[10]—"but at least she saw damn all Europe/and rode on that mule in Tangiers/and in general had a run for her money" (Canto 84). (A photograph of the "redoubtable" relative astride the mule remained in Ezra Pound's possession, found its way post-St. Elizabeths to his tower suite atop Schloss Brunnenburg, his daughter's castle in northern Italy, and then, in 1961, to his third-story studio in Venice.)[11]

Their voyage, recorded by Pound in letters home, had all the makings of a Baedeker Grand Tour—London, Brussels, Cologne, a journey down the Rhine to Bingen and Mainz, a stay in the Alps (Lucerne and Como), a side trip to Tangiers, and finally Naples, Rome, Florence, and Venice. It was this last port of call—"the Queen of the Adriatic"—which was to play so vital a role as major segment and locus of the poet's luminous dream: "Venice struck me as an agreeable place —as, in fact, more agreeable than Wyncote, Pa., or '47th' and Madison Avenue. I announced an intention to return. I have done so. I do not know quite how often. By elimination of possible years: 1898, 1902, 1908, 1910, 1911, 1913, 1920" (*Indiscretions*, 1923).

The next junket abroad, following his freshman year at college, was made with his father in 1902 and featured, in addition to the return trip to Venice, a visit to London's Royal Mint. Both Americans were struck by the reserve and sobriety of their British hosts: "There was none of that congenial 'You can have it if you will carry it out,' with which the, I think, 10,000-dollar-size bag used to be treated." This notation, also from his autobiographical jottings, is a passing reference to the Philadelphia Mint, where the standard game among workmen was to tell the visitor he could keep one of the bags of gold provided he could carry it away, a feat which invariably proved, to the victim's dismay, impossible to accomplish.

On the strength of a University of Pennsylvania Harrison Fellowship in Romance Languages, Pound crossed the Atlantic a third time, in 1906, to gather material at the British Museum and at the Royal Library of Madrid for a projected doctoral thesis, ultimately aborted, on the dramatic works of Lope de Vega.[12] The remainder of his seven-month sojourn was spent tramping about Provence, the Spanish countryside, and the lake-and-hill interior of northern Italy. In the course of his travels, Pound came to think of himself as a modern-day troubadour (a "finder"), whose job it was to dig up and rechannel the terrain of a long-extinguished medieval past: "A man may walk the hill roads and river roads from Limoges and Charente to Dordogne and Narbonne and learn a little, or more than a little, of what the country meant to the wandering singers; he may learn, or think he learns, why so many canzos open with speech of the weather, or why such a man made war on such and such castles" ("Troubadours—Their Sorts and Conditions," 1913).

In rethinking twelfth-, thirteenth-, and fourteenth-century modes and conventions, the wayfarer made a strategic discovery: the Middle Ages, as he came upon them in 1906, did not exist in woven tapestry alone, nor in the period romances he had so assiduously pored over in a graduate seminar the year before. There was in Provence a life like our own: "Men were pressed for money; there was unspeakable boredom in the castles." This schematic interpretation of the spatial and temporal flow of history ("all time is eternally present;" "all ages are contemporaneous") helps to explain, among other things, how a poem of potentially epic proportion could hope to proceed and cohere without so much as an initial blueprint. It is clear that *le jeune* had already begun to fasten his gaze, if only remotely, upon his lifelong love and labor, the ideogrammically linked *Cantos*.

I knew at fifteen pretty much what I wanted to do. . . . I resolved that at thirty I would know more about poetry than any man living, that I would know the dynamic content from the shell . . . what part of poetry was "indestructible," what part could *not be lost* by translation . . . what effects were attainable in *one* language only and were utterly incapable of being translated.

In this search I learned more or less of nine foreign languages, I read Oriental stuff in translations, I fought every University regulation and every professor who tried to make me learn anything except this or who bothered me with "requirements for degrees."

Of course, no amount of scholarship will help a man write poetry, it may even be regarded as a great burden and hindrance, but it does help him to destroy a certain percentage of his failures. It keeps him discontented with mediocrity.

—"How I Began," 1913

Ezra Pound, William Carlos Williams writes in his autobiography, was basically shy, but hearty and good-humored, headstrong and hopeful. Above all, he was self-confident and certain of his future. Knowing, as

Ezra attests he did, that he wanted to become a man of letters, he persevered to take two degrees (Ph.B. Hamilton, 1905; M.A. Pennsylvania, 1906).[13] In June 1907, for reasons never explained, the University of Pennsylvania discontinued his graduate fellowship, forcing his withdrawal from the doctoral program. "So far as I know I was the only student who was making any attempt to understand the subject of literary criticism," he later protested, "and the only student with any interest in the subject." Underlying this assertion from an unpublished 1930 Pound essay was a tone of grave and endured bitterness. The poet "was to spend much of the next two decades putting the facts he had been taught in school together again" in a chronometrical pattern of his own design, relearning the elementals of learning, and excoriating American universities as though they were all indistinguishable from "the U. of P. or the Wabash of Indiana."[14]

The Wabash (Wabash College, Crawfordsville, Indiana): "Whole d—d dept., French, Spanish and Italian, to run as I hang please,"[15] he wrote his parents shortly before departing for the fall semester to teach in the Department of Romance Languages. And six weeks later, having sampled his first morsel of unsophisticated Indianian Kulchur—"the sixth circle of desolation"—he wrote again: "There seems to be plenty to be done here. Of course if you can find . . . as good a job for me somewhere in the effete east I would be very likely to abandon me 'igh callin' and skidoo to paats more plush-lined than Hoosier."[16] Pound need not have fretted: within four months of his arrival in Crawfordsville his year-long instructor's contract had been voided.

The story, soap-operatic as it now appears, is that he had fed and lodged a penniless young girl from a stranded burlesque show, whom he had found in a blizzard. The Misses Hall, from whom he had rented the rooms, went up—after his departure the next morning—for the usual cleaning and discovered the sleeping girl. They were maiden ladies in a small Midwestern town and had let the quarters before only to an elderly professor. They telephoned the president of the college and several trustees; the affair became public; only one outcome was possible.[17]

Pound had wanted to leave the country eventually, had said as much before and after Wabash, in conversation and by letter. "I am by natr thank god IMPATIENT, if I hadn't been, I shd. still be teaching half wits in a desert beanery, at Crawfurd'sville, Indiana, which is lowern hell,"[18] read a February 1935 message to Stanley Nott. The Wabash incident provided him with the needed impetus. He traveled by cattle boat from New York, and by early spring of 1908 reached Gibraltar. He had $80 in his pocket, a manuscript of poems, the cloying desire to see those poems in print, and the determination to reach London by way of Venice.[19]

2

I stood still and was a tree amid the wood.
—"The Tree," 1907

Will I ever see the Giudecca again?
    or the lights against it, Ca' Foscari, Ca' Giustinian
or the Ca', as they say, of Desdemona
or the two towers where are the cypress no more
        or the boats moored off le Zattere
or the north quai of the Sensaria . . .
(Canto LXXXIII)

Scanning the view of roof tiles, sky-tones, mud-green tidal influx, cats perched like miniature stone lions on balconies, the voyager felt that he had made a sage choice: Venezia, harbor of dreams, was "an excellent place to come to from Crawfordsville, Indiana"—or from any other place, for that matter. With the aid of a detailed map, Pound explored the near and far reaches of the city: the maze of filigree back alleys, secluded courtyards, bridges, archways, winding passages, dead ends, quaysides, dark overhung side streets, and sudden sunlit open squares. Like *The Cantos*, Venice is a circumfluent labyrinth, a topographical mosaic of incredible intricacy. The observer's art is easy to cultivate in such surroundings; the eye is easily pleased.

He lived over a bakery at 861 Ponte San Vio, close to the Grand Canal, on the way from the Accademia Bridge to Santa Maria della Salute; he moved, during the latter part of his stay, to a room in the San Trovaso section, in the Calle dei Fratti, only a quarter of a mile from San Vio. Immediately opposite his window in San Trovaso, on the other side of the narrow canal, was the workshop "where day and night the gondolas are repaired and repainted still," memories of which, mingled with scenes from later visits, haunt those moments in *The Cantos* given over to Venice:[1]

And the waters richer than glass,
Bronze gold, the blaze over the silver,
Dye-pots in the torch-light,
The flash of wave under prows,
And the silver beaks rising and crossing.
        Stone trees, white and rose-white in the darkness,
Cypress there by the towers,
      Drift under hulls in the night.
               (Canto XVII)

Drift and flow are everything where water is chief. The gondolas in drydock in the vast Piazza San Marco were a reminder for Pound that this canalport was born of illusion, a stone Aphrodite risen from the sea, and that what man took from the sea, the sea would repossess.

He walked by the sea that summer and had no money; he sat on the steps of the Dogana di Mare, the ancient customs house, and watched the changing lights and colors. He ate frugally—an order of baked sweet potatoes at a corner cook-stall for lunch and for supper a bowl of *minestra d'orzo*, barley soup: "in my time/an orzo" (Canto 102).

He wrote, but was not entirely confident about, his maiden book of verse, *A Lume Spento* ("With Tapers Quenched"), then in the process of being printed at his own expense:

> by the soap-smooth stone posts where San Vio
> meets with il Canal Grande
> between Salviati and the house that was of Don Carlos
> shd/I chuck the lot into the tide-water?
>   le bozze A Lume Spento/
>   and by the column of Todero
>   shd/I shift to the other side
>   or wait 24 hours . . .
>   (Canto LXXVI)

He waited. He did not chuck the lot into the tidewater, and *A Lume Spento* emerged shortly in a limited edition of a hundred copies. The period of self-advertisement was under way. Pound's ambitions, for both the book and his own career, were gigantic. "The American reprint," he wrote in a letter home in June, "has got to be worked by kicking up such a hell of a row with genuine and faked reviews that Scribner or somebody can be brought to see the sense of making a reprint. I shall write a few myself and get someone to sign 'em."[2]

At this point, Pound's stiff-wristed Rossetti-and-Swinburne lyrics and Browning-and-sugar-water monologues were not any better or worse than anyone else's. What distinguished this particular poet was his immense will power, his drive and determination, and his intention to set literature and literary trends in order.

To have gathered from the air a live tradition . . .
(Canto LXXXI)

He *is* America. His crudity is an exceeding great stench, but it *is* America. He is the hollow place in the rock that echos with his time. He *does* "chant the crucial stage" and he is the "voice triumphant." He is disgusting. He is an exceedingly nauseating pill, but he accomplishes his mission. . . . He is content to be what he is, and he is his time and his people. He is a genius because he has vision of what he is and of his function. He knows that he is a beginning and not a classically finished work.
—"What I Feel about Walt Whitman," 1909

With his reddish hair and beard and his refined hieratic features, the modern troubadour plunged into the life of the metropolis. Arriving in London in September 1908, he took up residence first in a room at 48 Langham Street, not far from the British Museum, and a year later moved to a small flat at No. 10 Church Walk in Kensington. He soon procured himself a position lecturing on "Developments of Literature in Southern Europe," at the Regent Street branch of the Polytechnic Institute, not with the intention of going back into teaching but simply as a means of supporting himself while he continued to write.

He had come to England, he later said, to meet William Butler Yeats, whose work he greatly admired; within six months he was meeting everyone. He lunched with Laurence Binyon, with Maurice Hewlett; had tea with the novelist May Sinclair; was a guest at a Poets' Club dinner, where he heard George Bernard Shaw expound on the Abbey Theatre; frequented the renowned Square Club; went to literary functions at the home of Ernest Rhys, an original member of the Rhymers' Club of the 1890s—at one of these, when Yeats was also present, Ford Madox Ford brought D. H. Lawrence. "The town seems to want to treat me white," Pound wrote his parents in February 1909. And in May, to William Carlos Williams, the Seafarer scrawled, "There is no town like

London to make one feel the vanity of all art except the highest."³ Several months earlier he had delivered a newly completed manuscript to Elkin Mathews, the *fin-de-siècle* publisher of such Edwardian stellars as Arthur Symons, Lionel Johnson, and Thomas Hardy. *Personae*, a slender volume of sixty-six pages bound in beige boards engraved with gold letters and bearing the lasting dedication—"This book is for Mary Moore of Trenton, if she wants it"—appeared in print mid-April 1909 to the tune of critical raves. At the age of twenty-three Ezra Pound was a moderately recognized poet of rank.

It was through Olivia Shakespear (the Diana Vernon of Yeats's *Memoirs*) that "Old Billyum" and "Ez" were formally introduced. The two, though Yeats was twenty years Pound's senior, were to see a good deal of each other, united by common interests, by Pound's marriage in 1914 to Dorothy Shakespear (Olivia's daughter), and by the marriage of Yeats, three years later, to Georgie Hyde-Lees, the step-daughter of Mrs. Shakespear's brother.

Shortly after meeting Yeats, the younger poet began regularly to attend the elder's Monday evening "at homes" in Woburn Buildings. He evidently made an impression on his host, for Yeats wasted no time in writing Lady Gregory (December 1909) about "this queer creature Ezra Pound, who has become really a great authority on the Troubadours [and] has I think got closer to the right sort of music for poetry than Mrs. Emery [Florence Farr]—it is more definitely music with strong marked time and yet it is effective speech."⁴ And Pound was similarly advising Williams and everyone else he knew to read Yeats's critical essays, and in May 1911 reaffirmed his admiration for the Irish poet in a note to Homer Pound: "Yeats I like very much. I've seen him a great deal, almost daily. . . . He is, as I have said, a very great man, and he improves on acquaintance."

Histories and hagiographies of the period, including those by Douglas Goldring, Richard Aldington, Phyllis Bottome, Edith Sitwell, Brigit Patmore, and Wyndham Lewis, have sufficiently testified to Pound's literary endeavors in London during the years before World War I. William Carlos Williams, who visited the British capital early in 1910, recalled that Pound "lived the poet as few of us had the nerve to live that exalted role in our time." Having scarce funds, he wore a seal-lined "directoire overcoat" indoors and out during cold weather, and a broad-brimmed troubadour hat. To complete the effect, he donned a pince-nez in imitation of Yeats, while one long, single-stone earring flopped across a cheek. At a social gathering he asked a hostess: "Why do you give us solid stuff like roast beef and plum pudding for lunch?" He inquired of the company: "Would you like to see how an American eats an apple?" and proceeded to quarter his and gobble it. At a literary breakfast in one of London's great houses, as Padraic Colum used to relate the tale, Pound, after refusing all offers of food, methodically ate with fork and knife the petals of a rose from the table centerpiece; finding them to his liking, he reached for another rose, and concluded his meal with an exuberant recital of "Ballad of the Goodly Fere." His dashing appearance and alluring manner helped make him the rage of cultivated gatherings. He was trying to master London intellectual society as Oscar Wilde had several decades before. And he possessed all of the prerequisites: enthusiasm, a piercing voice, a shattering laugh, a witty natural-born teacher's gift for provocative pronouncements ("I believe in technique as the test of a man's sincerity"), and a connoisseur's eye for the absurd.[5]

The *Punch* cartoon poses and masks, and the outrageous buffoonery, however, were all show, all part of the charade: Pound, the autocrat, was deadly serious in his purpose. He wanted to overhaul the whole face of poetry. He sought tautness and compactness—every word that was not functional, each superfluity merited elimination. His war was for a quintessential hardness that had been lost, an edge and sense and brevity such as the classics, "ancient and modern," possessed. Poetry, he declared, should have all the virtues of good prose: "There must be no book words, no periphrases, no inversions . . . objectivity and again objectivity, and expression: no hindside-beforeness, no straddled adjectives (as 'addled mosses dank'), no Tennysonianness of speech; nothing —nothing that you couldn't in some circumstance, in the stress of some emotion, actually say."[6] Above all, he had the "precise word" (Flaubert's *le mot juste*) in mind, regardless of the stratum of its origin, regardless even of the language of its origin, whether foreign or English —a preciseness of expression (the critic Jeannette Lander wrote) of which a corresponding exactness of rhythm must be an integral part: "To paint the thing as I see it."

In trying to rid the language of archaisms and similar impediments Pound was assisted by T. E. Hulme, the British doctrinaire philosopher and occasional poet. Hulme and his followers—Joseph Campbell, Francis Tancred, Edward Storer, F. S. Flint—formed a group which met weekly in a small Soho restaurant to discuss the latest trends in literature and to propound new and formidable ways of dealing with the old and conventional "rubble" which then passed for verse. Pound attended these gatherings off and on for a two-year period (1909–11), during which time he also returned briefly and uneventfully (1910) to the United States—the visit was to be his last for three decades.

Hulme's Bergsonian *Speculations*, gleaned from his notes by Herbert Read and published in 1924, seven years after the philosopher's untimely death in the trenches of France, depict him as having sensed, with astonishing accuracy, "a new spirit in the arts—a turn away from the romantic and the rhetorical, and toward the concrete, the geometrical and the precise."[7] The most important political principle which can be gathered from Hulme's writings is that he was a determined authoritarian: "Nothing is bad in itself except disorder; all that is put in order in a hierarchy is good."[8] He saw the changes of his own time—in philosophy (from rationalism to antirationalism); in art (from representationalism to abstraction); in poetry (from rhetoric to precise statement); in politics (from woolly-minded liberalism to hard-edged conservatism)— as constituting a single change, "the destruction of oppressive forces, the installation of a new and improved order."[9] To this end, Hulme's most important contribution to Pound's pre-imagist stance might well have been the authority of a philosophy, or rather the notes for a philosophy.

Another influence on Pound, probably the most profound literary influence, was Ford Madox Ford, the outspoken editor of *The English Review*; like Hulme, he communicated his ideas predominantly through conversation. At first, however, "Pound seems to have prized Ford's conversation mostly for the tales and anecdotes, not for the theories about writing; in fact, he resisted Ford's literary ideas for a number of years."[10] Pound wrote to his mother (August 1911) that he disagreed with Ford "diametrically" on every question: "art, religion, politics, and all therein implied."[11] It is easy to see how and why they were opposed. Ford complained that "most of the verse . . . written today deals in a derivative manner with medieval emotions" (a remark probably directed at Pound) and set himself completely against the kind of poetic diction that showed through some of Pound's early work.[12] Ford was all for an atomically "charged" language, "a sort of *pointillisme*," words shot through with electricity, friction created by ricochet, by the placement of words, one word rubbing up against another. Ford also advocated using "a contemporary spoken or at least speakable language" for literary purposes, the objective being "to register [one's] own times in terms of [one's] own time."

How much Pound came to respect Ford's advice can be deduced from a statement he offered Donald Hall in their 1960 *Paris Review* interview, which was published in 1962: "I made my life in London by going to see Ford in the afternoons and Yeats in the evenings. By mentioning one to the other one could always start a discussion." It was Ford's influence, as much as Pound's, which was so instrumental in Yeats's final emergence out of the incantations of the Celtic Twilight: "As far as the change in Yeats goes, I think that Ford Madox Ford might have some credit. Yeats never would have taken advice from Ford, but I think that Fordie helped him, via me, in trying to get toward a natural way of writing."

Pound's role in the updating of Yeats began at first innocently enough. In October 1912, having recently accepted *Poetry* magazine's offer to become foreign correspondent, he convinced Yeats to give the Chicago journal a boost with a selection of new work. Yeats sent several poems to Pound for transmittal, attaching a note to ask that the punctuation be checked. Pound, finding it difficult to resist temptation, made a number of changes in Yeats's wording. Yeats was infuriated, but then forgave his presumptuous young friend.

During the three winters and springs of 1913–16, E.P. lived and served as "Uncle William's" personal secretary at Stone Cottage, in Ashdown Forest, Sussex, attending to the older poet's needs, reading to him, writing from his dictation, and in general "instructing" him in ways of being more "definite and concrete" in his poetry. Pound wrote his mother (November 1913) that he regarded the position "as a duty to posterity." When Pound married, in April 1914, he brought his wife to live at Stone Cottage. Yeats enjoyed hearing Ezra and Dorothy haggle over modern critical doctrines. He was hardly enthusiastic about *les imagistes*, the group which Pound helped found, but admired their "satiric intensity."[13] He also admired Pound's astounding energy and disinterested intelligence. In 1913, Ernest Fenollosa's widow had entrusted the young instigator with her husband's draft translations of Chinese verse and Japanese noh drama. It was exhilarating for Yeats, always on the prowl for new methods of employing occult research, to learn that the Japanese plays were full of spirits and masks, and that the crisis in the plays usually occurred when a character who had appeared to be an ordinary mortal was suddenly revealed to be a god or spirit.[14] "These plays, or eclogues," noted Pound, "were made only for the few; for the nobles; for those trained to catch the allusion."[15] Yeats called them "an aristocratic form." Pound's redactions of the noh translations had a considerable influence on Yeats, and were responsible for the new phase in his career as a dramatist characterized by *Four Plays for Dancers*.

In 1916, Yeats handed over his father's letters for Pound to edit for the Cuala Press, saying that he represented "the most aggressive contemporary school of the young." And for good reason: by 1916 Pound had either discovered, sponsored, or helped launch ("boomed") the likes of D. H. Lawrence, Rabindranath Tagore, H.D. (Hilda Doolittle) and her husband Richard Aldington, Robert Frost, James Joyce, and T. S. Eliot. In addition, he had championed two major literary movements ("schools"); edited anthologies; rendered translations (or "rehandlings," by G. S. Fraser's reckoning); "Westernized" the Japanese verse forms tanka and hokku; published well-received critical studies (*The Spirit of Romance* and *Gaudier-Brzeska: A Memoir*); contributed to and had his hand in running a number of little magazines, including *The English Review, Poetry, The Egoist* (formerly *The New Freewoman*), and the *Fortnightly Review*. As if all this were not enough, there was also his verse; since *Personae*, he had managed to produce nearly one volume per year—*Exultations, Provença, Canzoni, Ripostes*, and *Lustra*. Horace Gregory called him "the minister without portfolio of the arts"; and Wyndham Lewis described him as "a Demon pantechnicon driver, busy with moving of old world into new quarters"—in Forrest Read's words, "a kind of moving van or storage warehouse" methodically transporting the language of poetry forward out of the old and into the new century.[16]

3

As to Twentieth century poetry, and the poetry which I expect to see written during the next decade or so, it will, I think, move against poppy-cock, it will be harder and saner, it will be what Mr. Hewlett calls "nearer the bone." It will be as much like granite as it can be, its force will lie in its truth, its interpretive power (of course, poetic force does always rest there); I mean it will not try to seem forcible by rhetorical din, and luxurious riot. We will have fewer painted adjectives impeding the shock and stroke of it. At least for myself, I want it so, austere, direct, free from emotional slither.

—"A Retrospect," 1918

An image of Lethe,
   and the fields
Full of faint light. . . .
—"The Coming of War: Actaeon," 1915

"Imagisme," in somewhat dubious French, was a term invented to describe the objective quality of H.D.'s early verse, her ability to get to the nucleus of the word, to present images without representing them.[1] Later called "the perfect Imagist," Hilda Doolittle had turned over to Pound, at his urging, a bale of her latest work. Perusing her "Hermes of the Ways," he made a number of deletions, then scribbled "H. D. Imagiste" at the bottom of the page before posting it (October 1912) to the pioneering Harriet Monroe at *Poetry:*[2]

The hard sand breaks
And the grains of it
Are clear as wine.
Far off over the leagues of it
The Wind,

Playing on the wide shore,
Piles little ridges,
And the great waves
Break over it. . . .

"It is the laconic speech of the Imagistes," read his appended memorandum. "Objective—no slither—direct—no excess of adjectives, etc. No metaphors that won't permit examination. —It's straight talk—straight as the Greek!"[3]

It is doubtful whether Miss Monroe knew at this stage what an "Imagiste" was supposed to be, but she introduced the literary sobriquet to America with the printing of "H. D. Imagiste's" poems in vol. I, no. 4 (January 1913). In the same issue was an article by Pound ("Status Rerum"), in which he referred to the imagists as a live literary group in London, but did not mention his connection with them.

He did not, for that matter, publish a formal declaration, an *ars poetica*, until March 1913. With the appearance in *Poetry* of "A Few Don'ts by an Imagiste," the movement began to define itself: "An 'Image,' is that which presents an intellectual and emotional complex in an instant."

A second article ("Imagisme")—the actual manifesto—signed by F. S. Flint but ghosted by Pound, cited as inspirational lights Sappho, Catullus, and Villon, and reduced the school's rules to three:

1. Direct treatment of the "thing," whether subjective or objective.
2. To use absolutely no word that does not contribute to the presentation.
3. As regarding rhythm: to compose in the sequence of the musical phrase, not in sequence of the metronome.

Clustered around each of these directives were various proscriptions and interdictions. Essentially a compilation of dicta expressed previously in *The Spirit of Romance* and such early essays as "I Gather the Limbs of Osiris" and "Prologomena" as well as the Introduction to *The Sonnets and Ballate of Guido Cavalcanti*, the rules moved directly against the post-Swinburne convention of fusing vague sensation with a regular beat and reinforcing the lines accordingly with trite epithets and meaningless clichés. Primarily, it was a plan designed to do away with the basic component of traditional English verse, the iambic pentameter, and replace it with a less contrived form that would give the poet greater freedom to develop his own style and method.[4]

It was only a matter of time before the movement got off the ground. Richard Aldington joined H.D. and Pound to form a microcosmic avant-grade of three. F. S. Flint stepped forward, as did Skipwith Cannéll, Allen Upward, and John Cournos. Ford, Williams, and James Joyce were drafted. Then, in the spring of 1913, plump, wealthy, cigar-smoking Amy Lowell of Brookline, Massachusetts, dropped in briefly at movement headquarters. Pound hailed the newcomer as "our only hippopoetess." To argue with her, Carl Sandburg mused, was "like arguing with a big blue wave." One of her poems was included in *Des Imagistes*, the movement's definitive, Pound-edited anthology (March 1914). Dissatisfied with the general handling of the publication, Miss Lowell returned from America to England in July. The best way to help other poets, she argued, was to reissue the anthology employing the same contributors, if possible, as before, but the same amount of space this time to be allotted to each, final selections determined by vote of all. In the confusing days which followed, it is difficult to determine whether she escaped with the group or Pound from it; the offshoot, in any case, was the American publication of three successive "Amygistic" anthologies with the appropriated title *Some Imagist Poets*, all of the volumes funded and edited by Amy Lowell; not one of the three, suffice it to say, contained work by Pound.

Having outdistanced the static movement of the "radiant node or cluster," the innovator marched on. The next *ism* erupted with a *BLAST*: it was called "Vorticism," a word of Pound's invention, and *Blast*, edited by Wyndham Lewis, was "A Review of the Great English Vortex." Writing to James Joyce, Pound referred to it as the "new Futurist, Cubist, Imagiste Quarterly." The aim of *Blast*, No. 1 (June 1914), according to Harriet Monroe's editorial in that August's *Poetry*, was "to blow away, in thick black capitals half an inch high, the Victorian Vampire." In place of romance and sentimentality, "the great opusculus" proposed patterned and power-charged energy—the energy of the "Vortex," as Pound labeled its transmedia electroshock troops: himself, Lewis, Ford, Henri Gaudier-Brzeska, Jacob Epstein, Edward Wadsworth, Arnold Dolmetsch, Rebecca West, and others; even Dorothy Pound, with her Lewis-inspired hard-edged cover designs for *Ripostes* and *The Catholic Anthology*, would come to be associated with the group.

The size of a telephone directory, and printed on coarse yellow paper, its cover a "damn-your-eyes" shocking pink, the movement's tabloid threatened—in huge writhing black letters—destruction and ruin to all those forces that it held responsible for 1914. Aristocracy and proletarianism, Victorianism, Rousseauism, the bourgeoisie, Christianity, even rhyme and form, humor and sport, museums and art—everything must be blasted up in smoke. "Blessings" were reserved for the "Seafarer," the great ports, "restless" machinery (cranes and lighthouses and factory walls), and one or two writers—Shakespeare, "for his bitter Northern Rhetoric of humour," and Swift, "for his solemn, bleak wisdom of laughter"; a special "blessing," as if to signify the school's sardonic nature, was granted the hairdresser, icon of some future and more liberal age.[5]

Conversely, there was a serious side to the movement, and here the connection between vorticism and its forerunner, futurism, becomes more readily apparent. Whereas the vorticists were either indifferent or opposed to many of the principles governing futurism,[6] the two movements did have certain things in common, especially insofar as both encouraged the artist, regardless of his medium, "to break up the surface of conventional art," to rebel against it thereby creating a swirl of artistic activity, one revolutionary practitioner influencing the work of another.

The first futurist manifesto[7] had called for speed, praised machines and war, glorified youth—as Mussolini was to do—and advocated the upheaval of all conventional art forms and institutions. A fervent F. T. Marinetti, supported by a fervent C. R. W. Nevinson, had sounded the battle cry for "the destruction of syntax. . . . Unbridled imagination. . . . Geometric sensibility." The emphasis, as in the Vortex, was on the importance of volition with direction, the conscious eschewal of "the static and mimetic for the dynamic and creative."[8] In "The Serious Artist" (1913), Pound dictates the *a priori* set of conditions basic to a full appreciation of vorticism: "We might come to believe that the thing that matters in art is a sort of energy, something more or less like electricity . . . transfusing, welding and unifying." Then: "A force rather like water when it spurts up through very bright sand and sets it into swift motion." Along similar lines, the Vortex may be described as "the point of maximum energy," the point of concentration of will, of apprehension, the creation of a single supraimage "from which, and through which, and into which, ideas are constantly rushing."[9] It is clear that Pound had been paying rapt attention to the scientific inventions and inventors of the day—Roentgen, Planck, Marconi, and the Curies—and that his oft-reiterated example of the magnet making a rose pattern in the iron filings was not a "random curiosity" but a whole way of looking at the world.

The second, and last, issue of *Blast* appeared in July 1915. This issue featured, as had the first, essays, illustrations, and notes by Lewis and poetry by Pound, but lacked the good cheer and exuberance of the previous year's publication—the staff and contributors were too conscious of the violence taking place on the battlefields of Flanders and France for that.[10] The War (as a hapless world called it) shattered the security that had both nurtured and provoked the artistic rebels.[11] *Blast's* second issue, for example, contained a continuation from the first of the elucidating and innovative art manifesto by the gifted twenty-four-year-old vorticist sculptor Gaudier-Brzeska, together with the announcement that he had been killed in action on June 5 at Neuville-Saint-Vaast.[12] His final *Blast* holograph, written from the trenches shortly before the end, began:

I HAVE BEEN FIGHTING FOR TWO MONTHS and I can now gauge the intensity of life.

HUMAN MASSES teem and move, are destroyed and crop up again.

HORSES are worn out in three weeks, die by the roadside.

DOGS wander, are destroyed, and others come along.

WITH ALL THE DESTRUCTION that works around us

NOTHING IS CHANGED, EVEN SUPERFICIALLY. LIFE IS THE SAME STRENGTH, THE MOVING AGENT THAT PERMITS THE SMALL INDIVIDUAL TO ASSERT HIMSELF.

4

My problem is to keep alive a certain group of advancing poets, to set the arts in their rightful place as the acknowledged guide and lamp of civilization.

—Letter to Harriet Monroe,
January 1915[1]

The layman does not realize that a change in literary tastes imperils a lot of electroplates, and that a more efficient mode of expression is just as dangerous for the deciduous or stilted as is a new mechanical invention for a firm which has all its capital sunk in old-fashioned machinery. . . . And so the world goes on being poisoned with dead thought.

—Letter to Henry Allen Moe,
March 1925[2]

In 1912 an American poet, Robert Frost—witty, dedicated, and ambitious—moved to England, discouraged because he was approaching middle age and still could not get his work published in the United States. His first volume, *A Boy's Will*, appeared in London in March 1913. When Pound saw that Frost in his verse had the ability to speak simply in his own voice, and to describe things clearly, he wrote to Alice Corbin Henderson, assistant to Harriet Monroe: "Have just discovered another Amur'kn. VURRY Amur'k'n, with, I think, the seeds of grace."[3] Pound reviewed *A Boy's Will* for the May issue of *Poetry*, using the review format as a means, not only of bolstering and boosting Frost, but of lambasting the American literary establishment. It was the first review of Frost's work to appear in the United States: "There is another personality in the realm of verse, another American, found, as usual, on this side of the water, by an English publisher long known as a lover of good letters. David Nutt publishes at his own expense *A Boy's*

Will, by Robert Frost, the latter having been long scorned by the 'great American editors.' It is the old story."

Later in the piece the critic grew more personal by way of introducing and quoting from the poetry itself, but the kernel of his argument moved against what at another point he termed "America's inertia, timidity, lack of good will, and hatred of the unfamiliar in the arts," the country's seeming reluctance either to endorse or support the more talented of her literary hopefuls. When Frost's book of dramatic dialogues *North of Boston* was published in May 1914, Pound again took to the battlefield; his review appeared in the December issue of *Poetry*, and read in part:

> . . . It is natural and proper that I should have to come abroad to get printed, or that "H.D."—with her clear-cut derivations and her revivications of Greece—should have to come abroad; or that Fletcher [John Gould Fletcher]—with his *tic* and his discords and his contrariety and extended knowledge of everything—should have to come abroad. One need not censure the country; it is easier for us to emigrate than for America to change her civilization fast enough to please us. But why, IF there are serious people in America, desiring literature of America, literature accepting present conditions, rendering American life with sober fidelity—why in heaven's name, is this book of New England eclogues given us under a foreign imprint?

Introduced to Pound by F. S. Flint, Frost very soon became aware that their respective temperaments were so markedly different that they could get along well for only a short time. The first rift between them, Lawrance Thompson informs us, was caused by Frost's resentment of the *Poetry* review of *A Boy's Will*; the second was caused by Frost's jealousy over Pound's celebrations of the newly formed imagist group. Giving vent to his sudden anger, the newcomer proceeded to unburden himself in an explosive note to John T. Bartlett (*ca.* April 4, 1913): "And Ezra Pound, the stormy petrel . . . has found me and sent a fierce article to Chicago denouncing a country that neglects fellows like me. I am afraid he over did [*sic*] it and it may be a mercy all round if it isn't printed."[4] He followed up this assault with a second Bartlett-bound directive (*ca.* June 16, 1913): "I object chiefly to what he [Pound] says about the great American editors. Not that I have any love for the two or three he has in mind. But they are better ignored—at any rate they are better not offended. We may want to use them some time."[5]

Nor did Frost's counterblasts stop there. On July 17, he wrote to Thomas Mosher, an American small-press publisher, once again railing against Pound, assailing him for his review of *A Boy's Will*: "If any but a great man had written it, I should have called it vulgar . . . it is so stupidly wide of the mark. . . ."⁶ And in the same month he sent F. S. Flint two playfully serious *vers libres* parodies mocking the modernist. Flint was vaguely amused by the poems but tried to dissuade Frost from showing them to Pound. Ultimately, they remained confidential, although Frost kept finding new evidence for negative feelings. Another letter was mailed to Mosher (October 28): "Pound is an incredible ass and he hurts more than he helps the person he praises";⁷ and another to Bartlett (*ca.* November 5): "I want to be a poet for all sorts and kinds. I could never make a merit of being a caviare to the crowd the way my quasi-friend Pound does."⁸

During the remainder of his stay in England, Frost continued to think of Pound as his immediate adversary. He carefully avoided making contact with his friend–enemy, and when he returned with his family to the United States early in 1915, he departed without bidding Pound farewell. In retrospect, all this represented rather peculiar and bewildering behavior on the confirmed New Englander's part. Pound had been the first writer of any consequence to take notice of Frost; as much as anyone, he helped establish the visitor's name. It would take Frost nearly forty-five years to acknowledge his debt.

Some time in 1912 Pound, unearthing tidbits of modernity wherever he could find them, produced a quatrain of invocation:

> Sweet Christ from hell spew up some Rabelais,
> To belch and . . . . . and to define today
> In fitting fashion, and her monument
> Heap up to her in fadeless excrement.
> —*Guide to Kulchur*, 1938

The Rabelaisian "spew" soon began to arrive in the work of an impoverished thirty-one-year-old Berlitz teacher living in Trieste, an accomplished linguist, by name James Joyce. Pound first heard of Joyce from Yeats, who showed him his fellow countryman's poem "I Hear an Army Charging." Finding it much to his liking, Pound wrote to Joyce, offering to include the poem in the anthology *Des Imagistes*, and inquiring if he had any additional material to spare. This encouraged the Irish Nighttowner to make the final corrections on the opening chapter of *A Portrait of the Artist as a Young Man* and send it on to Pound, together with a copy of *Dubliners* and news that he would presently have a play (*Exiles*) ready. Pound reviewed *Dubliners* in *The Egoist* (July 1914), placing Joyce's "hard and clear" prose in a class with Stendhal, James, and Flaubert—one of the few favorable reviews accorded the short stories—and he arranged for the same journal to publish *A Portrait*, both serially and in book form.

Determined that Joyce should not do the kind of piecemeal hack journalism he himself was forced to do, but should devote himself wholly to the perfection of his "enormous-megalo-scrumptious-mastodonic" masterwork, Pound made Joyce's impoverished financial state his personal business, drumming up the necessary aid and support from a variety of sources. In 1915, aided by Yeats, he succeeded in obtaining a subsidy of £75 for Joyce from the Royal Literary Fund; that same year Pound sent him an anonymous gift of £25 and arranged for the Society of Authors, British Parliament, and John Quinn (a wealthy New York attorney and art patron) to make contributions of generous amounts.

In July 1915, the Dubliner moved from the embattled city of Trieste to Zurich, to be able to get on with the creation of *Ulysses*. Because of the war, the twin Odyssean mentors of modern fiction and poetry would not meet until June 1920, when Pound persuaded Joyce to come to Sirmione, Catullus's resort on the Lago di Garda. In the intervening years, the instigator kept up a steady stream of correspondence both to Joyce and, on his behalf, to others, promoting his work in various reviews and literary journals. As London editor of Margaret Anderson and Jane Heap's *Little Review*, a post assumed at the end of March 1917, Pound negotiated and set up the partial publication of *Ulysses*. He later "brought Joyce to the attention of *The Egoist*'s publisher, Harriet Weaver—indeed 'thrust him down her throat,'" Wyndham Lewis testified—"and in time she set aside a sum of money that enabled Joyce to live comfortably in a Paris apartment" and finish his magnum opus.[9] "The magician in this Arabian Nights Tale was undoubtedly Ezra," contended Lewis. "Without Pound, the author of the *Portrait of the Artist* would perhaps never have written *Ulysses* or *Finnegans Wake*." In 1932 Joyce declared of his finder: "Nothing could be more true than to say that we all owe a great deal to him. But I most of all surely. It is nearly twenty years since he first began his vigorous campaign on my behalf and it is probable that but for him I should still be the unknown drudge that he discovered—if it was a discovery."

"And Eliot, Thomas Stearns, last comer to the Vortex, *que faisait-il dans cette galère?*"[10] He presented himself on September 22, 1914, at Ezra and Dorothy Pound's small triangular flat at 5 Holland Place Chambers, Kensington. The meeting had been suggested by Conrad Aiken, who had tried unsuccessfully to get Eliot's poems printed and who knew that Pound had connections with publishers. Eliot, a Harvard doctoral candidate in philosophy taking courses at Oxford, impressed Pound with his erudition. "An American called Eliot called on me this P.M.," Pound wrote to Harriet Monroe. "I think he has some sense tho' he has not yet sent me any verse."[11] A few weeks later, having read "The Love Song of J. Alfred Prufrock," an ecstatic Pound immediately transmitted his joy to the hearty editor of *Poetry*. It was, he said, "the best poem I have yet had or seen from an American. PRAY GOD IT BE NOT A SINGLE AND UNIQUE SUCCESS."[12] Pound dispatched the poem to Miss Monroe in October 1914, but she had her own ideas of what constituted publishable verse; she and Pound exchanged letters on the subject for six months before she acquiesced, tucking "Prufrock" away toward the back of the issue for June 1915, where it stood out like a diamond in the rough.

This was not, of course, to be Eliot's "single and unique success," but the commencement of one of the most sterling literary careers of this or any other century. The atmospheric receptivity Pound created encouraged Eliot to go on, enabled him to accomplish far more than he otherwise might have. At Pound's behest, Wyndham Lewis published "Preludes" and "Rhapsody on a Windy Night," two Eliot poems, in *Blast* No. 2. By September 1915, the pantechnicon driver had placed "Portrait of a Lady" in Alfred Kreymborg's *Others*; a month later Harriet Monroe used three more of the Missourian's poems; and in November all of Eliot's *Poetry* contributions to date and one of the two from *Blast* were collected in *The Catholic Anthology*, compiled by Pound in order to get "sixteen pages of Eliot into print at once." It was also through Pound's concerted efforts that "Possum's" first book, *Prufrock and Other Observations*, forty pages in stiff buff-paper wrappers, was published by the Egoist Ltd. Press in June 1917.

If it had been up to his family, Eliot would have resumed his education at Harvard, finished up his doctorate, and joined the ranks of the American professoriate. He did complete his thesis (on the metaphysician F. H. Bradley)—"to please his parents," according to his second wife, Valerie Eliot—"but dreaded the prospect of a return to the academy." It required little prodding on Pound's part, therefore, to persuade him to remain in London, although it was the imagist, in the final analysis, who saved Eliot for poetry.[13]

There were further discretions. Eliot left Oxford at the end of the spring semester 1915, having in the meantime married an Englishwoman, Vivienne Haigh Haigh-Wood. That fall, he took a job for a single term at the High Wycombe Grammar School outside London (salary £140 per annum with dinner) and the next semester at the Highgate Junior School (salary £160 per annum with dinner *and* tea). He was forced to supplement his income by giving evening lectures and by writing reviews and articles for technical and literary magazines. His wife's health was "delicate," and neither his family nor hers could offer much financial assistance. Bertrand Russell, whom Eliot had known at Harvard and with whom the couple lived in the early months of their marriage, noted: "She says she married him to stimulate him, but finds she can't do it. Obviously he married in order to be stimulated. I think she will soon be tired of him. He is ashamed of his marriage, and very grateful if one is kind to her."

Over these years Vivienne's health declined further; she complained of neuralgia, of insomnia. Although Eliot had advanced in March 1917 to a financially more secure post at Lloyds Bank of London, his personal tribulations continued to mount. Pound observed, with growing anxiety, that Eliot would soon be lost to poetry under the burdens of his wife's invalidism and the fierce schedule required to pay her physicians. "No use blinking the fact that it is a crime against literature to let him waste eight hours' vitality per diem in that bank," he wrote to John Quinn. "His wife hasn't a cent and is an invalid always cracking up, and needing doctors, and incapable of earning anything—though she has tried. . . ."[14] These were the circumstances, then, in the fall of 1921, when Eliot, near collapse, set out on an enforced three-month rest cure, first at Margate and then at a sanitarium in Lausanne, Switzerland. It was during this period that he completed *The Waste Land.*

5

And so that you don't continually misunderstand—usury
and interest are not the same thing. Usury is a charge
made for the use of money regardless of production and
often regardless even of the possibilities of production.

—"Ezra Pound Reading," vol. 2.,
Caedmon Records, 1962

The Evil is Usury. . . .

—Addendum for Canto C,
Drafts and Fragments, 1962

Preparing an autobiographical sketch for the 1949 edition of the *Selected Poems of Ezra Pound*, the author expostulated: "1918 began
investigation of causes of war, to oppose same."

Soon after his initial inquiry, he discovered a root cause—or
so he thought. Late in 1918, in the offices of A. R. Orage's *The New
Age*, Pound encountered Major Clifford Hugh Douglas, formerly chief
construction engineer of the British Westinghouse Company in India,
and the "inventor" of a new system of economics, called Social Credit.
To Douglas's mind, both war and lack of money had been caused by
financiers' manipulations—usury—and his mathematically drawn pana-
cea, or at least the main one, called for the distribution through central
banks of national dividends. Pound was easily convinced:[1]

> . . . With usura hath no man a house of good stone
> each block cut smooth and well fitting
> that design might cover their face,
> with usura
> hath no man a painted paradise on his church wall
> *harpes et luz*
> or where virgin receiveth message

32

and halo projects from incision,
with usura
seeth no man Gonzaga his heirs and his concubines
no picture is made to endure nor to live with
but it is made to sell and sell quickly
with usura, sin again nature,
is thy bread ever more of stale rags
is thy bread dry as paper,
with no mountain wheat, no strong flour
with usura the line grows thick
with usura is no clear demarcation
and no man can find site for his dwelling.
Stone cutter is kept from his stone
weaver is kept from his loom
WITH USURA

. . . .

They have brought whores for Eleusis
Corpses are set to banquet
at behest of usura.

(Canto XLV)

He adopted the vital cause because he was distressed about the war, disillusioned with the "botched civilization," disappointed with his own role as a poet. His prevailing mood, combined with postwar conditions, especially those imposed by the Versailles Treaty of 1919, brought to the surface a sudden awareness of the very dangerous position of the artist and alerted him to the possibility that the Great War was due principally to poor fiscal management and an accordant failure of intelligence. Intelligence was society's most valuable resource, and artists were the "antennae of the race." What ultimately counted was the overall cultural level of civilization and Douglas, claimed Pound, was the first economist "to postulate a place for the arts, literature, and the amenities in a system of economics" (*The Criterion*, January 1935). This, the poet added, ought to endear him to the highbrows, provided "their foreheads aren't mere façades."

It was a question also of being up in arms against a degenerating publishing system, American as well as British, which over the years had catered to commercial interests at the expense of the more creative forces of contemporary arts and letters. Money, and such matters, could never have been far from the writer's mind. In 1915, for example, a year of significant production for him, his total income from writing was £42. "My American royalties amount to about one dollar 85 cents per annum," he announced one year later. In order to pay the rent and replenish the larder he felt obliged to accept funds from both his father and wife, and where and when available, from those Wyndham Lewis belligerently called "The Apes of God"—patrons of the arts. Out of financial necessity, then, Pound was forced to found his own writing factory, assembling and churning out articles, essays, reviews at a prodigious, machine-like rate. His bibliographer, Donald Gallup, lists 71 periodical items for 1917, 117 for 1918, 189 for 1919, 89 more for 1920.[2] "One buys leisure time to work by selling one's stuff for what one can," he advised Marianne Moore at a time when he was helping her break into print. Because it was so totally devoid of humor, Pound's situation lent itself to serio-comedy: "Orage's 4 guineas a month . . . wuz the SINEWS, by gob the sinooz."[3] Orage, for whose *New Age* he had actually been toiling since 1911, was his bread and butter.

Given this set of hard-core particulars, one can begin to understand the poet's growing preoccupation with fiscal affairs, his effort to incorporate the Douglasite formula (the "A + B theorem")[4] and monetary reform in general into the main thrust of his daily comings and goings. According to Pound, usury, the foremost malefaction in the postfeudal world, was the underlying cause of the ruin of all human values, the most serious of which was undoubtedly the cancerous decay of the arts. The very existence of "the palsied shadow of usura" could be traced to the poor organization of distribution: capital was stagnating in the banks; the consumer lacked purchasing power; monopolies thrived; and credit was accorded to specific individuals and interest charged on it so that banks and lending institutions were creating money *"ex nihil,"*[5] out of nothing. Based on his consultations with Douglas, Pound was convinced that the problems of labor and distribution could be solved simultaneously. "The working day," he inculcated in the *ABC of Economics*, "should be kept short enough to prevent any one man doing two or three men's *paid* work," while the State should provide "honest certificates of work done." It stood to reason: the simplest means of keeping money distributed was to keep work distributed. As a result, the unemployment problem would be alleviated, the desires of the moneylenders thwarted, and capital shared equitably and fairly among all those entitled to it.[6]

Technically, Social Credit, as the name implies, was concerned with the role of credit in society. The belief of Douglas and his followers, as spelled out in numerous books and pamphlets, was that the "real" credit of a nation resided in a people's capacity to produce needed goods and provide necessary services, but "money" had been "cornered," so that "financial" credit (the credit of the bankers and financiers) controlled "real" credit. Orage, in full accord with Douglas's argument, postulated that "this disharmony between real credit and financial credit" was what lay at the root of the world's social and economic troubles. An explanation followed: "Real Credit is a product of Production and Consumption, and . . . its final source is the Community as a whole. . . . Financial Credit, that should be, and was designed to be, the handmaid of Real Credit and only exists at all because of Real Credit, is the monopoly of a comparatively few individuals, scarcely more than 1 in 100,000 of the population."[7] This omnipotent minority, Orage went on to imply, was made up largely of Jews. Indeed, he maintained, and both Pound and Douglas seem to have agreed with him, that the entire modern system, in which usury was predominant, was essentially Semitic-inspired.[8] For the poet-turned-economist, this idea became, at length, an obsession. Then came the long downward slope to rabid anti-Semitism, fascism, and paranoia. It ended in a locked ward for the criminally insane inside a madhouse atop a hill overlooking the bleak outskirts of the District of Columbia.

In the summer of 1910, when Ezra Pound made his brief return visit to the United States, he was reminded, aboard ship, of Henry James's view in *The American Scene*, particularly of "the awfulness that engulfs one when one comes, for the first time unexpectedly on a pile of all the *Murkn* magazines laid, shingle-wise, on a brass-studded, screwed-into-place, baize-covered steamer table."[9] In *Patria Mia* (1912), a robust account of his hastily put together safari, Pound recalled an abbreviated meeting he had had in London with James in which the novelist remonstrated against America: "It is strange how all taint of art or letters seems to shun that continent."

Taking his cue from the "Passionate Pilgrim," the imagist picked up approximately where he had left off with Frost: the bravado, the sarcasm directed against his homeland, poured out of him, were purposeful overcharges that touched again and again to keep the senses alive—his own and the senses of others—to the disorder, the demand of experience for a higher order of form. Having had the will power to discipline and educate himself, he was convinced that he was doing a salutary job by doing the same for his countrymen.

Pound, gazing across the Atlantic at the America he had left behind in 1908, and again two years later, admired his country's pervasive energy "but failed to find in it a 'guiding sense,' a 'discrimination in applying force.'" That "the force" was present, "everyone who had looked at the country, whether with sympathy or indignation, agreed," regardless of his persuasion or position. Redirecting this force was something else again.[10]

Lamenting the need for change, Pound had made this the central and key issue of an enduring literary campaign. Before and during World War I, he spoke and wrote endlessly of America's shortcomings —her "intellectual malaise" and "cultural isolation," her "defunct academic standards" and "catatonic gummed-up mind." "The Old Gang"— that carnivorous three-headed dragon comprised of publishers, editors, and educators—had done nothing to advance the possibilities of a *Risorgimento*, an American awakening: William Dean Howells, Frank Norris, Stephen Crane, Jack London, and Theodore Dreiser, as a group, were by no means in the same weight-class as Hawthorne, Melville, Thoreau, and Twain. And though Pound acknowledged Whitman's role on behalf of American free verse, he felt that the "barbaric yawp" was not enough: "We can't stop with the 'yawp.' We have no longer any excuse for not taking up the complete art." In his belabored "Pact" with Walt Whitman (1915), he admitted that "Whitman had helped to make the break from the past ('It was you that broke the new wood'), but [Pound] wanted now to go on to the task of refining the language and making it more precise ('Now is a time for the carving')."[11] Unhappily, his lament fell on deaf ears; he had found nothing but passivity in America's writers and critics, and "intimidating, dogmatic force on the part of those who might have made an artist's life tolerable."[12]

If America lacked a vigorous writing force, so too did England, and Pound's post-1918 grievances against the British were similar to those he had lodged previously against his own country. Where once there had been artistic energy and spontaneity, there was now waste and debris.

Things in London had changed. When the war was over and the smoke had cleared, all that remained was a smattering of the old. Spirits hovered in the air: Joseph Conrad, Edward Thomas, E. M. Forster, Virginia Woolf, Lytton Strachey, the Sitwells. The Vortex had dissipated. An aspect of Pound's job was done. His eye trained on the European mainland, he wrote to Rutherford, New Jersey, and William Carlos Williams (January 1919): "All sorts of 'projects' artoliteresque in the peaceconferentialbolshevikair. Switzerland bursting into Dadaique Manifestos re the nothingness of the All."[13] In 1921 he "embraced these currents," "bottling" London in favor of Paris, although for the present "he remained aloof, 'rejoicing in vacancy,' skeptical and unattached."[14]

Richard Aldington, who had returned from the trenches, found Pound seriously depressed, suffering from melancholia. He was stretched out on his bed and complaining of intellectual gout, stroking his Adam's apple, and declaring that the brains of the English stopped short there.[15] To Williams, he howled that there was no intellectual life left in England, save what thrived in his own room. He suggested to W. H. D. Rouse that the great passion of the great majority of Englishmen was for "a boot, any damn boot, to lick," and told Margaret Anderson that he was "bored to death with being any kind of editor," and that he "longed to hear the music of a lost dynasty."[16]

His fascination with England was over. Pound was dead weary; he had reached his saturation point. The "hell" Cantos, 14 and 15, written five years after his departure from England, "are specifically LONDON," he wrote to John Drummond (February 1932), "the state of [the] English mind in 1919 and 1920."[17] More precisely they mirror the state of Pound's mind in those years. The poet's wrath, at one point directed primarily against literary England ("an old bitch gone in the teeth . . ."), widens out here to include Fabians, bishops, *agents provocateurs* (the murderers of the Irish rebels Pearse and MacDonagh), vice crusaders, liars, pedants, those who do not believe in Social Credit, lady golfers, conservatives, and imperialists; and all "those who have set money-lust before the pleasures of the senses." Caught in a stasis of the most devastating conditions imaginable, the prisoners of Pound's monolithic cellblock wallow in their own excretion of filth. The bleak setting —"without dignity, without tragedy"—is unrelieved by that beauty of simile which keeps each of Dante's concentric circles free of squalor and rank.[18] To some extent the utter hopelessness of the modernist's inferno demonstrates just how high his hopes for Britain had originally been and how deeply disappointed he had become with that land.

Out of the despair and bitterness at the increasing indurability of Britain, out of fear and loss of hope for the individual overcome by modern civilization, Pound wrote not only the lower-depths segment of his epic but *Homage to Sextus Propertius* (1917) and *Hugh Selwyn Mauberley* (1920). Both cycles of poems, depicting as they do the desiccation of modern life, demonstrate to a greater extent than any of his other work the influence of Eliot. The innocent, clipped, rhymed strophes of *Mauberley* are rife with irony. *Homage*, full of the same quality, is, however, less bitter in tone. By 1920, more than a decade of London had pumped through Pound's heart; *Mauberley* is his quittance with the age and the place:

> The age demanded an image
> Of its accelerated grimace,
> Something for the modern stage,
> Not, at any rate, an Attic grace;
>
> Not, not certainly, the obscure reveries
> Of the inward gaze;
> Better mendacities
> Than the classics in paraphrase!
>
> The "age demanded" chiefly a mould in plaster,
> Made with no loss of time,
> A prose kinema, not, not assuredly, alabaster
> Or the "sculpture" of rhyme.

And *Homage* is his quittance with the past and its style; there is much talk of death:

> Annalists will continue to record Roman reputations,
> Celebrities from the Trans-Caucasus will belaud Roman celebrities
> And expound the distentions of Empire,
> But for something to read in normal circumstances?
> For a few pages brought down from the forked hill unsullied?
> I ask a wreath which will not crush my head.
> And there is no hurry about it;

I shall have, doubtless, a boom after my funeral,
Seeing that long standing increases all things regardless of quality.
. . . . . .
Nor at my funeral either will there be any long trail,
            bearing ancestral lares and images;
No trumpets filled with my emptiness,
Nor shall it be on an Atalic bed;
        The perfumed cloths shall be absent.
A small plebian procession.
        Enough, enough and in plenty
There will be three books at my obsequies
Which I take, my not unworthy gift, to Persephone.

Vain and caustic, yet eager for public acclaim, Propertius, a friend of Virgil and Ovid, represented a fitting mask behind which Pound could pose. The points of similarity between the two are striking—their "amorous passion, tragic sense of transitoriness, and savage indignation at pomp and official stupidity"[19] unite them. They are further united by the strong umbilical likeness that generally existed between Latin and English culture. Poets such as Catullus and Propertius, Pound wrote, "have approximately the same problems as we have: the metropolis, the imperial posts to all corners of the known world."[20] *Homage*, he averred, "presents certain emotions as vital to me in 1917, faced with the infinite and ineffable imbecility of the British Empire, as they were to Propertius some centuries earlier, when faced with the infinite and ineffable imbecility of the Roman Empire. These emotions are defined largely, but not entirely, in Propertius' own terms."[21]

The twelve-section series ran into the same storm of protest from philologists and literary critics as had formerly been lodged against Pound's translation of *The Seafarer* and his rendering of Chinese verse in *Cathay*. Only T. S. Eliot, of the early reviewers, possessed a coherent understanding of what Pound was trying to do. *Homage* was not a literal translation, but "a new *persona*, a creation of a new character, re-creating Propertius in himself, and himself in Propertius." Pound, Eliot perceived, possessed the boldness and resource to effect a new mode of translation, building upon the old, but permanently extending the bounds and strictures of English verse.

Hugh Selwyn Mauberley, written during the final stages of the poet's twelve-year residence in London, was likewise heralded by Eliot: "A great poem. . . . It is compact of the experience of a certain man in a certain place at a certain time, and it is also a document of an epoch; it is genuine tragedy and comedy; and it is in the best sense of Arnold's worn phrase, a 'criticism of life.' "[22] The sequence is made up of eighteen independent albeit intimately linked poems, presented in two sections, each section modifying the other. Its rhythm is Corbière instead of Laforgue, as in the "Possum's" *Lovesong*. There is a fragment from Sappho, a couplet from Ronsard, a quote from Homer in Greek, a line from Flaubert in French, and many paraphrases and excerpts from Bion, Cicero, Nemesianus, James, Gourmont, and Gautier. The poems in the sequence, ultimately autobiographical in conception (at the least this is a *poème à clef*), coalesce to form a unified picture of a passing age. As an aesthetic accomplishment—a singular, short-range endeavor—*Mauberley* is almost certainly the high point of Pound's entire literary career, a nexus between his most definitive pre-Canto work and the molten, "ply over ply" framework which holds *The Cantos* themselves together.

Ezra Weston Pound,   Philadelphia, Pa.
"Ezra"
"Bib's" pride.   Leader of the anvil chorus at
the Commons.   Oh, how he throws those
legs!   Peroxide blonde.

Top: The house built by Homer Pound in Hailey, Idaho, in which Ezra was born. (*Courtesy Harry Meacham.*)

Center: Ezra Pound in 1904/05, as a member of the Hamilton College Chess Club. (*Courtesy the Burke Library, Hamilton and Kirkland Colleges.*)

Bottom: Ezra Pound in 1905. From the Hamilton College Year Book. (*Courtesy the Burke Library, Hamilton and Kirkland Colleges.*)

Ezra Pound in 1908, the year he left the United States for England. (*Courtesy Humanities Research Center, University of Texas at Austin.*)

Pound in London, 1916. (*Courtesy Humanities Research Center, University of Texas at Austin.*)

Pound in his Paris studio, 1923. (*Courtesy U.S. Information Agency.*)

Above: The poet standing in the courtyard of his Paris studio, 1923. (*Courtesy U.S. Information Agency.*)

Opposite, top: James Joyce, Pound, Ford Madox Ford, and John Quinn, Paris, 1923. (*Courtesy U.S. Information Agency.*)

Opposite, bottom: Sample of the money-scrip issued by the Union Lumbering Company, Chippewa Falls, Wisconsin, owned by Ezra's grandfather, T. C. Pound. (*Courtesy Humanities Research Center, University of Texas at Austin.*)

6

Further investigations about contemporary history and further study of
Major Douglas's critique of economic practices had confirmed for
Pound what he had already pointed out in "The Revolt of Intelligence"
(1919) and reaffirmed the attitude implicit in *Mauberley*.[1] Paris promised vitality and a renewed center of gravity for artistic heroism; the final
"break" with London was slow in coming, was subject to the gradual
turn of seasons. As early as 1918, Pound had been intrigued by the stir
of life in such able French authors as André Breton, Louis Aragon,
and others, who were closely allied with the dadaists and cubists; from
Zurich they had begun to distribute newspapers and journals that sati-
rized "the holy church of our century (journalism)" and "the sanctimonious attitude toward 'the arts.' "[2] They had begun to explore and
publicize various aspects of the new economics—*metallurgie*, bankers,
financiers, munitions manufacturers. "They have given up the pretense
of impartiality. They have expressed a desire to live and to die, prefer-
ring death to a sort of moribund permanence."[3] When, after the war,
Breton, Aragon, and their group returned to Paris, Pound became convinced that London was no longer the literary capital of Europe. New
directions, both in his own life and outwardly in the life of the Continent,
were imminent.

Pound traversed the Channel a few times before settling in Paris
with his wife early in 1921. Their permanent residence was a moderate-
sized studio at 70 *bis* rue Notre-Dame-des-Champs, the same street
where Whistler had lived as a young man. The studio was in the courtyard *pavillon*, bottom floor, rental $10 a week. As always, the poet was
very poor; fame, or the kind of fame Pound enjoyed, did not pay the
bills. He made his own furniture, much of it out of wooden boxes and
crates. Dorothy Pound bought a used bassoon for her husband's birthday, which, when it was not being played, stood prominently in the
center of the room, next to the Dolmetsch clavichord brought over from

Kensington. In his spare time he hammered at egg-shaped drifts of marble ("the poet as sculptor"), split them, and produced jagged-edged abstractions which lay about the floor. His wife's paintings and drawings by Wyndham Lewis and Gaudier-Brzeska decorated the walls. The epitome of bohemian nonconformity—a flowing cape of extravagant dimensions, his beard cut to an even sharper point than before, his lion's mane wild—he was a human landmark on the Paris boulevards and in the sidewalk cafés. He made himself accessible to all visitors, resumed the role of cicerone and literary marshal that he had created for himself in London, at the same time furthering his career as poet, editor, and correspondent.[4]

The first enterprise was an attempt to reconstitute the bankrupt *Little Review* as a quarterly, beginning with material from local Parisian writers and art work by the Rumanian sculptor Constantin Brancusi; Pound informed Marianne Moore that it was also to serve as "a protest against the imbecile suppression of Joyce's *Ulysses*." The expatriate induced the Paris bookstore owner Sylvia Beach to start a small publishing firm in order to bring out the long-awaited Bloomsday chronicle, and then threw himself into the promotion of the project by soliciting subscriptions for the book from everyone he knew, including the adamant George Bernard Shaw. "Do I have to do everything you like, Ezra?" Shaw sneered. And finally: "I take care of the pence and let the Pounds take care of themselves."

He was translating Remy de Gourmont's 1903 *Physique de l'amour: essai sur l'instinct sexuel*, under the title *The Natural Philosophy of Love*, and was working on what was to become his opera *Le Testament*, based upon incidents in the life of François Villon, putting the vagabond's words and deeds to his own music. He published a collection of new verse, *Quia Pauper Amavi* (which included "Homage à la Langue D'Oc," "Moeurs Contemporaines," and the early versions of Cantos 1–3), and *Instigations*, a retrospect of his prose of 1917–1918. *Poems 1918–1921* covered that three-year period, and *Umbra* (1920) was a new collection of the best of his pre-*Lustra* work. In October 1921, his controversial "Paris Letter" was made a regular feature in *The Dial*; here and elsewhere he continued to emphasize the "economic factor" and Major Douglas's Social Credit theories and maintained his omnibus attack against the "chief offenders" of the "Kulchur-al Tradition"—Britain and the United States.

As in Kensington, he came to know a new and exciting crowd—

Cocteau, Picabia, Picasso, Berenson, Braque, Man Ray, Léger, Tristan Tzara, Hilaire Hiler. He also met E. E. Cummings, Archibald MacLeish, Samuel Putnam, Ernest Walsh, Frank Harris, Kathleen Cannéll, Natalie Barney, and Stella Bowen. Old friends reappeared: Wyndham Lewis, Richard Aldington, and James Joyce. Through Joyce he met another Irish exile, Samuel Beckett, but did not get along. Ford Madox Ford moved to Paris to edit the *Transatlantic Review*, and with Pound directing him, managed to boost a number of lesser-known American expatriates, including Robert McAlmon, Katherine Anne Porter, Glenway Wescott, Elizabeth Madox Roberts, and Caroline Gordon. Yves Tinayre, an opera singer with whom the poet had been acquainted in London, arrived to help put the finishing touches on *Le Testament*; impressed with the execution of the libretto, Villon's ballads, the music, the novel instrumentation ("2 cellos, 2 bassoons, 1 trombone, percussion, one fiddle, oboe, saxophone, etc., anything from 8 to 16 instruments for small house"), Tinayre sang the tenor role, both in the partial performance of the opera in 1924 (Pound accompanied on the drums) and in the first complete performance in 1926. Another musician, the American composer George Antheil, also had a large hand in the composition of the work; in return, Pound procured a concert hall for the young musician, reviewed his early experimental performances (including *Ballet Mécanique*), and afterward wrote a book entitled *Antheil and the Treatise on Harmony* (1924) to find the composer a larger audience and set down his own thoughts on music theory.

A central figure among the American expatriates, when E. P. set foot in Paris, was Gertrude Stein, who undoubtedly saw the new arrival as a potential threat to her pre-eminent position in local literary society. Perhaps she perceived, too, that he did not belong to the generation of the "lost," at any rate, not to the rank and file. They met twice. After their initial meeting, Miss Stein remarked that she liked Pound but "did not find him amusing." Their second encounter, however, was less successful. Pound chose to talk of Japanese prints, Oriental music, and political economy, though not necessarily in that order. The hostess ("our second Miss Lowell") felt bored and irritated. Thoroughly unpleasant for her, as well, was her guest's brash attempt to explain the paintings that hung on her wall. When, in a pique of violent excitement, "the village explainer" toppled out of her favorite armchair, she decided she would never invite him to her rue de Fleurus home again. Thus the views of at least two biographers: J. Landers and H. Greenfeld.

Another American, Ernest Hemingway, then a foreign correspondent for the Toronto *Star Weekly*, settled in Paris in December of 1921. Hemingway admired Pound's work and was eager to meet him. Sometime in late January or early February 1922, they did meet for the first time, at Sylvia Beach's bookstore, Shakespeare and Company, where they were introduced by the owner. A few weeks later Hemingway brought Pound the manuscript of one of his short stories—"Up in Michigan"—and the poet praised it warmly. In March, Pound sent six of Hemingway's poems to Scofield Thayer of *The Dial* and accepted a story for *The Little Review*. He helped agent Hemingway's first book, *Three Stories and Ten Poems* (1923), selling the rights to Robert McAlmon's Contact Publishing Company, and, as editor, supervised the production by William Bird's Three Mountains Press of *In Our Time*.

The two authors spent a good deal of time together discussing writers and technique and engaging in Hemingway's favorite pastime: athletics—playing tennis and trading fencing for boxing lessons. Although these extraliterary pursuits did not add much to Hemingway's expertise, they were important in laying a foundation for friendship and in making Hemingway receptive to criticism from the poet.[5] To be sure, it was Pound, Hemingway always claimed, who taught him "more about how to write and how not to write" than anyone else: "Ezra . . . was the man I liked and trusted the most as a critic . . . the man . . . who had taught me to distrust adjectives as I would later learn to distrust certain people in certain situations."

Pound, for his part, responded enthusiastically to Hemingway's talent. He felt that his new-found companion was on the verge of success, and he sincerely wished to see him recognized and rewarded. T. S. Eliot explained this aspect of Pound's personality, his zeal in coming to the aid of all those whose work he respected, as a "passionate desire . . . to live in a period in which he could be surrounded by equally intelligent and creative minds."[8] In addition, Pound probably was convinced that he could put Hemingway's "violent American" energy and rawness to good use "as part of the battle against the philistines."

In the course of these years they were involved in other joint efforts. Shortly after meeting him, Hemingway began to help Pound with his Bel Esprit project, a plan designed to free Eliot from the bank so that he could devote himself to his poetry. The scheme, involving voluntary contributions by practicing writers, actually became a nuisance and a source of embarrassment to Eliot, although in the end the publicity he received from it may well have resulted in his being granted the 1922 *Dial* Award of $2000.

Then, in the winter of 1923, Hemingway and Pound, accompanied by their wives, went on a walking tour of the ancient Italian battlefields, including Piombono and Ortobello. Hemingway, an authority on such matters, explained the battle strategy and campaigns of the Renaissance *condottiere* and art patron, Sigismundo Malatesta. The excursion was the beginning of Pound's decision to leave Paris and live in Italy, and in Malatesta he found a new hero for beatification in *The Cantos*.

Finally, the most memorable and enduring, and certainly the most meritorious of the poet's accomplishments during his Paris stay, was his editing job and reworking of Eliot's *The Waste Land*, still the marvel of the age. Gauging from the facsimile and transcript of the original drafts published in 1971,[8] what Pound apparently first saw of the poem, when Eliot arrived with it in Paris late in 1921, was a mass of manuscript and typescript (written on an assortment of paper) about twice the length as it first appeared in *The Criterion* (October 1922), of which the central core would seem to have been basically the five-part sequence we have —but with three additional long passages—with some eight miscellaneous poems, varying in length from five to seventy-three lines, also included, as well as certain individual lines, phrases, and words in the central section that were later altered or transposed or cut entirely. In his initial blue-penciling of the material, Pound marked some sections as unworkably bad, others as doubtful, and advised Eliot to weed out the shorter poems, suggesting lines here and there that could be salvaged by incorporating them into the main body of the work. With typical Pound élan, he noted: "The thing now runs from 'April . . .' to 'shantih' without a break. This is 19 pages, and let us say, the longest poem in the English langwidge. Don't try to bust all records by prolonging it three pages farther."

A critic, examining the results of the Pound–Eliot collaboration, described the process as one of pulling "a masterpiece out of a grabbag of brilliant material"; Pound, on the other hand, described his participation as a "Caesarian Operation." However described, Eliot was of course extremely grateful. One month before *The Waste Land*'s *Criterion* appearance, he presented the original manuscript to John Quinn for safekeeping, declaring it "worth preserving in its present form solely for the reason that it is the only evidence of the difference which his

[Pound's] criticism has made to the poem."[9] He dedicated *The Waste Land* to Pound with the plaudit *"il miglior fabbro"* (the better craftsman), the same inscription which Dante had used in reference to Arnaut Daniel. Explaining this dedication, and reaffirming his conviction of Pound's genius, Eliot wrote in 1938: "I wished at that moment to honor the technical mastery and critical ability manifest in [Pound's] . . . work, which had also done so much to turn *The Waste Land* from a jumble of good and bad passages into a poem."

7

Pound and his wife left Paris in the fall of 1924. After some traveling to and fro—Florence, Assisi, Rome, Taormina, Syracuse, Palermo[1]—the couple settled in Rapallo, a quiet resort town on the Riviera di Levante, the Riviera of the Rising Sun, seventeen miles southeast of Genoa. By February 1925, they had rented an apartment five flights up on the roof of the Albergo Rapallo, with a view of the sea—"Rapallo's thin line of broken mother-of-pearl" in Yeats's description. The apartment had a large terrace; Gaudier-Brzeska's monumental head of Pound, cut out of a solid block of marble and completed shortly before the sculptor's death, was set up at one end of it. The workroom, looking out on the terrace, was strung with overhead cords to which were attached a row of envelopes and sheafs of manuscript; *il miglior fabbro* called it his "active" filing system. And when he went out for his constitutional, *il signor poèta* donned a cape and a broad-brimmed hat with which he saluted other promenaders on the *lungomare*, "Cavalier style, with a dramatic swoop and sweep."[2]

It is not easy to say precisely what drew Pound to Italy, or, rather, it is difficult to point to a single overriding motive. He told visitors that he had reached a cul-de-sac in Paris; he was fed up with the rat race, weary of the literary maelstrom. "It was time for him to stop doing so much for other men and for literature in general, stop trying to educate the public and simply write," Malcolm Cowley reported in *Exile's Return*. Pound's unceasing activity on behalf of the age, his selfless whirling of people, movements, ideas, and styles, had prevented him from getting on with his "real" work—the composition and setting down of *The Cantos*. And then, too, he was disenchanted with city life in general. "Civilization usually comes from the metropoles," he wrote to a correspondent in the States, "but CAN sprout in small communities (e.g., as in Rimini or in Mantua) if there is determined individual effort."[3] So while one wandering generation—Hemingway, Fitzgerald, Dos Passos, Cummings, Thornton Wilder, Faulkner, Thomas Wolfe, and Edmund Wilson—was preparing to reclaim America, Ezra Pound was immersing himself still further in the thick of European culture, securing for himself a private retreat in an Italian town whose center was as far removed from the vectors of modern society as one could hope to get. Rapallo—by the "green clear and blue clear," the seaside hamlet described in "Ode on a Grecian Urn" by Keats—was to be his home for the next four lustrums (twenty years).

Amid these peaceful surroundings Pound was at last in a milieu that suited him, and for a few years at least seemed moderately content. The landscape and the climate soothed him, relaxed him. "The senses," he was shortly to write, "seem at first to project for a few yards beyond the body. Effect of a decent climate where a man leaves his nerve-set open or allows it to tune in to its ambience, rather than struggling, as a northern race has to, for self-preservation."[4] His "inclination" toward Italian landscapes was "fundamental, a temperamental *donnée*."[5] The sea, cypress, mountains covered with vines; "light, color, air"; skylines and the distant outlines of trees and hills: he "knew paradise when he saw it."[6]

His group of friends decreased in isolated Rapallo, but his correspondence was immense, and there was, when needed, an enthusiastic and ready audience. Richard Aldington, George Antheil, Ford Madox Ford, Stella Bowen, and Phyllis Bottome were occasional visitors; Father Desmund Chute and Max Beerbohm (*Mauberley*'s "Brennbaum the Impeccable") lived there; Gerhart Hauptmann, Emil Ludwig, Franz Werfel, Tibor Serly, Gerhart Münch were new-found acquaintances; Basil Bunting, Louis Zukofsky, Robert Fitzgerald, Ronald Duncan, Henry Swabey, and James Laughlin were among *"les jeunes,"* the young writers and scholars who appeared from time to time to enroll at the "Ezuversity," "Ez's" personal rendition of the ancient and traditional Socratic symposium, the venerable art of query-and-response. For the most part Pound did both.

As time progressed, his dialogue became more distinctly a catalogue of pet peeves, a deliberate campaign set against the twin sins, usury and Mammon. Some of Pound's younger followers responded to the calling by embracing the whole of the new philosophy. Certain old friends were less avid in their embrace. William Butler Yeats, who visited Rapallo with his young wife in 1928, was among those puzzled by Pound's political and economic ideas. He expressed his bewilderment to Aldington. "Here is a man," he said, "who produces the most distinguished work and yet in his behavior is the least distinguished of men. It is the antithetical self." Yeats was not too surprised when another confrere, Wyndham Lewis, attacked Pound in *Time and Western Man* as "that revolutionary simpleton." To Lady Gregory, Yeats wrote: "I see Ezra daily. We disagree about everything." He compared the Great Bass to Maud Gonne, the Irish rebel whom he had idolized and pursued for so many years. Again he wrote to Lady Gregory: "Ezra has most of Maud Gonne's opinions (political and economic) about the world in general." More: "He has even her passion for cats."[7]

---

think not that you wd/gain if their least caress,
were faded from my mind
I had not loved thee half so well
Loved I not womankind'
                              (Canto LXXIX)

whereas the child's face
is at Capoquadri in the fresco square over the doorway
                              (Canto LXXIV)

A privacy and an interlude. In 1922 in Paris, at a recital, Pound had been introduced to the concert violinist Olga Rudge. She was an American expatriate, Ohio-born, wealthy-bred. According to one source she "thought him the most handsome man she had ever seen," and found him "reciprocating her regard."[8] The expression he beheld was that of "a dream passing over the face in the half-light." A "profile 'to carve Achaia,'" hers was "the line of the cameo." In his verse she took her place besides lesser female lights as "a great goddess," a Persephone renewed. In his life, where before women had always come and gone (both Yeats and Joseph Conrad could testify to the heavy *Verkehr*), she was to occupy a permanent and vital niche. Impulsively, he plunged into her grief: "*Her* affairs don't bear looking at. *His* affairs don't bear looking at. The past is forgotten, the future is ominous, the present is beyond words. . . . Need I go into details. I need not."[9]

There were reverberations: the responsibility of two families promised the certainty of uncertainty and confusion. Olga Rudge bore Pound's daughter, Mary, in 1925. The child was born in Bressanone, just north of Bolzano in the Italian Tirol, and was brought up on a farm by a peasant family, the Marchers, in nearby Gais. The other family was Dorothy's. Her son, Omar Shakespear, was born in 1926 at the American Hospital in Neuilly and was soon afterward given into the care of his maternal grandmother in England.

An interfamilial vendetta of silence, an Ezraic vow: during this period Dorothy Pound was to spend a portion of each year in London visiting with her son and her mother; her husband was to spend summers in Venice and Gais with Olga Rudge. Omar, attending a purgatorial English boys' school, was excluded from the Master's fold; Mary, raised with a stern paternal hand, was nevertheless dutifully watched over and cared for, angelically memorialized in "Babbo's" lifelong poem. Flickers of paradoxical and seismic complexity: the public poet versus the private man.

I personally think extremely well of Mussolini. If one compares him to American presidents (the last three) or British premiers, etc., in fact one can NOT without insulting him. If the intelligentsia don't think well of him, it is because they know nothing about "the state," and government, and have no particularly large sense of values. Anyhow, WHAT intelligentsia?

—Letter to Harriet Monroe, November 1925[10]

Mussolini has steadily refused to be called anything save "Leader" (Duce) or "Head of the Government," the term dictator has been applied by foreign envy, as the Tories were called cattle-stealers. It does not represent the Duce's fundamental conception of his role. His authority comes, as Eirugina proclaimed authority comes, "from right reason" and from the general fascist conviction that he is more likely to be right than anyone else is.

—*Jefferson and/or Mussolini*, 1935

The struggle to survive—familywise as well as in the public eye—began to take on new proportions for Pound. His letters, postcards, even his books and pamphlets, were now invariably dated Fascist style, from the "March on Rome" in late October 1922. His letterhead bore a cubist pen-and-ink drawing of him by Gaudier-Brzeska and a motto by Mussolini: "Liberty is a duty not a right." Pound's first attempt to enter into contact with Mussolini was in 1932. On April 23 of that year he wrote from Rapallo to Alessandro Chiavolini, Mussolini's private secretary, announcing his desire to communicate and meet with the Italian leader, to present him with "his own impressions" of Italy.[11] On April 26 he received a reply informing him that, due to previous and pressing engagements, the Duce could not receive him; it was requested, however, that he send a letter to Mussolini outlining the topics he wished to discuss. Three days later, Pound wrote to Chiavolini again, stating that he wished to discuss "the following subjects, according to the time available":

I. Details which I have observed traveling throughout Italy during the last decade, and which demonstrate to me the obstacles overcome by Fascist effort (land reclamation, restoration of buildings, etc.).

II. Two pressing problems.

A. Working conditions in Sicilian sulphur mines, with the exception of the modernized one visited by His Excellency seven or more years ago.
B. Productivity in the cork industry, as compared proportionally with that of Portugal, Spain and France.[12]

The letter was transmitted to Mussolini and a belated interview was arranged for Monday, January 30, 1933, at 5:30 p.m., in the Palazzo Venezia in Rome. In the course of the meeting, Pound presented Mussolini with a vellum edition of *A Draft of XXX Cantos*, published three years earlier by Nancy Cunard's Hours Press in Paris. He also handed the dictator a monograph containing a detailed eighteen-point program which summed up the basic concepts of his political ideology.[13] While Mussolini paid scant attention to his visitor's political suggestions, he did seem to welcome the verse. Insisting that he found what he had seen of Pound's poetry *"divertente"* (entertaining), "the Boss," as the poet called him in Canto 41, made an instant and lifelong believer out of Pound. Here was proof, as if proof were actually required, of Mussolini's greatness, of his ability to lead and to discern what others (even artists) could not discern:

'MA QVESTO'
said the Boss, 'è divertente.'
catching the point before the aesthetes had got there . . .

Although Pound would not have the opportunity to meet personally with Mussolini again, he did keep up a steady and ongoing correspondence with the Palazzo Venezia and later with the Duce at Salò during the last days of the Republic. What Pound saw in Mussolini was a statesman of tremendous energy and will, "an OPPORTUNIST who is RIGHT, that is who has certain convictions and who drives them through circumstance, or batters and forms circumstance with them," an ardent Muscle Man "driven by a vast and deep 'concern' or will for the welfare of Italy, not Italy as a bureaucracy, or Italy as a state machinery stuck up on top of the people, but for Italy organic, composed of the last ploughman and the last girl in the oliveyards...."[14]

The poet also admired the many-sided Mussolini because he seemed to him to be a man concerned not only with power and order but with organization, in this case the organization of the state. Here was someone who desired to create an Italy with a functioning train schedule but without miles of useless swamp and marshland. Here was someone who seemed willing to do battle with crime, who wanted to rid the country of its rapacious usurers and munitions makers, and at the same time fight off a decadent and money-hoarding aristocracy. Mussolini's "continuing artistic and political revolution," Pound wrote, had the "material and immediate effect" of "*grano, bonifica, restauri*, grain, swamp-drainage, restorations, new buildings, and, I am ready to add off my own bat, AN AWAKENED INTELLIGENCE in the nation and a new LAN-GUAGE in the debates in the Chamber."[15]

Shaped by his faith in Mussolini and the new Italian state, Pound's views on financial and political affairs poured forth to premiers, cabinet ministers, senators, congressmen, bankers, economists, editors, journalists, and generally to anyone who ventured a response of any kind. He wrote Professor J. H. Rogers, a member of President Roosevelt's Brain Trust who was in London attending a conference: "18 Sept Anno XI. I don't care what you DO, so long as it isn't on my conscience that you are an Abroaded innocent/trusting in British vipers, Genevan mandrakes, and ignorant of Douglas, and ras moneta (stamp scrip). I am prob/ younger'n you are, tho' not much, but by god I'll spit on yr/tombstone if some attention isn't given to contemporary economics."[16] He signed himself "cordially yrn/" and enclosed a form for reply. Afterward, ruminating on his attack, Pound explained in print ("Money Pamphlet, Number Four"): "The London Economic Conference also got nowhere."

He approached higher-ups; he had once admonished Woodrow Wilson by letter;[17] he now wrote on a postcard to Franklin D. Roosevelt:

Lest you forget the nature of money/i.e., that it is a ticket. For the govt. To issue it against any particular merchandise or metal, is merely to favour the owners of that metal and by just that much to betray the rest of the public. You can see that the bill here photod. has SERVED (I mean by the worn state of the note). Certificates of work done. That is what these notes were in fact/before the bank swine got the monopoly. Thus was the wilderness conquered for the sake of pork-barrelers who followed.[18]

The front of the card showed a reproduction of the fifty-cent scrip originally issued by Thaddeus Pound's Union Lumbering Company, Chippewa Falls, Wisconsin. Pound's parents, having retired to Rapallo in 1928, had brought the sample bills over with them, reminding the poet of his frontier heritage. This meant something to him; "he was no longer a lone American calling for reform, or member of a clique, but began to see himself as part of a solid historical tradition."[19]

On the other hand, it was apparent that Pound felt a profound alienation from almost all facets of American creative activity. In 1927, with savings accumulated from his long-overdue *Dial* Award, he proceeded to edit his own little magazine which he called, appropriately, *The Exile*. A number of items in the four issues of the journal suggest that he was no longer "a dazzling littérateur" of precociously advanced sensibilities but was devoting an inordinate amount of attention to his peculiar set of nonliterary obsessions. The periodical featured articles on politics and commerce, with a strongly anti-American bias, and supplementary pieces on Prohibition and sex.[20] "Quite simply," the iconoclast insisted, "I want a new civilization." And in the final issue of *The Exile* (Autumn 1928) he wrote, "The job of America for the next twenty years will be to drive back the government into its proper place, i.e., to force it to occupy itself solely with things which are the proper functions of government."

What literature there was, he seemed to be saying, should concern itself with economics and politics and with what was going on at the given moment: "Preserving public morality is more important than exploring psychological hinterlands."[21] Attempting to perpetuate this "*Rappel à l'ordre*," the chronicler denounced Milton and Wordsworth and wrote *How to Read* (1928); he denounced Freud and Marx and wrote the *ABC of Economics* (1933). The impetus of his contact—direct or indirect—with contemporary history had its far-reaching effects. He felt a sudden "resurgence of energy and a crystallization of the 'totalitarian synthesis.' "[22] He was ready, he wrote in "Date Line" (1934), "to take rash chances, to put . . . money on this year's colts." The year of his didactic *How to Read* he also published a translation of *Ta Hio, The Great Learning,* annotations of Confucian political doctrine. And after his audience with "the Boss," there followed, over the next decade or so, a potpourri of socioeconomic scatterings: *Alfred Venison's Poems: Social Credit Themes by the Poet of Tichfield Street* (1935); *Jefferson and/or Mussolini* (1935); and the highly opinionated *Money Pamphlet* series, six booklets written in Rapallo, the first, second, fourth, and sixth in Italian: *An Introduction to the Economic Nature of the United States* (1944); *Gold and Work* (1944); *What is Money For?* (1939); *A Visiting Card* (1942); *Social Credit: An Impact* (1935); *America, Roosevelt and the Causes of the Present War* (1944). Even his *ABC of Reading* (1934), based substantially on letters to Iris Barry, Marianne Moore, and others, and *Guide to Kulchur* (1938), a compendium of brief essays on government and the arts, were not so much academic texts as expressions of near-dictatorial brashness, full of the dictator's own whim and fancy.

In 1934, William Butler Yeats, then in his sixty-ninth year and in need of critical encouragement, returned to Rapallo. He had not written any verse for over two years and had not seen Pound for five; now, with all but the last of the lyrics for his drama *The King of the Great Clock Tower* completed, he began to wonder. He decided, as he later confessed, "to get the advice of a poet not of my school who would, as he did some years ago, say what he thought." He invited Pound to dine with him and tried to engage him in literary conversation; Pound resisted. "He said apropos of nothing 'Arthur Balfour was a scoundrel' and from that on would talk nothing but politics. All the modern statesmen were more or less scoundrels except 'Mussolini and that hysterical imitator of him Hitler.'" Yeats objected to Pound's "violence," but Pound, carrying on in the same vein, told him to peruse the works of Major Douglas, "who alone knew what caused our suffering." Their dialogue ended abruptly when Pound denounced Dublin as "a reactionary hole." Nor was his final verdict of the new Yeats play any the more promising; in a slashing scrawl he wrote the word "Putrid!" across the front page and the next day deposited the manuscript at Yeats's hotel.[23]

Later in the same year, an agitated and excitable Pound paid a brief visit to Paris to seek out old friends, among them James Joyce. Convinced that Pound was "mad," and "genuinely frightened of him," Joyce asked Ernest Hemingway to join them for supper. It was to be the last time that Hemingway would actually see Pound. Recalling the occasion, Hemingway noted that Pound was erratic and distracted, that he spoke the entire evening of nothing but politics and economics and of the imminent collapse of Europe. Joyce, very likely with the same meeting in mind, wrote to Harriet Weaver: "I am afraid poor Mr Hitler-Missler will soon have few admirers in Europe apart from your nieces and my nephews, Masters W. Lewis and E. Pound."[24] And when Mussolini invaded Ethiopia in October 1935 the Dubliner wrote to his daughter-in-law, Helen Joyce, joking about Pound's political passion and push: "May the 17 devils take Muscoloni and the Alibiscindians! Why don't they make Pound commander-in-chief for Bagonghi and elect me Negus of Amblyopia?"[25]

Following Mussolini's attack on Ethiopia, Pound had rushed inevitably to Italy's defense—out of sympathy for Italy but also because of his paranoid distrust of the League of Nations and of what he believed to be the hypocrisy of the British "Judo-cratic" press.[26] Within less than a year, he produced no less than twenty-five articles for *The British-Italian Bulletin* (a supplement to *L'Italia Nostra*, an Italian newspaper published in London) and a spate of articles for numerous journals and news magazines, all of his journalese pro-Mussolini and loudly proclaiming the Italian cause.

8

"Beer-bottle on the statue's pediments!
"That, Fritz, is the era, to-day against the past,
"Contemporary."

(Canto VII)

... For forty years I have schooled myself, not to write an
economic history of the U.S. or any other country, but to
write an epic poem which begins "In the Dark Forest,"
crosses the Purgatory of human error, and ends in the
light, and "fra i maestri di color che sanno. . . ."

—An Introduction to the Economic Nature
of the United States (1944)

Melopoeia, logopoeia, phanopoeia: the screw wrenches and claw ham-
mers of Pound's engineering bench had been primed and readied, due
architectonic preparation for the composition of a "fifty years epic."
Begun in 1915 and abandoned in 1961—thus unfinished and possibly
unfinishable—*The Cantos* appeared progressively in eight sections
under separate headings. The poem's origins can be traced back to
1904, to fleeting, half-forgotten conversations between the poetician and
his university mentors. A letter written to his mother from London in
1909 pinpoints the poem's growth in the poet's mind. "An epic in the
real sense," he offered, "is the speech of a nation thru the mouth of one
man."[1] In *Make It New* (1934) he would reconsider: "An epic is a
poem including history. No one can understand history unless he understands economics."

One false start in 1917: three ur-Cantos appeared that summer in
Poetry, afterward to be partly revised, partly scrapped. The first book-
length issue of *The Cantos* consisted of sixteen brought out by the Three
Mountains Press of Paris in 1925. Four years later, in the midst of the
leviathan project, he tried to explain the poem's structure to Yeats. He

showed the Irish poet a photograph of a fifteenth-century mural by Cosimo Tura, in three compartments: above, the Triumphs of Love and Chastity; in the middle, the zodiacal signs; beneath, certain seasonal rites of Cosimo Tura's day. Pound told Yeats that in *The Cantos* the Triumphs were replaced by archetypal persons, namely the civilization builders (Confucius, Sigismundo Malatesta, Mussolini, Napoleon, John Adams, Thomas Jefferson); the zodiacal signs were replaced by the epic's fixed elements (descent into Hades, the metamorphosis, etc.); and various modern events and rites took the place of the rites in Tura's time.[2] When completed the creation would display a structure "like that of a Bach fugue"—there would be "no plot, no chronicle of events, no logic of discourse." And in 1960, pondering the fate of his work, the craftsman reaffirmed his choice of a fugal or contrapuntal symphonic effect: "Only a musical form would take the material and the Confucian universe as I see it is a universe of interacting strains and tensions."[3]

In *The Spirit of Romance* he had presented the same argument on behalf of Dante's *Divine Comedy*, pointing to its structure as an example of a "great symphony." But he had also admitted the impossibility of re-creating a design parallel to Dante's, and if he had roughly simulated the Florentine's tripartite organization, the methodology employed was strictly his own. He had ordered *The Cantos* according to what he called the "ideogrammic" or "ideogrammatic method," based on the Oriental schema of juxtaposition used in creating new and multiple ideograms. As outlined by Fenollosa in *The Chinese Written Character as a Medium for Poetry*, two or more ideograms, or word pictures, are conjoined to form a new ideogram; understood as a whole, they create a new meaning, a completely new morphology. This also is often the methodology used in Chinese verse whereby seemingly disparate objects are described in series and the transitions from one thought to another are made with the bewildering rapidity and irregularity of a dream. Poetry of this type functions not merely as a medium of expression but at the same time as a medium of discovery in which the reader is as much involved as the writer, for he must help develop the poem's connections, must help make the poem cohere.

Pound leaps through the ages and from place to place because he wants to create a poetic synthesis, a montage of times past and present. By juxtaposing and interlocking ideas, images, quotations, languages, facts, and themes, *il miglior fabbro* has set out to X-ray the modern mind, to go deep into it by an examination of the roots in history of its patterns of actions and change. And the technique of this examination, as the ideogrammic method prescribes, is a continual process of collation and cross reference, a sort of evaluation by comparison. Pound's vision of "the process"—like Spengler's, Toynbee's, or Ortega y Gasset's—does not reside in the notion that history is something over and done with, but in its permanence as an active force, a living organism, forever fluid and capable of renewed metamorphoses.[4]

That, anyway, was the theory—to live the poem as he wrote it, to capture the essence and quality of life "alive." The practice was more haphazard: anything that came to hand or mind at the moment of composition was more or less heaved into the epic, and became therefore relevant, although the only importance many of the fragments had was in the poet's passing, private associations.[5] Somehow, in piecing his poem together, Pound had allowed himself an overabundance of license. The method he had so carefully chosen and worked out conspired, in one sense, to work against him. What had once seemed high-hearted and truly noble now seemed childish and beside the point. Suddenly, almost without his realizing it, *The Cantos* were full of hate:

> The tale of the perfect schnorrer: a peautiful chewisch poy
> wit a vo-ice dot woult
> meldt dh heart offa schtone
> and wit a likeing for to make arht-voiks
> and ven dh oldt ladty wasn't dhere any more
> and dey didn't know why, tdhere ee woss in the
> oldt antique schop and nobodty knew how he got dhere
> and venn hiss brudder diet widout any bapers
> he vept all ofer dh garpet so much he
> had to have his clothes aftervards pressed
> and he orderet a magnifficent funeral
> and tden zent dh pill to dh vife.
>
> (Canto XXXV)

>   . . . Bismarck
> blamed american civil war on the jews;
> particularly on the Rothschild
> one of whom remarked to Disraeli
> that nations were fools to pay rent for their credit
>
> (Canto XLVIII)

Remarked Ben: better keep out the jews
    or yr/ grand children will curse you
jews, real jews, chazims, and *neschek*
also super-neschek or the international racket
           (Canto LII)

    the yidd is a stimulant, and the goyim are cattle
in gt/ proportion and go to saleable slaughter
    with the maximum of docility. but if
a place be versalzen , , , ?
With justice,
by the law, from the law or it is not in the contract
     Yu has nothing pinned on Jehoveh
          (Canto LXXIV)

Democracies electing their sewage
till there is no clear thought about holiness
a dung flow from 1913
and, in this, their kikery functioned, Marx, Freud
    and the american beaneries
Filth under filth . . .

          (Canto 91)

Ultimately, there is no explaining away—no need to explain away—passages such as these. They are simply there, "right in the middle of the poetry," as Allen Tate would have it. Yet there are also, as we know, superb passages in *The Cantos*, brilliantly recorded dialogue, keen fragments of action, richly cadenced lyrics. And though they do not begin to offset the appalling lapses of tone and the strange, offensive obsessions, they do reflect, in Donald Davie's words, an undeniable "quality of tenderness," "an attitude of reverent vigilance." Everything considered, Pound is, in a real sense, a nature poet, whose inhumanity is the inhumanity of the world, but whose sensitivity, the signs of his intense and persistent attention to the cosmos, can be found on almost any page of the *œvre*:[6]

Thus the light rains, thus pours, *e lo soleils plovil*
The liquid and rushing crystal
        beneath the knees of the gods.
Ply over ply, thin glitter of water;

Brook film bearing white petals.
The pine at Takasago
       grows with the pine of Isé!
The water whirls up the bright pale sand in the spring's mouth
"Behold the Tree of the Visages!"

                     (Canto IV)

Autumn moon; hills rise about lakes
against sunset
Evening is like a curtain of cloud
a blurr above ripples; and through it
sharp long spikes of the cinnamon,
a cold tune amid reeds.
Behind hill the monk's bell
borne on the wind.
Sail passed here in April; may return in October
Boat fades in silver; slowly. . . .

             (Canto XLIX)

With clouds over Taishan-Chocorua
      when the blackberry ripens
and now the new moon faces Taishan
one must count by the dawn star
     Dryad, thy peace is like water
There is September sun on the pools. . . .
         (Canto LXXXIII)

bare trees walk on the sky-line. . . .
         (Canto CX)

   . . . a partridge-shaped cloud over dust storm. . . .
         (Canto CXIII)

9

Pound continued through much of the 1930s to engage, if only part time, in various aspects of the arts. Early in the decade he organized his festive chamber-music series in Rapallo's town hall, the main purpose of which was the rediscovery of a number of "forgotten" composers—Dowland, Janequin, Pergolesi, Monteverdi, Vivaldi. In 1932 he published *Guido Cavalcanti Rime*, in 1933 the *Active Anthology*, in 1937 *Polite Essays* and *Confucius, Digest of the Analects*. He had added the Swiss naturalist Louis Agassiz (1807–73) and the German anthropologist Leo Frobenius (1873–1938) to his hand-picked pantheon, and was helping W. H. D. Rouse and Laurence Binyon with their respective translations of *The Odyssey* and *The Divine Comedy*. Among the literary magazines he assisted during these years were *Broletto*, an Italian quarterly devoted to new writing; Lincoln Kirstein and R. P. Blackmur's *Hound and Horn*; and Ronald Duncan's *Townsman* (London), to which he contributed articles of his own and helped to get contributions from others. As a final measure, he backed the newly launched Objectivist Movement, arranging for the publication of "precisionist" poets such as Bunting, Zukofsky, Carl Rakosi, Charles Reznikoff, George Oppen, and René Taupin, at the same time supporting a number of objectivist doctrines and manifestoes. But all this, compared to the constancy of his previous output, was marginal, and by the middle to late 1930s Pound's retreat from the cultural front was all but complete.

Sensing the outbreak of war, Pound gradually lost interest in poetry and literary criticism and began to write "stop the war" propaganda, heaping inexorable abuse upon the democratic leaders and upon what he called the "gonorrhoeal elements" of international finance. He proceeded to propagate his ideas in a bevy of periodicals whose orientations were often in direct opposition one to the other. He wrote for Communist newspapers and magazines, "left wing" weeklies, Fascist reviews, "right wing" journals, Italian technical organs such as *Rassegna Mone-taria*—he wrote, that is, for any publication that would open up its pages to him: *Delphian Quarterly, Aryan Path, America, Sante Fe New Mexican, Il Mare, New Masses, Japan Times, The New Review, Front,* even established periodicals like *Esquire* and the *Times Literary Supplement.*

Not enough that he bombarded these periodicals with his manifold dissertations on war and peace, poverty and prosperity, but he continued to write, as he had for some years, literally thousands of letters to persons of influence to set his ideas in motion. He continually felt he was on the verge of discovering someone who would take notice and could act.[1] He wrote to Paul de Kruif: "If Roosevelt thinks he can borrow the nation out of debt, he is a fool. And if he knows he can't and goes on as if he could, he is a traitor. Do send me items, and also criticize what I say; I want to make a just estimate, based on facts."[2] He wrote to Senator Arthur H. Vandenberg: "War is caused by finance, not by guns. Your committee is doing fine work, but so far as the press lets one learn anything, no sign that it has got down to bedrock."[3] To Senator William E. Borah: "I don't hold ANY theories about money that I am not ready to drop if anyone can and will stand up and show that I am in error."[4] To Congressman George Holden Tinkham: "I am very glad to read that you mean to show up the Carnegie Endowment. The Rockefeller, I know less about but would be glad of details. . . . Those buzzards have spent half a million a year taxed out of the people and they have steadily avoided exposing or investigating the economic causes of war."[5] To William E. Woodward: "Do it strike you as gauge of the economic illiteracy of the country if you (on the advisory board) don't know what an auxilliary currency is? And that F. D. R. is probably equally vague. The only defence a people has against 'tyranny,' i.e., gettin' rushed into war and having its eye teeth cheated out of it in peace time: is a diffusion of econ. knowledge."[6]

The more information he collected from his correspondents and followers and the closer he got—or thought he got—to understanding any problem, the greater his desire for action. He wanted action, some simple solution that would do away with the horror of a world that was not capable, given the conditions and facts of twentieth-century existence, of the relatively austere and ordered life of the mandarin society of Confucian China or even of the agrarian breath of the colonial American founders. The real stumbling block was that since he had taken up residence in Rapallo, and especially since the threat of war had become real, he had begun to lose personal contact with his friends in the United States, England, and France; he therefore became increasingly suscepti- ble to the distorted and often outrightly deceptive accounts of political and economic affairs as reported in newspapers, journals, and maga- zines, and to the unbalanced reports he received from the adherents of the Fascist regime.

He did make one concerted effort to assimilate information and guidance directly and on his own. A questionnaire was printed up in August 1934, headed "Volitionist Economics," which contained eight questions with space for replies—and this he subsequently distributed en masse:

> Which of the following statements do you agree with?
> 1. It is an outrage that the state shd. run into debt to individuals by the act and in the act of creating real wealth.
> 2. Several nations recognize the necessity of distributing purchasing power. They do actually distribute it. The question is whether it shd. be distributed as favour to corporations; as reward for not having a job; or impartially and per capita.
> 3. A country CAN have one currency for internal use, and another good both for home and foreign use.
> 4. If money is regarded as certificate for work done, taxes are no longer necessary.
> 5. It is possible to concentrate all taxation onto the actual paper money of a country (or on to one sort of its money).
> 6. You can issue valid paper money against any commodity UP TO the amount of that commodity that people want.
> 7. Some of the commonest failures of clarity among economists are due to using one word to signify two or more different concepts: such as, DEMAND, meaning sometimes WANT and sometimes power to buy; authoritative, meaning also responsible.
> 8. It is an outrage that the owner of one commodity can not ex- change it with someone possessing another, without being impeded or taxed by a third party holding a monopoly over some third substance or controlling some convention, regardless of what it be called.

Replies came in from people with a number of different opinions, rang- ing from A. R. Orage, who was then editing the *New English Weekly*, and H. L. Mencken, the vociferously opinionated journalist, to James P. Warburg, the New York banker and administrator. Some of those to whom he sent the form had ideas similar to his own and answered accordingly; others dissented, quibbled, ridiculed, or suggested that the queries were weighted in favor of Pound's own leanings.[7] But what encouraged him more than anything else was the fact that his survey met with an almost total response. He concluded, perhaps not unjustifiably, that interest in monetary affairs had reached a new plateau.

His most outspoken views on money and related themes, with the exception of the Italian radio broadcasts, were probably contained in Pound's six *Money Pamphlets*, composed between 1935 and 1944. In the first, *An Introduction to the Economic Nature of the United States*, the author pre-empts his discussion with an introductory thought: "The true history of the economy of the United States, as I see it, is to be found in the correspondence between Adams and Jefferson, in the writings of Van Buren, and in quotations from the intimate letters of the Fathers of the Republic. The elements remain the same: debts, altering the value of monetary units, and the attempts and triumphs of usury, due to monopolies, or to a 'Corner'." All of these references, as well as others similar in tack, had become the source of copious note-taking and quotation in *The Cantos*, an indication that Pound's economic and historical writings, particularly the prewar ones, were merely parallel texts or, at the least, commentaries and footnotes to the epic.

By the time he wrote the third pamphlet—*What is Money For?*—he had begun to show interest in Silvio Gesell's anarchist theory of the velocity of money circulation, or *Schwundgeld*—"shrinking money"—a paper-money system by which everyone was obliged, on the first of the month, to affix a stamp on every note he possessed equal to one per cent of the note's face value. The German economist's invention was no more than a gimmick designed to combat inflation, but Pound—always on the lookout for unorthodox ploys and devices—saw in it "an alternate way of getting money away from the strangle-hold of the banking community, besides reducing taxes for the general population."[8] Principally designed to keep money in circulation, *Schwundgeld*, or stamp scrip, never really caught on with Social Credit enthusiasts, who argued that mere motion of money would not make up the gap between cost and selling price. Pound was of a different opinion. "I am particularly keen on Gesell," he wrote, "because once people have used stamp script they HAVE a clear idea about money. They understand tickets better than men who haven't used stamp scrip." He was so keen on Gesell, in fact, that he journeyed, on the advice of Hugo Fack, a small-press publisher from Texas who had published an English translation of Gesell's book *The Natural Economic Order*, to a town where *Schwundgeld*, or something like it, had been tried out—Wörgl, in the Austrian Tirol, a place, he afterward advised, which had "sent shivers down the backs of all the lice of Europe, Rothschildian and others."

It was also in the third *Money Pamphlet* that he included his "Introductory Text Book," a mini-capsulated prolegomenon for the study of American history, which he considered important enough to enclose separately with all his other mailings, and which in its entirety reads as follows:

CHAPTER I

"All the perplexities, confusion, and distress in America arise, not from defects in their constitution or confederation, not from want of honour and virtue, so much as from downright ignorance of the nature of coin, credit, and circulation."

John Adams.

CHAPTER II

". . . and if the national bills issued, be bottomed (as is indispensable) on pledges of specific taxes for their redemption within certain and moderate epochs, and be of *proper denomination* for *circulation*, no interest on them would be necessary or just, because they would answer to every one of the purposes of the metallic money withdrawn and replaced by them."

Thomas Jefferson (1816, *letter to Crawford*).

CHAPTER III

". . . and gave the people of this Republic THE GREATEST BLESSING THEY EVER HAD—THEIR OWN PAPER TO PAY THEIR OWN DEBTS."

Abraham Lincoln.

CHAPTER IV

"The Congress shall have power; To coin money, regulate the value thereof and of foreign coin and to fix the standards of weights and measures."

Constitution of the United States, Article I
Legislative Department, Section 8, page 5.
Done in the convention by the unanimous consent of the States, 7 September 1787, and of the Independence of the United States the twelfth. In witness whereof we have hereunto subscribed our names.

George Washington.
President and Deputy from Virginia

In a brief addendum to these citations, the polemicist recommends a few of his favorite economic texts: C. H. Douglas, *Economic Democracy*; Willis Overholser, *History of Money in the U.S.*; R. McNair Wilson, *Promise to Pay*; P. Larrañaga, *Gold, Glut and Government*; M. Butchart, *Money*; and Silvio Gesell, *The Natural Economic Order*. Further along in the same afterword, Social Credit and *Schwundgeld* are reconciled, as it were, in a single drawn breath: "Douglas' proposals are a sub-head under the main idea in Lincoln's sentence, Gesell's 'invention' is a special case under Jefferson's general law."

Other gists and piths from the *Money Pamphlet* series:

In *A Visiting Card*, published in Rome and addressed to Italians, Pound writes: "I insist on the identity of our American Revolution of 1776 with your Fascist Revolution. Two chapters in the same war against usurers."

In *Gold and Work*: "This war was no whim of Mussolini's, nor of Hitler's. This war is a chapter in the long and bloody tragedy which began with the foundation of the Bank of England in far away 1694."

In *What is Money For?*: "USURY is the cancer of the world, which only the surgeon's knife of Fascism can cut out of the life of nations."

In the thirteenth year of the Fascist era Pound published his controversial text *Jefferson and/or Mussolini*. The title? "The fundamental likenesses between these two men are probably greater than their differences. . . . Jefferson was one genius and Mussolini is another." What else had they in common? Their attitude toward agriculture, the "sense of the 'root and the branch,' readiness to scrap the lesser thing for the thing of major importance, indifference to mechanism as weighed against the main purpose without regard to abstract ideas, even if the idea was proclaimed the week before last." Confucius served as binding yoke. In keeping within the tangents of Kung's doctrine, both Jefferson and Mussolini were aware that the crisis was "OF, not IN the system."

In a letter (September 1935) addressed to Chiavolini, Mussolini's personal secretary, Pound wrote: "The book (*Jefferson and/or Mussolini*) has been written, as everyone knows, in a year in which too many learned men, etc., members of the so-called Italian intelligentsia, ignored the constructive qualities of a new era." Pound took pride in the work. His foreword, written for the 1935 Stanley Nott edition, reads: "The body of this ms. was written and left my hands in February 1933. 40 publishers have refused it. No typescript of mine has been read by so many people or brought me a more interesting correspondence." Forty publishers were assurance enough of the book's controversiality. After its publication, three copies were shipped off to heads of state—two to Il Duce, the third to President and Mrs. Franklin Delano Roosevelt.

Dedicated to Basil Bunting and Louis Zukofsky ("a Quaker and a Jew"), *Guide to Kulchur* was put together rather haphazardly by Pound. Chapters and sections were strung together ideogrammically in the same manner as *The Cantos*, and like the epic the *Guide* is an amalgam of euphoric highs and alarming lows, the lows in this instance dominant. From his desultory examination of Socrates' *Ethics* onward, the incline of his line of attack is all downgrade:

> Form-sense, 1910–1914. Fifteen or so years later Lewis [Wyndham] discovered Hitler. I hand it to him as a superior perception. Superior in relation to my own "discovery" of Mussolini.

> Great intelligence attains again and again to great verity. The Duce and Kung fu Tseu equally perceive that their people need poetry; that prose is NOT education but the outer core of the same.

> America (the U.S.) has not paid its debt even in thought to the men who kept the U.S. OUT of the League at Geneva. If we have Susan B. Anthony in the rogue's gallery recently shoved onto our postage stamps, we shd. think up something better, some really honorific memento, say a monument really well sculpted, for Lodge, Knox, Borah and George Holden Tinkham, for having kept our fatherland out of at least one stinking imbroglio.

"Race prejudice is red herring. The tool of the man defeated intellectually and of the cheap politician": this excerpt, also from *Kulchur*, gives rise to a second problem—the immediate and ponderous question of Ezra Pound's alleged anti-Semitism. It was natural for him to link the Jews with usury, but often when he made this association, he did so in an exceedingly ambiguous manner. In 1938, for example, he wrote in the *British Union Quarterly* (formerly the *Fascist Quarterly*), that "our worst evil is the aryio-kike who is able to take a dirty line and stick to it without deviation or shadow of turning with none of the Jews' moments of pity, excitement or need of opulent display," and in his *Congressional Record*-inspired "American Notes" column for the *New English Weekly* he wrote that "Usurers have no race," and then added: "How long the whole Jewish people is to be sacrificial goat for the usurer, I know not."

His letters of the period were equally ambiguous. In February 1935 he wrote to Virginia Rice, his American literary agent: "Danger of jews. Not that they mayn't be O.K. individually. STATE of mind induced by being surrounded by nothing but."[9] And to James Taylor Dunn, editor of the *Globe*, a small journal, he vouchsafed (March 1937) that "if the jews wd. take any sort of part in econ/ reform as distinct from communistic obscurantism and financial obscurantism there wd. be no need of any anti-semitic stuff at all."[10]

Yet as the war drew near Pound became more and more partisan in favor of both Mussolini and Hitler, and more irrational in his hatred of Semitic cultural and financial influences. In December 1938, he told Louis Zukofsky: "Why curse Adolph [sic], why not git down to bedrock?.... As always jewish outlaw and crook leads the sheriffs posse back to the ghetto."[11] The following year (August 1939) he wrote an article for Sir Oswald Mosley's magazine, *Action*, in which he lauded the Third Reich: "The natural civilizer of Russia is Germany. No less gusty and active people would bother about educating the Mujik." And in *What is Money For?* he asks the reader to "note the paragraph from *Mein Kampf* magnificently isolated by Wyndham Lewis in his [1931] *Hitler*—'The struggle against international finance and loan capital has become the most important point in the National Socialist programme: the struggle of the German nation for its independence and freedom.' "

To try to find out why the author of *The Cantos* came to produce his virulent anti-Semitic lucubrations does not really take one far. Robert Fitzgerald suggested (*Encounter*, July 1956) that "only a man working in isolation, without criticism or ignoring it, could have failed to see the fretfulness and poverty of argument in some of these letters and essays." Certainly it is significant that Pound—always so keenly tuned to the problem of linguistic decay—did not grasp these symptoms either in Mussolini's or in Hitler's puffed-up and self-aggrandizing rhetoric, to say nothing of his own. Perhaps, to locate one cause, he had simply taken on too much, become too multiple, wasting himself in the process, dispersing himself beyond his human limitations. It was as though he had badly misinterpreted the tone of some important aesthetic occasion,[12] and in the agonized and agonizing yatter which emanated daily from Via Marsala 12-5, his friends and acquaintances noticed the error of tone more often now—the tone, many surmised, of a man no longer in touch.

10

... the collapse of our civilization in the war of the 1860's. ... The total democracy bilge, by which I mean the clichés, the assumptions, the current cant about "the people" arose from sheer misunderstanding or perversion. Perversion of ideas by means and by misuse of words. The disequality of human beings can be observed. ... There is no more equality between men than between animals.

—"National Culture—A Manifesto 1938"

Italy believes in "Libertà Economica, con responsibilità civica," economic liberty, and civic responsibility. It is this *Civic* Responsibility, this sense of responsibility, every man to himself *and* to the nation, that has been lost in both England and America. Therein is the decline of democracy.

A strong Italy is the keystone of Europe for peace, for the good life, for civilization.

No man living has preserved the Peace of Europe as often as has Benito Mussolini.

—"A Keystone of Europe," 1935

The penchant for camouflaging despair beneath harsh, commanding tones was not Pound's alone. Yeats, Lewis, Eliot, and D. H. Lawrence were all stanch reactionaries in whose writings can be found traces, and in some cases more than traces, of a snide and demeaning anti-Semitism. The same can be said of Claudel, Colette, Maurras, Morand, and Giraudoux. A third set—Céline, Hamsun, Hauptmann, Otto Abetz, Gottfried Benn, and Henry Williamson—were for the most part ardent Hitlerites, whereas Marinetti, Belloc, Gentile, d'Annunzio, G. K. Chesterton, and Pirandello were all members of Mussolini's camp. What distinguished Pound from the rest was his unfettered determination to see his utopia through to the end. The others, realizing their mistake, had drawn back in time—or at least had waited until it was over to repent and retreat. Only Pound persevered, supporting Italy while she was at war with the United States, and afterward (Alastair Hamilton writes), following her defeat and conciliation.

Precisely to what extent he mistook Black Shirt oratory for truth, concepts for deeds, is difficult to say. It was a question of maintaining faith right to the end of the Fascist era that before he died, and when he was completing the last of the seriatim *Cantos*, he would be able to point to the anti-Keynesian Douglasite vision as having been implemented in an existing country, and that country would be Italy.[1] So strong was his conviction, so blinding, that he often ignored, discounted in fact, those whose views differed from his own. In June 1937, when Nancy Cunard distributed from Paris her Spanish Civil War questionnaire asking 148 well-known authors whether they were "for, or against, the legal Government and the People of Republican Spain . . . for, or against, Franco and Fascism?" Pound responded that he felt "Neutral" about the entire matter. In an accompanying letter he explained why he thought so little of Miss Cunard's questionnaire and those who had signed it—writers such as Wells, Auden, and Stephen Spender. "Questionnaire an escape mechanism for young fools," he chided, "who are too cowardly to think; too lazy to investigate the nature of money, its mode of issue, the control of such issue by the Banque de France and the stank of England. You are all had. Spain is an emotional luxury to a gang of sap-headed dilettantes."

In sum, his promulgations and post-Vortex muscle-flexing served essentially to alienate him from his confederates. It had reached the point where even his fellow Social Creditors were fed up with him. John Hargrave, coleader with C. H. Douglas of the Social Credit Party of Great Britain, wrote to Gorham B. Munson, his Yankee counterpart, stating that Pound's propaganda for the movement was "worthless"—"it was like a series of explosions in a rock quarry." Munson, editor of *New Democracy*, the official organ since 1933 of the New York New Economics (Social Credit) group, to which the poet was a frequent contributor, likewise censored him, condemning him for his efforts to link Social Credit democracy with Fascist political totalitarianism. Pound's antics had grown so out of proportion by this time that Major Douglas himself took umbrage:

London
January 7, 1936

Dear E.P.,

Pending engaging a whole-time secretary to correspond with you, I suggest that you concentrate on the subject of taxation as a form of modern highway robbery combined with iniquitous interference with the freedom of the individual.[2]

E.P.'s response to this taunting epistle was predictable enough; deploying Silvio Gesell as portentous Rock-Drill, he mutinied against the former Westinghouse engineer, pouring his ammunition into the pages of the *British Union Quarterly* (April–June 1937): "If Douglas really does not understand Gesell then Douglas is done for. If his clique is afraid to discuss Social MONEY, then we must dismiss them as impotent sectaries, who have had their uses in sectional education."

All attempts to curtail Pound's myriad predatory activities fell short. Believing in his own fervent and oracular way that consciousness does determine being,[3] he continued to storm the barricades. During 1938 and 1939, he not only sent out a swarm of letters to politicians like Borah and Taft, who were against America getting involved in the war in Europe, but kept up his more serious inquiries into American social history, writing to historians, for example, Charles Beard and Davis R. Dewey; to Beard, on one occasion, urging him to begin a series of pamphlets on American economic history along the lines of his— Beard's—recent study, *Economic Origins of Jeffersonian Democracy*; and to Dewey, author of *Financial History of the United States* (1907), seeking further information about various matters mentioned in that work.[4] Among the then-current crop of fiscal reformers contacted by Pound were Arthur Kitson, Gladys Bing, Frederick Soddy, Claude Bowers, Christopher Hollis, and Lincoln Steffens. He wrote to Henry Ford and Gerald L. K. Smith, to Father Charles E. Coughlin and Governor Huey Long. He was in touch throughout with an international brigade of proto-Fascist rabble-rousers, some of them Syndicalists, some anarchists, but all anti-Semites: Leese, Williamson, Chamberlain, Mosley, Forgan, and Drinkwater of Britain; Ciano, Pardi, Pavolini, Polvarelli, Por, Ricciardi, Delcroix, and Stefani of Italy; Gottfried Feder and Hjalmar Schacht of Germany, two of the important formulators of Nazi economic policy.

There was so much to do and so little time that Pound was all but devoured. One role could not suffice him, no absolute self, nor fixed identity. He lectured at a number of Italian universities (Bologna, Milan, Rome); borrowed a second-hand printing press in order to expedite the production of his own fliers and pamphlets; acted as liaison between the various monetary reform sects, gathering data and information from one and disbursing it to all. He became involved in a world of self-delusion over which he ruled as per regulations of his own making. "Following Aristotle, Hume, Berkeley, and Anthony Trollope, my first step in any enquiry is now economic. I look to the cost and the profits," he wrote in the April 1938 issue of *The Delphian Quarterly*. Earlier he had written, "There is too much future, and nobody but me and Muss/and half a dozen others to attend to it."[5] His attitude and demeanor were such that even his daughter detected about him what one of the examining government psychiatrists at his sanity hearing in Washington in 1946 typed an air of "confabulation"—he was obsessive, dogmatic, unduly egocentric: "Sometimes Izzo* brought some shy young man interested in poetry. Babbo would immediately challenge the newcomer by pulling out a ten-lira note and telling him to look at it carefully, to read the fine print. What did it mean, what did it say, what did he know about the nature of money? Nothing. Unless he understood the nature of money he could not understand or write good poetry. Then followed a list of assignments. The young man seldom came a second time."[6]

In the sense that it monopolized his every thought and action, the economic-and-political factor had become a kind of objective correlative for Pound, an all-consuming passion which threatened now to rule his life. Although to some extent an outsider, he had managed to place himself, by virtue of his direct involvement in metapolitical happenings, at the crossroads of the holocaust. His Promethean expressions of will were uttered with such frequency and ferocity that almost no one could tell whether they were aimed to terrify, bemuse, alarm, or simply devastate. Intruders (and who now was not an intruder?)[7] came away perplexed and bewildered. If he remained uncharacteristically silent about events as newsworthy as the much-publicized Moscow Trials of 1936–38 or the signing of the short-lived Nazi–Soviet nonaggression pact of

---

* Carlo Izzo, a professor of English and American literature, living in Venice, was a close associate of Pound's during the 1930s.

1939, it was because he had riveted his attention on other, more immediate target areas.

America's welfare was still the central point of concentration for the poet. Surprisingly, the type of government that he favored for the States was no more than a continuation of the old democratic tradition, but one, he cautioned, that "works." He did apparently want to see established in America one or two Fascist ideas, but these only to improve the existing system, so that when he urged representation in Congress according to trades and profession, rather than representation according to geographic distribution, he was not urging this because it was to be found in fascism but as a means of carrying out better the original goals of Jefferson, Adams, Jackson, and Van Buren.[8] Pound's conviction that somewhere along the line the Constitution had been corrupted and the American Dream shattered gnawed at him now with increasing persistence. It was with this thought in mind that he decided, shortly before the outbreak of the war, to return to the United States. The trip, for all intents and purposes a self-styled mercy mission, was to be his first visit home in nearly three decades. It began in Genoa on April 13, 1939, aboard the Italian liner *Rex*.

Inferno

(1939–1945)

1

William Carlos Williams, Ford Madox Ford, and H. L. Mencken had been trying for years to get Pound to return home, if only for a brief visit. He had toyed with the prospect before, but at the last moment had always reneged, insisting that the lumpish American scene was worth avoiding. But by January 1939, having recently returned from London to Rapallo,[1] he experienced a change of heart. In a note to Wyndham Lewis, written at approximately this time, he announced his intention to "invade the States." Lewis was living in New York and Pound wanted to join him. With Europe drifting toward war, he was eager, as Noel Stock put it, to play his part in keeping the peace between Italy and the United States and also thought it was time that he went personally to see American leaders, to point out to them the road to economic as well as political sanity.

What infuriated him was the inexorable fact that not one American in a thousand knew his Constitutional rights. No one, for example, was aware that the United States had not, since 1913, issued its own money, but was instead borrowing money issued by the Federal Reserve Bank, and that part of the onerous taxes which American citizens paid their government was actually interest on this alleged perpetual loan. Pound felt that if the people could ever know that they were being "duped" into paying unlawful taxes and encouraged to fight needless wars "they would rise up in revolution, purify the government and return to a simple, taxless federation of states, ruled by laws, locally passed and locally enforced."[2] Such was the trigonometry of his vision, and in order to see it through he was prepared, if need be, to accept an advisory post in government and to spend some months each year in his own country.

Later he would come to regret having made the voyage at all. In the muck and mire of the Detention Training Center outside Pisa, sifting through isolated memories now buried under the collapse of history, he would think back on the venture as a complete and utter failure and would record it as such in *The Pisan Cantos*. At St. Elizabeths, reaffirming his apprehensions, he explained to visitors that he had arrived on American soil too late and in the wrong frame of mind. In the final analysis, the 1939 trip served essentially to convince him of the hopelessness of the general political situation and resulted, upon his return to Italy, in his taking up the microphone in defense of the forces of National Socialism. Projecting the *Rex* periplum in strictly mythological terms, he came to see it as the descent into Hades, his *Nekuia*, the Seafarer in transit, in search of home—*nostos*—and himself on that infernal expedition as Odysseus/Pound, a traveler, "a man of no fortune and with a name to come." And, what is worse, this painful image continued to dog him for years to come.

And then went down to the ship,
Set keel to breakers, forth on the godly sea, and
We set up mast and sail on that swart ship,
Bore sheep aboard her, and our bodies also
Heavy with weeping, and winds from sternward
Bore us onward with bellying canvas,
Circe's this craft, the trim-coifed goddess.

(Canto I)

He arrived in New York harbor on April 21, eight days after leaving Italy. Aboard ship he had occupied a first-class suite. He said in a newspaper interview twenty years later that he had booked to travel second class but had been given the suite for $160 because the ship was empty.[3] He had taken, he said, only one suitcase and a rucksack and had not needed porters; he had spent only $5 over and above his fare.[4]

Gorham Munson sent a wireless message advising, "Give economic but not political views to the press when interviewed," and John Cournos sent a welcoming telegram when the liner docked. Munson also went to meet Pound but missed him; by the time he arrived, the poet had cleared customs and departed for 4 Patchin Place in Greenwich Village, home of E. E. Cummings. Before he left he met the press.[5]

The question uppermost in everyone's mind was put to him by one of the ship reporters: Would there be a war?

"Nothing but devilment can start a new war west of the Vistula.

I'm not making any accusation against anyone. But the bankers and the munitions interests, whoever and wherever they may be, are more responsible for the present talk of war than are the intentions of Mussolini or anyone else." Mussolini, he said, "has a mind with the quickest uptake of any man I know of except Picabia." And who was Picabia? "Picabia is the man who ties the knots in Picasso's tail."

The usual queries followed about contemporary books and writers.

"I regard the literature of social significance as of no significance. It is pseudo-pink blah. The men who are worth anything today are definitely down on money—writing about money, the problem of money, exchange, gold and silver. I have yet to find a Bolshevik who has written about it."

What did he think of James Joyce?

"When Joyce was writing I ballyhooed him. Not since he retrogressed."

Ernest Hemingway?

"Hemingway is a good guy, but I don't suppose we'd want to meet personally. Spain."

Poets?

"I can name only one poet writing today. I mean E. E. Cummings."[6]

Pound stayed in New York for only a few days, before proceeding to Washington, D.C. President Roosevelt was too busy to see him so he saw Secretary of Agriculture (afterward Vice President) Henry A. Wallace, to whom he was introduced by letter by Paul de Kruif. Wallace later recalled the meeting for Charles Norman: "Pound had some ideas as to proper economic organization but I have forgotten what they were. . . . Pound seemed normal enough when he called on me but rather pessimistic as to the future of the U.S. I was much surprised to learn later that he had broadcast for Mussolini. I do not think that he intended to hurt the U.S.A. But I do think he operated in a different world from most of us."[7]

While he was in Washington he met and discussed monetary reform with almost everyone: Senators Taft, Vandenberg, Byrd, and Bankhead (Tallulah's uncle), Representatives Hamilton Fish, Jr., Martin Dies, and H. J. Voorhis. Voorhis, who the previous year had used in a House debate the quotation from John Adams which Pound employed as chapter one of his "Introductory Text Book," proved more cooperative than the rest.

Pound felt, after attending a session of Congress, that the nation would do well to broadcast legislative hearings, and he pressed Voorhis to push this issue in the House with good speed. Voorhis attempted to drum up interest in the proposal but with little success. With another sympathetic politican, Senator Burton Wheeler, Pound discussed Roosevelt's New Deal policies; he later quoted Wheeler as claiming that Roosevelt had packed the Supreme Court "with Justices who would declare Constitutional anything that he did":

> "Has packed the Supreme Court
>   so they will declare anything he does constitutional."
>   Senator Wheeler, 1939
>   (Canto 100)

In a 1945 affidavit in support of an application for bail, his counsel stated that in 1939 Pound, the grandson of a Congressman, "saw such statesmen as Bankhead, Borah, Bridges, Byrd, Downey, Lodge, Mac-Leish, Tinkham, Voorhis, and Wallace, all in a vain effort to move the nation's policies toward paths which he thought were the paths of peace." Pound told the district judge at his initial hearing in 1945 that he had made the 1939 journey "to keep hell from breaking loose in the world." But not all had gone according to plan. When he saw Senator Borah, he apparently discussed his desire to serve the country in some official capacity. Borah's testy response, together with some samples of Bankhead's frank but noncommittal conversation on Roosevelt, were reproduced in the last of the *Pisan Cantos*:

> "an' doan you think he chop an' change all the time
> stubborn az a mule, sah, stubborn as a MULE,
> got th' eastern idea about money"
>   Thus Senator Bankhead
> "am sure I don't know what a man like you
>   would find to *do* here"
>   said Senator Borah
> Thus the solons, in Washington,
> on the executive, and on the country, a.d. 1939.
>   (Canto LXXXIV)

And as part of an *American Hour* radio broadcast from Rome, June 19, 1942, another glimpse, equally sour, of his stay in the nation's capital:

Among my American memories is that of a fallen gentleman in shabby overcoat in a Washington bar. Wishing to get something other than editorial and congressional views and the results of the New Deal and subsequent Americanisms in the year 1939, in fact, about cherry time, I inquired of him . . . what he thought of it all, and I got the indubitably incontrovertible reply, "Ah, we're all mixed up, this generation." That undoubtedly represented the real man in or at that moment very slightly and momentarily removed from the street, as contrasted with the BBC "hand-picked." And any man's clarity must start inside his own head.

After Washington, there was a great deal of traveling back and forth. The wife of E. E. Cummings recalled seeing Pound toting around a pair of rolled-up pajamas in an envelope tucked under his arm. John Slocum, to whom he had been introduced by James Laughlin in Austria four years earlier and at whose residence he was now staying in New York, recalled a trip to Englewood, New Jersey, where he and Pound picked up the daughter of an old friend, then returned and tried to get into Sherman Billingsley's Stork Club. They were turned back at the plush-covered rope across the entrance because of Pound's attire. He wore no tie (the equivalent of full frontal nakedness in the New York of those days)[8] and an open-neck shirt with broad purple stripes.

He began to drop in on such friends as Ford Madox Ford and Tibor Serly, both of whom were temporarily living in New York, and to frequent the Museum of Modern Art, where Iris Barry was in charge of the new film library. He was often seen in the company of Wyndham Lewis and met Marianne Moore for the first time, although they had written one another for nearly twenty years; he saw Katherine Ruth Heyman again, a concert pianist whom he had known since 1904 but not seen since 1908; he ate lunch with H. L. Mencken and traveled to New Haven, Connecticut, to visit James Angleton, who printed the "Introductory Text Book" in the first issue of his journal *Furioso* (Summer 1939). In Greenwich, Connecticut, he gave an interview and wrote an article, "The Cabinet of a Dream, and Congress Should Go on the Air," which was published in the *Greenwich Time* of July 13.[9]

One night he stayed at the home of William Carlos Williams. He tried so hard to ram economic innuendo down his host's throat that Williams wrote a letter (June 7, 1939) to James Laughlin in which he expressed distress and concern:

The man is sunk, in my opinion, unless he can shake the fog of fascism out of his brain during the next few years, which I seriously doubt that he can do. The logicality of fascist rationalization is soon going to kill him. You can't argue away wanton slaughter of innocent women and children by the neo-scholasticism of a controlled economy program. To hell with a Hitler who lauds the work of his airmen in Spain and so to hell with Pound too if he can't stand up and face his questioners on the point.[10]

Although Pound told the press otherwise, the possibility of war in Europe preyed heavily on his mind and one day in May he dined with the Polish Ambassador, Count Jerzy Potocki, cautioning him against Winston Churchill whom he thought a threat. "God help you," he told the Ambassador, "if you trust England." On another occasion he visited Fordham University in the Bronx. There, he discussed the Church's attitude to economics with two Jesuits, Father Moorhouse Millar and a Father Murphy. Father Millar read through *What is Money For?* and, according to Pound, in a letter the following year, "was good enough to express interest and to catch a couple of slips." In a second letter he described Father Millar as "one of the most serious characters I saw in U.S."[11]

From New York he visited Cambridge, Massachusetts, where he stayed with the poet Theodore Spencer, an assistant professor of English at Harvard. At the university, Pound had a chat with the chairman of the economics department and agreed to requests from the English department to give a reading and from the department of speech to make a recording.[12] James Laughlin, then a student at Harvard, was present at the reading, which was held in a lecture room in Sever Hall. Four years later, Laughlin, by then publisher of New Directions, related to FBI special agents that Pound, "after noticing that the preponderance of the audience consisted mainly of Jews, changed the poems he planned to read to definitely anti-Semitic poems."[13] A second observer, also interviewed by the FBI, noted that he read as if he wanted to pick a fight with the audience.

Again in New York, he dined with Gorham Munson and Paul Hampden, the Social Credit economist, at the Players Club next door to the National Arts Club on Gramercy Park. He was disconcerted because he had not enjoyed the success in Washington that he thought he might have, either with regard to monetary reform or in finding a suitable position through which he might place his knowledge of history and economics at the disposal of his country. He was in a better frame of mind the day he went to see Virginia Rice, a literary agent who had placed four of his books, including two collections of *Cantos* and *Jefferson and/or Mussolini*. According to Miss Rice, her renowned client at one point chimed, "I don't want to roast little babies; I just happen to like the Fascist money system."[14] She, too, when the time came, would provide the FBI with much-needed information.

Pound threw a dinner party at Robert's, a restaurant since closed on East Fifty-fifth Street, for Mr. and Mrs. E. E. Cummings and Mr. and Mrs. Max Eastman, whom he had requested Cummings to bring. All went well until the subject of Italian fascism came up. Mrs. Eastman—the late Eliena Krylenko, a painter—and Cummings exchanged a few general quips after which Max Eastman suggested that as a non-Italian Pound probably escaped the regimentation which was the essence of the system, adding that he could not imagine that Pound would greatly enjoy being regimented in the first place. To which the poet angrily retorted: "Fascism only regiments those who can't do anything without it. If a man knows how to do anything, it's the essence of fascism to leave him alone."[15] The remainder of the meal passed in silence.

Another confrontation soon ensued, this time with his devoted protégé Louis Zukofsky, whom he encountered at the studio of Tibor Serly. They had not seen one another since 1933. Arrogant and embittered, Pound was full of noisome chatter about the volatile political situation. He told Zukofsky that Mussolini represented the only logical answer to bourgeois materialism and Marxist determinism, both of which denied the poet's creative consciousness a revolutionary role. Zukofsky was of a different mind. He advised Pound that he did not doubt that his integrity had decided his political action, but, pointing to the older man's head, indicated that something had gone awry. When Pound asked him what he thought of the infamous radio priest and Christian Front booster, Father Charles Coughlin, Zukofsky answered, "Whatever you don't know, Ezra, you ought to know *voices*."[16]

It was while the expatriate was in Washington that he received, and accepted, the offer of an honorary degree from Hamilton College, Clinton, New York. Taking along a pair of black dress shoes borrowed from Tibor Serly, he departed for his alma mater on June 6. On June 9 he was interviewed by a reporter from the Utica *Observer-Dispatch*. "If God loved the American people," he told the young journalist, referring to the forthcoming election, "the Republican party would nominate for President George Hilden Tinkham, the representative from Massachusetts." He also talked "quite a little and fiercely about England." The interview took place at the College Hill home of Professor and Mrs. Edward Root where Pound was staying. He was having "a very delightful time." Much of it was being spent, it turned out, on the tennis courts behind the college gymnasium.

The commencement exercises were held on June 12 in the Georgian Colonial campus chapel. Pound was awarded the honorary degree of Doctor of Letters. The citation was read out:

> Ezra Pound: Native of Idaho, graduate of Hamilton College in the Class of 1905, poet, critic, and prose writer of great distinction. Since completing your college career you have had a life full of significance in the arts. You have found that you could work more happily in Europe than in America and so have lived most of the past thirty years an expatriate making your home in England, France, and Italy, but your writings are known wherever English is read. Your feet have trodden paths, however, where the great reading public could give you few followers—into Provençal and Italian poetry, into Anglo-Saxon and Chinese. From all these excursions you have brought back treasure. Your translations from the Chinese have, for example, led one of the most gifted of contemporary poets [T. S. Eliot] to call you the inventor of Chinese poetry for our time. Your Alma Mater, however, is an old lady who has not always understood where you have been going, but she has watched you with interest and pride if not always with understanding. The larger public has also been at times amazed at your political and economic as well as your artistic credo, and you have retaliated by making yourself—not unintentionally, perhaps—their gadfly. Your range of interests is immense, and whether or not your theories of society survive, your name is permanently linked with the development of English poetry in the twentieth century. Your reputation is international, you have guided many poets into new paths, you have pointed new directions, and the historian of the future in tracing the development of your growing mind will inevitably, we are happy to think, be led to Hamilton and to the influence of your college teachers. You have ever been a generous champion of younger writers as well as of artists in other fields, and for this fine and rare human quality and for your own achievements in poetry and prose, we honor you.

At the conclusion of these words, the president of the College, William H. Cowley, placed over the poet's head the traditional buff and blue hood commemorating the colors of the Revolutionary Army uniform.[17]

The exercises were followed by the annual alumni luncheon in the

Hall of Commons. The principal speaker was H. V. Kaltenborn, a veteran news analyst and radio commentator, who had also been honored with a degree. "It is written in history," he began, "that dictatorships shall die, but democracies shall live." Democracies, he went on, "are more expensive and less efficient in organizing for a single purpose, but they are not as wasteful of fundamental human values." He praised England, and referred to the "doubtful" alliance between Italy and Germany, whereupon Pound asked loudly what he meant by "doubtful." Kaltenborn tried to explain but Pound would not let him and in the heat of the exchange began to laud Mussolini and fascism. Professor A. P. Saunders, onetime dean of the college, who was sitting next to Pound, tried to calm him, but to no avail. To the amazement of everyone present, a seemingly innocent wrangle developed suddenly into a full-blown uproar. There was angry shouting on both sides, and it was not until President Cowley intervened that order was finally restored.[18]

Pound followed Kaltenborn as speaker. He described, according to the *Utica Daily Press*, the impossibility of obtaining the writings of John Adams, whereas the works of Marx, Engels, and Trotsky were readily available in selections costing mere pennies. "It is my conviction that you ought to be able to purchase the thoughts and writings of America's founders as easily and cheaply as you can those of subversive propagandists." In closing he offered as required reading his own "Introductory Text Book."[19]

Once back in New York, he became defensive about the incident upstate. In a letter to President Cowley he implied that Kaltenborn had goaded him into making the outburst. He began again the inevitable rounds of friends and associates, but the hopes and dreams for his homeland and himself that he had brought over with him two months before were now a thing of the past. It was a subdued, deflated reformer who, a few days later, rode to the pier to board the *Conte di Savoia* for the return trip to Genoa. Within two months of his arrival in Italy the immediacy of the world situation was driven home to him. At daybreak, on September 1, 1939, the powerful German armies swept across the Polish frontier and converged on Warsaw. Events which had once seemed permanently forestalled were finally taking their dreadful course; the world war was under way.

2

On March 31, 1940, in a letter to Ronald Duncan, editor of *Townsman* (London), Pound wrote:

> Blasted friends left a goddam radio here yester. Gift. God damn destructive and dispersive devil of an invention. But got to be faced. Drammer has got to face it, not only face cinema. Anybody who *can* survive *may* strengthen inner life, but mass of apes and worms will be still further rejuiced to passivity. Hell of a state of passivity? Or limbo?
>
> Anyhow what drammer or teeyater *wuz*, radio is. Possibly the loathing of it may stop diffuse writing. No sense in print *until* it gets to finality? Also the histrionic developments in announcing. And the million to one chance that audition will develop: at least to a faculty for picking the fake in the voices. Only stuff fit to hear was Tripoli, Sofia, and Tunis. Howling music in two of 'em and a cembalo in Bugarea.
>
> And a double sense of the blessedness of silence when the damn thing is turned off.
>
> Anyhow, if you're writin for styge or teeyater up to date, you gotter measure it all, not merely against cinema, but much more against the personae now poked into every bleedin' 'ome and smearing the mind of the peapull. If anyone is a purrfekk HERRRRkules, he may survive, and *may* clarify his style in *resistance* to the devil box. I mean if he ain't druv to melancolia crepitans before he recovers.
>
> I anticipated the damn thing in first third of Cantos and was able to do 52/71 because I was the last survivin' monolith who did not have a bloody radio in the 'ome. However, like the subjects of sacred painting as Mr. Cohen said: "Vot I say iss, we got to svallow 'em, vot I say iss, ve got to svallow 'em." Or be boa-constricted. . . .[1]

"The blasted friend" who brought the radio to Rapallo as a gift was Natalie Barney, a fellow American who had also expatriated to Europe and had founded her own literary salon in the heartland of the Left Bank of Paris. Among her better-known charges were Anatole France, Remy de Gourmont, and André Gide. And the dauntless "devil's box," which had so sorely tempted the last "survivin' monolith," would soon prove "both a challenge and a destructive influence" for him. Ultimately destructive, it represented an initial challenge, "mainly in terms of the poet's drive for recognition and esteem, in particular for the recognition and esteem of America."[2]

Pound's preoccupation with gaining the respect from America which he felt he deserved was such that he had made plans for a second return trip to the States. The failure of the first voyage still rankled, but in the end it was to remain his only voyage. Now that war had broken out, travel was difficult. Besides, Pound found himself once again involved in a flurry of activities.

For one thing, Daniel Cory had introduced him to the Spanish philosopher and former lecturer at Harvard George Santayana, who, like Pound, was a reverent fan of Mussolini. This pleased the poet no end. "Never met anyone who seems to fake less," the Great Bass wrote to T. S. Eliot, referring to his meeting with the philosopher.[3] For a time there was serious talk of a Pound–Eliot–Santayana collaboration for Faber and Faber on a book which would present the "Proper Curriculum for the Ideal University." This proposal had been inspired by Santayana's relating to Pound the comment made by Henry Adams about teaching at Harvard ("It can not be done"), but although Eliot reported the Faber committee as saying that "it ought to be a very queer book and it appeals to them," nothing came of the project.

Faber did publish, in 1940, *Cantos LII–LXXI*, the first gathering of Poundian verse to appear since *The Fifth Decad of Cantos*, three years before. Cantos 52–71 combine Confucian China with the wide world of John Adams and those citizens of Adams' milieu who constitute the American chapter of the *Sagetrieb*. Pound was enthused about the subject matter, but was down on the writing of poetry; as a result, these twenty Cantos are probably the weakest link of the entire collection.

Among other enterprises, he became a life member of the American Academy of Political and Social Science in Philadelphia and immediately began asking for cooperation by members in the "defining of economic terms and the study of other problems facing the United States and the world."[4] To the editor of *The Annals* of the Academy he wrote suggesting that space be set aside for the following vital matters:

1. Among the first rights of a man or nation is the right to stay out of debt.

2. (ref. Brooks Adams, an author whom the American universities have for 30 years refused to face.)

Dumping is an hostile act, whether it be dumping of wheat or of gold. Any attempt to force a nation to take a useless or at least unnecessary commodity like gold is a move towards war.

cordially yours

P.S. Are you touching problem of American responsibility for present war?[5]

He was similarly enthused with regard to the activities of the National Institute of Arts and Letters, bombarding members with frequent mailings, imploring them to give financial aid to Joe Gould, to form "committees of correspondence," and to consider the possibility that Eliot and Santayana be appointed European members.[6] He wrote to Pearl Buck: "The war is mainly for money lending and three or four metal monopolies."[7] To Eliot: "Naturally history without monetary intelligence is mere twaddle. That I think I have conveyed to you by now??"[8] To Lester Littlefield, a close friend of Marianne Moore's: "The point being the country won't feed its five or ten best writers."[9] And to J. D. Ibbotson, Pound's former professor of Anglo-Saxon at Hamilton College: "Will you consider the fact that at the present moment there is NO weekly in America to print me, and not even a monthly where I cd. print TWO pages a month. . . . It is inconceivable that in ANY other country a man in my position wouldn't have that convenience."[10]

Old complaints levied within a new context. As usual, he saw himself projected in the role of lawmaker, of deputy. In a letter to Louis Zukofsky he stated that the supreme test of poetry was: "can Ez read it?" and secondly, "can he read it with approval and/or pleasure?"[11] Sparse as his own literary output was at this time, he nevertheless took pleasure in occasionally recommending the work of others. Currently he was pushing *Eimi* by E. E. Cummings, *In the American Grain* by William Carlos Williams, and Henry Miller's *Tropic of Cancer*. Both Cummings and Williams had been influenced to a certain extent by Pound's economic ideas, and it was not long before Miller, a Mussolini supporter from the beginning, began to see the light regarding economics as well. Pound's correspondence with the ex-Brooklynite resulted in a new Miller essay, "Money and How It Gets That Way" (reprinted, 1962, by New Directions in *Stand Still Like the Hummingbird*, a collection of Miller's selected orientations): ". . . Upon reading *Tropic of Cancer*,

Ezra Pound wrote me a postcard in his usual Cabalistic style, asking me if I had ever thought about money, what makes it and how it gets that way. The truth is that until Mr. Pound put the question to me I had never really thought about the subject. Since then, however, I have thought about it night and day."

Other timely Pound letters included one to Senator Robert Taft, offering advice about Republican strategy in the elections; one to H. L. Mencken, in which he talked about his attitude to fascism in relation to the United States ("as I said and as wuz printed while I was in America, the danger for the U.S. is not fascism, the danger is in getting a god damned tyranny with none of the humanizing and constructive elements of the corporate state. No guilds, no representation of every man by someone of his own trade, no checking of monopolies and price ramps, no tribunal where a man can take a case of economic injustice, etc.");[12] a third to Burton Wheeler insisting that he (Wheeler) deserved due credit for his efforts to keep "young America" from being slaughtered.

In many of the letters and articles Pound wrote at this time, he spoke exultantly about a recently discovered book—*The Law of Civilization and Decay* (1895), by Brooks Adams—which provided new facts for some of the poet's by now old-hat ideas. Brooks, brother of Henry Adams, and direct descendant of John Adams, maintained that "at times of economic competition the capitalist and usurer become predominant in society and the producer of goods falls into debt and servitude."[13] His main thesis was that usury and money played key roles in the rise and fall of nations and civilizations. The Roman Empire, for example, did not crumble because of the weakness of its moral fiber but because its supply of money was gradually contracted and deflated, a process which took, according to the author, many centuries. Adams further concluded that this process was due to the excessive forces exerted by a commercial "special privilege" class whose financial practices vitiated the health and strength of the nation as a whole, a syndrome which has repeated itself through the ages from one civilization to the next.

The outbreak of war and Pound's resultant isolation forced him to rely on new outlets for his publications. Through Katue Kitasono and the so-called Vou Club poets of Tokyo, the Great Bass became acquainted with some prominent Japanese publications. Three of them— the *Japan Times*; the *Japan Times & Mail*; the *Japan Times Weekly*—

seemed anxious to have him among their contributors. His articles for these newspapers, on cultural morphology and the progress of the war, showed an increasing identification with Fascistic ideals.

On July 22, 1940, the *Japan Times* ran a Pound piece which spoke of the "essential fairness of Hitler's war aims"; taking Hitler's latest victories into account, Pound considered the Führer's aims relatively "mild." In the same article Churchill was presented as a "senile" and "mentally deranged" man, a mere "shopfront" for the Rothschilds and Sassoons. On August 12, in another exposition for the same paper, Pound posited this commentary: "Democracy is now currently defined in Europe as 'a country governed by Jews.' "[14] It is interesting to note that these blandly oversimplified jottings were sent to these periodicals only after being cleared through the higher echelons of Italian government channels. A notice about Pound from Luciano DeFeo of the National Institute of Cultural Relations to Guido Rocco of the Ministry of Popular Culture speaks for itself; it can be found in the FBI Ezra Pound general correspondence files:

> Rome, 10 May
> Anno XVIII
>
> Dear Rocco,
>
> I am enclosing an article that Pound would like to send to Japan and which he has submitted to Comrade [Camillo] PELLIZZI, and the latter sent to me in order to forward it to you.
>
> With cordial greetings.

Rocco added the following note to DeFeo's letter before forwarding the entire bundle—letter and article—to the Ministry of Foreign Press: "I think *it will do*. He [Pound] supports the legitimacy of the thesis of economic independence, especially of financial independence of poor Nations in respect to the oppression of international finance."

The bright and blinding, buccaneering energy which had made Pound a born initiator of literary movements had obviously been displaced. The bitter anger and ferocious machinations which currently ruled him were nowhere as evident as in his letters to Odon Por, whose Fascistic tract *Politica economico-sociale in Italia anno XVII–XVIII* (*Italy's Policy of Social Economics 1939/1940*) Pound translated into English under the dateline of September 1941. Por was a political theorist, originally a Hungarian Syndicalist, whom Pound seems to have trusted implicitly. As early as April 1934 the poet had made his stance known to Por. "Never lose sight," he wrote, "of the AIM of Fascism, and its great elasticity." In April 1939, he squibbed, "The perfect state should move like a dance," a phrase repeated several months later for the benefit of the *British Union Quarterly*. Early in 1940 he inquired of Por: "WHOM ought we to educate next?" In the same letter he referred to Roosevelt as "Jewsfeldt," and in a subsequent letter called him "stinkie Roosenstein." On May 22, 1940, he wrote to Por: "Whom did Jewsfeldt buy his gold FROM????" On May 29, he trained his sights on Churchill: "I hope they shoot 25 Steffs for every B.U. [British Unioner] that Churchill manages to push out railway trains or otherwise kill." Concerning France (September 7, 1940): "I see ole Pete Pétain has desituated FIVE bloody Rotschilds [sic]/ But there are 14 more sons of bitches who regented la Banque de Frogs." Nor did Pound hedge around when it came to closing his letters to Por. On at least one occasion (July 12, 1940) he employed the following benediction: "Heil Hitler, yrs. Ez."[15]

He hammered at more or less the same subjects and with an equal amount of vehemence in some ninety articles (May 1939–September 1943) for *Il Meridiano di Roma*, a newspaper edited by Cornelio di Marzio, director also of the Fascist Confederation of Artists and Professional Men. It was di Marzio who initially put Pound in touch with the Italian Ministry of Popular Culture and it was Pound's friend, Ubaldo degli Uberti, chief of the Navy Press Office in Rome, who had put him in touch with di Marzio. Pound's demonstrations in the *Meridiano* included such lively but awkwardly phrased excernments as:

(14 May 1939) I am writing without hope for an English or American notice of the citation from Confucius made by Hitler in his latest talk, and I don't even think Hitler himself *cited* it. The Führer has arrived at a millennial truth through his lively interest in the events of the day: "The place of a country abroad depends exclusively on its organization and on its internal cohesion." It is thus that history enters into the human mind.

(30 March 1941) There is no doubt that Roosevelt receives *direct* information. In part, however, he receives it from deluded individuals, to say nothing of malicious idiots, although we do not wish to speak in vague terms. *We* must concern ourselves not with imprecise information but with specific cases and the nature of the source of this information. I offer you a typical example: Some years ago, I was stunned to learn that

an old jew (an American ambassador, like so many other half-American jews) by the name of Straus had taken a young jew (head of the Department of State in Washington) to lunch with Rothschild (no less), in Paris, at the well-known underground refuge in the luxurious Rothschild palace. I don't believe that little Heine Morgenthau went to this luncheon with the specific intention of betraying France, his more or less temporary country, but I firmly believe that no little jew (considered a dimwit by his foxy father) could have dined in the Rothschild palace without feeling a certain exultation.

In fact, inasmuch as he was unable to run a fruit-growing concern, thus preparing himself to manage the richest revenue in the world, I think that little Heine actually *believed* what he was told by the . . . supreme head usurer, the son or the grandson of the dynasty of Meyer Anshelm, who spoke as though he were Moses on top of Mount Sinai.

I claim that it is in this way that lies have penetrated the diminutive brains of several pluto-dilettante ambassadors, not all of them necessarily of middle eastern origin.

(11 May 1941) Mussolini and Hitler follow through magnificent intuition the doctrines of Confucius. King Victor Emanuel is a Confucian sovereign.

Many of these *Meridiano* reports were later gathered together and printed (September 1944) as *Orientamenti* (*Orientations*) by the Casa Editrice delle Edizioni Popolari. But because of the collection's controversial political and economic nature it was decided by the Italian authorities soon after publication to destroy the entire edition of the book. Only a small number of copies escaped destruction. One of the surviving copies was seized, in May of 1945, by foreign agents of the Federal Bureau of Investigation, turned over to FBI headquarters in Washington, D.C., and translated in its entirety from Italian into English. Ironically enough, this translation, still part and parcel of the FBI archives, represents the sole English volume of *Orientamenti* in existence.

Located in these same FBI archives are additional articles by Pound, including a number of columns which the American poet penned for *La Vita Italiana*, a decidedly pro-Fascist journal, as well as a translation of a *Meridiano* article ("The Jews and This War") which appeared in the May 1940 issue of *News from Germany*. Pound also wrote, as the FBI files indicate, for *Il Giornale di Genova*, the Fascist daily paper of Genoa, and the *Libro e Moschetto*, a journal of Fascist groups in the universities, published in Milan. An article in *Moschetto* (April 20,

1940)—"Historical Parallels"—began by drawing attention to Mussolini's Confucian-like intuition and went on to discuss Italian intellectuals; their duty, it said, was not only to cooperate but also to savor the artistic values inherent in fascism as well as to analyze and respect the wisdom of the Duce. Drawing a comparison between American and Italian political systems, Pound pointed out, in the same piece, that American prejudice against fascism existed as a result of America's ignorance of her own history. Another article published a year later in the *Vedetta Mediterranea* was directed at this same intellectual crowd: "It is the hour of those whose critical sense has for years been occupied with analyzing the problems of building 'stukas.' When writers arrive at a comparable efficiency we shall also have 'a literature of the Era Fascista.' " This article, too, found its way into the FBI investigatory files.

As the first year of the war drew to a close, Pound found himself almost entirely cut off from outside sources of information. There are plaintive appeals in some of his letters of 1941 for news of events from both England and the United States. Letters from the Allied countries were now few and far between; even the delivery of newspapers and magazines was coming to a halt. Pound began to thirst for new and more effective ways of transmitting and receiving vital data and knowledge. Natalie Barney's appropriately timed gift loomed larger and larger in his mind. Radio, bereft of commercial advertising, represented a formidable classroom aid. Even more than that, it was an estimable addition to the propagandist's arsenal, an important mode of communication in the modern world. But as Pound was later to inform his friend, Harry Meacham, he arrived at the Italian microphone only after a struggle: "It took me, I think it was, TWO years, insistence and wangling etc to GET HOLD of their microphone. . . ."[16]

Even after he began broadcasting, in January 1941, there were serious questions raised as to Pound's suitability. Camillo Pellizzi, president of the Fascist Institute of Culture, was to report that Italian officials mistrusted Pound's broadcasts, even suspected that they contained a secret code language and that the poet was acting as a double agent, transmitting information to the Allied Central Intelligence Service. Two months after his first broadcast the SIM (Servizio Informazioni Militari, Military Information Service) declared itself opposed to Pound's participation on the radio, believing, as they formally put it, that his offer to collaborate was dictated by "ulterior motives." An investigation of Pound's activities by Colonel Cesare Ame of the SIM culminated in the following letter being written to the Ministry of War, with copies sent to the Ministries of Foreign Affairs and Popular Culture:

> It has been learned from a trustworthy source that Ezra Pound, together with the U.S. subject Hermann Moss, an officer of the American consulate in Genoa, who is known to have strongly anti-Italian sentiments, acquired a number of English books to send to British citizens interned in Italy. Moreover, the abovementioned writer, during a recent sojourn in Rome, had a long talk with the American Ambassador William Phillips. Our judgment with regard to his offer of collaboration is negative.[17]

As a result of this notice, the Ministry of War advised against accepting Pound's offer of collaboration, despite the fact that he had already made several broadcasts. They notified Celso Luciano, chief of Cabinet of the Ministry of Popular Culture, of their decision, and Luciano in turn dispatched an urgent memo to Giuseppe Pession, director of the Inspectorate of Radio Broadcasting, warning against the continued use of Pound.

Luciano was further alarmed by a second letter he received at this time about the poet, this one from the manager of the National Institute of Cultural Relations with Foreign Countries:

> There is no doubt in my mind that Ezra Pound is insane! He is a pleasant enough madman and he is certainly a friend of Italy, but in the course of two interviews I recently had with him, I heard criticism, circumspection, accusations, etc., that have rather alarmed me. Not because I believe what Pound told me, but because he likes to gossip. And it would be most unpleasant to have nasty rumors in circulation. If it is possible for you to have him called, inform him in a prudent manner (I am willing to assume the responsibility) that I have communicated to you his impressions, his circumspections—and his criticisms. It would not be a bad idea if you could make him talk.
> It is advisable that such things be stopped from the start. If there is a bit of truth in it, you must be informed and if there isn't he must openly be told what his task consists of and that he must not speak nonsense.[18]

Luciano forwarded this letter to Pession with the admonition that he, Pession, hear Pound out and then attempt to "pacify" him. Which is just what the director of the Inspectorate did. He called Pound into his office, and after listening to the poet's complaints, bade him to be more cautious during future conversations, especially with individuals not connected to the Ministry of Popular Culture.

In the course of his long-term dealings with the Italian Fascist government, Pound elicited more than one hostile response from Axis officials. In October 1935, passing through Rome, he deposited at the office of Mussolini his farfetched project for an international organization—"The League or Convention of Peoples"—which was to serve as substitute for the League of Nations, "a bunch of swindlers, slaves to British tyranny." The reaction by the Duce's office to Pound's plan was one of mock and derision. An internally circulated memo tells the story:

> It is an eccentric plan conceived by a foggy mind, lacking all sense of reality.
> The speck of truth upon which it is based gives its author the illusion of having discovered a formula of genius.
> Considering Pound's affection for Italy and his enthusiasm, it should suffice to point out to him:
> —that a League such as the one he proposes cannot be thrown together in 24 hours:
> —that in any event it would be necessary for the government in question to wage a campaign to convince the public of the virtues of the new League—and this also would take considerable time:
> —that, for the moment, Italy, Austria, and Hungary are members of the League of Nations, and are therefore bound to this organization for at least two more years:
> —that, nonetheless, the proposal will be borne in mind for possible future consideration of its particulars.[19]

Another proposal by Pound, presented to the Ministry of Popular Culture in November of 1939, netted a similar response. It concerned Pound's plan for a threefold publications project. The first part had to do with the publication of a series of studies on great American political figures of the past, men whose ideas paralleled the main functioning theories of fascism; the second was a proposal for the production in Italy of a magazine in English devoted both to Italian literature, art, and music and to the political and economic life of the country; the third project concerned the publication of a weekly bulletin that would summarize the best articles to appear in Italian dailies but which, for the most part, went unnoticed.

Luigi Villari, a specialist in Italian cultural relations with the United States, had been assigned to examine Pound's proposition. His summation of the plan (and of Pound himself) was not very encouraging. Submitted to the director general of Propaganda Services, it read in part:

> Mr. Pound is an American poet residing in Rapallo, with a strong affection for Italy and a great admiration for Fascism. . . . He is a man of ability and culture, and is completely well-intentioned, but he is a confused person, and moreover wants to concern himself with economic matters, about which he has only the most outlandish ideas.
>
> In the United States, Pound is recognized as a poet, but he is not taken at all seriously as a political or economic writer, and thus any undertaking conceived by him will not carry much weight.[20]

So Pound's initial ties with the Ente Italiano Audizione Radiofoniche (EIAR), the government-controlled radio broadcasting agency, were extremely tenuous. There were those in the higher reaches of the Italian government who were never fully convinced, for reasons of their own, of Pound's good will toward the Italian State. Others, however, especially those in the Foreign Press section, were confident of Pound's devotion. When all was said and done, the objections of the SIM to Pound's participation as a collaborator were dismissed by the directors of press and radio propaganda as being vague and without a solid enough foundation. It was decided to continue with Pound despite the unfavorable assertion of counterespionage.

His first broadcast, or the first reported broadcast, was made January 23, 1941, from EIAR studios in the Via Asiago, Rome. The name of the program was the *American Hour*. It was transmitted to Britain and much of central Europe as well as to the United States. Pound's segment of the program ran for seven minutes. His script began: "The United States should try to understand the last 20 years of European history, before going too far in finding themselves involved in the war. Democracy was created in America and this is the place where it must be saved. The peace of the world is set forth through the good government from the interior."[21]

He made, he later estimated, on the average of one radio speech every three days, or approximately ten per month. But it was not until October 2, 1941, that the Foreign Broadcast Intelligence Service of the Federal Communications Commission began to monitor these informal, crackerbarrel-sage talks. By this date it was clear that America was going to support British efforts against the Axis powers and was merely looking for an opportunity to enter the war. This no doubt helped calcify Pound's attitude toward his homeland. He was further distressed by the interposition on July 12, 1941, of the State Department, which that day gave orders to the United States embassy in Rome to extend his passport for six months only, and to limit it exclusively for return to the United States. By October, with three of six months expired, he was still residing in Italy and was still going strong as a radio propagandist. His broadcast of October 2 ran for twelve minutes. The reception was described by the transcriber as "Fair." The title of the talk was "The Last Ditch of Democracy":

> Pound speaking. It's a speech all right. Democracy has been licked in France. The "Frogs" were chucked into war against the will of the people. Democracy has been licked to a frazzle in England where it never did get a good lock-in anyhow. But even pseudo-democracy breaks down when a people is chucked into war against its will. And the Britons never voted Winston into the premiership. In fact, when did they ever have an election? Remember, it's the government in England that decides when to have an election. Think where we would be if Mr. Roosevelt would merely postpone elections till he got ready to have one.
> Well, Democracy is in her last ditch, and if she ain't saved in America no one is going to save her, not in her parliamentary form. As to uniting with England, taking on a lot of bad debts and new liabilities, one of the speakers on this radio was kind enough, that is he showed respect enough for American intelligence, yes even today he showed respect for American intelligence, by saying that only Britain was rooting for this "federation." On close examination the Britons themselves don't seem to be so numerous in the movement toward merger.[22]

His radio speeches elicited the same shock and sensation among the intelligentsia as did his previous cavalier theories on literature and the arts. Even Harriet Monroe's *Poetry* disclaimed Pound, denouncing him as a supporter of the enemy, if not an outright traitor. Conceivably it was only an outer defense, but Pound seemed to revel in his role, enjoying immensely the attention and notoriety he was receiving. He was used to going his own way and had been spouting his homespun economic and political theories for most of two decades. In the spirit of what in a 1943 essay he called "Freedom de Facto" ("Free speech without freedom of radio is a mere goldfish in a bowl"), the instigator went on flailing, filibustering, filling up the void with a fury of taunts and threats. Eschewing Arnoldian detachment for the direct and aggressive tactics of a Carlyle, the ideopraxist was intent on piloting the stunted, bifurcated Allied community into more navigable waters.

An example of his technique can be seen in his October 6 speech, rebroadcast October 7, and reported in a number of American and British newspapers. In this potshot-laden radio explosion Pound gunned down everyone and everything in sight, including a few of those supposedly on his own side: Victor Sassoon ("that Jewish pseudo-parsi head of the Shanghai rackets"); the "super-fatalism of slavs"; Tommy Atkins; "the Anglo-Judaic empire"; Field Marshals Wilhelm Keitel and Gerd von Runstedt; Chiang Kai-shek; Vidkun Quisling; Marshal Philippe Pétain; Charles de Gaulle; Pierre Laval; Walla Walla; the London *Times*; the New York *Herald Tribune*; not to mention the Chicago White Sox and Philadelphia Phillies!

He was not again monitored by the FCC until October 26, nearly three weeks later. This time he spoke for eight minutes, 12:17–12:25 p.m. His subject was Winston Churchill:

> Mr. Churchill, even Mr. Churchill hasn't had the brass to tell the American people why he wants them to die to save what. He is fighting for the gold standard, and monopoly. England is trying to starve the whole of mankind, and make it pay through the nose. . . . His gang, Churchill's, with a kike, gentile, or hybrid is not fit to govern. And the English ought to be the only people ass enough and brute enough to fight for him. . . .
> And Mr. Churchill and that brute, Rosenfeld, and their kike postal spies and obstructors distress me by cutting off my normal mental intercourse with my colleagues. But I'm not going to starve, I am not going to starve mentally. The cultures of the Occident came out of Europe, and a lot of it is still right here in Europe, and I don't mean archeology either. . . .

On November 4 he rattled on about Marx:

> Europe calling. Pound speaking. Subject, "The Golden Wedding". . . .
> Nobody on the Axis side denies that Marx discovered several genuine faults in the usury system. All we ask is a way to cure them; and the torture chambers in most countries where Stalin's power has reached, and in a few embassies in countries where he has never been able to get control of the total police force, rather indicate that the Bolshee system never got universal approval from its victim. However, why doesn't Stalin, with Rabbi Lehman and Shulman, Moses, Baugh, and the rest of the international bankers bring a few pages of the comrade's answers and read them between the caviar and the pheasant, and see if it don't enliven the dinner.

Sure, and it proves that Marx wanted to take economic, political, cultural, and organizational measures. And seeing, as he puts them in that order, you'd expect me to fall for it. . . . Of course the Bolshees didn't. Anybody that comes into power probably puts organizational measures first; and economics along with the last of the almost inaccessible part of culture. So few people seem able to grasp simple economics without, as Senator Bankhead remarked, "About three centuries delay."

And on November 6, among other things, he assaulted the President of the United States:

Europe calling, Pound speaking. Subject, "This War on Youth and on the Eighth Generation". . . . Europe, according to the financial news of London, must be wiped out, or certain monopolies will disappear. Men will be able to eat the grain of their own fields, unless Europe is blown to blithers. . . . In the United States of America, the land of abundance, [what is needed] is internal reform. Not a war in Africa, or in Asia. Not a war for the mine-owners against reformers of Rhodesia. Not a war for the opium raiders in Shanghai and Singapore. Internal reform . . . and freedom. . . .
Will you look at the age of the chief war pimps? Roosevelt now says he saw war coming back in 1937. In 1937 there was no necessity of war. Roosevelt did all he could to make it inevitable. There is no record of a single act of Roosevelt's [made] in the spirit of staving off war. Ignorance of Europe. Government in charge of pigs. . . . Don't say that I affirm what he did. What I affirm is that he never showed the faintest inclination to learn the facts and come out for a just solution. That is a very conservative statement. He has never been neutral. But get down to this one point of age. How old are the blokes who are trying to throw America into the conflict? What is their business? What is their civic record?. . . . Have any of them ever come out for the just price, which is basic to all sane economics? Even the old laissez-faire or Whig economists believed from the start that free competition leads to the just price. The wheeze against it was worked partly by faking the freedom of that competition. If you start a ten year war, yes, IF you start a ten-year war, none of these old swine will be there at the end of it.

The palaver poured forth in a variety of tongues—flat, pedantic, scolding tones intermingled with exaggerated Southern drawls, Western plainsman lulls, Cockney growls. He switched from one to another without warning, breaking at times into a torrid rage, slurring his words, ranting at a low-pitched roar. Often the reception was poor and added to the bizarre vocal inflections, making it impossible for transcribers to distinguish between words. When they did understand what was being said they were often unfamiliar with the subject matter. Their transcriptions were full of errors.[23]

The first Sunday of December 1941, they went to work again. This time the short-wave broadcast was loud and clear. At 6:12 p.m., Rome time, following the briefest of introductions—"We next present a talk by Ezra Pound entitled 'Those Parentheses' "—the poet's voice came on the air:

> Europe calling. Pound speaking. Ezra Pound speaking, and I think I am perhaps still speaking a bit more to England than to the United States, but you folks may as well hear it. They say an Englishman's head is made of wood and the American head made of watermelon. Easier to get something into the American head but well-nigh impossible to make it stick for ten seconds. Of course, I don't know what good I am doing, I mean what immediate good, but some things you folks on both sides of the wretched ocean will have to learn, war or no war, sooner or later. Now, what I had to say about the state of mind in England in 1919 I said in my Cantos, Cantos 14 and 15. Some of your philosophists and fancy thinkers would have called it the spiritual side of England. I undertake to say "state of mind."

He spoke on liberalism and his own devout patriotism:

> I can't say my remarks were heeded. I thought I got 'em simple enough. Words short and simple enough. In fact, some people complained that several of the words contained no more than four or five letters, some six. Now I hold that no Catholic has ever been or ever will be puzzled by what I said in those Cantos. I have, however, never asked for any sympathy when misunderstood. I go on—try to make my meaning clear and then clearer—and in the long run people who listen to me, very few of 'em do, but the numbers of that small and select minority do know more in the long run than those who listen to, say, H. G. "Chubby" Wells and the liberal stooges. What I'm gettin' at is, a friend said to me the other day that he was glad I had the politics I have got but that he didn't understand how I, as a North American United Stateser, could have them. Well, that looks simple to me. Things often do look simple to me.

On Confucius and Confucianism:

> On the Confucian system, very few start right and then go on—start at the roots and move upward. The pattern often is simple. Whereas, if you start constructing from the twig downward, you get into a muddle. My politics seem to me simple. My idea of a state or empire is more like a

hedgehog or a porcupine—chunky and well defended. I don't cotton to the idea of my country bein' an octopus, weak in the tentacles and suffering from stomach ulcers and colic gastritis. . . .

On Versailles, Roosevelt, the Jews:

What I am ready to fight against is having ex-European Jews making another peace worse than Versailles with a new two dozen Danzigs. . . . The sooner all America and all England wake up to what the war birds and Roosevelt are up to, the better for the next generation and this one. . . . Roosevelt is more in the hands of the Jews than Wilson was in 1919. . . . Eight years ago he was a-sayin' nothing to fear but fear. Well, what has become of that Roosevelt? What has he done for three years but try to work up a hysteria on that basis? He has got his face into a paper called *Life*, eight or ten photographs. Why, Jim Farley would have been less nuisance in the White House than "Snob" Delano, who objected to Farley, not on moral or ethical grounds, but purely as snobbism. Didn't want there to be a henchman to succeed him. . . .

He moved on from Farley to finance: the latter was what he had wanted to discuss all along. Everything had led to this:

And as to American labor—when will American labor start looking into the currency question? Question—of course there oughtn't to be any interrogative element in it. Even a hod carrier ought to be able to learn why interest-paying debts is not so good a basis for money and its productive labor. Yes, but will they? . . . Looks to me even now as if the currency problem was the place to start saving America, as I have been saying for some time back.

It was 6:24 p.m. in Rome. In Washington, where the talk had been monitored, it was 12:24 p.m., Eastern Standard Time. And in Hawaii it was the early morning of December 7. "The planes," reported *The New York Times*, "were burning on the landing strips of Honolulu; the U.S. Pacific Fleet smoldered in the waters of Pearl Harbor." The Japanese had launched their massive surprise attack; within a few days America would be actively engaged in the war.

A number of conflicting reports now fill in the gap of time, the hours, days, and weeks between the Pearl Harbor attack and the propagandist's next short-wave radio broadcast. What actually happened during this period is shrouded in mystery. Richard Rovere, reporting for *Esquire* (September 1957), wrote: "It is a matter of record that he [Pound] tried in 1942 to get aboard the last diplomatic train that took Americans from Rome to Lisbon. He was refused permission to board it. He had no choice but to stay in Rapallo."

Francesco Monotti, a journalist, reminisced in *Il Mare* (October 31, 1954):

> The American Government had notified American citizens scattered around the world, and the Pounds, like good citizens, were ready to obey and return to the United States. But at the consulate there must have been someone who thought of them as black sheep. In those supreme moments between day and night in their lives, something of grave consequence must have happened at the consulate at Rome. . . . He returned a completely changed man. . . . He decided quickly, [his] tickets were returned . . . Ezra Pound decided to remain in Italy.

Monotti insisted that Pound and his wife had arranged for a long absence. They had relinquished the lease to their apartment in Rapallo and had taken steps to assure themselves that books, manuscripts, and some valuable furnishings and pieces of art would be well looked after.

A third published statement substantiates the first two and supports Pound's later claim that he had made every conceivable effort to return to the United States at the time that America entered the war. This report appeared in *Current Biography, Who's News and Why* (1942), edited by Maxine Block: "Oddly enough, when Pound attempted to return to the United States in 1941 to lecture on Fascism he found himself unable to get transportation in spite of the fact that he said he had several sympathizers among members of the United States Senate whom he had met in 1939. In May 1942, when he tried to get permission to join a diplomatic train which carried large groups of Americans from Italy to Lisbon, he was again refused."

However, a Library of Congress report, issued in March 1958, indicates that the case might have evolved otherwise:

> Several writers have suggested that Mr. Pound attempted to return to the United States in 1941 and that he was denied permission to return to this country. An examination of pertinent State Department Passport Division files does not substantiate this claim. To the contrary, it appears that the State Department was officially eager to have Mr. Pound return to the United States and in 1941 his passport was extended for six months only, in order to compel his return. However, the documents in the State Department files do not preclude the possibility of the development of a

misunderstanding between Mr. Pound and a consular official which might
have unintentionally aborted Mr. Pound's "attempt" to leave Italy.[24]

Whose testimony to believe? A State Department memorandum
(Division of Foreign Activities), dated June 18, 1942, reads: "On July
12, 1941, this Department instructed the American Embassy at Rome to
limit Pound's passport for immediate return to the U.S. However, he
refused to return home and to the best of our knowledge is still residing
in Italy."

A second State Department memorandum in the same file, dated
October 11, 1941, refers to Pound as a "pseudo American"; it is signed
George Wadsworth, U.S. Chargé d'Affaires in Rome. This vindictive-
sounding statement would seem to suggest that there had indeed been a
difference of opinion between Pound and American representatives in
Italy. Two unidentified witnesses, interviewed by agents of the FBI in
the United States in May 1943, claimed to have seen Pound at both the
American Embassy in Rome and the American Consulate's Office in
Genoa. "On several occasions when he appeared . . . he made very
undignified remarks concerning the United States Government, and
when he entered and left the Consulate's Office (as well as the American
Embassy) he gave the Fascist salute."[25] This testimony, for what it is
worth, helps to explain how a rift between Pound and the consulate
might easily have developed and supports the theory that Pound was
actually his own worst enemy.[26]

It was the evening of December 7. The poet walked through the deserted
streets of Rome. His destination was the home of Reynolds and Eleanor
Packard, intelligent and likable Americans, the last of what had been a
fair-sized American community in Rome. Packard was the Rome correspondent for United Press. When Pound arrived he saw the open
suitcases. Packard's words came like bullets:

"The United States is at war. If you stay you will be a traitor."

It was an accusation. And in this tense moment of confrontation
Pound's status—"his relation to his own country and to other Americans
as fixed by law"—changed, although at the time he was not aware of
it.[27]

"I don't see why fascism is contrary to American philosophy," the
instigator countered. Seeing the astonished looks of the Packards, he

added: "I have nothing against the United States, quite the contrary. I consider myself one-hundred-per-cent American and a patriot. I am only against Roosevelt and the Jews who influenced him."[28]

The Packards returned to the United States.

And Pound stayed.

According to the monthly schedule of payments and salaries maintained by the Ministry of Popular Culture, the poet was paid 350 lire per broadcast—150 lire for writing the script and 200 lire for delivering it over the air. The equivalent of seventeen American dollars, this figure barely covered Pound's expenses. What few lire he managed to save, he either invested in Italian government bonds or gave to his parents, who had retired to Rapallo. The bonds would of course be rendered worthless with the collapse of Fascism.

The procedure for the payment of funds went as follows. After each broadcast Pound would proceed directly to the North American section of the Inspectorate of Radio Broadcasting to sign a *nota compensa* in triplicate stipulating that the broadcast had been delivered. One copy would go to the office of the Minister of Popular Culture (Alessandro Pavolini); another to Pound's immediate supervisor, George ("Giorgio") Nelson Page; a third to Giuseppe Pession of the Inspectorate of Radio Broadcasting. Pession or one of his assistants then approved the original *nota compensa* by affixing thereto an initialed stamp. The *nota compensa* would be sent directly to the central bursar's office, where a *mandato* or order of payment was issued in favor of Ezra Pound. From here the *nota compensa* and the *mandato* were forwarded to the Tesoraria Provinciale (Provincial Treasury) of Genoa on Via Brigata Ligura, which would in turn send them to the Ufficio del Registro (the Registry Office) in Rapallo. A notice would also be sent to Pound and he would bring his notice to the Ufficio del Registro and receive the amount indicated thereon. At the same time he would sign the *mandato* and the local registry office would send the signed document to the Provincial Treasury of Genoa, which would forward it to the Corte dei Conti, the accounting office of the Ministry of Popular Culture at Rome.

Much of the time he was involved in more than simply the writing and reading of his own Radio Rome speeches. The records indicate that Pound performed various functions. He wrote press releases for other broadcasters to read, edited manuscripts, created slogans, helped organize the network's propaganda campaign. At points he coauthored broadcasts and frequently shared the microphone with fellow announcers, participating in a number of news discussions and symposiums. And just as he had once churned out art and music criticism for *The New Age* under the pseudonyms B. H. Dias and William Atheling, he now broadcast, frequently, under the assumed name of Giovanni Del Bene.[29]

Despite the variety of his activities on behalf of the station and the frequency with which he made broadcasts, the material he did write for transmittal was subject to a thorough prebroadcast examination. EIAR officials "would read, study, and approve, or disapprove, any material for broadcasts submitted by Pound and others. If approved by these officials, the material would be submitted to the Minister [of Popular Culture] as a matter of form, and if the Minister approved it, then arrangements would be made, and a date set for the broadcast."[30] This testimony, by an EIAR technician, corresponded with the testimony submitted to the FBI in 1945 by other material witnesses, but clashed with Pound's own interpretation. One of the prevalent points of his defense would be that he had made broadcasts under his own impetus and solely as a free agent, an American citizen with America's national welfare his guiding light. Looking forward, it seems difficult to imagine that this line of abstract reasoning would have held firm under fire in a court of law.

Almost all Radio Rome broadcasts were prerecorded at EIAR studios on 78 rpm plastic playing discs, cartons of which were later recovered by U.S. counterintelligence officers and turned over to federal agents. It has also been ascertained that prior to the broadcast of December 7 several of Pound's radio talks were made directly from the recording facilities at the Ministry of Popular Culture. He purportedly composed the speeches at his home in Rapallo and edited them in restaurants, cafés, trains—wherever and whenever he could steal a moment of spare time.

His talks, as Charles Norman has said, had become a way of life. His cobroadcasters were among his close friends—Carmen Lilli, James ("Giacomo") Barnes, Nino Serventi, Olivia Rossetti Agresti, Natalia Troubetzkoy. Gabriele Paresce, of the Inspectorate of Radio Broadcasting, became a social intimate of Pound's and in 1945 offered to testify in his behalf. The poet was in frequent communication with General Manager Martucci of the Ministry of Communications and with Salvatore Aponte and Vittorio De Angelis of the Ministry of Popular Culture, as well as Alberto Lucini, head of the Division of Studies and Propaganda on Races. Perhaps his tightest bond with a high-ranking Fascist official was with Camillo Pellizzi. Interviewed by the FBI following Pound's capture in Rapallo in 1945, Pellizzi informed them that the poet had considered the Fascist system simply a means to an end. What Pound had sought was a kind of "utopia." Pellizzi added that while Pound was probably legally a traitor, he had never considered himself as such but rather thought it his "duty" to expose the Administration of the United States.[31]

In addition to radio personnel and party officials, Pound spent a good deal of time in Rome with a group of young dissidents, "leftist" or anarchist Fascists who ran a socio-political review called *Domani*, which was suppressed after a year of publication, and all or most of its organizers put in jail or *alla confine*. He was introduced to this group by Odon Por, who was a regular contributor to the publication. "Ezra Pound didn't come to meet the literary types but rather the political types," wrote Felice Chilanti, editor of *Domani*. "He came because he was interested in our unorthodox ideas on economics and society."[32] He also attended their meetings because he found the young tractable. Posing for the hundredth time as the unfrocked professor, he laid down the law: Picasso was an unrelenting Communist; Confucius and Mencius merited teaching in the schools; Wörgl in Austria had developed the most effective monetary system of modern times.

On January 26, 1942, seven weeks after the Japanese air attack on Pearl Harbor, Pound and his wife received word that they had been granted permission by the Italian Supreme Command to remain in Italy for the duration of the war. Three days later, at 9:30 p.m., EST, Pound made the first of his new, consecutive series of talks over Radio Rome. The brief introduction that had marked previous broadcasts had been replaced by an eloquently phrased, intricate preamble, carefully worded in English:

> ANNOUNCER: Rome Radio, acting in accordance with the Fascist policy of intellectual freedom and free expression of opinion by those who are qualified to hold it, has offered Dr. Ezra Pound the use of the microphone twice a week. It is understood that he will not be asked to say anything

whatsoever that goes against his conscience or anything incompatible with his duties as a citizen of the United States of America.

Pound replaced the announcer at the microphone:

Ezra Pound again speaking, speaking from Europe. Pearl Arbor Day, or Pearl Harbor Day, at twelve noon I retired from the capital of the old Roman Empire—that is, Rome—to Rapallo to seek wisdom from the ancients. I wanted to figure things out. I had a perfectly good alibi if I wanted to play things safe. . . .

. . . The United States has been for months . . . illegally at war through what I considered to be the criminal acts of a President whose mental condition was not, so far as I could see, all that could or should be desired of a man in so responsible a position or office. He has, so far as the evidence . . . available showed, broken his promises to his electorate. He had to my mind violated his oath of office. He had to my mind violated the oath of allegiance to the United States Constitution which even the ordinary citizen is expected to take every time he gets a new passport. It was obviously a mere question of hours between that day and time when the United States would be legally at war with the Axis.

I spent a month trying to figure things out. Well, did I? Perhaps I concluded sooner. At any rate I had a month clear to make up my mind about some things. I had Confucius and Aristotle, both of whom had been up against similar problems, both of whom had seen empires fall, both of whom had seen deeper into the causes of human confusion than most men. . . .

The United States has been misinformed. The United States has been led down the garden path and maybe down under the daisies. All through shutting out news. . . . Yes, I knew that this was what the war was about; I knew the war was about gold, usury, and monopoly. I said as much when I was last in America. I said then, "if the war is pushed on us." So now the United States has got pushed out of Guam and Wake, and I suppose out of the Philippines, and a Thirty Years' War is in progress. Is it? Is a Thirty Years' War what the American citizen thinks will do most good to the United States of America?

Or has somebody been misinformed? And if so, who misinformed him? According to the reports of the American press now available to the average European, someone in charge of American destiny miscalculated something or other. We hear that an inquiry is in progress, it being my private belief that I could have avoided the war with Japan if anyone had the unlikely idea of sending me out there with any thought of official powers. . . .

He concluded his speech with a final, somber toast to Adolf Hitler and the vagaries of madness:

The day Hitler went into Russia, England had her chance to pull out. She had her chance to say "Let bygones be bygones. If you stop this Muscovite order, we will let bygones be bygones. We will try to see at least half of your argument." Instead of which Hank Wallace comes up saying no peace till the world accepts the gold standard. . . . Whom God would destroy He first sends to the bughouse.

It was only the beginning. The broadcasts of record—those monitored by the FCC during the period of America's involvement in the war up to the time the Department of Justice moved to indict Pound—totalled 125. He was commuting now between Rapallo and Rome. He had taken a room at the Albergo d'Italia on the Via Quattro Fontane, across town from the antiquated eighteenth-century edifice which housed the radio station of Rome. His position as a radio "news" commentator entitled him to receive rate-reduction passes for use on Italy's national railway network, an indispensable item, considering the amount of traveling he did.

As for the radio speeches, their contents varied greatly from broadcast to broadcast. Old themes cropped up again and again. He attacked the privately owned Bank of England because it made money "breed"; he attacked Alexander Hamilton because of his financial speculations, J. Pierpont Morgan because he derived profits from the American Civil War, Henry Morgenthau because he was a money lord, the National Banking Act of 1863 because it favored private bankers, Pope Pius II because he was a usurer, the Rothschilds because they were usurers, Bernard Baruch because he was a Jew. He spoke of "Jewspapers and worse than Jewspapers," of "Franklin Finkelstein Roosevelt," of "kikes, sheenies, and the oily people." He noted that history had been "keenly analyzed" in *Mein Kampf* and recommended for reading purposes the forged *Protocols of the Elders of Zion*. Everywhere he looked he saw the ruins of "international money power," the horror of "the Jew, Disease Incarnate" (*"l'ebreo malattia incarnata"*). Several of the broadcasts were actually in the nature of "replies" to the speeches of American or British officials. Occasionally, he read from *The Cantos* or from a recently published article; or he would read excerpts from the half dozen *Money Pamphlets*. Often he talked about his literary friends—Joyce, Cummings, Cocteau, Lewis, Eliot. On May 14, 1942, he discussed Louis-Ferdinand Céline—"Ferdinand has GOT down to reality/Ferdinand is a writer"—but did not touch on Céline's support of Nazism. On July 6 he analyzed the "disease behind modern art." He lowed about old-fashioned "Yankee" independence and craftsmanship, about the vorticist movement, about Confucius, Kublai Khan, Jean-Jacques Rousseau, Albert Einstein, the "Morgenthau–Lehman gang," the Steffs and the Schiffs, Leo Frobenius (Pound's "look-alike"), about the Roman Catholic Church, about the Divine Mysteries, the Sienese bank known as the Monte dei Paschi, Aristotle's *Politics*, Browning's "Sordello." The admixture of names, terms, and themes must have been befuddling even for Pound. He announced during one broadcast (March 8, 1942): "I lose my thread at times, so much that I can't count on anyone's mind." He included his own. The ranting, puritanical, "do-gooding" American, whose propagandist line was more often Nazi than Fascist, frequently appeared to be talking to himself, rattling on for no good reason, jumping from one half-thought to the next.

At her home in Sant' Ambrogio, near Rapallo, he would read his talks to Olga Rudge and his daughter, whenever she was present, before taking the scripts to Rome; for a time he also gave the scripts to Dorothy Pound to read, but stopped doing so (she told Noel Stock) when she mentioned to him that because of the jumps he made they were sometimes difficult to follow.

Miss Rudge, herself a Mussolini devotee, found the broadcasts gratifying. While Pound was incarcerated at St. Elizabeths she gathered together a small selection of "Radio Roma" oddments; these she had printed at Siena in an edition of 300 ("If This Be Treason") and distributed them gratis among members of the academic community. Mary, when it came time for her to consider the implications of her father's condition, saw things differently. Her point of view was certainly the more objective of the two:

> He was losing ground, I now see, losing grip on what most specifically he should have been able to control, his own *words*.
>
> *lord of his work and master of utterance—*[33]
>
> —he was that no longer. And perhaps he sensed it and the more strongly clung to the utterances of Confucius, because his own tongue was tricking him, running away with him, leading him into excess, away from his pivot, into blind spots.[34]

The broadcasts need no further embellishment. They need only to be read to be believed.

February 3, 1942
You are at war for the duration of the Germans' pleasure. You are at war for the duration of Japan's pleasure. Nothing in the Western world, nothing in the whole of our Occident, can help you to dodge that. Nothing can help you dodge it.

February 19, 1942
That any Jew in the White House should send American kids to die for the private interests of the scum of the English earth . . . and the still lower dregs of the Levantine.

March 15, 1942
Parlando da Roma. Ezra Pound speaking from Rome. *Parlando da Roma.* . . . It is an outrage that any clean lad from the country—I suppose that there still are a few English lads from the country—it is an outrage that any clean lad from the country or any nice young man from the suburbs should be expected to die for Victor Sassoon. It is an outrage that even a drunken footman's by-blow should be asked to die for Sassoon.
As to your Empire, it was not always won by clean fighting; but however you got it, you did for a time more or less justify keeping it on the ground that you exported good government, or better government than the natives would have had without England. But you let in the Jew and the Jew rotted your Empire, and you yourselves outjewed the Jew. Your allies in your victimized holdings are the *bunya*, that is, the money lender. You stand for usury, and above metal usury you have built up bank usury, 60 percent as against 30 and 40 percent, and by that you will not be saved. . . .
Was it an instinct to save the butt end of the race by not fighting? Is there "a race" left in England? Has it any will left to survive? You can carry slaughter to Ireland, but will that save you? I doubt it. Nothing can save you, save a purge. Nothing can save you, save an affirmation that you are English.
Hore-Belisha is not. Isaacs is not. No Sassoon is an Englishman racially. No Rothschild is English, no Streiker is English, no Roosevelt is English, no Baruch, Morgenthau, Cohen, Lehman, Warburg, Kuhn, Kahn, Schiff, Sieff or Solomon was ever yet born Anglo-Saxon. And it is for this filth that you fight. It is for this filth that you have murdered your Empire. It is this filth that elects, selects, elects your politicians.

March 26, 1942
My job, as I see it, is to save what's left of America and to help keep up some sort of civilization somewhere or other. Ezra Pound speaking from Europe for the American heritage. F.D.R. is below the biological level at which the concept of honor enters the mind.

March 30, 1942

No one for the past 100 years had dreamed of threatening the United States of America with extinction. A damn fool or a half-hypnotized vacuum in our White House threatened Japan with starvation, sent silly school-girl notes to Mussolini and Hitler, threatened to starve the world, talked "tosh" to the Axis powers and to Japan. The world has seen that propaganda, smelt the stink.

April 16, 1942

For the United States to be making war on Italy and on Europe is just plain damn nonsense, and every native-born American of American stock knows that it is plain downright damn nonsense. And for this state of things Franklin Roosevelt is more than any other man responsible.

April 23, 1942

The drift of Mr. Archibald MacLeish's remarks toward the end of March seems fairly clear. He has been given a gangster's brief and he has been entrusted with the defense of a gang of criminals and he is a-doing his damnedest. I object and have objected to the crime, regardless of who may be related to the men who have committed it, and I accept the conditions of the debate, namely, that the Morgenthau–Lehman gang control 99% of all means of communication inside the United States and that they can drown out and buy out nearly all opposition, on top of which Roosevelt has, characteristically, resorted to blackmail. Any man who does not accept the gigantic frauds perpetrated by the Morgenthau–Roosevelt treasury is to be held up as a traitor to the United States.

The reply is that any man who submits to Roosevelt's treason to the public commits a breach of citizen's duty. There is no connection between submittin' to the Roosevelt–Morgenthau frauds and patriotism. There is no connection between such submission and winning this war—or any other. There is no patriotism in submittin' to the prolonged and multiple frauds of the Roosevelt administration and to try to make the present support of these frauds figure as loyalty to the American heritage, is just so much dirt or bunkum. Doubtless the tactics of evasion will be used to the uttermost—but if the American people submit to either or both of these wheezes the American people will be mugs.

There are several historic facts which the opulent of the Morgenthau–Lehman gang would do well to dig up. Our Mr. MacLeish has not gone out—all out—for the printing of the defects of American history in handy and available volumes, so there are several historic facts which the opulent of the Morgenthau swindle would be well advised to extract and use.

Of course, for you to go looking for the point—points—of my bi-weekly talk in the maze of Jew-governed American radio transmissions is like looking for one needle in a whole flock of haystacks. And your press is not very open. However, if some lone watcher or listener on Back Bay or on top of the Blue Ridge does hear me, I suggest he make notes and ask Advocate Archibald whether it does win anything to have the people pay two dollars for every dollar spent by the government. I ask whether the spirit of '76 is helped by a-floodin' the lower ranks of the Navy with bridge-sweepings; whether war is won by mercantilist ethics and, in any case, whether men like Knox and Stimson and Morgenthau can be expected to fill the heart of youth with martial ardor and spirit of sacrifice. I ask Archie to say openly why he handed out four billion dollars in excess profits on the gold [word or words missing] between 1932 and 1940, handing it to a dirty gang of kikes and hyper-kikes on the London gold exchange firms. Why is that expected to help America? Or why should it be regarded as a model of devotion to the American spirit? Or why should any honest American vote for the continuance of that swindle or of keeping in office the men and kikes who were responsible for putting it over the people? . . .

Had you had the sense to eliminate Roosevelt and his Jews or the Jews and their Roosevelt at the last election, you would not now be at war. That is one point. But to suppose that you will win the war by goin' on bein' mugs in any and every internal conflict, to suppose that you will strengthen the United States abroad by submittin' to continued internal bleedin' and swindlin' is just so much hokum or nonsense.

April 30, 1942
Don't start a pogrom. That is, not an old-style killing of small Jews. That system is no good, whatever. Of course, if some man had a stroke of genius, and could start a pogrom up at the top. I repeat . . . if some man had a stroke of genius, and could start a pogrom up at the top, there might be something to say for it. But on the whole, legal measures are preferable. The 60 kikes who started this war might be sent to St. Helena, as a measure of world prophylaxis, and some hyper-kikes or non-Jewish kikes along with them.

May 5, 1942
The kike, and the unmitigated evil that has been centered in London since the British government got on the Red Indians to murder the American frontier settlers, has herded the Slavs, the Mongols, the Tartars openly against Germany and Poland and Finland. And secretly against all that is decent in America, against the total American heritage. This is my war all right. I've been in it for twenty years—my gran'dad was in it before me.

May 10, 1942
The next peace will not be based on international lending. Get that, for one. The next peace will not be based on international lending, and

England certainly will have nothing whatever to say about what its terms are. Neither, I think, will simple-hearted Joe Stalin, not wholly trusted by the kikery which is his master.

May 26, 1942

Every hour that you go on with this war is an hour lost to you and your children. And every sane act you commit is committed in homage to Mussolini and Hitler. Every reform, every lurch toward the just price, toward the control of a market is an act of homage to Mussolini and Hitler. They are your leaders, however much you think you are conducted by Roosevelt or told by Churchill. You follow Mussolini and Hitler in every constructive act of your government.

June 8, 1942

I suppose if I go on talking to you kids long enough I'll get something into your heads. If I go on pounding from day to day, every day and in every way, I will finally teach you kids why you got dragged into this war—if you survive it. And when you know that you will know more than your fathers did by the end of the last one.

June 28, 1942

You are not going to win this war. None of our best minds ever thought you could win it. You have never had a chance in this war.

July 2, 1942

I am not arguing, I am just telling you, one of these days you will have to start thinking about the problem of race, breed, preservation.

July 6, 1942

There is so much that the United States does not know. This war is proof of such vast incomprehension, such tangled ignorance, so many strains of unknowing—I am held up, enraged by the delay needed to change the typing ribbon, so much is there that ought to be put down, be put into young America's head. I don't know what to put down, can't write two scripts at once. The necessary facts, ideas come in pell-mell, I try to get too much into ten minutes. Condensed form is all right in a book; saves eyesight. The reader can turn back and look at a summary. Maybe if I had more sense of form, legal training, God knows what, I could get the matter across the Atlantic, or the bally old Channel.

July 14, 1942

You are in black darkness and confusion, you have been hugger-muggered and scarum-shouted into a war, and you know nothing about it. You know nothing about the forces that caused it. Or you know next to nothing. I am in the agonized position of an observer who has worked twenty-five years to prevent it, but I'm not the only observer who has so striven. Apparently no man could prevent it, that is, up to the point that it was not prevented. But a belief in destiny does not necessarily imply a belief that we have no duty; that we should not attempt to learn; that we should sit supine before an age-old evil. Given a little more knowledge, given the elimination of a small number of shysters, the war need not have happened.

July 20, 1942

You ought not to be at war against Italy. You ought not to be giving the slightest or most picayune aid to any man or nation engaged in waging war against Italy. You are doing it for the sake of a false accounting system.

July 22, 1942

Europe calling. . . . Ezra Pound speaking. I hear that my views are shared, most of them, by a large number of my compatriots, so it would seem, or maybe an increasing number of my compatriots. And there is a comforting thought on a warm day in a fine climate. I should hate to think that all America had gone haywire. I should like to feel that the American race in North America, in the North American continent, had some wish toward survival. That they wanted there to be a United States of tomorrow. . . .

Well, you have been fed on lies, for 20 years you have been fed on lies, and I don't say maybe. And Mr. Squirmy and Mr. Slime are still feeding it to you right over the BBC radio, and every one of the Jew radios of Schenectady, New York, and Boston—and Boston was once an American city; that was when it was about the size of Rapallo. . . .

And how much liberty have you got anyhow? And as to the arsenal—are you the arsenal of democracy or of judeocracy? And who rules your rulers? Where does public responsibility end and what races can mix in America without ruin of the American stock, the American brain? Who is organized? What say have you in the choice of your rulers? What control of their policy? And who does own most of your press and your radio? E.P. asking you.

February 18, 1943

Don't shoot him, don't shoot him, don't shoot the President. Assassins deserve worse, but don't shoot him. Assassination only makes more murders. . . . Don't shoot him, diagnose him, diagnose him. It is not only your affair, but it is your bound duty as American citizens. Duty begins at home.

March 19, 1943

Just which of you are free from Jewish influence? Just which political and business groups are free from Jew influence, from Jew control? Who holds the mortgage, who is the dominating director? Just which Jew has . . . nominated which assemblyman indebted to whom? And which one is indebted to Jewry or dependent on credit which he cannot get without the connivance of Jewry?

April 27, 1943
Oh, yes, another ten- or twenty-year war, between the United States and Slavic Russia. It'll start just as soon as this one shows signs of relaxing.

May 4, 1943
What are you doing in the war at all? What are you doing in Africa? Who amongst you has the nerve or the sense to do something that would be conducive to getting you out of it before you are mortgaged up to the neck and over it? Every day of war is a dead day as well as a death day. More death, more future servitude, less and less of American liberty of any variety.

May 8, 1943
There is not one ounce or atom of honesty in either Churchill or Roosevelt. Most of the reasons for England and America being in the war are unconfessable and indecent. . . . A clean England and a clean United States might collaborate in a new world, but it will take a hell of a lot of *Sapolio* to wash off the mess made by Roosevelt and Churchill. I'm telling you, I'm not giving you the Axis point of view.

May 9, 1943
The Jew is a savage, his psychology is . . . may the stink of your camp drive you onward—herders—having no care but to let their . . . herds grouse and move onward when the pasture is exhausted.

The prolix abuse and incantatory fervor, both pro and con, carried him forward. On May 11 Pound commented, without apparently knowing he was on the air, on a recent speech by Undersecretary of State Sumner Welles: "And Mr. Welles quite definitely and clearly mentioned the common man's desire to have a house of his own and his own family. Now that is what we believe National Socialism stands for in Germany. It is what Italy stands for; it is quite emphatically what Communist Russia does not stand for and would not stand for." So eager was the broadcaster to reply to the speech of Welles that he could not remember where the Undersecretary of State had spoken; and not having had the opportunity to examine an actual transcript of the speech he was unfamiliar with its actual content. Yet the following day, sharing the microphone with Al Sanders, a British broadcaster also employed by EIAR, the poet sallied forth again.[35]

> ANNOUNCER: Around the microphone with me tonight are Al Sanders, whom you already know, and Ezra Pound, who spoke to you last time, on this same broadcast.
> POUND: I spoke to you, I thought. I was not talking to anybody but the boys around the microphone.

ANNOUNCER: Well, exactly; but you know perfectly well—at least we hope—that there might be a few people who want to get a little bit of learning into their heads, by benefiting from his wisdom [*aside to Sanders?*].

POUND: Shall we say something overheard, what?

ANNOUNCER: Something overheard—exactly. What did we speak about last time, Al?

SANDERS: Before we get into any particular subject, I have a question to ask Mr. Pound. I heard you last night on a broadcast to America.

POUND: Do you mean to say anybody here listens to my broadcasts to America?

SANDERS: I do. Of course. I—maybe I'm a special case. But I do.

POUND: I always thought you were a special case. But—even so.

SANDERS: Kidding aside, I want to know one thing. You kept on talking about a speech made by the Undersecretary of State of the United States.

POUND: Well, I mean he's called the Undersecretary, but I mean I don't imagine Mr. Hull has much to do with running that department.

SANDERS: I think Mr. Hull is a nice old guy. I remember reading a whole story of his life in *Life*.

POUND: His life—I mean to say—

SANDERS: Yes, he's a Tennessee boy and they give him quite a write-up.

POUND: No doubt they'd give him quite a write-up, but what does he do in the State Department?

SANDERS: He gives it tone.

POUND: He gives it tone?

(*Laughter*)

ANNOUNCER: What kind of tone, Al?

SANDERS: First, I want to get through with my question. Then we'll discuss Mr. Hull. (*To Pound*) I want to know why you call Mr. Sumner Welles Mr. Sumner Wel-les. Don't you know about it? Have you been here in Italy so long you don't even know how to pronounce your own countryman's name?

POUND: I suppose that if he puts that extra "e" in, he put it there for effect—I suppose he wanted people to pronounce it that way.

SANDERS: What do you mean, he put it in?

POUND: I didn't think he was born with an "e" in his name. I thought that "e" came out of a name of some Cabinet minister of early American historical times.

SANDERS: Sumner went "society" on us?

POUND: I don't know anything about "society." I mean, I've been out of that country for a long time. I thought it was—might say—historic, what do you call it, a bit of old-lace-and-lavender-Colonial touch, I suppose you might say. Qualifying for the Daughters of the American Revolution or something.

SANDERS: Now tell us, Mr. Pound, you really think that when Mr. Welles made his speech—where was it exactly, at Toledo, wasn't it?

POUND: I got mixed up. I kept calling it Toronto, but I think it was Toledo or—

SANDERS: What do you think, when he made that speech? Did he really take it that Europe, or rather the Axis countries, would take it seriously?

POUND: God knows, a man makes a speech in Ohio, in Toledo, Ohio, where the presidents come from—

SANDERS: Is that a hint for a future candidate, in case FDR gets sidetracked?

POUND: Well, I suppose Mr. Wel-les or Welles, if you want to call him that, looks for a continuation of his job and hopes for a Democratic victory some time or other.

SANDERS: But you think that he would hope for a continuation of his job with FDR in the seat?

POUND: I reckon those Democrats would like to keep the seat, though they don't care much who runs it, but as long as they've got a permanency, they'd keep it.

SANDERS: As long as we brought the subject up, what do you mean [by Democrats]? A couple of years ago there were a lot of Democrats who wouldn't recognize FDR as a Democrat, if he saw them.

POUND: Well, I mean the New Deal, er . . .

SANDERS. A description of *what* kind of a New Deal we can't put over the radio.

POUND: Some of the things in the New Deal were all right—I mean, even Mr. Hamilton Fish said the New Deal for—I think he said—it was all right for nearly two years. At any rate—

SANDERS: I dare say.

POUND: I'd call it socialist then, er, Mr. Roosevelt's prime aim in life. Which do you mean? Are you talking about the hard-shelled Carter Glass, who wanted to get back to gold because the Republicans dote on him?

SANDERS: I mean the average southern Democrat. I've talked with a good many Democrats who never believed that Mr. Roosevelt was much of a Democrat.

POUND: Not a Democrat in the dictionary sense of the word. He's not a man who cares anything about the welfare of his people, I don't think.

SANDERS: Well, his whole program was got up on a basis—

POUND: Yes, I know, he had a program, but maybe John Caldwell Calhoun was the last Democrat.

SANDERS: You said a very just thing, I think, Mr. Pound, when you said that he didn't really have the welfare of the people at heart. I think that is one of the main things one can find fault with FDR about. I think that a lot of people consider that FDR might have done very much better by his people if he hadn't pushed them into the war.

POUND: I didn't want him to get into the war. God knows, this war was not made for my comfort or for anybody else's that I can see.

SANDERS: Well now, the English, or rather the British—I wonder how they feel about it? There seems to be a slight discrepancy of ideas between the British and Americans at this moment.

POUND: If the British can't get a good lunch at the Savoy, why, I reckon they'd go round to the Berkeley.

SANDERS: Yes, that's right.

POUND: That is—well, I mean the English can go to the Savoy, where there are only English.

SANDERS: How many are there, what's the percentage of them, er?

POUND: It isn't a question of percentage—the English, after all, are a constitutional monarchy. The people in England haven't got anything to say about running it.

SANDERS: No, that's quite true, the way they haven't got anything to say about running it in the United States, either.

POUND: Haven't we? Remember those—no, you're too young. But when they were running—the "Yellow" crew—in the New York *Journal*, back in 1890—they used to run a funny kind of poem, in two lines, a little rhyme:

> In the days of Charlemagne
> Did the people drink champagne?

Guess again.

SANDERS: That rhyme can be applied every day.

POUND: "In the days of old champagne Did the people get away?" Nay, nay.

ANNOUNCER: Don't you think that, as Al says, that applies to people at the present time?

POUND: Not if the directors of Kuhn, Loeb & Co . . . Who are out in the front line trenches, getting decimated?

SANDERS: Well, the founders of Kuhn, Loeb—

POUND: The kernel of the whole business.

SANDERS: Kuhn, Loeb brings up to your mind, my mind, to every man with imagination, international finance. Now, we're all agreed that the international bankers, either part of one big family, or of one big sect or race or lodge, or whatever you want to call it—

POUND: There are family ties between some of them.

SANDERS: Are all tied together in the united nations. We are all agreed on that—I'm sure we agree so today and for the future. If that is so, as we say, how come that there's so much discrepancy of outside views among the different united nations, among the people of the united nations?

POUND: But the people get it in the neck all around. When they won't pay up 60 per cent interest, under the impression they're paying 6, then they get pressed into war, or they have Russia stirred up to blackmail the people who won't toe the line.

SANDERS: Don't you think the whole set-up is also a very convenient preparatory measure for any future wars? The united nations, on the surface, are fighting together, and on the under surface, as everyone sees, they are fighting against each other. The British are accusing the Americans of trying to grab the British Empire, and the Americans feel that they are being taken for a ride by the British.

ANNOUNCER: What about the Russians—what do they feel?

POUND: I don't understand the Slavic temperament, but the people who know least are the ones who get into the war quickest.

SANDERS: You know it's a fact, Mr. Pound, that there—the center of world finance used to be in the City of London?

POUND: There was a lot of finance in Paris that wasn't exactly separate. London became very dominant.

SANDERS: Don't you think that, now, has shifted slightly?

POUND: I thought it was generally agreed that the shift was scheduled and that—

SANDERS: You think it was scheduled?

POUND: I think a lot of Jews have now got their money in [transcriber's guess: Argentina].

SANDERS: Yes, I think that's probably true.

ANNOUNCER: How do you link up the so-called united nations? From the financial point of view, how do you get Russia into the picture?

POUND: They want Russia to kill off the Germans.

SANDERS: In other words—[Germans] to kill off the Russians?

POUND: Secondary, they don't mind Russia being weakened. But Russia is the hammer held over the head of these rebellious Germans and rebellious Europeans.

SANDERS: And rebellious Italians.

POUND: Yes—rebellious Italians, yes.

SANDERS: In other words, you think that there's a British-Russo *mariage de convenance*.

POUND: I don't know that I'd go as far as to call it a marriage—call it a liaison, if you like.

SANDERS: They go to bed together.

ANNOUNCER: Well, if you like to call it that, but they certainly don't see things eye to eye in many other things.

SANDERS: Oh no, the next war is very nicely secured—this er, er, Hank Wallace began to see signs of trouble on the horizon.

ANNOUNCER: Don't you think that any one war is made by just [words missing]. Wars are part of a process, take long preparation.

POUND: Not so long [words missing] to work a curve of acceleration.

SANDERS: In other words, we're fighting a war to start more wars.

POUND: Undoubtedly Italy was trying to stop that process. New York and London are undoubtedly fighting a war to maintain the process of having wars once in so often, whenever it suits international finance.

ANNOUNCER: Yes, I think that's very clear, Mr. Pound. I'm afraid that our time is up. I want to thank Mr. Pound for what he said, and Mr. Sanders. And good-night everybody.

Pound arriving back in New York aboard the liner *Rex* in 1939, after nearly three decades abroad. (*Wide World Photos.*)

Opposite: In front of his hotel in Rome, 1942. (*Wide World Photos.*)

Above: Row of security cages at the Detention Training Center near Pisa, Italy, 1945. A corner of Pound's cage, specially constructed of airstrip steel, is visible on extreme left. (*Courtesy Humanities Research Center, University of Texas at Austin. Signal Corps photo.*)

Above: The medical compound of the Detention Training Center. Late at night, Pound was allowed to use the dispensary typewriter, the same one on which he wrote the Pisan Cantos. (*Courtesy Stephan Chodorov. Signal Corps photo.*)

Opposite, top: Pound arrived in Washington, D.C., after a flight from Italy, November 18, 1945, in custody of U.S. Marshals. (*Wide World Photos.*)

Opposite, bottom: The prisoner immediately after his arraignment in District Court, Washington, D.C., November 20, 1945. (*Wide World Photos.*)

3

One day early in April 1943, Florence Williams came home to tell her husband that one of the tellers at the local bank had asked her if she knew anyone in Italy named Ezra Pound. The teller had heard a person of that name on the radio the night before say "something about 'ol' Doc Williams of Rutherford, New Jersey, would understand.' Something like that."

"What the hell right has he to drag me into his dirty messes," said William Carlos Williams to his wife.

"I'm just reporting what I heard," Floss said. "You're always getting mixed up in something through your friends."

Williams was anything but pleased. He was even less pleased when, several weeks later, an FBI agent turned up at his front door. The Bureau had been working on the Pound case for nearly a year, and the agent wanted to know, Williams noted in his 1948 *Autobiography*,[1] if he would be willing to listen to some records of Pound's Italian shortwave broadcasts in order to identify his voice.

Williams seemed reluctant at first. For one thing, except for brief and occasional visits, he had not spent much time with Pound for a number of years; he was not entirely certain he could recognize Pound's voice on what might be a poor recording. For another, he was not particularly enthused about the dour prospect of having to cooperate with the FBI. Although he had shortly before written an article for a small magazine called *Decision* in which he referred to Pound as Lord Ga-Ga and labeled him a "pitiable spectacle," a "fool," a "spoiled brat" and a "stupid ass," he had no desire now to turn informer.

"I can say that the recording I hear sounds like the voice of Ezra Pound," Williams bristled. "I can't say more than that."

"Are you a loyal American citizen?" the agent asked.

"Of course I'm a loyal American citizen. I've spent my whole life, generally speaking, for my country, trying to serve it in every way I know how."

Had the question intimidated Williams? Most probably it had. He indicated that he was willing to do what he could to help the FBI. Within the following weeks the agent paid two more visits to the poet's home. On neither occasion, however, did he subject Williams to Pound's venomous broadcasts. Nor did Williams, for his part, admit to the agent that he too had once been a dues-paying member of the Social Credit party which held its weekly meetings in New York at the private Fifth Avenue brownstone of Gorham Munson. Instead, the doctor produced a small packet of correspondence from Pound—a card, postmarked Rapallo, December 22, 1938; a letter, postmarked Washington, D.C., May 2, 1939; another letter, dated March 22, 1940, and postmarked Italy. These were subsequently confiscated by the FBI as documentation, proof that the broadcaster had returned to Italy of his own accord prior to the outbreak of the war.

Whether or not by volunteering this and other information Williams was in fact out to "get" Pound is now difficult to say. More than likely, he felt perplexed and bewildered by the entire twist of events, and possibly demoralized by the moral guilt feeling induced by actually having shared some of Pound's views on strict monetary reform. It was because of Pound's persistent prodding that he had joined the Social Credit party in the first place. No doubt he believed it was the political and economic elements of Pound's philosophy, and not Ezra Pound personally, that "they" (the government through the FBI) were trying to smash and with which he was willing to go along.

Such sentiments were commonplace among quite a few of *il miglior fabbro*'s close friends and associates. The KGB-like "disavowals and denunciations" elicited by the FBI from a number of Pound's confreres would seem to bear this out. James Laughlin, for example, the poet's chief American publisher, told special agents that "Pound's plight is the case of a man never adjusting himself to society, although having vast ambition and much ego. . . . As a result of Pound's extraordinary ego, he thinks he is the greatest poet since Dante. He, however, believes that people have persecuted him over a period of years. Therefore, he is now anxious to persecute the Jews."[2]

Laughlin, at one time also an avid Social Creditor and a contributing editor to Gorham Munson's Social Credit periodical, *New Democ-*

racy, may well have intended to steer FBI agents to a conclusion compatible with his own—that Pound was no longer in full command of his mental faculties and therefore not fully responsible for his deeds. In this endeavor, however, the publisher inadvertently became a prime source of information, supplying FBI investigators with a wealth of data concerning the author's private and wartime activities. So too did Archibald MacLeish, whom Pound had so unmercifully torn apart in one of his more fervid broadcasts. MacLeish, a friend of Pound's in Paris following World War I and a major force (as was Laughlin) in the battle to get the poet released from St. Elizabeths, was Librarian of Congress in 1939; in 1941, he was director of the U.S. Office of Facts and Figures, in 1942, assistant director of the Office of War Information, and in 1944, Assistant Secretary of State.

Thus, in 1943, the state of affairs was such that circumstance worked completely against Pound. MacLeish, whose verse play *Panic* attacked American bankers and usurers, probably also felt himself to be among those victimized by Pound, influenced by the expatriate's driving letters of the 1930s urging him as an attorney, statesman, and writer to look into himself and then to act accordingly, to take a firm stance on the nation's fiscal and political policies. Convinced that Pound was mad and therefore better off in an insane asylum, MacLeish supplied the FBI with photographs of the poet taken in Paris and Rapallo during the 1920s and 1930s. In a letter (September 10, 1943) to Harvey Bundy, Special Assistant to the Secretary of War, MacLeish wrote: "I am not asking you . . . to think of the problem in terms of Pound, or Pound's reputation. The real question seems to me to be a question of the way in which this government should treat as tragi-comic a figure. . . . There is, I think, no question but that his punishment will very precisely fit his crime."[3]

Others: Richard Aldington, like Williams, inundated the FBI with letters from the chief imagist which were full of political and economic babble, and responded affirmatively when asked if he would be willing to listen to records in order to identify Pound's voice; Virginia Rice likewise handed over a bundle of incriminating mailings, and recounted details of Pound's 1939 State-side visit and insulting anti-Semitic remarks; George Antheil supplied the Bureau with copies of the master's out-of-print books and provided the names of other potential material witnesses. Louis Zukofsky, Ronald Duncan, Tibor Serly, John Drummond, and John Slocum variously cited the poet for his particular brand of "anti-Americanism." Reynolds Packard and James Angleton spoke of his fondness for the Duce. E. E. Cummings, always one of Pound's stanchest public supporters, cooperated with the FBI to the hilt, railing against his friend for his patronage of the Fascist regime and his violent opposition to the Jews. Of *il miglior fabbro's* intimate vortex, only T. S. Eliot and Ernest Hemingway remained mute. The rest seemed at best undecided, at worst willing and able to testify against Pound in an effort to further the government's cause.

The last EIAR broadcast to be monitored by the FCC was aired July 25, 1943. The following day, in the District Court of the United States for the District of Columbia, an indictment for violation of the Treason Statute (Section 1, Title 18, United States Code, 1940 Edition),[4] was returned against Ezra Pound:

> The Grand Jurors for the United States of America duly impaneled and sworn in the District Court of the United States for the District of Columbia and inquiring for that District upon their oath present;
> That Ezra Pound, the defendant herein, at Rome, Italy, and other places within the territory of the Kingdom of Italy, and, as hereinafter described, in the District of Columbia, within the jurisdiction of this Court, and at other places throughout the United States and elsewhere, continuously, and at all times during the period beginning on the 11th day of December, 1941, and continuing thereafter to and including the date of the presentment and filing of this indictment, under the circumstances and conditions and in the manner and by the means hereinafter set forth, then and there being a citizen of the United States, and a person owing allegiance to the United States, in violation of his said duty of allegiance, knowingly, intentionally, wilfully, unlawfully, feloniously, traitorously, and treasonably did adhere to the enemies of the United States, to wit, the Kingdom of Italy, its counsellors, armies, navies, secret agents, representatives, and subjects, and the military allies of the said Kingdom of Italy, including the Government of the German Reich and the Imperial Government of Japan, with which the United States at all times since December 11, 1941, have been at war, giving to the said enemies of the United States aid and comfort within the United States and elsewhere.

It was the classic definition of treason. The indictment went on at considerable length, each of the specifications which followed terminating in similar fashion: ". . . said defendant asserted, among other things, in substance, that citizens of the United States should not support the United States in the conduct of the said war."

Seven other American citizens were indicted with Pound: Frederick Wilhelm Kaltenbach, Robert H. Best, Douglas Chandler, Edward Leo Delaney, Constance Drexel, Jane Anderson, Max Otto Koischwitz. All of them, with the exception of Pound, had broadcast from Germany. Following the mass indictment, Attorney General Francis Biddle held a press conference. "It should be clearly understood," he informed reporters, "that these indictments are based not only on the content of the propaganda statements—the lies and falsifications which were uttered—but also on the simple fact that these people have freely elected, at a time when their country is at war, to devote their services to the cause of the enemies of the United States. They have betrayed the first and most sacred obligation of American citizenship."[5]

Pound afterward told his counsel that he heard of the indictment via the BBC. He was not aware that his talks had been monitored. On August 4, while staying at Rapallo, he wrote Mr. Biddle a detailed brief making clear his present position. He left the letter with the Swiss Legation in Rome, which promptly forwarded it to the proper authorities:

> I understand that I am under indictment for treason. I have done my best to get an authentic report of your statement to this effect. And I wish to place the following facts before you.
>
> I do not believe that the simple fact of speaking over the radio, wherever placed, can in itself constitute treason. I think that must depend on what is said, and on the motives for speaking.
>
> I obtained the concession to speak over Rome radio with the following proviso. Namely that nothing should be asked of me contrary to my conscience or contrary to my duties as an American citizen. I obtained a declaration on their part of a belief in "the free expression of opinion by those qualified to have an opinion."
>
> The legal mind of the Attorney General will understand the interest inherent in this distinction, as from unqualified right of expression.
>
> This declaration was made several times in the announcement of my speeches; with the declaration "He will not be asked to say anything contrary to his conscience, or contrary to his duties as an American citizen" (Citizen of the U.S.).
>
> These conditions have been adhered to. The only time I had an opinion as to what might be interesting as subject matter, I was asked whether I would speak of religion. This seemed to me hardly my subject, though I did transmit on one occasion some passages from Confucius, under the title "The Organum of Confucius."

I have not spoken with regard to *this* war, but in protest against a system which creates one war after another, in series and in system. I have not spoken to the troops, and have not suggested that the troops should mutiny or revolt.

The whole basis of democratic or majority government assumes that the citizen shall be informed of the facts. I have not claimed to know all the facts, but I have claimed to know some of the facts which are an essential part of the total that should be known to the people.

I have for years believed that the American people should be better informed as to Europe, and informed by men who are not tied to a special interest or under definite control.

The freedom of the press has become a farce, as everyone knows that the press is controlled, if not by its titular owners, at least by the advertisers.

Free speech under modern conditions becomes a mockery if it does not include the right of free speech over the radio.

And this point is worth establishing. The assumption of the right to punish and take vengeance regardless of the area of jurisdiction is dangerous. I do not mean in a small way; but for the nation.

I returned to America before the war to protest against particular forces then engaged in trying to create war and to make sure that the U.S.A. should be dragged into it.

Arthur Kitson's testimony before the Cunliffe and MacMillan commissions was insufficiently known. Brooks Adams brought to light several currents in history that should be better known. The course of events following the foundation of the Bank of England should be known, and considered in sequence: the suppression of colonial paper money, especially in Pennsylvania! The similar curves following the Napoleonic wars, and our Civil War and Versailles need more attention.

We have not the right to drift into another error similar to that of the Versailles Treaty.

We have, I think, the right to a moderate expansion including defence of the Caribbean, the elimination of foreign powers from the American continent, but such expansion should not take place at the cost of deteriorating or ruining the internal structure of the U.S.A. The ruin of markets, the perversions of trade routes, in fact all the matters on which my talks have been based is [sic] of importance to the American citizen; whom neither you nor I should betray either in time of war *or* peace. I may say in passing that I took out a life membership in the American Academy of Social and Political Science in the hope of obtaining fuller discussion of some of these issues, but did not find them ready for full and frank expression of certain vital elements in the case; this may in part have been due to their incomprehension of the nature of the case.

At any rate a man's duties increase with his knowledge. A war between the U.S. and Italy is monstrous and should not have occurred.

And a peace without justice is no peace but merely a prelude to future wars. Someone must take count of these things. And having taken count must act on his knowledge; admitting that his knowledge is partial and his judgment subject to error.

Pound's letter to the Attorney General, lucid and reasonably temperate, nonetheless contained two basic flaws. Although his post-Pearl Harbor Day talks were prefaced by the announcer's paragraph about Fascist hospitality and freedom of expression, this did not in any way exempt Pound from his duties as an American citizen. The announcer's introductory statement, in fact, had no legal bearing whatsoever. Yet Pound took the statement about "his not being asked to go against his conscience or say anything incompatible with his duties as an American" as proof of his innocence of treason, and he continued to cite it as such for years to come.[6] He maintained, also, as he had in the letter, that the Constitutional guarantee of freedom of speech justified his actions. In addition, although he made claims to the contrary, his broadcasts were beamed to American troops at home and abroad. His comments, especially about the landings and battles in North Africa in April and May of 1943, were heard by soldiers and sailors—French, British, and American—directly involved in these bloody battles. That he did not succeed in persuading American soldiers to desert or malinger is actually beside the point.

On July 25, 1943, a coup led by King Victor Emmanuel and Marshal Pietro Badoglio, hero of the Ethiopian invasion, forced Mussolini to resign. "Our culture," Pound wrote, "lies shattered in fragments." By early August, Badoglio had replaced Mussolini, and the Allied armies, having landed on the boot of southern Italy, were inching their way north. Pound's final broadcast for Radio Rome was made during the first week of September. He had manned his post until the end. Now, with the German military occupying Rome and Italians fleeing in every direction, he prepared to take leave of the city.

He returned to the Albergo d'Italia to pay his bill and leave his leather briefcase and wide-brimmed Borsalino hat with the clerk at the front desk. From the degli Uberti family he borrowed a knapsack, sturdy walking stick, military road map, and heavy hiking boots. At noon on September 10—two days after the announcement of the signing of the Armistice—he appeared at the home of another friend, Naldo Naldi, whose wife Nora was from London.

(In an unpublished account written some years later and recorded by Noel Stock in his Pound biography, Naldi described how at first when the doorbell rang he and his wife hesitated before answering; they had no idea whom to expect. When they opened the door, in walked Pound, his knapsack on his back. He told them he was going to visit his daughter in Gais. They tried to dissuade him, offered to put him up until one knew what was going to happen. The war might be over in a few days, a treaty might be signed. But Pound had already made up his mind. The Naldis fed him and filled up his knapsack with eggs, fruit, bread. He had come, he told them, not for food but to see a familiar face and to get some information on the most expedient way to leave the city. Naldi marked Pound's map for him. The poet was visibly upset as he prepared to leave. Naldi accompanied him along the street for several minutes. "At the corner [reads Naldi's manuscript] I showed him the right way to go. He shook my hand, without speaking. It is so difficult to find the right words when things are enormously complex. I watched him go off, his stick striking the footpath regularly . . . I did not see him again.")[7]

During the following days, as he made his way north, he was given food by kindly peasant women and spent his nights sleeping under the sky. He slept in an air-raid shelter in Bologna. The next morning he boarded a train which took him to Verona. The man "out of Naxos past Fara Sabina" walked the rest of the way, dirt and dust covering his face, his feet all blisters. It was during this part of the flight that he was helped by Carl Goedel, an official in the English section of Radio Rome, who afterward joined forces with the Salò Republic. He recalled Goedel in Canto 78: "Goedel's sleek head in the midst of it"—and again on the first page of Canto 79: "(to Goedel in memoriam)/ Sleek head that saved me out of one chaos."[8]

A few days later, Pound reached the Tirolean village of Gais: " 'Gruss Gott,' 'Der Herr!' 'Tatile ist gekommen!' " He was exhausted, but he had journeyed this great distance for good reason. There was something pressing he felt compelled to tell his daughter. She was old enough now to know that there was another family: a wife in Rapallo, with a son in England. In time he would set things right—"If this war ever ends . . . ," he informed Mary.

The situation in the north, with its volatile Austro–Italian population, was just as uncertain as it had been in Rome. Soon after his arrival at Gais, two members of the SOD (*Südtiroler Ordnungs Dienst*), carrying rifles, appeared at the Marcher farmhouse, apparently with the intention of arresting the poet. One of them, a wood carver, felt sympathetic toward Pound. The two soldiers decided to let him stay until his feet had healed, and suggested that he then go to Germany or possibly over the Alps into Switzerland. He occupied himself during this period by doing odd jobs around the house: he repaired a chicken coop and a flight of stairs connecting the stable to the barn. After news arrived of Mussolini's daring liberation in mid-September by German parachutists and of the partial resurrection some weeks later of the Fascist regime, at the Lago di Garda, the Great Bass made up his mind to return to Rapallo. He also made up his mind, while passing around Lake Garda on his way home, to get in touch with the new regime, still in the process of being formed.

A story by Damaso Riccioni that appeared in *Il Nazionale* on September 4, 1955, under the title "Con Ezra Pound al Lago di Salò" tells of Pound's visit with Serafino Mazzolini, Salò's Minister of Foreign Affairs. Riccioni reports that he found the poet and the minister engaged in heated conversation at the latter's villa. The subjects discussed ranged from imagism and Italian poetry to the latest on Mussolini, Hitler, and Stalin. When the subject of Pound's indictment by an American grand jury came up, the poet grew defensive. He cited Socrates as an example of a private citizen who refused to subordinate his own feelings, regardless of the cost, when his country was at war. The poet spoke of being guided by an interior light and claimed that his ideas were neither impious nor subversive. He told Riccioni that eventually his own countrymen would come to see the light.[9]

Back in Rapallo he was hard at work again—reading, translating, producing pamphlets, articles, manifestoes, and posters. In the summer of 1941 he had rendered into English the initial volume, entitled *Moscardino*, of the multi-volumed saga, *Il romanzo di Moscardino*, by Enrico Pea. Among the material he was translating now—from English into Italian—was an unpublished book on economics by the British poet J. P. Angold called "Work and Privilege" ("Lavoro e Privilegi"); he tried to interest an Italian publisher in the project but the attempt failed. He was greatly interested in spreading the ethic of Confucius ("Better gift can no man make to a nation/ than the sense of Kung fu Tseu"), so offered his reading public an Italian version of the opening chapter of *Ta Hio*, which he renamed *Ta S'eu* or *Dai Gaku*, and which appeared in the *Meridiano di Roma* under the title "Studio Integrale," in expanded book format as *Testamento di Confucio*; there was also the Confucian *Ciung lung, L'asse che non vacilla* ("Chung Yung, The Unwobbling Axis"), a twist on the "Pivot" of the original English title.

With the establishment of the Fascist regime at Salò, there arose a battery of newspapers and journals devoted solely to charting the resurgence of the movement: *Il Secolo XIX; Il Secolo–La Sera; L'Idea Sociale; Il Popolo di Alessandria.* Pound wrote for all of these publications but most frequently and avidly for *Il Popolo.* Beginning in November 1943, and for the next sixteen months, some thirty-five of his boisterous illuminations appeared in the pages of the Alessandrian newspaper, covering the usual and expected mélange of themes—banking, usury, fascism, the race question. Excerpted in the November–December 1972 issue of *La Destra,* a neo-Fascist periodical printed in Rome, the *Popolo* pieces have the same ring and twang as many of Pound's radio broadcasts, smack at times of Madison Avenue ad-land campaign *loquela:*

March 28, 1944

It is difficult to define with any real precision property rights in Russia under the jurisdiction of the Stalin-Judaic state.

Stalin is a clear thinker, but this does not mean that a Judaic administration will be of much use to the workers.

April 30, 1944

Arguments arise because of the ignorance of *all* the participants.

A friend compliments me on my "original" writing. It isn't that it's original; it is simply informed. . . .

The Fascist dictum was defined years ago; we believe in the freedom to express an opinion on the part of those qualified to hold an opinion.

June 8, 1944

Civic order arises out of ethical order.

The Italian Risorgimento was a light in the world. That light will shine again.

November 21, 1944

Brothers! Let us unite against the influence of corrupt foreigners who seek to dominate us!

Do you believe in law? Very well, but remember the eternal law of nature; the strong shall dominate the weak.

January 9, 1945

Enough of that form of economy praised by the usurocracy and eulogized by the dirty *Times* of London, by Lippmann and other filthy jews, covered with excrement; and so proud of being forever cited by the Italian press, in defiance of Fascist thought. . . .

The goal of every stinking Roosevelt, Churchill, Eden, Lehman, Baruch, or B'nai Brith is to suppress all independence.

January 23, 1945

The Italians were poisoned by the *wrong books imported from abroad.* Churchill and Roosevelt made sure that the *real* English and American books were kept hidden, and that the few copies that reached Italy caused no curiosity. The critic Linati, who was lazy, and Mario Praz, a Bloomsbury snob, who had a monopoly on Anglo-American literary criticism in Italy, ignored these *real* books. The so-called Italian "intelligentsia" preferred a Walpole to an E. E. Cummings, and a Wodehouse to a Brooks Adams. Now you are paying for it. . . .

Usurers are all cousins.

Pound's belief in what he was doing was so firm, his notion of the way things should be so divorced from the way things were, that he was incapable of separating right from wrong, fact from fiction. It never occurred to him that, on the one hand, Italy had been conquered by the Allies and, on the other, commandeered, at least in the north, by Major Albert Kesselring and whole squadrons of Hitler's desperate troops. If anything, Pound was more hopeful now than before, more confident that his vision of the ideal republic was within reach. His attachment to the Salò Republic and the Veronese Charter were complete. It was more than a luminary pipe dream; he believed, with an almost religious fervor, that given the proper support, Italy and Germany could still rule the world.

His first duty was to educate the still educable masses. Giovanni Gentile, formerly Minister of Education, had been appointed president of the new Florentine Academy. Pound wrote to Gentile, enclosing a three-page proposal for a national education program in literature. The syllabus listed not only Homer, Catullus, Ovid, Dante, Chaucer but also a full agenda of "readable" historians and economists. A copy of the proposal was forwarded by Gentile to the Duce at Salò, who promptly appended the name of Plato, whose *Republic* he had recently read and pondered.

In accordance with Jeffersonian democratic dogma, Pound never once wavered from his belief that the individual comprised the mainstay of the State. The more aware and well informed the individual, the more advanced and liberated the society in which that individual circulated. In this regard, Pound wrote (January 3, 1944) to the regime's new Minister of Popular Culture, Fernando Mezzasoma, complaining that his (Pound's) efforts to rid Italy of her clinging ignorance had been unsuccessful; the older generation was no less ignorant than the new, and Pavolini's attempts to instill learning and knowledge while he was still Minister of Popular Culture had been equally blocked. Another letter (February 1, 1944) covered much of the same ground: "A suggestion: everyone in the country, when not able to take part directly in specific advancements of the Republic, should attempt to maintain the level of intellectual life, and should communicate with someone else who can collaborate in the maintenance of civilization."[10] In specific terms, Pound was concerned with those in Italy most qualified to carry on the tradition of the cult of intelligence—namely, those citizens with some kind of advanced university degree:

> To the Italian intelligentsia is given over the Republican task of insuring Italy that she will never be without an inspired group of men capable of informing the government and the people of the currents of contemporary thought . . . and of the latest reforms. . . .
>
> Study, inform yourselves, publish as much as you can and prepare in silence if you are in invaded territory, even if you are in danger; study the truth which we want to see disseminated and which the enemy fears.
>
> The major flaw of democracy is not that it records and follows the will of the people but that it does not. The flaw in the electoral system is not that it serves to express the will of an informed public but that it expresses the imbecilities of a public that is ill-informed and which bases its opinions on the most incompetent strains available.
>
> The corporative system employs men who are qualified in one field to set the rules and standards acceptable for other fields, about which they usually know nothing. The purpose of an assembly is not to reach a compromise between measures, but to group together the accumulated and various aspects of knowledge of a nation's varied groups and trades. . . .
>
> In other words, I would launch an appeal to all those who could do something useful for the future of Italy. We want facts; we want truth. We are against usurers and monopolists. Only an autonomous nation can resist the infamy of universal usury. Anyone who has texts useful for the enrichment of our invaded territory should study them, publish them, distribute them.
>
> —Letter to Fernando Mezzasoma, November 1944[11]

Pound's letters to Mezzasoma arrived at Fascist headquarters in Salò almost daily. At times he enclosed copies of his recently published articles in support of the regime, at other times requests for general information in order to complete these articles. Frequently, in his role as unofficial admonitor to the Duce and the Salò Republic, he sent specific recommendations on how the government might better prepare itself for the reconstitution of the state.

A letter dated January 11, 1944, from Pound to Mezzasoma, bitterly assailed Italian journalists for their ignorance of economic and financial affairs. Two days later he wrote again, this time calling for propagandists and radio broadcasters more devoted and responsive to the Republican Fascist cause. On January 15 he castigated Ermanno Amicucci, director of the *Corriere della Sera,* for not considering him as a prospective contributor; Mezzasoma had recommended Pound to Amicucci, but the Milanese editor thought the poet's Italian "incomprehensible" and thus unpublishable. On February 27 and again on March 1, 1944, Pound sent Mezzasoma composite lists containing suggestions for the improvement of the ministry's propaganda machine ("Propaganda should aim for the creation of a state of mind conducive to action"), and asking that university students be primed for future induction into the broadcasting corps. He also had in mind a plan whereby Rapallo would be allocated funds for the publication of its own weekly newspaper, a proposal quickly thwarted when Mezzasoma informed him that the country was in the middle of a serious paper shortage.

The flow never stopped. In June, Pound wrote asking the government to publish in book form his more than 300 Radio Rome broadcasts to be distributed gratis to potential movement supporters. On November 16 he wrote, urging Mezzasoma to consider the Italian writer and publisher Giambattista Vicari for a position with the Ministry of Popular Culture. A second mailing the same day discussed the advisability of producing a microphotographic edition of the works of Vivaldi, a project which Pound thought would convince a dubious public that the Social Republican government was "at peace with itself." And in still another letter written that month, the poet discussed the possibility of amnesty for both the rebels and intellectuals, and for those who, because of lack of political sophistication, ignorance of history, incomprehension of the Fascist revolution, were still among the ranks of the enemy. The idea was that the radio, now sending propaganda from Milan, should broadcast an appeal directed at these groups and invite them to take part in the eternal struggle.

While most of Mezzasoma's responses to Pound were merely conciliatory in substance (March 6, 1944: "I wish to thank you once more for your observations and your suggestions which are always greatly appreciated and which I find very useful"),[12] he did go to a good deal of trouble to see that the poet's views were given proper consideration and that they were dispatched with due haste to the proper authorities. On December 4, 1943, Mezzasoma sent the following memo to the Ministry of Communications:

> The collaborator Ezra Pound, American writer, old and proven friend of Italy in the service of which he has placed his intellectual bearing, has advised this Ministry as follows:
>
> "The proposal for an autobus from Spezia to Salò via Genoa, Tortona, Piacenza and Cremona, will give the Republic a new backbone.
>
> "Liguria is now completely cut off from all modes of communication. Even before, one had to take three trains to get from Rapallo to Milan.
>
> "In order to give the impression that this new Government actually exists, an improvement in communications, as well as a direct route, would certainly be of help. It is important that we at least attempt to improve the conditions which existed prior to December 8."
>
> This office would like you to give the above communication all due consideration.[13]

On January 24, prompted by the arrival of another letter from Pound, this one in the form of a Service Note, Mezzasoma's staff distributed a set of reports to the offices of various government agencies. The first went to Nino Sammartano, director general of the Cultural Exchange Division of the Ministry of Popular Culture:

> We would like to bring to your attention the following excerpt from the January 15, 1944, dispatch sent by the collaborator EZRA POUND:
>
> "There is no doubt in my mind that treason was in existence and exists today in Italy. Proposals for the education of prisoners were approved but never carried out. It seems to me that this resulted in a great loss of time.
>
> "It should be noted that the Russian Revolution was fomented during the Russo-Japanese War by means of printed material which was distributed among the Russian prisoners-of-war.
>
> "Based on certain historical facts as well as current events it is my conviction that Roosevelt is a dog and that he deserves to be tried and given a sentence as harsh as the one meted out to Ciano.
>
> "I hope that after the 13th of this month we will experience a

propagandistic upswing. I don't know when the printing presses will run again, but we should begin to solve certain bureaucratic problems which slow us down: these are Sammartano's words.

"While waiting for the presses to begin we might decide what to print. . . . I enclose herewith a brief summary of EDUCATIONAL MATERIAL.

"It is useless to present propaganda that is so obviously propagandistic. . . .

"The History of Fascism by G. Volpi has been translated. I have offered to correct the hundreds of typographical errors which mar this second edition (free of charge, for the sole purpose of seeing a good book in circulation). I was asked to translate a book which would create havoc among the Americans and Englishmen.

"Because my name is associated with pro-Fascist efforts I did not add my *Jefferson and/or Mussolini* to the enclosed list. . . .

"But after what has happened I tend to think that a translation of this book might find readers in Italy. . . ."

Be so kind as to let us know what you think.

A second report was forwarded to the office of Dr. A. Del Prato of the Ministry of Propaganda:

> We would like to bring to your attention the following excerpt from a dispatch dated January 15, 1944, sent by the collaborator EZRA POUND:
> "The most useful books with which to combat the expressed opinions of the Anglo-Saxon-Jewish-Yankee press are . . . :
>> BROOKS ADAMS: The Law of Civilization and Decay
>> The New Empire
>> KITSON: The Bankers' Conspiracy
>> OVERHOLSER: History of Money in the U.S.A.
> "My rough drafts are in the hands of Pellizzi, who accepted translations of Adams' two books in order to have them published by Barbera.
>> WYNDHAM LEWIS: The Apes of God
>> E. E. CUMMINGS: EIMI."
> We would appreciate it if you would take an interest in this matter and advise us accordingly.

And a third report was sent to the office of the director general of Foreign Press and Radio:

> We would like to bring to your attention the following excerpt from the dispatch of January 15, 1944, sent by the collaborator EZRA POUND:

"The provisions of the 13th appear to me to signify the fact that 'The die is cast.' Opposition will come from the mercantile industrialists, usurers, etc. And about these will gather the uneducated, or the badly educated, those nourished on Jewish-Times-Nouvelle-Revue-Française propaganda.

"Without a printing press and a microphone it is difficult to educate these people and break them of their resistance—conscious or unconscious, active or passive, habits.

"The facts of history support Fascism."

Perhaps this material will be of help to you: let us know.[14]

During this entire period, Pound's personal allegiance to the Italian Republic never flagged. He directed letters of support to many of the leading functionaries of the Salò command—Gilberto Bernabei, Head of the Cabinet of the Ministry of Popular Culture; Alessandro Pavolini, Party Secretary; Arturo Bonucci, Commissioner of the Confederation of Professional Men and Artists; Alfredo Cucco, Commissioner of the National Institute of Fascist Culture. A shower of demonstrative mailings went out to Giovanni Dolfin, Mussolini's new private secretary, and to Mussolini himself. On several occasions he requested personal meetings with Il Duce, only to be told that Mussolini was indisposed. He did meet at least once, however, with Gampietro Domenico Pellegrini, Salò's Minister of Finance, to discuss Fascist and Nazi economic policies. And there were others with whom he was in contact: Ugo Manunta of the Ministry of Labor; Archimede Mischi, Chief of Staff, Army of the Salò Republic; Piero Parini, Mayor of Milan; Margherita Sarfatti, Mussolini's former mistress.

At the same time, a second wave of new quarterlies was launched in whose pages Pound registered his pedagogical peeves: *Il Lavoro*; *La Provincia Lavoratrice*; *La Fiamma Repubblicana*. From them, it was clear that both in form and texture his articles—as well as his letters— had deteriorated markedly. They were no more than a random compilation of ill-tempered woofs and tweets, standard expressions, as devoid as could be of aesthetic and philosophical depth: "We must look for the source of the poison; we must locate the poisoners"; "Our first job is to mobilize the troops, to stabilize the land"; "What is needed is a printing press that functions." Confucius and Cavalcanti served as inspiration for a set of display posters Pound had printed at his own expense; written in Italian, they sported such maxims as "The archer who misses the bull's-eye turns and seeks the cause of his failure in himself" and "So live that your children and their descendants will be thankful." Also: "A Nation that will not get itself into debt drives the usurers mad." With the collapse of his empire not far off, he began to sound more and more like another word-dealer of paratactic, hyper-naïve slogans: the *Wake*'s Humphrey Chimpden Earwicker (HCE), Joyce's version of *1984*'s Big Brother.

During 1944, the poet published and distributed twin manifestoes, both of them sanctioned by a small band of Italian writers who called themselves "Gli scrittori del Tigullio" ("Writers of the Tigullio," after the Gulf of Tigullio, on which Rapallo is situated). Signed by Gilberto Gaburri, Edgardo Rossardo, Giuseppe Soldato, Michele Tanzi, and Ezra Pound, the first of the two documents appeared in *Il Popolo di Alessandria* for February 27 and was later issued as a broadside. Authored by Pound, the four-part statement opened with a salute to the other writers of Italy and then launched into a declaration which began: "The live thought of the era is permeated by the Fascist spirit." No doubt based in part on Pound's involvement during these years with certain German propagandists, this first manifesto cited Frobenius, Thaddeus Zielinski, Cruet, and Confucius as prime examples of the international appeal of Fascist thought. Expanding on this thesis, the handout stated that "every writer working outside the Axis countries who was at one time or is still really alive, is openly in favor of Fascism." The circular pointed to the program of the Salò Republic as the essence of perspicacity and Mussolini as the Republic's only true leader. The Duce would be succeeded, the manifesto read, by "THE REPUBLICAN IDEA." As for slogans, there were two: "The treasure of a nation is its honesty" and "The philosophy of a man is demonstrated more in his actions than in his words."[15]

The second manifesto, also probably the work of Pound, began: "It is to be noted that no writer of worth in England or in America has declared himself in favor of Roosevelt or of Churchill; no writer of note has praised the infamous usuro-monopolistic system which Churchill and Roosevelt represent." A hodgepodge of propagandistic oversimplification, the circular centered on the lack of objectivity in the American press, Judaic control of Allied radio and newspaper conglomerates, uses and abuses fostered by public gatherings and assemblies. "He has the right to speak," the document closed, "who possesses knowledge which the others do not." Copies of both manifestoes were later forwarded to Mussolini at Salò.

"Jactancy, vanity, peculation to the ruin of 20 years' labour": such colloquial syncopation became the rueful subject of Canto 77 and other segments of the Pisan set. The new Veronese program, clear and strict—although from Pound's point of view perhaps not clear or strict enough—nevertheless needed backing. Thus while the British and Americans methodically, so it seems, and heedlessly bombed Italy's wondrous cities—and Sigismundo's Temple in Rimini—the poet, just as methodically (and heedlessly) kept up the struggle.[16] He was the lone, relentless ant, fighting his own battle—or as he came to see it years later, "the last American living the tragedy of Europe."[17]

By December 1, 1943, La Repubblica di Salò, on orders from the Reichstag, established its own radio propaganda center in Milan, first in the Via Rovani and then at Via Antonini 50. During their first week in operation, while the radio network was still under strict German military control, Pound went to see station officials. He arrived at Via Rovani bearing a letter of introduction from Nino Sammartano which he presented to a Signor Daquanno, the station's newly appointed general manager. It was Daquanno's expressed opinion that Pound would best serve the movement and himself by broadcasting for the German radio network either from Paris or Berlin. Pound was opposed to this idea. He was determined to make his stand with Italy. Then, on December 10, during the half-hour "Tunis" series, a program beamed to American troops in Europe and North Africa, Daquanno agreed to turn over the microphone to him. Pound's radio speech, rather a long one entitled "Being Able to Detect Crime," dealt almost exclusively with the Italian *gerarchi*—Grandi, Ciano, Bottai, Badoglio, and others—accused by the Germans of having betrayed the Axis cause. The only sensible way to deal with the defectors, Pound warned, was to take decisive and expedient action. After expanding on this theme and building up to a high-fever pitch, the orator terminated the broadcast with a vilifying crunch of random rhetoric. He concluded: "Every human being who is not a hopeless idiotic worm should realize that fascism is superior in every way to Russian Jewocracy and that capitalism stinks."[18]

His next contact with Radio Milan occurred during the month of February 1944, at which time the director general of the station, a man by the name of Tamburini, sent a message to the General Office for Foreign Press and Radio, a branch of the Ministry of Popular Culture, advising them of the station's decision to offer Pound a paid position. Included as part of the FBI files, the note reads:

Memo for the Head of the Office

23 February
Anno XXII
    With reference to our recent conversation, I wish to advise you that Radio Division IV in Milan has recently invited the collaborators Ezra Pound and Giacomo Barnes to join them. They will each send two or three messages per week to Milan; these messages will be of a polemic nature suitable for insertion into news reports in foreign languages. . . .
    The Administrative Office has provided for payment in favor of Ezra Pound.

The Director General
Tamburini

    Interrogated by FBI and G-2 agents (May 1945), Tamburini proceeded to illuminate a few of the mysterious facts surrounding Pound's liaison with the radio station (in particular with a program called *Jerry's Front Calling*), an affiliation which was to last until April 1945, long after the program had been moved to Fino Mornasco on Lake Como:

    . . . Pound started sending me manuscripts consisting of comments and short news items which he asked me to use . . . and sometimes he would create slogans such as "America is running herself into debt." The material he furnished us with was often anti-Semitic in nature. I would recognize the short items he contributed. . . . I used parts of them in the scripts for *Jerry's Front Calling*.
Between November of 1944 and April of 1945, I wrote Pound two or three letters telling him I had used this or that line which he had contributed. I remember . . . that Pound created a character known as "Mr. Dooley." Pound would think up humorous remarks for "Mr. Dooley" to make on the radio.
    . . . Pound continued sending these short items regularly until about April of 1945. After I left Milan to go to Fino Mornasco, Pound would send his items to the German Consulate which was located in the Hotel Principe di Savoia, Milan. The German Consulate would then forward the articles to me at Fino Mornasco.
The German authorities in Italy never paid Pound any money because he was receiving a regular monthly check from the Italian Ministry of Popular Culture. The German and Italian propaganda officials worked [together] very closely. . . .[19]

With the exception of these few documents, little is known about the eighteen months Pound spent working as a speech- and slogan-writer for the last outpost of Fascist radio warfare. There are, we have already seen, letters to sundry government clansmen dealing with the general topic of Italian radio propaganda, which in some instances afford specific advice on the general subject matter, but little in the way of personal rendition or anecdote. One letter which has been recovered, from Pound to Giorgio Almirante (May 16, 1944), of the Ministry of Popular Culture, suggests that a good deal of pressure had been exerted on the poet to move to Milan so as to participate more directly and persuasively in the radio broadcasts. No doubt the Fascist chiefs of staff were convinced that an American's voice would lend weight to their campaign. Pound, on the other hand, appears to have been torn between remaining in Rapallo and moving to the northern metropolis to pick up where he had left off in Rome:

> It is the composition and content of the speeches which are of primary interest to me. My physical strength is not what it used to be. . . . I was invited to move [to Milan] by automobile in December, but the time was not right. . . .
>
> The minute I am convinced that my voice should be heard over the radio I will find the means—or at least I will attempt to find the means—to get there. . . .
>
> I was quite ready to speak on a regular basis in December, even though this would have meant falling from three to six months behind in my work. I am currently completing two manuscripts for Sammartano. . . . Also, I write every day for the radio, but it simply doesn't pay to sacrifice quality for quantity.
>
> The system which worked best for me prior to July 25 was to write approximately twenty-five speeches at a sitting. . . . I would spend about fifteen or twenty days at a time in Rome recording these broadcasts; each speech was then played three times. . . .
>
> What I would eventually like to do . . . is to go to Milan occasionally by camion for two or three weeks at a time. In other words, I want to use the same system which worked so well for me before. Since I can no longer lift or move heavy suitcases I would need some sort of porter service. I know this sounds foolish, better fit perhaps for old ladies and young girls, but it is enough to throw off the delicate balance of my radio speeches.[20]

About the time Pound wrote this letter to Almirante another wrench was thrown into the works. The poet and his wife, by decree of the German military, were ordered out of their waterfront apartment in

Rapallo to make room for some German troops who were fortifying the beach with bunkers and tank traps in preparation for the inevitable Allied sweep into Germany. The accumulation of twenty years of books and papers, letters, manuscripts, drawings, was all slowly carted uphill to Casa 60, Olga Rudge's rented two-story, two-family house in Sant' Ambrogio, with its olive press on the ground floor. For the duration of the war, the Pounds and their hostess lived à *trois*, sharing household duties and lives. Olga Rudge makes mention of their coexistence in passing in a letter to Ezra's attorney written in 1947, referring to the kindness of her own hospitality toward Dorothy Pound at the time. But with this exception, and perhaps one or two others, almost nothing has been said or written about this period, the prevailing consensus being that nothing need be said or written.

Whether Pound knew it or not, his days were numbered. A wide dragnet had been cast, and it was only a matter of time before he would be apprehended, either by Italian *partigiani* or American troops. Following the July 1943 indictment he became the subject of numerous communiqués and letters between Washington and the U.S. forces in Europe and Africa. A cable dated September 17 informed the Commanding General of the North African Theater of Operations, General Jacob L. Devers, of the action taken by the Washington grand jury against Pound. Devers sent a carbon of the cable and an accompanying note of explanation to the Commanding General of the U.S. Fifth Army. The flow of these events is recorded by Charles Norman in his book *The Case of Ezra Pound*; many of the documents involved can be found in the U.S. State Department files, Washington, D.C.

On January 24, 1944, Attorney General Biddle asked Henry L. Stimson, Secretary of War, for prompt notification should Pound be taken into custody by the military. The letter from Biddle further stipulated that Pound was to be "thoroughly interrogated concerning his radio broadcasting and other activities on behalf of the Italian Government." On February 9, Biddle's request was forwarded to General Devers, together with a capsulated personal history, physical description, and an FBI photograph of Pound. Attached to this material was a letter from the desk of the Adjutant General:

> It will be noted that the Attorney General wishes certain action taken in the event that Pound should be taken into custody, and that upon the

receipt by the Department of Justice of the requested information, further consideration will bé given to the advisability of effecting Pound's return to the United States.

General Devers replied on February 25:

> Reference to your letter of 9 February 1944 concerning activities of Dr. Ezra Pound and desire of Attorney General for certain information in the event of his capture, you are advised that the Commanding General of the United States Fifth Army has again been informed . . . that he [Pound] is wanted on an indictment charging him with treason and in the event of his capture to notify the Theater Commander immediately.
>
> The F.B.I. photograph of Dr. Pound is being reproduced. It will be distributed with other descriptive data through the Provost Marshal and G-2 sections.

The "descriptive data" included: height, five feet ten and one-half inches; forehead, broad; eyes, gray-green; nose, straight; mouth, mustached; chin, bearded; complexion, fair; face, oval.

In the last months of the Salò Republic, Pound returned to poetry; he labored diligently translating *The Cantos* into Italian. He had already translated his decade-old work comparing Jefferson and Mussolini into "the language of the people among whom he lived." And he was busy supervising the production and publication by the Casa Editrice delle Edizione Popolari, in Venice, of six of his books and pamphlets, including a number of the *Money Pamphlets*, many of which were destroyed soon after printing by the Ministry of Popular Culture as being inopportunely controversial.

Toward the end of the war he completed Cantos 72 and 73, both written in Italian, neither included in the epic as published prior to 1976.[21] Their absence creates a lacuna which has become an integral part of the poem, "a fault line," observes Hugh Kenner, "a record of shifting masses." With the war as *mise en scène*, the two cantos salute a swarm of Ezra's Fascist friends: Manlio Dazzi, F. T. Marinetti, Gioacchino Nicoletti, Ubaldo degli Uberti (*"chi muore oggi fa un uffare"*). Dante, or a version of Dante, speaks in Canto 72; and 73 is given over to Cavalcanti, to what he sees and hears in Italy in 1942–43.[22] Both Cantos were forwarded to Mussolini at Salò with an accompanying letter from Pound placing his talent at the Duce's feet. He also sent the poems to his daughter, who by the end of the war was working in a German military hospital at Cortina d'Ampezzo.

So the Great Bass labored and dreamed the Republic ("actual only in the mind"), while Churchill, Roosevelt, and Stalin actively pursued victory and unconditional surrender.[23] In Rapallo, there had been the usual wartime hardships but not much in the way of direct attack. "Bombs fell," the poet would write in *The Pisan Cantos*, "but not quite on Sant' Ambrogio." A church and an orphanage were hit, and an old priest killed.[24] The damage was mild compared to the heavy destruction which took place in Genoa and all along the Italian coast where the bridges fell and the Aurelia road was uprooted.

Then, on April 28, 1945, Pound's universe crumbled completely. Benito Mussolini, attempting to escape, was caught and killed on the shore of Lake Como by angered partisans. His corpse and that of his mistress Claretta Petacci were carted to the Piazzale Loreto in Milan and desecrated. A day or two later, without firing a shot, the Americans occupied Rapallo.

The poet, in formal attire, went down from Sant' Ambrogio into the town to greet his countrymen and make his knowledge of modern Italy available. He spotted a number of military men—officers mostly— at a local café. Nobody seemed to know what he was talking about, certainly no one cared very much. On the street, a solitary black infantryman, separated from his unit, tried to sell the poet the bicycle on which he was perched. Pound returned to Sant' Ambrogio.[25]

The next day they came for him. They were not American soldiers but Communist *partigiani* from the *commando* in Zoagli. There were two of them, both armed with Tommy guns. The poet, his Legge *Four Books* opened wide on the desk, was working on a translation of the *Book of Mencius*. Olga Rudge had gone into town to buy the paper; Dorothy Pound was paying her weekly visit to Ezra's aging mother in Rapallo. Rumor has it the gun butts sounded twice against the door. Pound went to open, then *"Seguici, traditore."* Ezra slipped the Confucius and the Chinese dictionary into his pocket and left the keys with the girl who lived on the first floor. He preceded the two men down the winding mountain trail to a waiting car. He was handcuffed and driven away.[26]

4

Serenely in the crystal jet
　　　　as the bright ball that the fountain tosses
(Verlaine) as diamond clearness
　　　　　　How soft the wind under Taishan
　　　　　　　　where the sea is remembered
　　　　　　out of hell, the pit
　　　　　　out of the dust and glare evil
　　　　　　Zephyrus/Apeliota
This liquid is certainly a
　　　　　property of the mind
nec accidens est　　but an element
　　　　　　　　　　　　in the mind's make-up
est agens and functions　　dust to a fountain pan otherwise
　　　　　Hast 'ou seen the rose in the steel dust
　　　　　　　　　(or swansdown ever?)
so light is the urging, so ordered the dark petals of iron
we who have passed over Lethe.
　　　　　　　　　　　(Canto LXXIV)

If the hoar frost grip thy tent
Thou wilt give thanks when night is spent.
　　　　　　　　　　　(Canto LXXXIV)

Because the people who generally talk about it were not there, folklore surrounds the arrest.[1] It is said that a half-million-lire reward had been placed on Pound's head and that the two partisans had taken him prisoner in order to collect. But this was mere conjecture, unsubstantiated. The *partigiani* wanted only to ask him a few questions. They were after bigger game: Fascist shop stewards and local petty bureaucrats. He was driven from Zoagli to Partisan Central Headquarters at Chiavari and released as being of no interest to them. He had then demanded to be taken to the U.S. command post at Lavagna to turn himself in; the partisans obliged. The following day, MP's drove him to the CICHQ—

the Counter Intelligence Center—in Genoa. The first entry in the May 17 G-2 Journal, Headquarters 92nd Infantry Division, listing "Incidents, Msgs, Orders, etc.," reads: "Ezra Pound in custody of CIC, 92nd Div. since 3 May 45."

Retracing the poet's steps—from Zoagli to Chiavari to Lavagna—Olga Rudge was able to locate him in Genoa. She found him at the CIC, handcuffed, in a large waiting room among a crowd of people. By nightfall only a few people remained, but Pound had not been interrogated. A guard told the couple they could spend the night in the room. He brought them blankets and they slept on the wooden-slat benches. The next morning Pound's interrogation began. In the evening he was returned to the waiting room. Olga Rudge refused to leave until she was told what would be done with him, where they would take him. At the end of the second full day of questioning, she was summoned to the office of an FBI special agent. The agent, an American by the name of Amprim, was polite and considerate, but firm. He told her she must go home and keep herself at the disposal of the American authorities, ready to testify in case of a trial. But where, when? He did not know. All he could tell her was that Pound would be placed under house arrest; he was not to see or communicate with anyone until further notice.[2]

Two days later, May 7, Amprim appeared in Sant' Ambrogio. He had come to examine Pound's private files and papers. When he departed three days later, having also interviewed Olga Rudge and Dorothy Pound, he took with him a slagheap of material, nearly 7000 pages, enough to fill up the better part of fourteen volumes of FBI files.

Among the confiscated items was Pound's typewriter, an Everest portable, with a misaligned "t" and a page of the *Book of Mencius* still in it. The salesman who had sold Pound the typewriter was later interviewed by Amprim. Yes, he could remember making the sale in February of 1938, at Pound's home in Rapallo. The poet had requested an especially sturdy machine; he sometimes typed for three days without a break.

Included in the Sant' Ambrogio haul were a number of typewritten specimens—letters, scripts, articles—all typed on the confiscated model. During further interrogation at Genoa, Pound dated and initialed these samples, a procedure he repeated in connection with an assortment of documents and holdings, including EIAR *note compenso* and *mandati* gathered by the Psychological Warfare Branch in Rome. An examination of a single page of Amprim's inventory of materials seized that day from Sant' Ambrogio demonstrates just how formidable and meticulous a case was being prepared against Pound:

> Two pencils and a black (Swan) fountain pen and ten sheets of paper bearing the known handwriting and handprinting in ink of Ezra Pound.
> Fifteen sheets of paper bearing the known handwriting and handprinting in ink and pencil of Ezra Pound.
> Six sheets of paper and one card bearing typewriter specimens from an Everest portable typewriter, Model 90, serial no. 27780, in blue and black ink, two sheets of carbon paper, one sheet of thin white paper and two sheets of paper containing handwriting in a foreign language.
> Five sheets of paper containing typewriter specimens taken from an "Olympia Buromaschinenwerke A. G. Erfurt" serial number 451393, in blue and black ink, two sheets of carbon paper and one thin white piece of paper.[3]

The second machine, the Olympia office model, was identified as having been found in one of the offices of Rome's Ministry of Popular Culture which Pound had used while broadcasting for Radio Rome.

Another page of inventory from the Amprim report, with names deleted by the FBI in accordance with the regulations imposed by the Freedom of Information Act, provides a list of quasi confessions and admissions elicited by CIC agents from Pound in the course of further interviews at Genoa:

> 1. Five-page signed statement by Pound furnished to   ,
> Counter Intelligence Agent of the 92nd Division, U.S. Army, [and to] Special Agent   of this Bureau on May 6, 1945, at Genoa, Italy.
> 2. Five-page signed statement by Pound furnished to   ,
> Counter Intelligence Agent of the 92nd Division, U.S. Army, and Special Agent   of this Bureau on May 7, 1945, at Genoa, Italy.
> 3. Two-page signed statement by Pound furnished to Special Agent   of this Bureau on May 8, 1945, at Genoa, Italy.
> 4. Five-page "outline" dated May 8, 1945, furnished by Pound to Special Agent
> 5. Two pages of material captioned "Further Points" dated May 8, 1945, in which Pound further explains some of his views.
> 6. One-page signed statement furnished Special Agent   on May 6, 1945, at Genoa, Italy.[4]

What Pound said during these interrogations remains under lock and key in the archives of the Department of Justice, Washington, D.C.

Convinced of his innocence, he probably spoke freely; he spoke freely to an American reporter who was permitted to interview him at the CICHQ on May 8.

On that occasion he stated that if a man valued his beliefs, he valued them enough to die for them, and if they were worth having at all, they were worth expressing. He then voiced the belief that if he could only meet with President Truman or Premier Stalin he could save the Western world untold postwar misery. A German official, he said, had arranged for him to join the International Investigation Commission which, in 1942, went to Katyn. He had volunteered with high hopes of being permitted to see Stalin, but at the last minute his application was blocked, he was barred from the commission.

The reporter asked Pound if he thought there was a chance Truman or Stalin would grant him an interview now. He replied:

"One might say that I am in an unfavorable position at the present time to be received at the White House. If I am not shot for treason, I think my chances of seeing Truman are good."

Once embarked on the subject of politics there was no holding him back:

"There is no doubt which I preferred between Mussolini and Roosevelt. In my radio broadcasts I spoke in favor of the economic construction of fascism. Mussolini was a very human, imperfect character who lost his head.

"Winston [Churchill] believes in the maximum of injustice enforced with the maximum of brutality.

"Stalin is the best brain in politics today. But that does not mean that I have become a Bolshevik."

And Hitler?

"Hitler was a Jeanne d'Arc, a saint. He was a martyr. Like many martyrs, he held extreme views. . . . He and Mussolini were successful insofar as they followed Confucius; they failed because they did not follow him more closely."

Finally, when asked what he expected his chances would be if forced to stand trial for treason, he said:

"I do not believe that I will be shot for treason. I rely on the American sense of justice."[5]

However justified his faith in American jurisprudence might have been, disposition of his case had slowed to a standstill. More than two weeks had elapsed and the poet was still in the hands of the Military Government and Intelligence branches of the U.S. Army. A torrent of dispatches now flew back and forth between Allied Force Headquarters and the Mediterranean Theater of Operations message center, Caserta, Italy:

May 19, 1945
FROM: 15 ARMY GROUP
TO: ALLIED FORCE HEADQUARTERS, INFO G-5
  For G-2
  Doctor EZRA POUND captured 3 May by partisans is now in custody of CIC 92 Division. Amprim has obtained signed statement and pertinent documents and is awaiting decision from WASHINGTON regarding disposal.

May 21, 1945
FROM: FIFTH ARMY
TO: COMMANDING GENERAL, MEDITERRANEAN
    THEATER OF OPERATIONS
  Awaiting orders for disposition from your Headquarters for DR. EZRA POUND, War Criminal, held by 92 Division.

May 21, 1945
TO FOR ACTION: ADJUTANT GENERAL, WAR
                DEPARTMENT, WASHINGTON
SIGNED: EARL ALEXANDER, ALLIED COMMANDER
  In custody Provost Marshal here is EZRA POUND.
  Reference AGWAR [Adjutant General, War Department] cable of 14th May.
  Investigation completed. Statement by POUND and documentary evidence airmailed FORNEY 21st May. Request information POUND's further disposition soonest.

Instructions arrived the following day:

May 22, 1945
TO FOR ACTION: COMMANDING GENERAL,
                FIFTH ARMY
                COMMANDING GENERAL,
                REPLACEMENT AND TRAINING
                COMMAND
SIGNED: COMMANDING GENERAL, MEDITERRANEAN
        THEATER OF OPERATIONS
  American Civilian Doctor EZRA LOOMIS POUND reference Fifth Army cable 2006 under federal grand jury indictment for treason.

Transfer without delay under guard to MTOUSA Disciplinary Train-ing Center for confinement pending disposition instructions. Exercise ut-most security measures to prevent escape or suicide. No press interviews authorized. Accord no preferential treatment.

The order was carried out:

May 27, 1945
FROM: FIFTH ARMY
TO: COMMANDING GENERAL, MEDITERRANEAN
    THEATER OF OPERATIONS
  Doctor EZRA POUND delivered to MTOUSA DTC 1500 hours 24 May this year.

The Detention Training Center, Mediterranean Theater of Operations, U.S. Army, lay between Viareggio and Pisa on the coastal plain, within sight of the Via Aurelia. Inside the confines of this dusty, one-half-mile-square compound, surrounded by barbed wire and guard towers, were the killers, brawlers, rapists, and deserters from line and service outfits, 3600 of the most hard-headed, recalcitrant soldiery the Army had to offer. Some of them were sent on to federal prisons in the United States, some to the gallows at Aversa, and others were shot down in futile attempts to escape. There was no escape from the DTC. *Yank* (the Army weekly) proclaimed it "the toughest training detail in the Army . . . tougher even than front-line combat." Here, "trainees"—those not bound for prison or execution—were given a last chance to redeem themselves and return to honorable status in the Army and then to civilian life. Their season in hell consisted of "one year of training, 14 hours a day (not counting close-order punishment by night), one year of terrible dis-cipline, unbroken regimentation, unbearable monotony." This was truly the First Circle.

The night before his arrival at the camp, acetylene torches used to reinforce a cage gave off a blue light that lit up the sky. There was a row of such cages, ten to the row, each of them reserved for a man about to be executed. His was the tenth cage of the ten, at the extreme end of the column, a specially constructed, grilled "security cage," heavy-duty air strip welded over galvanized mesh. Pound called his cell the *"gab-bia,"* gorilla cage. Like the others, it measured six feet by six and a half. A tarpaper roof provided little shelter from sun or rain. By night a special reflector poured glaring light onto his cage alone. He slept on the cold cement floor. He was fed meager rations once a day. His toilet was a tin can.

He was the only civilian prisoner in camp. The commandant during his incarceration was Lieutenant Colonel John L. Steele, whose name crops up in *The Pisan Cantos*, as do the names of other prisoners and guards. From the start he was placed under twenty-four-hour surveillance. He wore an Army fatigue uniform, unbuttoned at the neck. His trousers hung loose and his shoes were unlaced (belts and shoelaces were not permitted in the death cells). He stared out at the Aurelian Road, or watched insects weave patterns in the Pisan air. He walked back and forth in the cage, two paces by two paces, relearning its dimensions with each step. He slouched or sat. He read his Legge Confucius or the Chinese dictionary he had brought with him from Sant' Ambrogio. He was not allowed out of the small cubicle, so he exercised within its binding perimeters: he shadow-boxed, fenced, played tennis with imaginary opponents. Later, when moved to larger quarters, he found an old broom handle that became a tennis racquet, a billiard cue, a rapier, a baseball bat to hit small stones, and a stick which he swung out smartly to match his long stride.[6]

For three weeks he was kept in the cage, a victim of the glare, dust, and isolation. One afternoon, after a drenching rain, the guards opened his door and gave the old man a narrow military cot; it kept him off the ground but not out of the cold of night. The next day, they packed a pup tent into the cage. Bible, cot, pup tent: even with these comforts his constitution would not bear the strain. He collapsed. "He lost his memory," his attorney would write for the benefit of the court. "He became desperately thin and weak until finally the prison doctor feared for him." He was taken out of the cage and transferred to a large pyramidal tent in the Medical Compound section of the camp.

If conditions here were easier, they were still far from ideal. His furniture consisted of a cot and a small wooden packing crate; later, another packing crate and a table were added. During his first week in the tent he kept mostly to himself. His food, eaten from an Army mess kit, was handed to him through the Medical Compound fence. His eyes, badly inflamed from the glare and dust, were given proper medical treatment, although he was not permitted to go to see the doctors until they were finished with the other prisoners. The idea was to keep him as isolated as possible from the general prison population.

Despite these efforts and precautions, the myth of the poet-convict soon spread. He was acclaimed an instant hero among the trainees when it was discovered that he had made a "fool" of the Army psychiatrist who had examined him, twisting his questions around so drastically that the examiner became confused. The DTC psychiatrist eventually pronounced Pound sane, although a bit "exotic," a medical opinion which differed radically from the one offered by the government-appointed psychiatrists who examined him after his return to the United States.

The camp medics provided Pound with a ready-made audience. He told them that he would never be brought to trial because he "had too much on several people in Washington" for the government to allow him to testify in court. He admitted that he had spoken over the Italian radio network but insisted that his broadcasts were in no way treasonable. As usual, he raved about the "dunghill usurers" and "usuring cutthroats." His feverish green eyes snapped as he shouted that the American people had been swindled by their leaders. Wars could be avoided if the true nature of money were understood. "When," he asked, "will the United States return to Constitutional government?" No one ventured a response.

Late at night, after taps, he was allowed to use the dispensary typewriter. He wrote letters for other prisoners—several for men about to be executed—and typed out English versions of *The Unwobbling Pivot* and *The Great Digest*.[7] During the torpid summer months, with the experience of the war and the cage still fresh in his mind, he composed the remarkable eleven Cantos (74–84), the moving and enduring *Pisan Cantos*.

"The constant clanging and banging of the typewriter, which he punched angrily with his index fingers, was always accompanied by a high-pitched humming sound he made as the carriage raced the bell. He swore well and profusely over typing errors"—that, Robert Allen has divined, was the method; the technique came just as naturally. He wrote as if he would not survive the experience, as if he expected to be shot at any time:

> till the shrine be again white with marble
> till the stone eyes look again seaward
>> The wind is part of the process
>> The rain is part of the process
> and the Pleiades set in her mirror

Time is not, Time is the evil, beloved
Beloved the hours βροδοδάκτυλος
      as against the half-light of the window
      with the sea beyond making horizon
                (Canto LXXIV)

A fat moon rises lop-sided over the mountain
The eyes, this time my world,
      But pass and look *from* mine
        between my lids
          set, sky, and pool
          alternate
          pool, sky, sea . . .
             (Canto LXXXIII)

The Bard's songs soared above "Taishan"—the distant mount—like a phoenix. In a highly compressed style the poet set down his thoughts on a wide range of disciplines, reconnecting himself to history —the world's as well as his own. As *Hugh Selwyn Mauberley* had been a literary gravestone to the civilization that produced and endured World War I, *The Pisan Cantos* were an elegiac and tragic monument to Europe in 1945. Europe had failed him. Italy, the repository of his final hopes for the Continent, had likewise let him down. His disappointment, represented by the "enormous tragedy" of Mussolini's fall, provided the poet with his opening lines for Canto 74:

The enormous tragedy of the dream in the peasant's bent shoulders
Manes! Manes was tanned and stuffed,
Thus Ben and la Clara *a Milano*
      by the heels at Milano
That maggots shd/ eat the dead bullock
DIGENES, διγενές, but the twice crucified
            where in history will you find it?
yet say this to the Possum: a bang, not a whimper,
      with a bang not with a whimper,
To build the city of Dioce whose terraces are the colour of stars.

The manner of the Duce's death was also taken up in Canto 78:

but was hang'd dead by the heels before his thought in
                         proposito
    came into action efficiently

And in Canto 80 he remembered Mussolini at Salò during the Republic's final days, the dictator surrounded by a motley crew of cohorts:

> and as to poor old Benito
> > one had a safety-pin
> one had a bit of string, one had a button
> > all of them so far beneath him
> half-baked and amateur
> > or mere scoundrels
> To sell their country for half a million
> > hoping to cheat more out of the people

The collapse of history, of the world as he knew it and wanted it to be, became the "abiding spectre" of this unit of poems.[8] "Nothing matters," Pound writes in Canto 76, "but the quality of the affection—/ in the end—that has carved the trace in the mind/ dove sta memoria." The *quality of the affection*: there is plenty of that. Wave upon wave of affectionate memory has been locked away inside his mind, to remain there, *"Formato locho."* These kaleidoscopic memories are his sole stayings against the world's flux:

> Lordly men are to earth o'ergiven
> > these the companions:
> Fordie that wrote of giants
> > and William who dreamed of nobility
> > and Jim the comedian singing:
> > > "Blarrney castle me darlin'
> > > you're nothing now but a StOWne"
> and Plarr talking of mathematics
> > or Jepson lover of jade
> Maurie who wrote historical novels
> > and Newbolt who looked twice bathed
> > > are to earth o'ergiven.
> > > > (Canto LXXIV)

> by Babylonian wall (memorat Cheever)
> > out of his bas relief, for that line
> we recall him
> > and who's dead, and who isn't
> > and will the world ever take up its course again?

very confidentially I ask you: Will it?
    with Dieudonné dead and buried
not even a wall, or Mouquin, or Voisin or the cake shops
    in the Nevsky
                    (Canto LXXVI)

      so that I recalled the noise in the chimney
as it were the wind in the chimney
    but was in reality Uncle William
downstairs composing
that had made a great Peeeeacock
    in the proide ov his oiye
    had made a great peeeeeeecock in the . . .
made a great peacock
    in the proide of his oyyee

proide ov his oy-ee
as indeed he had, and perdurable

a great peacock aere perennius
    or as in the advice to the young man to
breed and get married (or,not)
        as you choose to regard it

at Stone Cottage in Sussex by the waste moor
(or whatever) and the holly bush
    who would not eat ham for dinner
because peasants eat ham for dinner
    despite the excellent quality
and the pleasure of having it hot

well those days are gone forever
                    (Canto LXXXIII)

    As always for Pound, past and present merged; Proustian scents of days gone by joggled him back to the reality of machine-gun towers and barbed wire strung from post to post. Amidst the ruins, against this cameo of thieves and killers, an old man who has been "hard as youth sixty years" is forced to learn humility—to pull down his vanity—the hardest way possible: "not arrogant from habit/ but furious from perception." Encaged he turns to the world outside his immediate world, the miniaturized green universe sung by Wordsworth and Coleridge,

Hopkins and Yeats. "In nature," Pound writes, "are signatures/ needing no verbal tradition"—

> and there was a smell of mint under the tent flaps
> especially after the rain
> > and a white ox on the road toward Pisa
> > > as if facing the tower . . .
> > > > (Canto LXXIV)

> And now the ants seem to stagger
> > as the dawn sun has trapped their shadows,
> this breath wholly covers the mountains
> > it shines and divides
> it nourishes by its rectitude
> does no injury
> overstanding the earth it fills the nine fields
> > to heaven
> . . . .
> and in the warmth after chill sunrise
> an infant, green as new grass,
> has stuck its head or tip
> out of Madame La Vespa's bottle
>
> mint springs up again
> > in spite of Jones' rodents
> as had the clover by the gorilla cage
> > with a four-leaf
>
> When the mind swings by a grass-blade
> > an ant's forefoot shall save you
> the clover leaf smells and tastes as its flower
> > > (Canto LXXXIII)

Contrasted to his responding senses and the small natural phenomena of ants and wasps is the jarring drama of the stockade, re-created in these Cantos in startlingly realistic terms. Pound never forgets where he is or why he is there. To this end, there are numerous references in the sequence to persons and locales connected with the stockade. "Till" of "Till was hung yesterday/ for murder and rape with trimmings" was St. Louis Till, one of the incorrigibles who shared the death cells with Pound. The protagonist of " 'Ah certainly dew lak dawgs,/ ah goin' tuh wash you'" was Whiteside, the camp turnkey; he is not addressing Pound here but an unwilling canine. There was also a camp cat:

> Prowling night-puss leave my hard squares alone
>   they are in no case cat food
>   if you had sense
>   you wd/ come here at meal time
>   when meat is superabundant
>   you can neither eat manuscript nor Confucius
>   nor even the hebrew scriptures
> (Canto LXXX)

And further ado: "a bag o' Dukes" concerns the prison custom of using cigarettes or "roll-your-own" tobacco as the unit of exchange in all commercial transactions; to be "boxed" meant two weeks on bread and water with a blanket and a bucket in the seven-foot square concrete cubes behind the death cells; work on the "honey wagon," which collected excrement from the stockade latrines, was a speedy and popular way for the trainee to earn good marks and eventual clemency.[9] Thus the caged panther, recording the monotonous beat of the "bumm drum" in the prison band, reached his simplest, most humane conclusion under conditions not fit for man or beast. His formal, almost Biblical summation occurs in Canto 83—[10]

> Nor can who has passed a month in the death cells
>   believe in capital punishment
> No man who has passed a month in the death cells
>   believes in cages for beasts

—And with Pisa still on his mind, a further declaration is made much later in *Drafts and Fragments*:

> To be men not destroyers.
> (Notes for Canto CXVII *et seq.*)

The summer had passed but no one had heard from him, nor knew his whereabouts, or even if he was still alive. Eventually he was allowed to write to his wife. She had returned to Rapallo from Sant' Ambrogio and was living at Via Marsala 12-5 with Ezra's widowed mother. A short note, written in pencil, informed Dorothy of his imprisonment and indicated that she would be allowed to visit him. Wearing a mackintosh which had belonged to Homer Pound, she arrived at the camp on October 3—his first visitor after many months' imprisonment; when she told the guard at the front gate who she was, he rang through on the sentry-box telephone: "Tell Uncle Ez his wife is here to see him."[11] They were permitted thirty minutes together in a small office with guards posted at the door.

Two weeks later, Olga Rudge and their daughter, Mary, came to visit; they had made the trip from Rapallo in an Army jeep with American soldiers. On November 3, four days after her husband's sixtieth birthday, Mrs. Pound paid a second visit to the camp. And Omar Pound, on leave from the U.S. Army, also made his way to Pisa; he arrived at the prison camp the day after Pound's removal and return to Washington to stand trial for treason.

Meanwhile, news of his internment at the DTC had reached James Laughlin in America, and early in September he asked a friend, Julien Cornell, a thirty-five-year-old New York City attorney well versed in the field of civil liberties, to defend the writer. During the same month, Pound received a letter from his late father-in-law's firm, Shakespear and Parkyn, London solicitors who had handled the poet's previous legal affairs. Arthur Moore, Pound's adviser at the John Street firm, feared that his former client might try to take on his own case; he advised Pound to retain counsel and stand mute at such time that the case should be heard. Pound wrote back on October 5. Judging from his response, he was not aware of Laughlin's involvement and was weighing the possibility of hiring the prominent criminal defender, Lloyd Stryker, to represent him. Although not brief, Pound's letter was certainly clear and to the point:

> Gentlemen:
> I am very glad to get your letter of the 7th ulto: re-sent on the 24th which is the first that has reached me from the outer world, though Dorothy was permitted to visit me two days ago and brought the good news of Omar. I am very much pleased with his independence and initiative in all ways.
> Also glad to observe from your stationery that John St. has not been bombed out of existence.
> I am not sure that your advice is given in full knowledge of certain essential facts of my case.
> For example, I was not sending axis propaganda but my own, the

nucleus of which was in Brooks Adams' works 40 years ago, in Kitson's published 25 years ago, and in my own pre-war publications.

This was sent and stated to be sent at least over the medium wave, on various occasions, with the preface:

"On the principle of free expression of opinion on the part of those qualified to have an opinion, Dr. Pound has been granted the freedom of our microphone twice a week. He will not be asked to say anything contrary to his conscience or contrary to his duties as an American citizen." The twice was extended to 3 & more times. These conditions were faithfully observed by the Rome radio. I never was asked to say anything.

The investigator for the American Dept. of Justice expressed himself as convinced that I was telling him the absolute truth months ago, and has since with great care collected far more proof to that effect than I or any private lawyer could have got at.

My instinct all along has been to leave the whole matter to the U.S. Dept. of Justice, the good faith of whose agent I have had no reason to doubt.

I do not know how this will strike you, but the fantastic conditions in Italy have been such that someone who has come here and examined the facts can probably form an opinion more easily than anyone, however perspicacious at a distance.

I had hoped to see Mr. MacLeish in Washington in May while he was still in the State Dept.

You will see that there are elements in the case far more interesting than my personal welfare.

I have very cordial recollections of Lloyd Stryker, he is now, I believe, one of the best known big lawyers in the U.S. whose fees are probably far beyond anything I could pay.

40 years ago, about 1905, when his father was President of Hamilton College, Lloyd and I must have been among his prominent headaches, Lloyd in the home, and I in the classroom. BUT I should much prefer to see Mr. MacLeish before deciding on so important a step as NOT speaking on my own behalf. I believe MacLeish is himself a lawyer, and in any case he can write to me at this address. If he writes as my lawyer I would certainly be permitted to answer him as I am now answering you.

My most complete fog, my difficulty is my ABSOLUTE ignorance of what had happened in the U.S.A. and in England from 1940 to 1945.

With Mr. Dalton at the Exchequer, with the Labour Party not only "In" but also OUT of what to me always appeared to be its obscurantism. I mean, with the public ownership of the Bank put first on its program. A great deal of what you probably considered my moonshine (if you ever considered it at all) must now be made open to the British public.

All over the place what were 20 years ago considered heresies of my friends are now admitted as fact. The "A" plus "B" theory of Maj. C. H. Douglas is tacitly accepted in all proposals for government spending. The public has learned a great deal, but it still has the right to know MORE. If that be over my dead body, so much the worse both for me and for the public.

BUT the suppression of historic fact has NOT been useful, it neither helped to preserve peace nor to carry on the war. Given the present tension, no one is more ready than I to admit that certain facts should perhaps not be dragged into the limelight at this moment. BUT that does not apply to other facts that are simply ignored. I mean that the men in charge both of England and the U.S.A. seem still unaware of them. And that after 25 years of study I can no longer be treated as a whimsical child in these matters.

I am sorry to take up so much space, but I cannot tell from your letter whether you have had enough information to see clearly.

The agent of the Dept. of Justice started by saying that they proposed to consider my past 30 years' work. I do not know whether Mr. Stryker would be prepared for such labour, and·without it, I do not know how he could tell the Court what the case is about.

The picture painted by propaganda has been such, that I do not know whether you can conceive that FREE SPEECH was preserved precisely where the British Public would least expect it, namely in Italy by a few unknown, I suppose you would call them "liberals," working inside the Italian framework. I do not think it is an occasion for great skill in presenting a case so much as for great patience in making clear the bearing of known and knowable facts. Which facts, I am not sure whether you yet grasp, if you will pardon a rather flat statement.

What I am in absolute ignorance of is: whether anyone actually heard my broadcasts; whether they did any good, by which I mean whether they in any way contributed to the better understanding of certain economic fundamentals. Which better understanding is definitely shown now in public pronouncements in England and the U.S.A. (As C. H. Douglas used to say after the other war: "If they don't do it now, they will have to do it after the next one".)

I do not know whether the public HEARD, or if hearing they understood one single word of my talks. The only auditors I know of were foreigners in Florence. Plus whatever education one could insert in Berlin. Yes, the RE-education of Europe. Any enlightenment on that point that you can give me, I would be most grateful to receive. And, of course, seeing that "my program" is going through all over the place, I can not know that those who are putting it through are in any way conscious of my existence, or that they would be pleased to know that I had been on their side of the battle for enlightenment.

Don't gasp, I know it will take time for this strange view to get through the probable mist of prejudice that has been raised by the jingo press.

But a great deal that could in 1938 only be printed in outcast periodicals of small circulation, is now in print and will increasingly be printed in the more general press.

I want very much to know the source or reason for your opinion that I should not address the Court. Is it due to your not knowing what I actually said on the air?

I will send you a copy of this letter in 2 days' time and if you receive both copies you can send one to Mr. MacLeish. If you receive only one copy, would you please have it copied and send him a copy?

It seems to me he might also communicate with Roger Baldwin of the Civil Liberties Union, as the question of Freedom of Speech on the air, together with other constitutional points should interest them.

Emphatically I want to see Mr. MacLeish and have been given to understand that it would be possible once I were in the U.S.A.

BUT the simplest plan would be for him to write to me as my lawyer (if I am correct in supposing that he is a lawyer), at any rate he has known my work for 20 years and has some concept of what I have been driving at . . . am not in the least sure that Ll. Stryker has, or could have.

Can Omar do anything towards getting his mother's passport put in order? There seems to be some circumlocution re the formalities.

Have I a balance at Faber and Faber that could be sent to Dorothy pending the release of her own funds?

Also can you ask Mr. Eliot whether Faber will be ready to print another volume of Cantos? or at any rate "The Testament of Confucius". This is a new translation of the Ta S'eu; and the first proper translation of the Chung Yung, plus an abridgment of the analects and of Mencius.

He may understand from the Cantos on the Chinese Dynasties, that this text of Confucius, having been read at the root of the DOUBLE chinese dynasties is the ONLY basis on which a world order can work.

The Chinese Empire during its great periods offering the ONLY working model (and having served repeatedly as proof of being a working model) that can possibly serve in the present situation.

This may sound a large order, but we have come through a very large war. And someone has got to use adult intelligence in dealing with the world problem.

Confucius started as market inspector, and rose to be Prime Minister AND resigned. He gave more thought to the problem of vast administration than any simple high-brow philosopher.

I do not know that I would have arrived at the centre of his meaning if I had not been down under the collapse of a regime. But at any rate the work is serious. I mean the translation. Both the First and Second book have been published here, I mean my Italian translation of the Ta S'eu with the Chinese text facing it and my Italian version of the Chung Yung. I was working on the Mencius when the partigiani came to the front door with a tommy-gun.

Another point that you may not know, i.e. that I was not fleeing from justice. You may still be under innumerable misapprehensions.

I don't want to extend the present letter indefinitely.

Sincerely yours,
Ezra Pound

About the same time that he wrote to Shakespear and Parkyn he began to send parcels of his hand-corrected Cantos to Dorothy Pound at Rapallo, who would pass them on to his daughter for retyping. The fresh manuscripts would then be sent back to the camp and returned to the poet.[12] Innocent as this procedure appeared, it apparently alarmed the censor at the Detention Center, who suspected that *The Pisan Cantos* were coded messages to the outside world. The result was a second Pound letter, this one directed to the wary camp censor, assuring him that the manuscript contained no cryptic messages. The document, which appeared for the first time in 1962 in *The Paris Review*, serves also as a primer on the reading of these poems:

E. Pound

NOTE TO BASE CENSOR

The Cantos contain nothing in the nature of cypher or intended obscurity. The present Cantos do, naturally, contain a number of allusions and "recalls" to matter in the earlier 71 cantos already published, and many of these cannot be made clear to readers unacquainted with the earlier parts of the poem.

There is also an extreme condensation in the quotations, for example

"Mine eyes have" (given as mi-hine eyes hev) refers to the Battle Hymn of the Republic as heard from the loud speaker. There is not time or place in the narrative to give the further remarks on seeing the glory of the lord.

In like manner citations from Homer or Sophokles or Confucius are brief, and serve to remind the ready reader that we were not born yesterday. The Chinese ideograms are mainly translated, or commented [on] in the english text. At any rate they contain nothing seditious.

The form of the poem and main progress is conditioned by its own inner shape, but the life of the D.T.C. passing OUTSIDE the scheme cannot but impinge, or break into the main flow. The proper names given are mostly those of men on sick call seen passing my tent. A very brief allusion to further study in names, that is, I am interested to note the prevalence of early american names, either of whites of the old tradition (most of the early presidents for example) or of descendants of slaves who took the names of their masters. Interesting in contrast to the relative scarcity of melting-pot names.[18]

The patchy gray fall weather brought cold winds and rain. Pound was uncomfortable in his tent. His request for more blankets was delayed for a week while an officious corporal pondered the matter. On October 22 a message was sent to the War Department saying that unless instructions were received soon, the Detention Training Center would be forced to release its civilian prisoner. Pound had been kept in custody, the radiogram said, while the FBI investigated his case; but now their investigation was complete. Once again, the bureaucratic machine began to roll. In early November, Pound read, in the Mediterranean edition of *Stars and Stripes*, that seven Italian radio technicians and officials were being flown to Washington to testify against him. His case was receiving wide publicity in the American press. It was being handled at the highest official level and was being accorded top priority by the government. On November 5, a War Department memorandum was received by the Commander of the Peninsula Base Section:

> The Department of Justice shortly will ask for return to the UNITED STATES of EZRA POUND, 14 November probable target date. We will give you about 3 days notice of date for POUND's arrival here. Legal jurisdiction requires that plane returning prisoner land at Bolling Field in the District of Columbia and NOT at National Airport or other airports in the UNITED STATES.
>
> Arrangements to be made here for relinquishing POUND to Federal Bureau of Investigation upon arrival at Bolling Field.
>
> Advise this office of destination of plane and time of departure of Italian witnesses in EZRA POUND case.

The projected target date came and went and still no word was received. Pound became extremely depressed. Whereas he had originally hoped for a speedy trial and verdict, he now despaired of ever leaving Pisa. But within forty-eight hours, the long-awaited directive arrived; it had come from the Office of the Judge Advocate General of the War Crimes Division, Washington, D.C.:

> 16 November
>
> Return of EZRA POUND is subject.
> Secretary of War directs that ATC pick up POUND on highest priority

on regular flight leaving ROME 17 November and arriving US 18 November.

Pound is to be transported under military guards until relinquishment to federal authorities in US.

Most important that first landing of plane must be at Bolling Field in District of Columbia and NO other.

Advise ATC to communicate their Headquarters WASHINGTON of plane designation and probable time of arrival at Bolling Field.

Request immediate reply.

The importance placed on where the plane transporting Pound was to land had been explained in a November 15 letter from the Attorney General's office to the Secretary of War:

> As you know, jurisdiction over crimes committed outside the United States is in the District in which the defendant is found or first brought. It is therefore of the utmost importance that Pound be brought directly to the District of Columbia and that the airplane in which he is returned should not land in the United States prior to arrival at Bolling Field. Should a forced landing elsewhere become necessary, custody over Pound should be retained by military authorities until he can be released to officials of this Department in the District of Columbia. It is desired to point out, also, that jurisdiction over the National Airport is questionable and that under no circumstances should the airplane be landed there.

On the night of November 16, after six months' imprisonment, the poet was handcuffed and taken by jeep to the airport in Rome. There, he was kept in isolation for nearly twenty-four hours, and then placed aboard an airliner scheduled to arrive in Washington the evening of the eighteenth after a short stopover in the Azores. Recalling the flight for McNair Wilson thirteen years later, Pound wrote that the provost marshal in charge was delighted to discover afterward that the party "he kicked out of the front seats reserved for the captive and a guard" was the French ambassador and his wife, both of whom, in turn, were amused by the "AMOUNT of armed force required to receive the handcuffed prisoner in Washington."[14]

As he stepped from the plane photographers and reporters clustered around. He appeared grizzled and red-eyed, wearing a baggy gray coat and trousers, a soiled U.S. Army sweatshirt and GI shoes too large for his feet, and carried a hat, heavy overcoat, and small leather case. From Bolling Airfield he was taken to the District of Columbia jail. The next day, he was brought before Chief Judge Bolitha J. Laws. When the prisoner asked permission to act as his own counsel he was told the charge was too serious for that. Judge Laws set November 27 for a formal arraignment, and Pound was returned to his cell.[15]

He did not meet his counsel until the following day. Reporting to James Laughlin on their initial encounter, Julien Cornell wrote: "I found the poor devil in a rather desperate condition. He is very wobbly in his mind and while his talk is entirely rational, he flits from one idea to another and is unable to concentrate even to the extent of answering a single question, without immediately wandering off the subject." Cornell encouraged his client to talk freely, and Pound, after months of being cooped up, obliged. He rambled on about Confucius, Jefferson, and the economic and political implications of their ideas. He was convinced that certain powerful government officials, with whom he had no acquaintance whatever, might interest themselves in his case if they could be persuaded of the soundness of his views. Among others, he wanted Archibald MacLeish and Henry Wallace, both of whom he did know, to testify on his behalf in court. He told Cornell that whether or not he was convicted he could be of great help to President Truman, because of his knowledge of conditions in Italy and Japan. The attorney was convinced that Pound was still suffering the aftereffects of his collapse at Pisa. As Cornell wrote in his book, *The Trial of Ezra Pound*: "It was apparent to me that he was in no state to stand trial or even plead to the indictment but was in need of medical care and hospital treatment."[16] When he asked Pound how he felt about the possibility of pleading insanity as a defense, the poet stated that he had no objection. He told Cornell that the idea, in fact, had already occurred to him.

Purgatory

(1945–1958)

1

Pound later confided to reporters that he had not expected to spend half a year with murderers and felons inside a prison colony within eyeshot of Pisa's leaning wonder. From Genoa's CICHQ he had expected to be flown directly to the United States. Even when the vehicle carrying him stopped at the DTC, he thought that his visit would end as soon as a plane was readied at the nearest airfield. By the same token, he had never imagined having to spend thirteen years in a snake pit with catatonics and schizophrenics, locked away behind brick walls the color of clay, a few miles from the White House, on a hill overlooking the wedding-cake dome of the Capitol. That ironic event was recorded in pen by the friendly psychiatrist, a stranger who had taken the time and trouble "to write out instructions for a sane man condemned to live among the insane."[1]

At the same time he supposed he was lucky to be alive. Guy Davenport reminds us that at St. Elizabeths, Pound sustained himself by remembering C. Musonius Rufus slinging a pickax in the chain gangs that dug the canal across the Isthmus of Corinth. He remembered Tasso, Raleigh, Cervantes, and John Bunyon writing in their cells. The charge of treason, he recalled, had been leveled against Blake, Dante, Galileo, and Socrates. And madness? That affliction was the common property of all artists. Rimbaud had a split personality, Verlaine was a psychopath. Van Gogh killed himself, as did Mayakovsky, Modigliani, Hart Crane, and Virginia Woolf. And Christopher Smart, Hölderlin, Nijinsky, and Antonin Artaud spent years in lunatic asylums.

"Crazy as a fox," intoned one madhouse crasher who visited Pound at St. Elizabeths; "Crazy as a Fascist," cried another. Diagnosed insanity might have saved his life. It did not save his soul. Even without a trial he suffered the indignities of conviction. He had foreseen the paradox himself years before in a poem called "Sub Mare" (1912): "It is, and is not,

I am sane enough." He was sane enough to suffer the pangs of internment; a court of law decided he was not sane enough to be released. In
1958, the same court overruled itself; Pound was released as incurably
insane, but not dangerous. And so, twelve years, eleven months, and two
weeks after being taken into custody near Rapallo, the poet was once
again a free man.

> That the wave crashed, whirling the raft, then
> Tearing the oar from his hand,
>   broke mast and yard-arm
> And he was drawn down under wave,
>   The wind tossing,
> Notus, Boreas,
>   as it were thistle-down.
> Then Leucothea had pity,
>   "mortal once
> Who now is a sea-god:
>   νόστου
> γαίης Φαιήχων, . . ."

(Canto 95)

With Pound's arrival in Washington, which followed by six days the
arrival of the Italian radio technicians and officials who had been imported to testify against him, a new true bill was issued, charging the
prisoner with nineteen overt acts of treason. The second indictment,
handed up on November 26, 1945, superseded the previous indictment
issued on July 25, 1943. Neither the poet nor his counsel had seen a copy
of the superseding document when he was arraigned the following day:

> The Grand Jurors for the United States of America duly impaneled
> and sworn in the District Court of the United States for the District of
> Columbia and inquiring for that District upon their oath present:
>   1. That Ezra Pound, the defendant herein, was born at Hailey, Idaho,
> October 30, 1885, and that he has been at all times herein mentioned
> and now is a citizen of the United States of America and a person owing
> allegiance to the United States of America.
>   2. That the defendant, Ezra Pound, at Rome, Italy, and other places
> within the Kingdom of Italy and outside the jurisdiction of any particular
> state or district, but within the jurisdiction of the United States and of
> this Court, the District of Columbia being the district in which he was

found and into which he was first brought, continuously, and at all times beginning on the 11th day of December 1941, and continuing thereafter to and including the 3rd day of May 1945, under the circumstances and conditions and in the manner and by the means hereinafter set forth, then and there being a citizen of the United States, and a person owing allegiance to the United States, in violation of said duty of allegiance, knowingly, intentionally, wilfully, unlawfully, feloniously, traitorously and treasonably did adhere to the enemies of the United States, to-wit; the Kingdom of Italy and the military allies of the said Kingdom of Italy, with which the United States at all times since December 11, 1941, and during the times set forth in this indictment, have been at war, giving to the said enemies of the United States aid and comfort within the United States and elsewhere, that is to say:

3. That the aforesaid adherence of the said defendant, Ezra Pound, to the Kingdom of Italy and its military allies and the giving of aid and comfort by the said defendant, Ezra Pound, to the aforesaid enemies of the United States during the time aforesaid consisted:

(a) Of accepting employment from the Kingdom of Italy in the capacity of a radio propagandist and in the performance of the duties thereof which involved the composition of texts, speeches, talks and announcements and the recording thereof for subsequent broadcast over short-wave radio on wave lengths audible in the United States and elsewhere on ordinary commercial radio receiving sets having short-wave reception facilities; and

(b) Of counselling and aiding the Kingdom of Italy and its military allies and proposing and advocating to the officials of the Government of the Kingdom of Italy ideas and thoughts, as well as methods by which such ideas and thoughts could be disseminated, which the said defendant, Ezra Pound, believed suitable and useful to the Kingdom of Italy for propaganda purposes in the prosecution of said war;

That the aforesaid activities of the said defendant, Ezra Pound, were intended to persuade citizens and residents of the United States to decline to support the United States in the conduct of the said war, to weaken or destroy confidence in the Government of the United States and in the integrity and loyalty of the Allies of the United States, and to further bind together and increase the morale of the subjects of the Kingdom of Italy in support of the prosecution of the said war by the Kingdom of Italy and its military allies.

4. And the Grand Jurors aforesaid upon their oath aforesaid do further present that the said defendant, Ezra Pound, in the prosecution, performance and execution of said treason and of said unlawful, traitorous and treasonable adhering and giving aid and comfort to the enemies of the United States, at the several times hereinafter set forth in the specifications hereof (being times when the United States were at war

with the Kingdom of Italy and its military allies), unlawfully, feloniously, wilfully, knowingly, traitorously and treasonably and with intent to adhere to and give aid and comfort to the said enemies, did do, perform, and commit certain overt and manifest acts, that is to say:

1. On or about September 11, 1942, the said defendant, Ezra Pound, for the purpose of giving aid and comfort to the Kingdom of Italy and its then allies in the war against the United States, spoke into a microphone at a radio station in Rome, Italy, controlled by the Italian Government, and thereby recorded and caused to be recorded certain messages, speeches and talks for subsequent broadcast to the United States and its military allies; that the purpose of said messages, speeches and talks was, among other things, to create dissension and distrust between the United States and its military allies; and that in said speeches, messages and talks the said defendant asserted, in substance, that the war is an economic war in which the United States and its allies are the aggressors.

2. On or about December 10, 1942, the said defendant, Ezra Pound, for the purpose of giving aid and comfort to the Kingdom of Italy and its then allies in the war against the United States, spoke into a microphone at a radio station in Rome, Italy, controlled by the Italian Government, and thereby recorded and caused to be recorded certain messages, speeches and talks for subsequent broadcast to the United States and its military allies, and that the purport of said messages, speeches and talks was to create racial prejudice in the United States.

3. On or about February 4, 1943, the said defendant, Ezra Pound, for the purpose of giving aid and comfort to the Kingdom of Italy and its then allies in the war against the United States, spoke into a microphone at a radio station in Rome, Italy, controlled by the Italian Government, and thereby recorded and caused to be recorded certain messages, speeches and talks for subsequent broadcast to the United States and its military allies.

4. On March 19, 1943, the said defendant, Ezra Pound, for the purpose of giving aid and comfort to the Kingdom of Italy and its then allies in the war against the United States, spoke into a microphone at a radio station in Rome, Italy, controlled by the Italian Government, and thereby recorded and caused to be recorded certain messages, speeches and talks for subsequent broadcast to the United States and its military allies, and that the purpose of said messages, speeches and talks was, among other things, to cause dissension and distrust between the United States and England and Russia.

5. On or about May 12, 1943, the said defendant, Ezra Pound for the purpose of giving aid and comfort to the Kingdom of Italy and its then allies in the war against the United States, spoke into a microphone at a radio station in Rome, Italy, controlled by the Italian Government, and thereby recorded and caused to be recorded certain messages,

speeches and talks for subsequent broadcast to the United States and its military allies, and that in said messages, speeches and talks the said defendant asserted, among other things and in substance, that Italy is the natural ally of the United States; that the true nature of the Axis regime has been misrepresented to the people in the United States and that England, Russia and the United States are aggressor nations.

6. On or about May 14, 1943, the said defendant, Ezra Pound, for the purpose of giving aid and comfort to the Kingdom of Italy and its then allies in the war against the United States, spoke into a microphone at a radio station in Rome, Italy, controlled by the Italian Government, and thereby recorded and caused to be recorded certain messages, speeches and talks for subsequent broadcast to the United States and its military allies, and that the purport of said messages, speeches and talks was to create racial prejudice and distrust of the Government of the United States.

7. On or about May 15, 1943, the said defendant, Ezra Pound, for the purpose of giving aid and comfort to the Kingdom of Italy and its then allies in the war against the United States, spoke into a microphone at a radio station in Rome, Italy, controlled by the Italian Government, and thereby recorded and caused to be recorded certain messages, speeches and talks for subsequent broadcast to the United States and its military allies, and that in said messages, speeches and talks the said defendant praised Italy, urged the people in the United States to read European publications rather than the American press and to listen to European radio transmissions, and stated further that he spoke "from Rome, in a regime where liberty is considered a duty. . . ."

8. Between July 29, 1942 and July 25, 1943, the said defendant, Ezra Pound, for the purpose of giving aid and comfort to the Kingdom of Italy and its then allies in the war against the United States, on a day and date to these Grand Jurors unknown, and in the presence of Armando Giovagnoli and Giuseppe Bruni, spoke into a microphone in a radio station at Rome, Italy, controlled by the Italian Government, and thereby recorded and caused to be recorded certain messages, speeches and talks for subsequent broadcast to the United States and its military allies.

9. Between July 29, 1942 and July 25, 1943, the said defendant, Ezra Pound, for the purpose of giving aid and comfort to the Kingdom of Italy and its then allies in the war against the United States, on a day and date to these Grand Jurors unknown, and in the presence of Armando Giovagnoli and Fernando de Leonardis, spoke into a microphone in a radio station at Rome, Italy, controlled by the Italian Government, and thereby recorded and caused to be recorded certain messages, speeches and talks for subsequent broadcast to the United States and its military allies.

10. Between August 22, 1942 and July 25, 1943, the said defendant, Ezra Pound, for the purpose of giving aid and comfort to the Kingdom of

Italy and its then allies in the war against the United States, on a day and date to these Grand Jurors unknown, and in the presence of Walter Zanchetti and Giuseppe Bruni, spoke into a microphone in a radio station at Rome, Italy, controlled by the Italian Government, and thereby recorded and caused to be recorded certain messages, speeches and talks for subsequent broadcast to the United States and its military allies.

11. Between August 22, 1942 and July 25, 1943, the said defendant, Ezra Pound, for the purpose of giving aid and comfort to the Kingdom of Italy and its then allies in the war against the United States, on a day and date to these Grand Jurors unknown, and in the presence of Walter Zanchetti and Fernando de Leonardis, spoke into a microphone in a radio station in Rome, Italy, controlled by the Italian Government, and thereby recorded and caused to be recorded certain messages, speeches and talks for subsequent broadcast to the United States and its military allies.

12. Between December 11, 1941 and July 24, 1943, the said defendant, Ezra Pound, for the purpose of giving aid and comfort to the Kingdom of Italy and its then allies in the war against the United States, on a day and date to these Grand Jurors unknown, and in the presence of Fernando Luzzi and Giuseppe Bruni, spoke into a microphone in a radio station at Rome, Italy, controlled by the Italian Government, and thereby recorded and caused to be recorded certain messages, speeches and talks for subsequent broadcast to the United States and its military allies.

13. Between December 11, 1941 and July 25, 1943, the said defendant, Ezra Pound, for the purpose of giving aid and comfort to the Kingdom of Italy and its then allies in the war against the United States, on a day and date to these Grand Jurors unknown, and in the presence of Fernando Luzzi and Giuseppe Bruni, spoke into a microphone in a radio station at Rome, Italy, controlled by the Italian Government, and thereby recorded and caused to be recorded certain messages, speeches and talks for subsequent broadcast to the United States and its military allies.

14. Between December 11, 1941 and July 25, 1943, the said defendant, Ezra Pound, for the purpose of giving aid and comfort to the Kingdom of Italy and its then allies in the war against the United States, on a day and date to these Grand Jurors unknown, and in the presence of Giuseppe Bruni and Fernando de Leonardis, spoke into a microphone in a radio station at Rome, Italy, controlled by the Italian Government, and thereby recorded and caused to be recorded certain messages, speeches and talks for subsequent broadcast to the United States and its military allies.

15. Between April 1, 1942 and July 23, 1943, the said defendant, Ezra Pound, for the purpose of giving aid and comfort to the Kingdom of Italy and its then allies in the war against the United States, on a day and date to these Grand Jurors unknown, conferred and counselled with

Salvatore Aponte and Adriano Ungaro, officials of the Ministry of Popular Culture of the Kingdom of Italy, for the purpose of securing their approval of manuscripts composed by said defendant to be used in the making of recordings for subsequent broadcast to the United States and elsewhere.

16. On or about July 11, 1942, the said defendant, Ezra Pound, for the purpose of giving aid and comfort to the Kingdom of Italy and its then allies in the war against the United States, accepted and received payment and remuneration in the sum of 700 lire from the Kingdom of Italy for compiling and recording messages, speeches and talks for subsequent broadcast to the United States and elsewhere from a radio station in Rome, Italy.

17. Between December 11, 1941 and May 3, 1945, the said defendant, Ezra Pound, for the purpose of giving aid and comfort to the Kingdom of Italy and its then allies in the war against the United States, on a day and date to these Grand Jurors unknown, accepted and received payment and remuneration from the Kingdom of Italy, in an amount to these Grand Jurors unknown, for compiling and recording messages, speeches and talks for subsequent broadcast to the United States and elsewhere from a radio station in Rome, Italy.

18. On or about June 24, 1942, the said defendant, Ezra Pound, for the purpose of giving aid and comfort to the Kingdom of Italy and its then allies in the war against the United States, accepted and received payment and remuneration in the sum of 350 lire, from the Kingdom of Italy for compilation of notes and comments for broadcast to the United States and elsewhere from a radio station located in the Kingdom of Italy.

19. Between December 11, 1941 and May 3, 1945, the said defendant, Ezra Pound, for the purpose of giving aid and comfort to the Kingdom of Italy and its then allies in the war against the United States, on a day and date to these Grand Jurors unknown, accepted and received payment and remuneration from the Kingdom of Italy, in an amount to these Grand Jurors unknown, for compilation of notes and comments for broadcast in the United States and elsewhere from a radio station located in the Kingdom of Italy.

The defendant, Ezra Pound, committed each and every one of the overt acts herein described for the purpose of, and with the intent to adhere to and give aid and comfort to the Kingdom of Italy, and its military allies, enemies of the United States, and the said defendant, Ezra Pound, committed each and every one of the said overt acts contrary to his duty of allegiance to the United States and to the form of the statute and constitution in such case made and provided and against the peace and dignity of the United States. (Section 1, United States Criminal Code.)

This protracted judgment, important because it constituted the bulk of the government's case against Pound, was signed by the foreman of the grand jury, and by the following: Edward M. Curran, United States Attorney in and for the District of Columbia; Isaiah Matlack, Special Assistant to the Attorney General; Samuel C. Ely, Special Assistant to the Attorney General; Donald B. Anderson, Special Assistant to the Attorney General, and Theron L. Caudle, Assistant Attorney General.

The inclusion of the names of the Italian radio employees—Salvatore Aponte, Giuseppe Bruni, Armando Giovagnoli, Fernando de Leonardis, Fernando Luzzi, Adriano Ungaro, and Walter Zanchetti—is noteworthy insofar as the law requires the testimony of two witnesses for each act of treason. Yet because there never really was a trial, these seven witnesses never presented their testimony in court. Department of Justice invoices indicate that they were well remunerated for their time and trouble, housed and fed in first-class hotels and restaurants in and around the Washington area, where they remained for nearly two months. When it became evident that no trial was forthcoming, they were placed aboard a government airliner and returned to Italy.

*

The days he spent in the dank cell block of the District of Columbia jail must have brought back whatever unpleasant memories remained with him of Pisa. Julien Cornell writes that on November 23, Pound was taken in a police van to the "bull pen" at the courthouse and kept there all day, shut in with a group of disorderly prisoners—presumably because the grand jury was that day in the process of indicting him. On November 24 and 25 he was kept locked in his cell, as were other prisoners, because of an attempted jail break in another wing of the prison. He suffered extremely, as he had before, from claustrophobia, and was admitted to the jail infirmary, where he spent the nights of November 25 and 26. The morning of the twenty-seventh, the day scheduled for the formal arraignment, Cornell found his client in a state of "almost complete" mental and physical exhaustion. When the attorney informed Pound that the arraignment was to take place that afternoon, the poet became visibly upset. He insisted that he felt ill and asked to be returned to the infirmary.

Several hours later, at the proceedings themselves, Cornell informed the court that his client was not sufficiently well to enter a plea.

Under the law, a plea of "not guilty" was entered for him by Chief Judge Laws. The government, represented by Assistant Attorney General Isaiah Matlack, did not object. To Matlack, and to Judge Laws, Cornell now handed copies of two documents he had prepared for the occasion: an affidavit in support of the motion for bail, and a memorandum of law "submitted in support of the defendant's application for admission to bail pending trial on the indictment." Cornell presented the gist of the affidavit orally to the court, reading much of the time from notes:

> I am an attorney at law of New York and have appeared herein for the defendant, Ezra Pound, at the request of his London solicitors, and with the permission of the court, for the sole purpose of this arraignment. I do not defend his actions, nor do I approve his sentiments. I do not feel that I can properly try his case. But in accordance with my duty as a lawyer, I have felt obliged to comply with a request that I confer with this man accused of crime.
>
> I must report that the defendant, Ezra Pound, after his arrest on a charge of treason last May, has been continuously held incommunicado in solitary confinement, under such extreme conditions that he suffered a complete mental collapse and loss of memory. Although he has partially recovered his health, I believe that he is still insane and that if he remains in prison he may never recover, and not only will he be unable to stand trial on this indictment, but one of the greatest literary geniuses of these times will be permanently eclipsed.
>
> I urge this court to order his removal at once from the District of Columbia jail, where he is now confined, to a civilian mental hospital or sanatorium under bail, or that if bail is not permitted, he be removed to a civilian mental hospital or sanatorium operated by the United States and placed in custody of a civilian physician. I believe that such action is imperative, and that if it is not taken immediately, he will never recover his senses sufficiently to defend himself against the indictment which has been handed up to the court. . . .
>
> It is not necessary to recount the story of Pound's downfall. I need only say that his extraordinary conduct, his vilification of the nation's leaders during the war time, his vainglory and vituperations, his anti-Semitic and vulgar utterances, as broadcast over the Rome radio, cannot be explained on any basis of mere venality but only on the ground that Pound is an old man no longer in the full possession of his mental powers. I am led to this belief not only because the mentality of the man in his prime and the ridiculous broadcasts of his old age are utterly incompatible, but also because his private correspondence is unmistakable, and in the opinion of many of his close friends and associates, his

mind has been deteriorating for a number of years, far beyond mere senility or eccentricity.

It was this streak of mental weakness in Pound, which had long been evident to his friends, that led him, I believe, into mental collapse when he was subjected to the rigors of imprisonment.[2]

Having established the current facts of the case, Pound's attorney proceeded to trace the poet's background, accomplishments, recent ordeal, and present disability—with good effect, Charles Norman points out. Cornell's summation emphasized the seriousness of his client's condition, and again made the point that without proper and immediate medical attention, Pound would be unable ever to stand trial. The Memorandum of Law on Application for Bail demonstrated Cornell's familiarity with the statutes and Constitutional provisions which pertained to the crime of high treason. Precedents were rare, but the attorney managed to uncover two cases—one of treason in 1795, the other of piracy in 1813—which seemed to relate to the situation at hand. What was interesting about the piracy case was that the 1813 court admitted to bail a subject whose failing health made continued imprisonment dangerous. (See Appendix IV.)

Following a brief recess of the court, Judge Laws delivered his decision:

> I have considered the motion filed in behalf of the defendant that he be admitted to bail or in the alternative that he be removed from his present place of imprisonment in the Washington Asylum and Jail to the custody of a hospital or other institution operated by the United States or the District of Columbia. From the showing made before me by counsel for the defendant, it appears advisable to have an examination and observation of the defendant made by physicians and that pending such an examination and report of their findings and pending the granting of opportunity to counsel for the prosecution to reply to the motion for bail, no action should be taken on such motion.
>
> Accordingly, the defendant is ordered remanded to Washington Asylum and Jail with the recommendation that he be transferred to Gallinger Hospital or such other hospital as may be designated by authorized officials of the United States for examination and observation and for treatment, if found necessary. The motion for admission to bail is continued for further hearing until December 14, 1945; counsel for the United States will submit on or before December 10th any showing which they may desire to make in opposition to the said motion.

On December 4, as directed, Pound was removed to Gallinger Municipal Hospital, and installed in a private, locked room. There, he was examined (individually and jointly) by four doctors—three representing the government and the fourth retained by Cornell. They were Dr. Winfred Overholser, superintendent of St. Elizabeths Hospital, Washington's federal government asylum for the insane; Dr. Marion King, medical director of the U.S. Health Service; Dr. Joseph Gilbert, head of the division of psychiatry at Gallinger Hospital; and Cornell's choice, Dr. Wendell Muncie, associate professor of psychiatry at the Johns Hopkins Hospital, Baltimore. After conferring among themselves they composed the following report, outlining their initial findings, for the benefit of the court; it was addressed to the Honorable Bolitha J. Laws, Chief Justice, U.S. District Court, and supported the defense's contention that the defendant was suffering from a paranoid state which rendered him mentally unfit to advise properly with counsel or to participate intelligently and reasonably in a trial and, therefore, he should not be tried but should instead be placed in a mental institution where he could and would be given proper medical care:

December 14, 1945

Sir:

The undersigned hereby respectfully report the results of their mental examination of Ezra Pound, now detained in Gallinger Hospital by transfer for observation from the District Jail on a charge of treason. Three of us (Drs. Gilbert, King and Overholser) were appointed by your Honor to make this examination. At our suggestion, and with your approval, Dr. Wendell Muncie, acting upon the request of counsel for the accused, made an examination with us and associates himself with us in this joint report. Dr. Muncie spent several hours with the defendant, both alone and with us, on December 13, 1945, and the others of us have examined the defendant each on several occasions, separately and together, in the period from his admission to Gallinger Hospital on December 4, 1945 to December 13, 1945. We have had available to us the reports of laboratory, psychological and special physical examinations of the defendant and considerable material in the line of his writings and biographical data.

The defendant, now 60 years of age and in generally good physical condition, was a precocious student, specializing in literature. He has been a voluntary expatriate for nearly 40 years, living in England and France, and for the past 21 years in Italy, making an uncertain living by writing poetry and criticism. His poetry and literary criticism have achieved considerable recognition, but of recent years his preoccupation with monetary theories and economics has apparently obstructed his literary productivity. He has long been recognized as eccentric, querulous, and egocentric.

At the present time he exhibits extremely poor judgment as to his situation, its seriousness and the manner in which the charges are to be met. He insists that his broadcasts were not treasonable, but that all his radio activities have stemmed from his self-appointed mission to "save the Constitution." He is abnormally grandiose, is expansive and exuberant in manner, exhibiting pressure of speech, discursiveness, and distractibility.

In our opinion, with advancing years his personality, for many years abnormal, has undergone further distortion to the extent that he is now suffering from a paranoid state which renders him mentally unfit to advise properly with counsel or to participate intelligently and reasonably in his own defense. He is, in other words, insane and mentally unfit for trial, and is in need of care in a mental hospital.

Respectfully submited,
Joseph L. Gilbert, M.D.
Marion R. King, M.D.
Wendell Muncie, M.D.
Winfred Overholser, M.D.

While Pound was being detained at Gallinger, his attorney returned to New York. Aside from the usual and expected difficulties connected with a case of this sort there were added problems. There was the matter of mounting expenses and frozen funds. Because of the war, Dorothy Pound's bank account in England had been seized by British authorities, and the poet's American account with the Jenkinstown Trust Company, Jenkinstown, Pennsylvania, was in the hands of the Custodian of Alien Property. In Rapallo, the family safe-deposit box had been shut down by order of the Allied Command. James Laughlin and other friends advanced certain funds but the largest contribution by far came from E. E. Cummings, who presented Cornell with a one-thousand-dollar check; Cummings obviously felt differently about Pound now than he had in 1943 when first interviewed by the FBI. For an article about Pound which appeared in the newspaper *PM* (New York) on November 25, 1945, Cummings voiced this humane sentiment: "Every artist's strictly illimitable country is himself. An artist who plays that country false has committed suicide; and even a good lawyer cannot kill the dead. But a human being who's true to himself—whoever himself may be—is immortal; and all the atomic bombs of all the anti-artists in spacetime will never civilize immortality." Although his thousand-dollar donation was intended as an outright gift rather than a loan, Mrs. Pound insisted on repaying Cummings when her funds were later released.[3]

In an effort to bolster Pound's case, to make certain that the insanity plea stuck, Cornell wrote to some of Pound's friends and acquaintances—Allen Tate, Tiffany Thayer, Ernest Hemingway—hoping to procure letters written to them by Pound before the war, full of the obscenities and anti-Semitic slurs with which he had become associated. Cornell was eager to demonstrate that his client's problems were deeply rooted and that it was unlikely there would be any considerable change in the near future. He was also interested in any recent Pound correspondence he could find, confident that it would demonstrate the same lack of cohesion he had recently detected in Pound's speech.

Not one of the triad of writers Cornell contacted was able to locate pertinent material. Tate made some alternate suggestions, and Thayer said he would continue to search his house. Hemingway wrote from the Finca Vigia in Cuba that he had received no letter from Pound after 1936, and that any previous correspondence would have been stored away in Paris. Hemingway added that he could attest to Pound's madness and believed that his friend's mind and judgment had become progressively impaired over the past ten years with, he noted, occasional flashes of brilliance. He called Pound "one of the greatest poets that ever lived." Hemingway blamed the poet's condition partially on the false flattery of an unscrupulous few who had taken advantage of his "ever-mounting vanity." (December 11, 1945: Beinecke Library, Yale.)

The evidence Cornell sought—that Pound was no longer of sound mind—arrived unexpectedly in the form of a brace of notes written by Pound, and addressed to Cornell, while the poet was locked away in the bowels of St. Elizabeths, shortly after being transferred there from Gallinger. Scribbled in pencil, in short staccato lines, on sheets of cheap ruled paper, the letters (dated January 1946) convey the tone of a desperate and frightened man:

> Problem now is
> not to go stark
> screaming hysteric . . .
> relapse after comfort of
> Tuesday = & mute.

olson saved my life.
young doctors absolutely
useless.
must have 15
minutes sane
conversation daily . . .
velocity after
stupor *tremendous.*
enormous work
    to be
done.
& no driving
    force
& everyone's
  inexactitude
very
fatiguing.
. . . . .

        Dungeon
        Dementia
mental torture
constitution a religion
a world lost
grey mist barrier impassible [*sic*]
    ignorance absolute

            anonyme
futility of might have been
coherent areas
       constantly
        invaded
   aiuto
        Pound[4]

[*Aiuto*: "Help!"[5]]

The motion for bail placed earlier was heard and denied on December 21. Under federal statute, prisoner #76028 was transferred the same day to Howard Hall, the criminal lunatic ward of St. Elizabeths Hospital. It was from here that he had written the two notes to Cornell.

Howard Hall was a grim, 1880s building with locked doors and gratings at the windows, the entire structure surrounded by a massive wall. Outside the building, but within the confines of the wall, was a small exercise yard. Like the other inmates, Pound was permitted a brief daily exercise period in the yard. At all other times he was padlocked into his cell. The thick black steel door, which separated him (perhaps mercifully) from the lunatics in slippers and strait jackets, was pierced by nine peepholes cut into it in three horizontal rows. Medics, so inclined, could observe the poet inside his cell by peering in at him.

Charles Olson, one of the poet's first visitors at the hospital, kept a journal of these early days of Pound's ordeal. The prisoner apparently complained more than once (to the projectivist practitioner) of the never-ending psychiatric examinations, the mind probes performed on him by one staff psychiatrist after another. To add to his misery, he had left his personal effects behind at Gallinger, so that for several weeks he was without reading glasses or books. Among the reading material which Olson later provided was *The Fountainhead* by Ayn Rand. Someone else brought Pound a Georgian primer: he wanted to learn the language, he told Olson, so that he could correspond with Stalin. And Harry S. Truman: Who was he, he wanted to know. Was he the one behind his own current troubles? "Does his name happen to be Warren Gamaliel?" he asked, the question a thrust at the Harding Administration. "You will have to take his name as it sounds," replied Olson.[6]

He had other early visitors to the "hell-hole"—Katherine Proctor, H. L. Mencken, Theodore Spencer, Caresse Crosby, William Moore, Jim Farley, Eileen Lane Kinney (a friend of Brancusi's). Ida and Adah Lee Mapel, two old Virginia ladies whom Pound had first met in Spain in 1906, also visited regularly. The majority of his guests came away appalled and shocked by what they had seen. Madmen roamed the corridors. The open ward steamed with heat and reeked of bile and sweat. Quite often Pound seemed oblivious to it all. As in days of old his conversation piped and droned and ran the gamut. He talked about a younger Yeats, warning him to keep his own nose clean of politics; about the American Indian on the ward, who ran around talking about killing people; about the Jews, usury, C. H. Douglas. He talked about Gaudier-Brzeska, Katyn, *Newsweek*, Congressman George Holden Tinkham, the indictment, Westbrook Pegler, and Ford Madox Ford. He recommended books for reading (Ronald Duncan's *Journal of a Husbandman* and the stories of Mary Butts) and discussed ramifications of the war ("Radar won the war, production was second and military strategy third").[7] But when not entertaining visitors, when alone in his cell at night or during the day, he suffered greatly from claustrophobia and loneliness and the feeling that he was going mad. On at least one occasion his "clear conscience" provided him with a moment of happiness, despite his surroundings. "I remember," he wrote to R. McNair Wilson in April 1958, "a moment of quite irrational happiness in the hell-hole."[8]

It appeared, for a time, as if the case of the United States of America versus Ezra Pound was over. But the Department of Justice had put too many hours of hard labor into this, the first postwar case of treason, to simply let the matter drop. Then, too, there were those who believed that Pound had not been brought to trial on his indictment because of a sly arrangement which had been cooked up by certain government officials. Pressure was brought to bear on the Department of Justice by such periodicals as the Communist *New Masses*, which called for Pound's immediate execution. In truth, Pound had become a kind of scapegoat—the man who let everybody down. The Great Bass's figurehead publicity snowballed to the point where a public trial was owed the public. It was not so much the case of America versus Rabbi Ben Ezra (as Conrad Aiken, employing Browning's poem title, renamed him in *Ushant*) but of America versus the renegade intellectual, the Faust-man who dared tread on his country's heart and soul. And it was not just the trial of a modern-day poet—or even of a man who had remade poetry—but of the stuff, of the genre of poetry, itself. It was as much Milton's trial, or Blake's, or Dante's—as it was Pound's.

On January 16, 1946, the District Court heard and granted a motion by the Attorney General's office, represented by Isaiah Matlack and Donald B. Anderson, for a formal statutory inquisition into Ezra Pound's mental state. The inquisition was scheduled for February 13, before Judge Laws and a jury. The day before the inquisition, Cornell went to St. Elizabeths to see Pound and prepare him once again for the ordeal of appearing in court. After explaining to him what was going to happen, the attorney stopped by Dr. Overholser's office to pay his respects and discuss his client. As superintendent of the hospital, Overholser had access to the latest medical reports on Pound. He informed Cornell that some of the younger physicians on his staff—Ziman, Kavka, Griffen, Cruvant—had examined the poet and found him eccentric but sane enough to stand trial. In the same breath he added that he, however, was of a different mind. It was Overholser's feeling that Pound would never regain his sanity to the extent that he would be able to consult with an attorney in meeting the charges against him or be able to defend himself on a witness stand in a court of law.

Although the Department of Justice might have hoped otherwise, the Sanity Inquisition was well publicized and well attended. James Laughlin was present; Charles Olson was there, covering the proceeding for the *Partisan Review*. The courtroom was packed with newsmen.

The testimony presented by the four psychiatrists involved in the case fills more than a hundred pages. The excerpts which follow represent the substance of their respective statements concerning Pound's mental condition:

Dr. Wendell Muncie testifying:

Q. Will you state what symptoms you found in Mr. Pound?

A. There are a number of things which attracted my attention in examining Mr. Pound, and these are essentially the items that appeared to me:

He has a number of rather fixed ideas which are either clearly delusional or verging on the delusional. One I might speak of, for instance, he believes he has been designated to save the Constitution of the United States for the people of the United States.

Secondly, he has a feeling that he has the key to the peace of the world through the writings of Confucius, which he translated into Italian and into English, and that if this book had been given proper circulation the Axis would not have been formed, we would be at peace now, and a great deal of trouble could have been avoided in the past, and this becomes his blueprint for world order in the future.

Third, he believes that with himself as a leader, a group of intellectuals could have gotten together in different countries, like Japan, for instance, where he is well thought of, to work for world order. He has a hatred of bureaucracy which goes back a long way, and one may conclude that his saving of the Constitution draws a clear distinction between the rights of the people and those who govern the people. . . . In addition to that, he shows a remarkable grandiosity. He feels that he has no peer in the intellectual field, although conceding that one or two persons he has assisted might, on occasion, do as good work as he did.

Q. Did you at any time ascertain whether he understood the nature of the offense?

A. Whether he understands the meaning of treason, or not, I do not know. He categorically denies that he committed anything like treason, in his mind, against the people of the United States.

Q. Were you able to discuss it with him sufficiently to find out whether or not he had any grasp of the nature of his alleged crime?

A. Such discussions, and there have been several, always end up in bringing in all the matters I talked about, the economic situation, Confucius,

Japan, and so forth, but by no stretch of the imagination can you make
him realize the seriousness of his predicament, and that is the astonishing thing. If you touch on his case and hospitalization, Confucius and
these other things seem to get roped in, and you end up with a confusion of thoughts.

Q. In other words, he is not able to pursue a point logically, but he does
   confuse it with other ideas, is that right?

A. Yes.

Q. Were you able to discover whether any other mental difficulties had
   occurred in his previous life?

A. Well, all we know is from the record that he went through an unusual
   mental experience in a concentration camp in Italy, which, by all the
   records, must have been a profound emotional experience amounting,
   I suppose, to a panic state, but to suggest how it might be described
   technically, I don't know. But it was a rather severe emotional crisis he
   went through, at which time he was seen, I think, by some psychiatrists.

Q. Before that did you examine sufficient of his writings, and so on, to be
   able to determine whether or not this condition may have arisen in his
   earlier life?

A. I have read a great deal of his writings in connection with preparing
   this case, and it is my idea that there has been for a number of years a
   deterioration of the mental processes.

Q. Will you tell the jury what is your opinion as to Mr. Pound's ability
   to understand the meaning of a trial under this indictment for treason,
   and particularly his ability to consult with counsel and formulate a defense to the indictment?

A. I think he is not capable of doing any of those things.

Dr. Marion King, a specialist in criminal psychopathology, testified
next:

. . . After rather careful consideration of his [Pound's] life-long history,
and especially his progress during the last few years, it is my opinion that
he has always been a sensitive, eccentric, cynical person, and these char-
acteristics have been accentuated in the last few years to such an extent
that he is afflicted with a paranoid state of psychotic proportions which
renders him unfit for trial.

Q. I presume a person can be psychotic, might even have paranoid ten-
   dencies, and be eccentric and cynical, and still be able to stand trial, is
   that true?

A. Yes.

Q. What other considerations are there in his case which make him unable to stand trial, in your opinion?

A. He has deviated from his chosen profession in that he has become preoccupied with economic and governmental problems to such an extent that during discussion of those problems he manifests such a sudden and such a marked feeling and tone that he reaches the point of exhaustion, and this unusual propensity, intense feeling, is quite characteristic of paranoid conditions and is sufficient, in my opinion, to permit, at least create, considerable confusion; at least that was the situation when I examined him, so that it is very difficult for him to explain his theories and proposals in a clear and concise logical manner.

He also exhibited considerable distractibility, easily distracted from the subject of the conversation, and it was difficult for him to come back to the point under discussion.

Q. Have you seen such symptoms as those in other men under accusation of crime, or men convicted of crime?

A. I have seen many cases of this type not only among people who were charged with crime, or convicted of crime, but also among those who have not been charged with an offense.

Q. Do you regard this inability to reason properly, this condition of distractibility, as the major reason why it would be, in your opinion, impossible for him to stand trial?

A. One of the major reasons.

Q. What classification would you state for Mr. Pound's mental condition according to your classifications pertaining to mental illness?

A. I would say that would fall in the category of paranoid states, sometimes called paranoid conditions. That is not a very satisfactory term because it is part way between so-called paranoid schizophrenia or dementia praecox, paranoid type, and true paranoia. There are all types of gradations between the extremes, and it is my opinion that he falls in between those two extremes.

Q. Does he have a split personality?

A. No.

Q. Just what is it that makes you place him in that category?

A. He does not have the clear, well-defined systematized delusions of the paranoiac type; neither does he have the dissociation, the personal hallucinations or delusions, the disordered delusions that go with the dementia praecox, paranoid type, at the other extreme, but he does have a rather diffuse paranoid reaction which falls somewhere between those two fields, and that is the reason I would not classify him as a dementia praecox patient, or a case of true paranoia.

Q. What is his intelligence, or what is his I.Q.?

A. Very high. . . . There has been no impairment of the intelligence over the years. That again is a characteristic of the disorder we are describing. Paranoids are very apt to develop among those of high intelligence, whereas schizophrenia is more likely to occur in individuals with low I.Q.

Dr. King's statement that "There has been no impairment of the intelligence over the years" might seem to conflict with Dr. Muncie's previous observation that "there has been for a number of years a deterioration of the mental processes." None of the attorneys present that day noticed the discrepancy; two psychiatrists, Frederic Wertham and Thomas Szasz did, but long after the fact. Wertham made his discovery known in an essay entitled "Road to Rapallo: A Psychiatric Study" (*American Journal of Psycho-therapy*, 1949), whereas Szasz devoted a long chapter in his book *Law, Liberty and Psychiatry* (1963) to the same issue.

Dr. Winfred Overholser's testimony:

Q. Will you tell us the reasons which lead you to the conclusions that he is unable to participate in the trial of this indictment intelligently?

A. Of course, in the first place we have the background of his history and the Department of Justice has been very helpful in making available what files they have concerning the case.

Q. Do you remember before that, or had you seen the text of his alleged broadcasts?

A. Yes, and other things in addition. In the first place, it is quite obvious that the man has always been unusually eccentric through the years. He has undoubtedly a high regard of his own opinion, and has been extremely vituperative of those who disagree with him.

He has a very high degree of intelligence, there is no question on that score, and his relations with the world and other people during practically all his life have been those of a person who was very skeptical, to say the least.

He is extremely free in his conversation; he has not been reticent by any stretch of the imagination, but his production has been unusually hard to follow. He speaks in bunches of ideas.

Q. You mean his production of speech?

A. Yes, and rambling and illogical.

There was an episode shortly after he was taken into custody by the American Forces in Italy during which he was extremely agitated and anxious, and he has shown episodes such as that sometimes when he was under observation both at Gallinger and St. Elizabeths. At times he has been extremely restless, and at times his speech has been more disconnected than others.

The ideas, perhaps, which he expresses indicate some of his views in connection with the war. In the first place, he is thoroughly convinced that if he had been allowed to send his messages to the Axis, which he wished to send, prior to 1940, there would have been no Axis even. In other words, that if given a free hand by those who were engaged in stultifying him, he could have prevented the war.

He lays a great deal of his difficulty at the door of British Secret Service, and other groups, which have opposed him.

He assures me, too, that he served a very useful purpose to the United States by remaining at the Italian prison camp to complete his translation of Confucius, which he regards as the greatest contribution to literature.

He is sure that he should not have been brought to this country in the capacity of a prisoner, but in the capacity of someone who was to be of great benefit to the United States in its post-war activities.

I might state that this constitutes a grandiosity of ideas and beliefs that goes far beyond the normal, even in a person who is as distraught in his mind as he is.

From a practical view of his advising with his attorney, there would be the fact that you cannot keep him on a straight line of conversation; he rambles around, and has such a naïve grasp of the situation in which he finds himself, it would not be fair to him or his attorney to put him on trial.

Furthermore, due to the episode he had in Pisa when he was under confinement, I think there would be a much more violent reaction on top of this paranoid reaction if the trial was to proceed.

Now Mr. Matlack cross-examined Overholser. The subject: the medical reports submitted by Overholser's associates, those staff members of St. Elizabeths whose findings differed so markedly from his own:

Q. Doctor, I understood you to say that you based your opinion partly on your own observation and partly on examination of records at the hospital.

A. That is right.

Q. Do you have with you the records of the hospital showing his present condition?

A. Yes, sir.

Q. Could you produce them?

A. Surely, it is in my briefcase.

Q. Have you, yourself, treated Mr. Pound, or has that been left to your associates out there?

A. Partly to the associates.

Q. Are these records the records made by the staff?

A. That is right.

Q. And will you state by referring to them what the records show as to his present state of mental health?

A. It is a rather bulky record, as you see.

Q. Can you summarize it?

A. Essentially, it is that there has been very little change in his condition since he came in. A summary of the case from the time he came in is pretty much in line with what I said this morning, and the whole staff has seen him. There has been some discussion about him which has not been formal; in fact, no formal diagnosis has been made as yet.

Q. No formal diagnosis?

A. No.

It is a curious fact indeed that neither Matlack nor Anderson pushed or probed Overholser for further information concerning this specific issue. It was Cornell's contention that it would not have made any difference anyway if the conflicting reports of the young doctors had been read, as they would have been far outweighed by the opinions of Muncie, King, Overholser, and Gilbert, who expressed not the slightest doubt in their view that Pound was not sufficiently sane to stand trial, and never would be. At trial's end, therefore, Overholser left the courtroom, his bulky briefcase intact, the medical reports untouched and unread.

Dr. Joseph Gilbert was the final witness to be called. His testimony dealt with Pound's symptomatic behavior while under observation at Gallinger Hospital:

> . . . When I [saw] him he . . . complained that . . . he . . . felt unusually fatigued . . . he describes his feeling at the time as being unable to get flat enough in bed, and then during the various examinations he spoke of this fatigue and exhaustion very frequently, and more or less—I mean it was consistent, it was present all of the time he was interviewed, whether for a short or long period.
>
> While he was in the psychiatric department of Gallinger he remained in bed practically all of the time, with the possible exception of sitting up for his meals, or going to a bathroom nearby, and during long periods of interviews with him he remained reclining in bed, with the additional symptom of restlessness, rather rapid movements about the bed, and suddenly sitting or rising to the upright sitting position, or to move quickly about from the bed to a table nearby to get some paper, book or manuscript, and then to as suddenly throw himself on the bed and again assume the reclining position. This fatigue and exhaustion, which he states was completely reducing him, as he said, to the level of an imbecile in his thinking capacity, was notwithstanding the fact that he was undergoing no amount of physical activity. His thinking and mental activities were so greatly interfered with during the long or short periods of interviews that he easily, and a number of times during longer periods, became quite exhausted, emotionally and physically, too.
>
> Along with that was a certain amount of rather marked restlessness notwithstanding the reclining position in bed, and quick movements either into bed, or movements of experimentation, or movements to as-

sume the sitting position, or movements to secure a book, a sheet of paper, or other articles in the room, in an agitated type of physical activity.

He spoke of his mental processes being in a fog, to use his own words, that he admits during these periods of severe fatigue that he was unable to undertake temporarily any mental activity, and also complained of pressure throughout various regions of the head, what he described as a feeling of hollowness, going through this gesture [indicating] with his fingers, describing the vortex of the skull, indicating that there was a feeling not only of pressure but of hollowness in that particular part of the cranium.

Q. Can you say whether in having him describe his symptoms and attitudes to you there was any suspicion whatever of malingering, or did he appear to be entirely open and truthful about it?

A. I did not feel that there was any element of conscious malingering in any of the symptoms that were expressed during my various examinations of him.

I have not so far gone into what might be called the purely psychiatric symptoms, but I did not feel that there was any conscious element of malingering.

Q. In other words, he may not himself have been testifying about his true physical condition, but the things he told you he actually believed to be true?

A. Yes, I think that is correct.

Dr. Gilbert's testimony was followed by a brief meeting before the bench between Cornell and Matlack in which it was decided not to call Pound as a witness. Judge Laws then issued a summary and brief explanation of the case for the benefit of the jury. He concluded with these words:

> . . . In a case of this type where the Government and the defense representatives have united in a clear and unequivocal view with regard to the situation, I presume you will have no difficulty in making up your mind. However it is my duty as the judge that whenever an issue is submitted to a jury to say to the jury that you are the sole judge of the facts, so when you retire to the jury room now select a foreman and try to make up your minds whether this defendant is presently of unsound mind, and when you make up your minds you answer the questions that the clerk will submit to you, and if you find that he is not of unsound mind you will return that kind of verdict.

The jurors retired at 3:55 p.m. and returned three minutes later to render the verdict:

THE CLERK OF THE COURT: Mr. Foreman, has the jury agreed upon its verdict?

THE FOREMAN OF THE JURY: It has.

THE CLERK OF THE COURT: What say you as to the respondent Ezra Pound? Is he of sound or unsound mind?

THE FOREMAN OF THE JURY: Unsound mind.

THE CLERK OF THE COURT: Members of the jury, your foreman says you find the respondent Ezra Pound of unsound mind and that is your verdict so say you each and all?

(All members of the jury indicated in the affirmative.)

(Thereupon, the hearing was concluded.)

Pound at St. Elizabeths Hospital, circa 1957. (*Courtesy Harry Meacham. This photo originally appeared in the* Richmond News Leader.)

Pound outside the District Court, Washington, D.C., April 18, 1958, just after the treason indictment had been dismissed. (*Wide World Photos.*)

2

I most certainly never "adhered to the Kingdom of Italy against the U.S.," but how the hell to make anyone understand ANYthing—without educating 'em from age of 6 to 60—beats me. 20 years' work to prevent the damn war starting, etc. God bless the survivors.

—Letter to E. E. Cummings,
December 1945[1]

It has been your habit for long to do away with good writers,/You either drive them mad, or else you blink at their suicides,/Or else you condone their drugs, and talk of insanity and genius,/But I will not go mad to please you.

—"Salutation The Third,"
1914

Dickens and Poe in tandem could not have designed a more forbidding, lackluster setting than St. Elizabeths. "That place, beginning with its great red-brick front gate," wrote Michael Reck, "is a lesson in ugliness." Massive brick hospital buildings connected by narrow, mudcolored footpaths reminded Reck of Mencken's dissertation on the American "libido for the ugly." Seen from afar, the asylum, in Washington's Congress Heights adjoining Bolling Air Force Base across the Anacostia River, resembled a barren medieval fortress.

Yet the grounds themselves, 400 acres of rolling grasslands, were densely wooded.[2] Giant elms, oaks, maples: this acreage had once been part of an arboretum, and the trees still bore identification plaques in English and Latin. There were outdoor tennis courts. And the institution was self-contained: the 7000-patient colony ran its own bakery, icehouse, laundry, library, machine and electric shops. It even operated a small railroad that was probably the last steam, coal-fed switch engine in the country in regular use; every fall and winter it ran along its mile of track to the main railroad, bringing the many tons of coal necessary to heat the 125 buildings on the hospital grounds.

The patients sprawled everywhere. On cold and rainy days they lined the gloomy, dark corridors; on warmer days they sat outdoors on benches or in roped-off enclosures on the grass beneath the trees. They wore a kind of gray prison garb with oversized house slippers or sneakers on their feet. Some crawled about on their knees or stood on chairs and howled. Most of them, their tranquilized faces drained of all expression, sat with their hands clasped between their knees, not moving at all, sunk in listless dejection.

So the poet had been remanded to St. Elizabeths, there to remain until restored to sanity; declared mentally and physically fit by the doctors and superintendent of the hospital, he would be released into the custody of the United States Marshal, and his case returned to the courts. He had considered the Sanity Inquisition a farce, albeit a means to an end, a necessary evil. In the course of the hearing he had exploded only once: the triggering word had been "fascism." "I never did believe in fascism, God damn it," Pound had yelled, jumping out of his seat. And then: "I am opposed to fascism." The eruption had added to the drama.

Now this sequel: he would have to learn how to survive within these walls, in this universe "where the dead walked/and the living were made of cardboard." He learned quickly that he could survive only by living inside his own head, or vicariously, via the news he received from the outside world, whether brought by visitors or by letter. "Gtst difficulty," he wrote to D. D. Paige, "is to get people to write me *enough* letters to keep me aware of life *outside* the walls."[3] To Eileen Kinney: "I can't hold two sides of an idea together but can live on memory if someone BRINGS it."[4]

At last, someone did bring it: in June of 1946, Dorothy Pound succeeded in having her lapsed passport renewed. She sailed to America aboard the S.S. *Marine Carp* and then flew to Washington, where she was met by the Mapel sisters. Previously, Julien Cornell had explained to Mrs. Pound that although the doctors who had seen her husband had found him paranoid, she would, when she saw him, find him his "usual self" ("... the mental aberrations which the doctors have found are not anything new or unusual, but are chronic and would pass entirely unnoticed by one like yourself who has lived close to him for a number of years").[5] Assurances aside, Mrs. Pound did not, quite, find him his usual self; he was far more agitated and incoherent than he had been before that summer in Pisa.[6]

Mrs. Pound wrote to Cornell (July 14, 1946):

> I have now seen Ezra three times—the first time for an hour. I find him very nervous and jumpy. I believe his wits are really very scattered, and he has difficulty in concentrating for more than a few minutes. During the one hour we spoke mostly of family odds and ends,—on Thursday of his Chinese translating chiefly, and I have introduced myself to the head of Ch. Dept. in Congressional Library who is much interested in Ezra's work. Today Ezra spoke of my trying to find out what was going on in the outside world. He has newspapers, but naturally hasn't much faith in that kind of news.
>
> I met the mother of a young man E.P. has talked with in St. Elizabeths. She was full of the idea of "going to the Women of the P.E.N. Club, and making them ask the President for clemency." I said it was important to choose the right moment.
>
> I do believe we must try to get Ezra *out* of that place. He himself says he'll never get well in there and has said so each time to me. He wants to know very much how far you understand the case. He does not feel, I rather gather, that you are "on to" all his economic learning. He has made the following statement to me—"Treason is not an extraditable offense."
>
> When he gave himself up in May, 1945, he volunteered to go to the U.S.A. "to give information to the State Dept." instead of which they handcuffed him and took him to prison. He says in passing that a man cannot be handcuffed in a moving vehicle.
>
> What I am wondering is how can E. be gotten into a private sanatorium, less imprisoned, and if he left St. Elizabeths, would those four doctors still be in a position to testify to his mental instability. What can be done as quickly as possible, in safety? He says he has had no contact with any "adult" mind. Of course 15 minutes makes a break—but that's all. T.S. Eliot evidently feels strongly he should be moved. I am writing to Laughlin by this post. What places are there? Dr. Overholser is still away.
>
> The Misses Mapel so very kind and helpful.[7]

Cornell responded immediately. He agreed that the poet would be better off in a private sanatorium but did not feel that the time was right to present a new motion for bail. He suggested waiting at least until the fall when public clamor in opposition to Pound would begin to subside.

He also assured Mrs. Pound that he had a sound understanding of the entire case, including Pound's economic theories and the motives underlying his broadcasts. He had made it a point, he said, to study not only Pound's poetry but his economic tracts and had read up on Social Credit in general.

On November 7, Pound, still confined to the hell-hole and allowed visitors for only fifteen minutes daily, received a letter from Cornell: "Now that the elections are over I am proceeding as planned to make application for your release since all concerned seem to be agreed that this is the most opportune time."[8]

What was open to question was the incarceration, seemingly for life, of an accused man who had not been tried.[9] "You are presumed to be innocent until proved otherwise," the November 7 letter said, "and since there is no prospect that you can ever be proved guilty, you cannot in my opinion be indefinitely confined merely because of the indictment." The attorney based his argument on Dr. Overholser's latest medical opinion: that Pound, although able to function, was permanently and incurably insane. Here was a neat distinction: the subject was too insane to stand trial but not so insane as to have to spend the rest of his natural life behind institutional walls.

The application for bail was drawn up January 3, 1947; the case was heard on the twenty-ninth:

"Comes now the defendant by his counsel, JULIEN CORNELL, and moves the court for an order admitting the defendant to bail and for the grounds of this motion respectfully shows:"

The pertinent paragraphs follow:

6. Defendant's attorney has been informed by Dr. Winfred Overholser, Superintendent of St. Elizabeths Hospital, based upon his examination and treatment of the defendant which covers a period of about one year beginning at about the time of his admission to Gallinger Hospital on December 4, 1945, that in his opinion (1) the defendant has been insane for many years and will never recover his sanity or become mentally fit to stand trial on the indictment, (2) the defendant's mental condition is not benefited by his close confinement at St. Elizabeths Hospital where he is kept in a building with violent patients because of the necessity for keeping him under guard, and it would be desirable from the point of view of the health and welfare of the defendant if he could be removed to a private sanatorium, and (3) the defendant is not violent, does not require close confinement and the public safety would not be im-

paired if he were allowed the degree of liberty which a private sanatorium permits for patients who are mildly insane.

7. It therefore appears from Dr. Overholser's opinion, based upon a full year of observation and treatment, that the defendant can never be brought to trial on this indictment and will for the rest of his life be presumed innocent in law, although he may remain under the charge of treason. It appears also from the medical standpoint that the continuance of his present incarceration is not desirable and his transfer to a private sanatorium would benefit him.

8. If on medical grounds the defendant should be released from custody, then to continue to hold him would be equivalent to a sentence of life imprisonment upon a man who is and always will be presumed innocent. He would be confined for the rest of his life because of an accusation which can never be proved. It is respectfully submitted that such confinement would be unlawful and unconstitutional.

Cornell's bid fell through; the application (motion) for bail was summarily denied. But the youthful attorney had foreseen a legal tug of war; he was not at all surprised and slowly began to prepare a petition for a writ of habeas corpus in which he repeated many of the same arguments. This petition was presented by Dorothy Pound, acting "as Committee for the person and estate of Ezra Pound," and was filed in District Court on February 11, 1948. It was, however, likewise dismissed, and the writ—against Dr. Winfred Overholser, as well as "aides and assistants and whoever has the custody of the body of Ezra Pound" —was not issued.

According to Cornell, this setback was also only temporary. He felt confident that the defense stood a reasonable chance of obtaining a reversal on appeal. The case would not be an easy one, he instructed his client, because there appeared to be no precedent and also because of popular feeling against the poet. "I want you to know that the appeal will be difficult," he wrote to Dorothy Pound, "and that while I am confident in the justice of our position, victory is by no means assured." The attorney's letter (March 4, 1948) concluded: "If it is necessary to carry the case to the United States Supreme Court, we will probably not have a decision until next fall, but the intermediate appellate court should reach a decision within the next two or three months."[10]

Cornell planned to base his appeal on more or less the same issues he had attempted to promote in the original petition for a writ of habeas corpus. The legal question here is important and is best illustrated by certain key passages to be found in the petition itself:

11. My husband, Ezra Pound, is held in custody pursuant to the authority of Section 211 of Title 24 of the United States Code which provides as follows:

"If any person, charged with crime, be found, in the court before which he is so charged, to be an insane person, such court shall certify the same to the Federal Security Administrator, who may order such person to be confined in Saint Elizabeths Hospital, and, if he be not indigent, he and his estate shall be charged with expenses of his support in the hospital."

12. The release from custody of persons so confined is provided in Section 211b of Title 24 of the United States Code which is as follows:

"When any person confined in Saint Elizabeths Hospital charged with crime and subject to be tried therefor, or convicted of crime and undergoing sentence therefor, shall be restored to sanity, the superintendent of the hospital shall give notice thereof to the judge of the criminal court, and deliver him to the court in obedience to the proper precept."

13. There is no provision in the statutes for the release from custody of a person who is found to be permanently insane and consequently unable to be tried, yet whose mental condition does not require confinement in a hospital or asylum. The statute does not prohibit release of a person confined under such circumstances, but merely fails to make any provision to cover such an eventuality.

14. I am informed by counsel that my husband has the legal and constitutional right to be released from custody, because there is no justification in law for his continued confinement. When a person has been accused of crime and found to be of unsound mind, he may be properly confined for the reason that (1) there is an indictment pending against him under which he may be brought to trial if and when he recovers his sanity, or (2) his mental condition is such that he requires hospitalization, or (3) it would be dangerous to the public safety for him to remain at liberty. In the first case, the state is exercising its police power under which it may apprehend and confine persons awaiting trial while in the other cases the state is acting as the guardian and *parens patriae* of persons who are unable to provide for their own welfare. But unless the state can properly bring to bear either its police power or its power of control over insane persons for the welfare of themselves and the general public, the state has no legal or constitutional right to hold in custody an insane person merely because he had been found to be insane. The Constitution still guarantees to him that his liberty shall not be taken away without due process of law, and if his own and the public welfare

does not require it, he may not be deprived of his liberty by confinement in an institution. In the case of my husband, Ezra Pound, there is no reasonable possibility that he will recover his sanity, and, therefore, he can never be brought to trial under the indictment. It is also clear that his insanity is of a mild sort which does not require his continued hospitalization. Under these circumstances, if my husband is held indefinitely in confinement, he will in effect be confined for the rest of his life, solely because an indictment is pending against him which can never be resolved by trial.

15. It is a fundamental principle of law that every person is presumed to be innocent until he has been found guilty, and also that no person may be imprisoned until his guilt has been determined by due process of law. Under these principles, the indictment against my husband is no evidence of his guilt, and he must be presumed innocent of the charge against him, and such presumption will endure for the rest of his life, because he will never be in condition for trial. As a result, a presumably innocent man is being held in confinement and will be confined for life, merely because he has been charged with crime, and has not sufficient mental capacity to meet the charge. His confinement on such grounds is nowhere authorized by statute, or by any principle of law, and would deprive him of his liberty without due process of law in violation of the Fifth Amendment to the United States Constitution.

WHEREFORE, your petitioner prays that a Writ of Habeas Corpus be issued by this court directed to Dr. Winfred Overholser, Superintendent of St. Elizabeths Hospital, to produce the body of Ezra Pound before this court, at a time and place to be specified therein, then and there to receive and do what this court shall order concerning the detention and restraint of Ezra Pound, and that he shall be ordered to be discharged from the custody of the respondent and released to the care of the petitioner, as the Committee of his person and estate.

Dorothy Pound
Petitioner

The appeal, however, based as it was on the original writ, was soon rescinded. On March 15, 1948, Cornell received a letter from Dorothy Pound: ". . . Please withdraw the appeal at once. My husband is not fit to appear in court and must still be kept as quiet as possible; the least thing shakes his nerves up terribly. I want nothing attempted now until the November elections are over."[11] For all practical purposes, this letter marked the end of Julien Cornell's involvement in the case.

It was later ascertained that Ezra Pound, and not his wife, had insisted that the case be handled in this fashion. Pound refused to place himself at the mercy of a "corrupt" Supreme Court. He had no faith in the American legal system, no faith in American legislators or the American way of life. What he was after was a Presidential pardon, a full pardon with all the trimmings, something approximating France's absolution of Voltaire. He was no Lord Haw-Haw, Tokyo Rose, or Axis Sally, but a man of benevolence and understanding. A pardon, on the other hand, entailed factors beyond anyone's control. Pound could not, in fact, be pardoned, because he had not been convicted of any offense and there was nothing to pardon him for.

The legal maneuvering was not all for naught. Following the January 1947 court action in which Cornell sought an application for bail, the poet was removed, by court order, from Howard Hall and placed (on February 4) in the more comfortable, less restrictive, Chestnut Ward (Center Building, second floor), where Pound occupied his own small, 8′ × 10′ cubicle with a view of the grounds. His visiting privileges were extended from fifteen minutes to two hours a day. He entertained his visitors in the noisy and crowded corridor outside his room; a screened-off alcove with round table and chairs served as his reception area.

It was to this site that the creators and followers of modern literature flocked. Charles Olson continued to visit for a time, until he could take Pound's anti-Semitic remarks no longer. Rudd Fleming, a young university lecturer, and his wife visited off and on for over nine years; Pound and Fleming worked together on a number of translations of Greek plays, including the *Electra* of Sophocles. These Pound renditions were never published, but they did point the poet toward another play which was published—*The Women of Trachis* by Sophocles. Two professors from The Catholic University—James Craig La Drière and Giovanni Giovannini—were among the regulars. Witter Bynner went to see him and found "the same great, booming boy, or so he seemed, who clutched me with a bear-hug and cried out, 'After forty years.' Time and the beard had made little change for me in his presence."[12] E. E. Cummings and his wife, Marion Morehouse, traveled to St. Elizabeths on several occasions; Cummings compared Pound's incarceration to his own imprisonment in France during 1917, backdrop for his stirring prose account, *The Enormous Room*. William Carlos Williams came to visit; he noted that Pound, his hair unruly and gray, had begun to resemble the beast in Cocteau's experimental film *La Belle et la Bête*. Despite antipathy for his friend's political and antihumanitarian biases, Williams never stopped lauding Pound's verse. He wondered, though, how the poet could remain so apparently unmoved by his own confinement, so undaunted by his surroundings, and so entrenched in the same ideas that had motivated him for years.

Whenever he was in the United States, T.S. Eliot made it a point to drop in on Pound. While strange, vacant-faced men drifted about, the Possum and the Brer Rabbit conferred. Over the years, the two poets had diverged markedly—Eliot toward the high Anglican church, Pound toward economics. But the warmth between them was still there. "There is always a core of solid sense in Mr. Eliot's talk," Pound told friends. He prized that solid core; it was what was most lacking in his own life these days.

Shortly after one of his visits, Eliot wrote to Julien Cornell, expressing grave concern over the dire conditions of Pound's incarceration:

November 24, 1948

My dear Cornell,

After my visit to St. Elizabeths Hospital I came away with one very clear notion of something that should be done for Ezra Pound which his well-being seems to me to require.

Mrs. Pound told me that Pound was only allowed out of doors at the times when the other inmates of his ward were allowed to go out, under the supervision of a warder. It seems to me that it ought to be permissible for him to go out alone in the grounds with his wife, and with her responsible for his returning in due time. This would, incidentally, give a relatively greater degree of privacy than is possible under the conditions in which he can be visited indoors. I am not in the least suggesting that he should be allowed to leave the grounds.

Could you take this point up with Dr. Overholser? I saw him only before I had visited Pound, and before Mrs. Pound had told me of this restriction. Surely he is entitled to have some fresh air daily, upon this condition.

I also think that it would be desirable to enquire whether there is not some other building on the grounds in which he could be confined, where he could have somewhat more normal conditions, and not be among patients of the types of insanity among which he is at present.

I am writing in some haste, as I have still to pack for my departure from Princeton tomorrow.[13]

Cornell sent a copy of the foregoing to Dr. Winfred Overholser at the hospital, and Overholser replied:

I have your letter of November 29th enclosing the inquiry from Mr. T.S. Eliot about Mr. Ezra Pound. I had a brief talk with Mr. Eliot at the time of his visit to Washington, but unfortunately, as he says in his letter, this was before he had seen Mr. Pound. I have some hesitation in accepting the suggestions made by Mr. Eliot. It remains a fact that Mr. Pound is under indictment for the most serious crime in the calendar and that he has at the present time far more privileges than any other prisoner in the Hospital. He is on a quiet ward, has a room by himself and is allowed a good deal of latitude in the way he occupies himself. His wife visits him very frequently. When I found that the walking parties had been suspended in the winter I saw to it that on days when the weather was good these were reinstituted, but I found that Mr. Pound refused to go out on any but the first.

He has supreme contempt for the patients on the ward regardless of the ward he might be on since he is inclined to be rather supercilious in his views of practically everyone with whom he comes in contact.

I can assure you that we shall do everything within reason for the comfort of Mr. Pound, but in spite of his being a well-known author, I question whether I should put myself in the position of giving unusual privileges to him over and above those which he already enjoys.[14]

A further influx of visitors to St. Elizabeths included: Achilles Fang, Allen Tate, Thornton Wilder, Conrad Aiken, Guy Davenport, Stephen Spender, Frank Ledlie Moore, Norman Holmes Pearson, Michael Lekakis, Elizabeth Bishop, Katherine Anne Porter, Bö Setterlind, Rolf Fjelde, and Langston Hughes. Marshall McLuhan made several visits from his home-base in Toronto and on one of them brought along a young literature student, Hugh Kenner, who soon thereafter wrote his landmark study, *The Poetry of Ezra Pound*. Robert Lowell, in and out of mental hospitals himself, came to see Pound. So too did poets Fred Seidel and Paul Blackburn. Juan Ramón Jiménez, who was to win the 1956 Nobel Prize in literature, made it a point to drop in on the prisoner while serving as professor of Spanish literature at the University of Maryland. At St. Elizabeths, the two authors conversed in Spanish. During one of Jiménez's last visits Pound told him "You are an exile *from* your country; I am an exile *in* my country."[15]

Marianne Moore secured permission from Dr. Overholser and came to visit. She brought Pound chocolates, which he was very fond of, and peanuts for the squirrels and blue jays on the lawn. She climbed up the spiral steel steps of Central Building and knocked on the locked door of Chestnut Ward. The official who admitted her said, "Mr. Pound is a great help to us with the other inmates. It is good of you to come to see him." Miss Moore replied, "Good of me? You have no idea how much he has done for me—and for other writers. It's the least I can do."

Pound helped her with her translations from La Fontaine. She told Charles Norman: "I was feeling fit and ready to die, and I thought of him. I have boasted that I have never asked anyone for help. But I sent him about six of the Fables." She included a note: "The editor in charge feels that I had better put the material away for a few years (I think he said ten). . . . I infer that my ear is not good. Will you take time to tell me if the rhythms grate on you?"

Pound answered on stationery bearing the device "J'Ayme Donc Je Suis":

"Yes m'dr Marianna/ the least taint of quality an/or merit upsets these blighters. Lez see the rest of 'em. I shd try Faber or at least some-one in London."

He sent another letter:

"Let E. P. attempt having 'em printed in one of the few periodicals he reads."

One year later:

"E. wd/be glad to help but cannot concentrate. [on back]: KICK OUT this god damned french syntax, with relative clauses. WRITE the sense in plain english, PROSE, and then versify the SENSE of your prose."[16]

Quoting Cicero, Marianne Moore contributed a Pound tribute to Noel Stock's *Ezra Pound: Perspectives* (1965):

"What Ezra Pound required of poetry, he exemplified in person, I think: Ut doceat, ut moveat, ut delectet: teach, stir the mind, afford enjoyment—his three offices of the orator."

Also a visitor was the Greek scholar Edith Hamilton, who, with chauffeur and limousine, appeared at the hospital once a month, for a time. One of her conversations with Pound was recorded for posterity by another party present on that occasion:

(Pound shows Miss Hamilton several of the Confucian ideograms.)
POUND: This ideogram means respect, the root of respect, respect for the kind of intelligence which enables the cherry tree to grow cherries. Now, this other ideogram represents the man carrying a lance and the spoken word from the mouth, meaning the crusade to find the rightly-aimed word. Yeats said to me that if they knew what we thought, they'd do away with us. They want their poets dead.
EDITH HAMILTON: A Chinese friend of mine was told in the examination

halls at Nanking of a great Confucian scholar, such a scholar that he wrote a letter, and there was only one man in all China who could understand it. That is not very democratic, I'm afraid. That is aristocratic, like you, Mr. Pound.

POUND: But it is democratic as long as it provides that anyone may have the opportunity to learn enough to read that letter.

EDITH HAMILTON: You always puncture my balloons, Mr. Pound.

POUND: You haven't been out since my latest theory that Dante was a real democrat and Shakespeare a bloody snob.

EDITH HAMILTON: I'm no Shakespearian, Mr. Pound, but I must quarrel with you there. I don't believe Shakespeare ever had that fixed an idea.

POUND: In the Inferno, Dante doesn't pay any attention to the class from which the characters sprang.

EDITH HAMILTON: But he didn't have any common men in his Inferno. They were all important people. He didn't portray the torturing of the common man.

POUND: Shakespeare was propounding this idea of a limited monarchy in his twelve histories.

EDITH HAMILTON: I don't think so. I think he was too careless a man to do anything like that. And I think that Mr. Dante was more aristocratic than Mr. Shakespeare. [She quotes Hamlet's Soliloquy.] The soliloquy was Mr. Shakespeare coming through—the only time I know where he really came through. By the way, is that Rousse translation of Homer a good one?

POUND: It doesn't have the movement or the sound or any approximation of one. Edwards in the Hudson has done the best translation, but it hasn't got the right quantities in it.

EDITH HAMILTON: Is anyone doing a good translation?

POUND: There are probably fifty or sixty people doing bad translations, and I know of five or six incompetent young men doing better translations that will not be good enough, but they are trying to make a good translation.

EDITH HAMILTON: Mr. Pound is such a naughty fellow (to MRS. POUND.) What do you do with him when he's like that? Does scolding do him any good?

DOROTHY POUND (laughs): Oh help, I gave that up long ago. (POUND grins, pleased at having amused the ladies.)[17]

One day, Louis Zukofsky came to visit, accompanied by his wife and son, Paul, a violin prodigy aged ten, who entertained the poet on the lawn of St. Elizabeths by performing solos of Bach, Mozart, Corelli, and the Janequin motet "Les Oiseaux," which Pound had transcribed at Pisa as Canto 75, the musical Canto.

Archibald MacLeish appeared at the hospital twice, the second time in December of 1955. For two hours the two poets talked peacefully and sensibly about literature and the state of the arts. The encounter apparently moved MacLeish. Later, he wrote eloquently of his dismay at witnessing "a conscious mind capable of the most complete awareness . . . incarcerated among minds which are not conscious and cannot be aware" and commented on "the patience and kindliness of the man who suffers it."[18] When he left the hospital that winter day, having spent an afternoon amidst the bedlam, he was determined to do his utmost to secure Pound's release from captivity as quickly as possible.

In the course of his incarceration, Pound became involved in two separate literary controversies: both shook the foundations of the academic community. The first occurred late in 1945 and concerned the Imagist and the publishing firm of Random House, which decided that year to exclude twelve Ezra Pound poems from their Modern Library Giant *An Anthology of Famous English and American Poetry*. Edited by William Rose Benét and Conrad Aiken, the anthology posted the following explanation in lieu of the poems:

> At this point Conrad Aiken included in the Modern Library edition of his anthology, on which the present text is based, the following poems by Ezra Pound: *Envoi (1919), The Tree, The Tomb of Akr Caar, Portrait d'une Femme, Apparuit, A Virginal, The Return, The River Merchant's Wife, The Flame, Dance Figure, Lament of the Frontier Guard*, and *Taking Leave of a Friend*. When the publishers insisted on omitting these poems from the present edition, he consented upon one condition: that it be clearly stated in print that his wishes were overruled by the publishers, who flatly refused at this time to include a single line by Ezra Pound. This is a statement that the publishers are not only willing but delighted to print.

Julien Cornell responded to this printed statement by writing a stern letter to Mr. Bennett Cerf, then president of Random House, threatening the publishing firm with a libel suit on the grounds that Pound had not been proven guilty of treason in a court of law. The matter did not rest there. When Cerf took the problem of censorship to the readers of his column in the *Saturday Review of Literature*, he was deluged with a flood of correspondence. So vehement were some of these letters that Cerf decided to include the dozen poems in the next edition of the anthology and made a public statement to that effect. The 1950 edition of the Modern Library anthology contained the poems, accompanied by this note:

> After the publishers of the Modern Library omitted the poems of Ezra Pound from the first edition of this volume, a veritable avalanche of praise and blame, equally divided, descended upon them.
>
> Nothing could have been further from the intention of the publishers than to exercise arbitrary rights of censorship. We now have decided to include these poems of Ezra Pound in order to remove any possible hint of suppression, and because we concede that it may be wrong to confuse Pound the poet with Pound the man.

Pound the poet versus Pound the man: that dichotomy was at the heart of the second controversy as well. This furor, the more publicized of the two, began with the bestowal in 1949 of the first Bollingen Prize for poetry to *The Pisan Cantos*, published by New Directions in 1948. The $1000 award, established by Paul Mellon through the Bollingen Foundation, was made by vote of the Fellows in American Letters of the Library of Congress, an advisory board appointed by the Librarian of Congress. The members of this board—Conrad Aiken, W. H. Auden, Louise Bogan, Katherine Garrison Chapin, T. S. Eliot, Paul Green, Robert Lowell, Katherine Anne Porter, Karl Shapiro, Allen Tate, Willard Thorp, Robert Penn Warren, Theodore Spencer, and Léonie Adams—issued this statement in defense of their recommendation that the prize go to Pound: "The Fellows are aware that objections may be made to awarding a prize to a man situated as is Mr. Pound. . . . [But] to permit other considerations than that of poetry achievement to sway the decision would destroy the significance of the award and would in principle deny the validity of that objective perception of value on which civilized society must rest."

The decision caused a storm. The critic Dwight Macdonald applauded the award as "the brightest political act in a dark period." Albert Deutsch, long a Pound opponent, denounced all those who had supported Pound as turncoats and compared the incarcerated poet to Benedict Arnold. William Barrett asked his readers how lines such as "Pétain defended Verdun while Blum/was defending a bidet" and "the goyim are undoubtedly in great numbers cattle/whereas a jew will receive information" merited a prize.

The question of the Pound award was stimulus for editorial and literary discussion in any number of varied magazines. For a few weeks at least, Pound and poetry were front-page news, and every man, woman, and child with an opinion felt compelled to comment. A symposium in *Partisan Review* (May 1949) made ax-and-hatchet politicians out of our mildest intellectuals:

W. H. Auden: "Anti-Semitism is, unfortunately, not only a feeling which all gentiles at times feel, but also, and this is what matters, a feeling of which the majority of them are not ashamed. Until they are, they must be regarded as children who have not yet reached the age of consent in this matter and from whom, therefore, all books, whether works of art or not, which reflect feeling about Jews—and it doesn't make the slightest difference whether they are pro or anti, the *New York Post* can be as dangerous as *Der Stürmer*—must be withheld."

Robert Gorham Davis: "If Ezra Pound's *Cantos* are read with a wider literary and historical sense than the 'new criticism' permits, they gain in meaning. As poetry they fail, despite Pound's sensibility. Their incoherence is real incoherence; it is not 'achieved form.' But against the author's intention they are highly revealing. They are a test case for a whole set of values, and stand self-condemned. They are important documents; they should be available, they should be read. But they deserve no prize."

Clement Greenberg: "Life includes and is more important than art, and it judges things by their consequences. I am not against the publication of *The Pisan Cantos*, even though they offend me; my perhaps irrational sensitivity as a Jew cedes to my fear of censorship in general, and to the anticipation of the pleasure to be gotten from reading poetry, and I have to swallow that consequence. But I wish the Fellows had been, or shown themselves, more aware of the additional consequence when they awarded their Bollingen Prize."

George Orwell: "He [Pound] was a contributor to Mosley's review, the *British Union Quarterly*, and accepted a professorship from the Rome government before the war started. I should say that his enthusiasm was essentially for the Italian form of fascism. He did not seem to be very strongly pro-Nazi or anti-Russian, his real underlying motive being hatred of Britain, America and 'the Jews.' His broadcasts were disgusting. I remember at least one in which he approved the massacre of the East European Jews and 'warned' the American Jews that their turn was coming presently. These broadcasts—I did not hear them, but only read them in the BBC monitoring report—did not give me the impression of being the work of a lunatic."

Karl Shapiro: "I voted against Pound in the balloting for the Bollingen Prize. My first and more crucial reason was that I am a Jew and cannot honor anti-Semites. My second reason I stated in a report which was circulated among the Fellows: 'I voted against Pound in the belief that the poet's political and moral philosophy ultimately vitiates his poetry and lowers its standards as literary work.' This statement of principle I would place against the official statement of the Fellows, which seems to me evasive, historically untrue, and illogical."

Dissenters dominated the scene, but there were other views. Hayden Carruth, for one, shared Dwight Macdonald's sentiment that Pound had earned his award. Under Carruth's editorship, *Poetry* magazine published a pamphlet in 1949 defending Pound against a vicious attack by Robert Hillyer, launched in the pages of the *Saturday Review of Literature*. *The Case Against the Saturday Review of Literature* contained statements by Allen Tate, Léonie Adams, and Luther Evans; also reprints by Malcolm Cowley, Aline B. Louchheim, and the editors of *The Hudson Review*; letters from Archibald MacLeish, Mark Van Doren, William Meredith, William Van O'Connor, Cleanth Brooks, and Yvor Winters. Included with it was a copy of a letter of protest from John Berryman directed to the editors of the *Saturday Review*, which read in part:

> . . . Under the pretense of attacking the award of the Bollingen Prize to Ezra Pound, you sanctioned and guided a prepared attack on modern poetry and criticism, impugning not only the literary reputations but the personal characters of some of its foremost writers. In the blanket attack you included persons not connected with the award in any capacity, as well as its donor. Through the technique of the smear and of "guilt by association" you linked the names of T.S. Eliot, Ezra Pound, Paul Mellon, and Carl Jung, and adumbrated a Fascist conspiracy, for which you did not produce the evidence, and by implication you included in this attack not only certain of the Fellows in American Letters of the Library of Congress, but also a larger group of unnamed writers who were participating in the conspiracy.

Seventy-three signatures were affixed to this brief; among them were Newton Arvin, R. P. Blackmur, Richard Chase, E. E. Cummings, Francis Fergusson, Wallace Fowlie, Joseph Frank, Stanley Edgar Hyman,

Randall Jarrell, Alfred Kazin, Harry Levin, Arthur Mizener, J. F. Powers, Philip Rahv, I. A. Richards, Mark Schorer, Delmore Schwartz, Donald Stauffer, Peter Taylor, Glenway Wescott, and Stark Young.

Before the stir subsided even Radio Moscow got into the act, commenting: "One is prompted to ask how low and miserable must be the quality of modern bourgeois poetry in America if even the insane and verified ravings of a confessed madman could win a literary prize?" (March 21, 1949).[19]

Only Pound, at St. Elizabeths, maintained his composure. Generally speaking, he was indifferent to the affair, referring to the Bollingen as the "Bubble-Gum Award." The government, however, refused to issue a second Bollingen Prize, and the administration of the award was taken over by Yale University. In explaining the government's position, Senator Theodore Green of Rhode Island, chairman of the Library Committee, informed a *New York Times* reporter (August 19, 1949): "We are opposed to the Government discriminating between individuals in the matter of taste. There are no standards to apply, only personal opinions." And the Honorable Jacob Javits, later U.S. Senator from New York State, inserted material in the *Congressional Record* of August 2, to the effect that it was his opinion that fascists were taking over the Library of Congress. He wanted to know what, if anything, was being done to counter their attack.

During all this, Pound occupied himself with his work. In 1947, New Directions published his Confucius: *The Unwobbling Pivot* and *The Great Digest*. A revitalized and enlarged *Personae* appeared shortly, as did a new volume of *Selected Poems*. In 1950, *The Letters of Ezra Pound*, edited by D. D. Paige, was published by Harcourt, Brace and by Faber and Faber a year later. A new edition of *Guide to Kulchur*, with a blurb on the dust-jacket written by Pound, was published in 1952. *The Translations of Ezra Pound* came out in 1953, the same year as his *Literary Essays*. In 1954, Harvard University Press issued his translation of the three hundred "Odes" of ancient China under the title *The Classic Anthology Defined by Confucius*. *The Hudson Review* published *The Women of Trachis* in its winter issue, 1953–54, and the BBC's Third Programme produced the Sophoclean drama on April 25, 1954, with one of Pound's active supporters, Denis Goacher, playing the role of Hyklos, son of Herakles and Daianeira.

His correspondence also continued full force. He wrote to everyone who wrote to him and to many who didn't. To a professor at Haverford College who wanted to start a "Catullian Quarterly" he sent a list of would-be backers and contributors. To a professor at Rutgers he sent a list of books by contemporary Italian writers which he felt merited translating. He wrote to George T. Slavin: "1. I shd LIKE to save the constitution   to that end have cert. stuck my neck as far as a man can without getting it broke. 2. I bloody well never adhered to the Kingdom of Italy."[20] To Mary Barnard: "Will they never civilize this . . . country. Even the fat-headed english have sense enough to eat @ some restaurant once a week/or month with a few people they dont particularly like in order that life persist—letters.—etc."[21] To J. D. Ibbotson "Nuts on socialism . . . constitution only alternative to Muscovite avalanche. Only *true* barrier."[22]

He wrote frequently to William Carlos Williams, addressing him as "Deer Bullll," "Voui, mon vieux coco," "My dear old Hugger-scrunch," "My Dear Old Sawbukk von Grump," and "Dr. Pedagogue." His blithe letters of former years—in which he spoke of "fresh meat on the Russian steppes" or referred to the war in Spain as being of "no more importance than the draining of some mosquito swamp in deepest Africa"—were replaced by less abusive but equally antagonistic notes. During February of 1946, for example, while still in the hell-hole, he wrote:

OK Dr. Pedagogue
2 simple questions

1. What do you think of Gesell?
2. Whom do you *agree* with?

What is the best book you have read in last 7 years? or at least tell me one good one.

EP[23]

And from Chestnut Ward came a letter which wound its way into Williams' *Paterson*, Book III—its focus: ". . . There must be one hundred books . . . that you *need* to read fer yr/mind's sake." And he went on to name a few of them: the Greek tragedies (Loeb editions), Frobenius, Gesell, Brooks Adams, and the Golding Ovid.

He wrote to Cummings: "I spoze with 25 years time lag it will—or rather someone by then will tell the . . . . that I was not at any time sending axis propaganda but my own."[24] To Henry Swabey: "What the

. . . hell CAN you say for a pen Empire that lets best poet of the generation Bunting (B. Bunting) disappear sans trace, and no breath of curiosity even among the ten alleged literates still on the dung heap."[25] To Jackson Mac Low: "What I am driving at is that some kike might manage to pin an antisem label on me IF he neglected the mass of my writing. BUT the dirtiest smear of all was to try to call Mussolini an anti-sem."[26]

Conversation was Pound's chief mode of recreation at St. Elizabeths. Whether seated in the windowed alcove off his corridor or perched in an aluminum deck chair on the hospital lawn beneath elms, his first love was the monologue. Often his talk was merely an anecdote from *The Cantos*. He was a fine mimic, and like most good actors, a ham at heart. With voice and facial expressions, he could re-create Eliot or James in London or the Boston-bred Henry Adams talking to the young Santayana, the latter informing the former that he planned to teach at Harvard. Pound imitated Adams' Boston brogue and the old man's palsied head-shaking as he responded: "Teach . . . at *Hah-vahd*? Teach (three-second pause) at *HAAH-VAHD*?? (Three seconds more.) It . . . (three seconds) . . . cahn't . . . (five seconds—vigorous cranial tremors) . . . be done."[27]

Anecdotes filled up the air. When he spoke of old friends his conversation was usually quite affectionate. He called *Finnegans Wake* "that diarrhoea of consciousness," but laughed joyfully recalling a drunken Joyce in Paris trying to kick down the chandelier. Yeats was "fond of spooks." Wyndham Lewis had been a good friend but a complete eccentric. Hemingway, having posed in shorts and T-shirt for a Rheingold beer commercial, became the butt of a private joke which never failed to amuse.

After a number of years in the hospital, Pound was granted new privileges: he was permitted "evening hours," which meant that he could sit outdoors until 8 p.m., and was allowed to play tennis on the asphalt courts. Many who knew him, including Noel Stock, have suggested that the poet rather enjoyed this period of his life, despite the obvious drawbacks. He certainly enjoyed being the center of attraction at the afternoon group gatherings which he hosted, and possibly he began to appreciate the services—including room and board—available to him as a result of his incarceration.

He was further gratified by the fact that he served as something of a guru for a cult of young disciples—wanderers, Social Creditors, rabid right wingers—who, through the years, became his most devoted and regular visitors at the hospital. It did not seem to disturb Pound that these avid communers represented the fringe of society. What counted was their willingness to work and learn, their desire to further the cause —to read for the cause, to write for the cause.

Thus the cause flourished: Dallam Simpson was publishing *Four Pages*; David Gordon was publishing the *Academia Bulletin*; T. David Horton was publishing *Mood*; William McNaughton was publishing *Strike*; Eustace Mullins was publishing *Three Hands*. In England, Henry Swabey was editing a Social Credit paper called the *Voice*. And in Melbourne, Australia, the vortex was proliferating in the pages of Noel Stock's *Edge* and in the four-page supplement to the weekly Social Credit paper, *The New Times*.

To these and similar publications Pound contributed innumerable political and economic notes, editorials, and commentaries, altogether of "quite indeterminable purport and [of] little, if any, visible effect," employing a variety of pseudonyms (Herbert Briscoe, W. Watson, Xavier Baylor), but all written in that unmistakably strident, tough, "pushy" style so representative of his correspondence. The publications, most of them printed by hand and distributed on street corners, served primarily to inform and educate Pound's immediate circle of followers. The understated message in all of them was that there existed an "evil conspiracy" in America, "the obvious way to combat which was by building up a counter-conspiracy." Nothing, of course, was ever very clearly defined—"it was part of this underground's mystique that it was never necessary to spell things out" (that, incidentally, also being one of the cardinal rules of *The Cantos*). The purpose of this clandestine countermovement was, however, made abundantly clear. Among its immediate aims were the following: to rescue the United States from the Left/ Liberal establishment and poetry from the free-versist Marxist usurpers who had taken it over in the mid-1930s and still held it captive; to restore sovereignty to the people from the monopolizers of credit; to investigate the Jews; to purge the Jews; to get Pound's work better known and understood and the poet released from St. Elizabeths.[28]

In addition to the writing of his own political and economic tracts, Pound took it upon himself to fill up these various publications with selections of historical interest and to line up a team of willing contributors of merit. *Edge* was graced, for instance, with the first publication of Pound's verse translation, "Five French Poems" (Rimbaud and Tailhade); a translation by S. V. Yankowski of Thaddeus Zielinski's "The Sibyl"; Alan Neame's translation of Jean Cocteau's *Léone*; passages from Henry Swabey's study "The Church and Usury"; and Pound's translation of a Mussolini diary ("Notebook of Thoughts"), written by the Duce during his captivity in La Maddalena and Ponza in 1943, before being rescued by the Germans. The first issue of Dallam Simpson's leaflet (*Four Pages*) contained a statement by Cummings: "Since you ask me, I'd love to experience a universe of individual human beings; where-and-when the privacy of each individual was honoured—not merely respected . . ." and also an item on economics from Olivia Rossetti Agresti, with whom Pound was in correspondence during the entire period of his incarceration. Among the journal's later contributors were Basil Bunting and the late Duke of Bedford, a monetary reformer who published frequently in a variety of economic journals.

Strike, edited in Washington by the young cabdriver-poet McNaughton, was Pound's most convenient outlet for prickly political pronouncements and the like. Each issue of the four-page monthly contained a liberal sprinkling of Poundiana. The contributions ranged in subject matter from favorable editorials on Joseph McCarthy and the House Un-American Activities Committee to anonymous reviews of individual books and authors. In the September 1955 issue of *Strike*, Pound wrote: "TRAVEL NOTE. Two zones have been located INSIDE Gunther. (1) the torcellian vacuum. (2) the vacuum absolute." One month later he reviewed a recent novel by another author: "There has been no adequate advertise of a novel called *Liberty Street*. It is badly written but it does deal with a useful topic, to wit, the grease in bureaucracy. The type of well-dressed illiterate who has never done anything but annoy the ill-starred members of the public who fall under his detailed control. This is not a local problem, all countries produce this type of vermin, which should provide material for whole flocks of aspiring historians." A political note appeared in *Strike* #7 (December 1955): "Thought grows, administrative arrangements decay. AFTER our Constitution had been betrayed by the traitor presidents Wilson and F.D.R. the idea of a vocational representation developed in Italy, after that came the Portuguese Labor Law. If we were a serious people, and if our universities and their faculties were serious organizations we would be more familiar with the

NATIONAL LABOR LAW OF THE REPUBLIC OF PORTUGAL."

There were other disciples and disciple-oriented activities. Out of the wilderness these lost sheep flocked to him. Sheri Martinelli was one of them. Painter, dropout, lover, she recorded her trek:

> I was going around t/world with the/clouds and t/air like Chief of All The Chiricahuas Apache: Cochise—when Ezra Pound (known to us as: "E.P.") "spoke to my Thoughts." I, too, "carried My Life on My Finger-Nails" and they were each & all a different colour because I was a working painter—a Fighter in The Ethical Arena wherein you KNOW what's Really Wrong because you did that yourself and you found out by The Way of Be-ing There. Artist.
>
> Maestro.
>
> Was There Ever Such A Man, Dear Goddess. A Man who found me Lost in Hellishness but FIRST I had been Made Trusting & Loving & Innocent & Ignorant "Love One Another Children" . . . so as not To Even Know for a split second that I *was* Lost. I was having a Ball. All Those Sweet-faced Indians! T/guiltless sex of animal desire; pure, simple & uncompli-cated by The Falsities of Any Other Facts! Freedom of Diet & No Two Days Running The Same.

And in the same letter:

> Today I remembered: His great Faith in Art when he said: "PAINT me out of here, Cara." So Painted E.P. in Paradise as he had sung me from Purgatory. . . . This is The Power of Art Work. With Out A Picture of It inside of your Mind—how can you Find It?[29]

That portrait of Pound—in reds and yellows and blues—appeared in a booklet of reproductions of paintings, *La Martinelli* by Sheri Martinelli, printed by Pound's young Milanese publisher, Vanni Scheiwiller, in 1956; Pound wrote the introduction. He also composed sections of *Rock-Drill* and all of Canto 90 with her in mind. "The stone taking form in the air/ac ferae,/cervi . . .": he painted her in reds and yellows and blues.

In addition to La Martinelli and the crew already named, there were other assorted local worshipers: Veronica Sun, David R. Wang, Reno "Skip" Odlin, Frampton Hollis, Jean-Marie Châtel, and Rex Lampman. Hollis was a young film-maker whose conversation amused Pound; Châtel was a university dropout "mobilized" by Pound to write the Great American novel; and Lampman, a fellow inmate at St. Eliza-beths, wrote the humorous "Epitaph" for the flyleaf of a new edition of *Pavannes and Divigations* (New Directions, 1958), an updated version of *Pavannes and Divisions* (Alfred A. Knopf, 1918): "Here he lies, The Idaho Kid,/The only time he ever did."

Another of Pound's younglings at St. Elizabeths was John Kasper who drifted in during the early 1950s from Columbia University. A course in early modern poetry with Babette Deutsch at the School of General Studies provided Kasper with all the introduction to Pound's poetry he would ever need. It was not *il miglior fabbro*'s verse but his politics which spurred him on. In a term paper for Miss Deutsch's class, Kasper wrote: "I thrilled at Nicolo Machiavelli, Friedrich Nietzsche and the political Ezra Pound. Hitler and Stalin are clever men and Wilson a fool. The weak have no justification for living except in service of the strong. What is a little cruelty to the innocuous when it is expedient for the strong ones who have the right to alter the laws of life and death before their natural limits?"[30]

This was the kind of mind Pound could mold. When Kasper joined the inner sanctum at St. Elizabeths he became its most sanctimonious member. In 1956, he started an "Ez for Prez" campaign and proffered the following advice in reaction to the Supreme Court's unanimous decision on integration:

JAIL NAACP, alien, unclean, unchristian
BLAST irreverent ungodly LEADERS
HANG 9 SUPREME COURT SWINE
(this year domine '56)
BANISH LIARS
Destroy REDS (ALL muscovite savages)
rooseveltian dupes
EXPOSE BERIA's "psycho-politics"
DEATH TO USURERS

This Pound-like pronunciamento, in imitation of the original Lewis–Pound *BLAST* manifesto, was issued under the imprint of the White Citizens Council of South Carolina, and ended with these words: "NOW DAMN ALL race-mixers/the stink: Roose, Harry & Ike . . . the pink punks, flatchested highbrows, homos, perverts, freaks, golf players, poodle dogs, hot-eyed Socialists, Fabians, scum . . . liars for hire, the press gang, degenerate liberals crying for the petrefaction of putrefaction." Some of these phrases were straight Pound, borrowed, among other places, from Cantos 14 and 15.

The Seaboard White Citizens Counsel, organized by Kasper, aimed to end "integration" in Washington, put the NAACP on the Attorney General's "subversive list," and abolish "rock-and-roll." Membership was open to anyone eighteen and white, who "believes in the divinity of Jesus Christ." Jews were not allowed.

It was only a beginning. In Louisville, Kentucky, Pound's newest devotee told a gathering of Southern segregationists: "They might have soul, they might have a right to pray. I know some men who claim they have seen niggers with tails."[31] He billed himself "Segregation Chief" and plunged farther south. In Clinton, Tennessee, he riled up another audience with taunts, threats, and a wave of cross-burnings. The next day the National Guard was dispatched, and Kasper was arrested on a federal warrant charging interference with court-ordered integration at Clinton High School. He was sentenced to a year in prison, but was quickly released on $10,000 bail raised by the White Citizens Council. He went to Florida, where he continued his campaign. This time it was not the NAACP he was after, but the Jews. "He told a rally Saturday night in Inverness he would demand that the Florida legislature raise voting requirements to five years' residence in the state, four years in the county, and three years in the precinct. The object, he said, is to 'deal with those Jews in Dade County [Miami] who keep moving back and forth and yet control the state machinery'" (*New York Post*, March 11, 1957).

Back in Tennessee, among the "real" people, Kasper again was arrested and charged with criminal contempt of the federal district court "on grounds he violated a permanent injunction against interference with peaceful integration of Clinton High School" (*The New York Times*, March 24, 1957). The ensuing publicity did not help Pound's bid for freedom. One comment on the Pound–Kasper liaison came from Ernest Hemingway: "I believe Ezra should be released and allowed to write poetry in Italy on an undertaking by him to abstain from any politics. I would be happy to see Kasper jailed as soon as possible" (*The Paris Review*, Spring 1958). As things developed, both of Hemingway's wishes were to come true.

In England, meanwhile, Peter Russell, editor of *Nine*, formed an "Ezra Pound Society" to help publicize the poet's plight. It was for this reason that he brought out English translations of a sextet of Pound's prewar and wartime writings; the collection, published under the group title

Money Pamphlets by £, included *An Introduction to the Economic Nature of the United States; Gold and Work; What is Money For?; A Visiting Card; Social Credit: An Impact; America, Roosevelt and the Causes of the Present War*. But the project backfired; the pamphlets reminded public and press alike of Pound's pernicious role during the war. Such was the case also with a second Russell enterprise, an anthology of ultra-conservative essays, titled simply *Ezra Pound*, which the freelance editor selected on the occasion of the poet's sixty-fifth birthday; the book was panned for its particular brand of political cant and rancor.

Another major publishing venture which did not sit well with the poet's critics was the Square Dollar Series, an experiment directed by Pound but carried out by T. David Horton and, until his arrest, John Kasper. The aim of this undertaking was to publish texts not widely enough read in American colleges and universities. The series featured an advisory committee consisting of Otto Allen Bird (University of Notre Dame), J. C. La Drière (Catholic University of America), L. R. Lind (University of Kansas), Marshall McLuhan (University of Toronto), and Norman Holmes Pearson (Yale). Each of the books in the series was priced at one dollar; these included: Fenollosa's *The Chinese Written Character* (in the same volume as Pound's *The Unwobbling Pivot* and *The Great Digest*); *The Analects of Confucius*, translated by Pound; *Gists from Agassiz* selected by John Kasper; *Barbara Villiers or A History of Monetary Crimes* by Alexander Del Mar, the late-nineteenth-century American economist whose work, Pound claimed, "had been made to disappear" by the usurocracy; *Bank of the United States* by Thomas Hart Benton; and Del Mar's *Roman and Moslem Moneys*.

In addition to selecting all the material published under the imprint, Pound composed the "blurbs" and advertising material. One of his circulars began:

> The boredom caused by "American culture" of the second half of the XIXth century was due largely to its being offered as "something like" English culture, but rather less lively; something to join Tennyson in "The Abbey" perhaps, but nothing quite as exciting as Browning, or Fitzgerald's Rubaiyat. . . . Square Dollar is starting with American writers who can hold their own either as stylists or historians against any foreign competition whatsoever. Agassiz, apart from his brilliant achievements in natural science, ranks as a writer of prose, precise knowledge of his subject leading to great exactitude of expression.[32]

The Square Dollar books were, the brochure pointed out, "A set of texts intended to foster the spirit of reverence for the intelligence working in nature" and also "Basic education at a price every student can afford." Del Mar, according to Pound, was America's most illustrious (and uncelebrated) historian: "He made great progress from Mommsen, and corrected Thorold Rogers. Along with Louis Agassiz and Leo Frobenius, he builds upon Alexander von Humboldt's 'art of collecting and arranging a mass of isolated facts, and rising thence, by a process of induction to general ideas.' "

Under Pound's guidance, Kasper and Horton published several other monographs: a small pamphlet containing the text of the American Constitution, a fourteen-page chapter from Del Mar, called *History of Netherlands Monetary Systems*, and *A Study of the Federal Reserve System* by Eustace Mullins. Plans were made for additional tracts. It was announced that "The basic sections of Blackstone necessary to a well-balanced study of the humanities will be published as soon as possible." The book did not appear at this time; nor did selections from *The Institutes* of the famous seventeenth-century jurist Sir Edward Coke, another of the poet's late discoveries. "Coke on Misprision" was the title of one essay the Imagist wrote following his release. It was Coke's contention that a man who knowingly did not report treason to the authorities was aiding and abetting the enemy and was thus guilty of a serious crime. Pound often cited *The Institutes* in defense of his own activities during the war, claiming that he was only doing his duty in drawing attention to Roosevelt's wrongdoings. "Misprision," he ventured, "is what I would have been guilty of had I not made the broadcasts."

David Rattray's "Weekend with Ezra Pound" (*The Nation*, November 16, 1957) draws a retrospective picture of what it must have been like to visit with the poet while he was a patient on the ward:

> Before we had a chance to talk about anything, Pound jumped up again: "You'll have tea, won't you?"
> I said that I would, and immediately he was everywhere at once, in a frenzy of activity, loading himself with jars of various sizes, tin boxes of sugar and tea, spoons and a saucer. I stood up in embarrassment, not knowing what I ought to do, but Mrs. Pound beckoned me from her corner: "Let's sit here and talk while he makes the tea." She was sitting behind a ramshackle old upright piano, so as not to see the people in the

hall or be seen by them. Miss Martinelli was making sketches for a portrait of her.

Suddenly Pound was standing before me, holding out a peanut-butter jar filled with hot tea. When we settled again, he glared up at me and said, "Well, what specific questions have you? Or did you just come to talk? I'd just as soon talk."

Pound talked and, in his usual fashion, jumped from one subject to another, beginning with Byzantine culture and ending with the toils of usury. Suddenly he rose from his chair and strode across the hall to his room, beckoning Rattray to follow. The cubicle was strewn with wadded papers, bits of envelopes, trampled books, pencils, lengths of string, cardboard files, trunks, old paint cans, jars filled with teabags or scraps of food. On the walls were paintings, some by Sheri Martinelli, and there was a broken-down dressing table with a large mirror. Pound gave his guest a copy of Del Mar's *Roman and Moslem Moneys* and then scrambled under the table in search of food-tins. These were filled with doughnuts and bread which he put into a paper bag for Miss Martinelli. A further search underneath his bed yielded a box containing hard-boiled eggs and salami, which he gave to Rattray to share with some of the other visitors in the alcove outside.

Eustace Mullins provides another glimpse of Pound, much more pastoral than the one Rattray paints, but in its own way equally telling:

> On summer afternoons, the Pounds created a little world of their own. . . . Usually they sat near a giant Japanese pine, but because of the ban on taking photographs, I was never allowed to take a picture of Ezra standing beneath this rugged tree, which was so much like him.
>
> Whenever they emerged from the ward, carrying their chairs, their string bags bulging with odd lots of food, books and letters for the visitors, their pet blue jays always set up a great screeching, wheeling above them as the chairs were arranged. Then the squirrels would come skipping down from nearby trees for their daily treat. Ezra would lure them up onto a bench with a peanut tied to a string. He taught them to take the nut from between his fingers, a practice that I considered reckless.
>
> During these afternoons, Ezra's manner was that of a deservedly popular professor at a small but highly-regarded school, who was having some of his star students in for tea. His *bonhomie* was always perfect for the occasion; he was a benevolent Socrates who as yet had no intention of drinking the cup of hemlock which his fellow citizens had offered him. Dorothy Pound was also as apt and self-effacing as a professor's wife, as

she poured tea, murmured "Shush" when the bluejays became too noisy, and produced little paper bags for the shells of hard-boiled eggs, so that we should not litter the lawn.[33]

Accurate as both of these portraits might be, neither conveys any sense of personal suffering. That Pound did suffer is self-evident. What few conveniences he appears to have enjoyed as a ward of the state were certainly overshadowed by the very presence of the place itself. Yet for all his torment, he seemed almost stoically determined to gain his freedom only on his own terms. There were those who began to wonder if he really wanted out. Among the skeptics was T. S. Eliot, who more than once wrote to Archibald MacLeish that their friend Pound seemed willing to approve the most harebrained schemes but to find objections to make to any scheme which offered any reasonable possibility of success.

Olga Rudge, also, found Pound's attitude bewildering. She came twice to the United States to visit the poet, once in the spring of 1952 and again briefly in the fall of 1955. From the beginning, she worked hard to help secure his release. At the end of the war, she went to Rome to see General Mark Clark to encourage him to intervene in the case. Then, in October 1948, she distributed a petition to Rapallo's citizenry attesting to Pound's honorable intentions during the war; the document was sent, via the American Embassy in Rome, to the State Department in Washington, D.C. It read:

> The undersigned having known the American writer Ezra Pound in Rapallo where he resided from 1924 declare that to their knowledge he took no part in Fascist activities in this town. He was never present at the local meetings or enrolled in the Fascist organizations.
>
> He was always considered as an American citizen, a friend of Italy, openly sympathizing with certain Fascist principles relating to political economy and in the fight against Communism which he held to be a danger to the United States themselves. During the war Mr. Pound continued to reside in Rapallo and from the tenor of his life it was evident that not only was he not benefiting from any special privileges but was suffering privations and economic hardship. The fact being evident that he had never acted from hope of gain enabled him to maintain the respect even of those among his fellow townsmen who disagreed with his political opinions.
>
> Mr. Pound's activity during the long years of his residence in Rapallo was always artistic and cultural as shown in his literary criticism and writings on political economy.

He always behaved with correctness and has never demonstrated anti-semitism.

The signers included many of Pound's friends and neighbors—doctors, shopkeepers, waiters, priests, farmers, municipal clerks, teachers, a lawyer, a painter, a newspaper editor. The final name on the petition was the mayor's, a man by the name of Maggio, an anti-Fascist, who added a postscript—Noel Stock writes—saying that he had appended his name "in consideration of the good that Mr. Pound had always done in Rapallo."

But petitions, pamphlets, mailings were not enough. Pound alone represented the controlling factor in his own case. Responsibility for the fact that he had never been brought to trial rested in the first instance with Pound himself and his lawyer, and thereafter with the psychiatric staff at St. Elizabeths. It was Pound who refused to accept anything but his own contention that he was sane—that, indeed, he had never been anything else except for a brief breakdown in 1945. At the same time he refused to plead anything but insanity—*mente captus*—and thus avoided the possibility of a trial through which he might eventually clear himself.

His daughter, Mary, married since 1946 to a Russo-Austrian nobleman by the name of Boris de Rachewiltz, made the trip to Washington in 1953. Sometime before her journey she had traveled to England to confer with T. S. Eliot, "the best-informed and most authoritative" of Babbo's friends:

> Tall, thin, stooping, with a sad enigmatic smile, he opened the door and led me into his study: ". . . you must forgive . . . a better welcome . . . I am just out of the hospital . . . we are alone in the house." I was struck by the austerity of the room. An imposing desk behind which he sat and behind him a blocked-up fireplace. A small electric—perhaps gas—stove burning. I felt awed and yet sorry for him, he should have been sitting in front of a blazing fire, that's what he needs, I thought. The room and his words felt chilly. After a while he went to fetch some tea: "Oh let me . . ." "No, no, stay where you are." *Inchiodata*. And stooping, he returned carrying a small tray with two cups and a tiny plate of very thin, very dry Saiva biscuits. And I inwardly: I wish I could give him some bread and butter. . . . He talked. Gently, uninterruptedly. Twice I dared put a question, he raised his hand and said: We'll come to it later. We never came to it. It was time to go.[34]

What the Possum said during the meeting lingered in her mind: "I fear your father does not want to accept freedom on any terms that are possible. The idea that you should be sent over to persuade him to sign a statement is a travesty."

Mary de Rachewiltz stayed in America three months and saw a number of people in connection with the case: Tiffany Thayer, Caresse Crosby, James Laughlin, Francis Biddle, Julien Cornell. Cornell set up an appointment for her with Arthur Garfield Hays and Osmond K. Fraenkel, counsel and associate counsel of the American Civil Liberties Union. She met with State Department and Department of Justice officials. But always the results of these meetings were the same. Nothing, nothing to be done.

He was not to get through hell (or purgatory) in a hurry but was to languish in his modern-day dungeon like Ozymandias in the desert, a living lesson of what happens when an artist meddles in business other than his own. The paideuma he fostered while in gaol kept him going. Labor Day, 1952, found him on the lawn beneath his favorite tree. He gave a reading that day of Provençal poetry and was recorded on equipment borrowed from a local radio studio. The session had been arranged by two recent college graduates, Marianne Mantell and Barbara Holdridge, publishers of Caedmon Records, under the condition that it would not be released while the poet was still confined. "Bird in cage does not sing," Charles Norman reports him as saying.

There were several Pound readings during this period, although none by Pound himself. "Ezra Pound, A Critical Study" was broadcast over the BBC in August 1954, followed shortly by a reading from Canto 88 (based on Benton's *Thirty Years' View*) and a Marius Goring recital of *Homage to Sextus Propertius*. "A Tribute to Ezra Pound," written and produced by Frederic D. Grab and Reid B. Johnson, both of whom had visited Pound at St. Elizabeths, was presented by the Yale Broadcasting Company on December 5, 1955, in celebration of the poet's seventieth birthday. The program included tributes from Auden, Hemingway, Williams, Cummings, MacLeish, and Stephen Spender. And Louis Dudek wrote a tribute for the seventy-year-old poet for the Canadian Broadcasting System, featuring readings from *The Cantos* and *Hugh Selwyn Mauberley*.

Bits and pieces of *The Cantos* appeared in a wide selection of American publications: *The Quarterly Review of Literature, The Rocky*

Mountain Review, The Yale Poetry Review, Sewanee Review, Virginia Quarterly Review. In 1953, Pound had helped draw up a manifesto on "the neglect of the Greek and Latin classics" and the need "to maintain language in a healthy condition"; the document was signed by some dozen university professors, headed by Hugh Kenner and Marshall Mc-Luhan. One of Pound's shadier enterprises was to help found an organization called "The Defenders of the American Constitution," the president of which was a retired Lieutenant-General of the Marine Corps, Pedro del Valle; *Task Force*, a publication edited by David Horton, became this group's monthly mouthpiece.

The poet continued to obsess over the Jews and was relentless in his efforts to warn select correspondents of their imminent infiltration. When not engaged in such distractions, he was either off on some other political or economic tangent, or intent on pressing forward one of many personal issues. In August 1955, Chestnut Ward TV carried news of the death of Wallace Stevens; Pound reminded his friends of Stevens' worth to poetry and encouraged Doc Williams to pen a feeling obituary. There were times when Pound worried about his own health. He suffered from chronic arthritis of the neck and back and was in constant search of a lasting cure. Ernest Hemingway was the recipient of at least one Pound note dealing with the subject of insane asylums. There was need of reformed asylum architecture, more fresh air and sunlight, improved facilities for the inmates. A similar letter went to Frank Lloyd Wright at Taliesin who, upon learning of the poet's plight, quipped something to the effect that America was intent on stifling its uncommon men; it would learn, he said, that it could not live without them.[35]

Further revelations: in 1956, a new devotee turned up. Marcella Spann, a young, quiet, and attractive graduate of a college in Texas, was an instructor in the English department of a junior college in Washington. She was to compete now with Sheri Martinelli for the position of Maestro's muse, and within a short period of time had taken over the job.

Another muse, this one permanently displaced, was the Maestro's wife. Dorothy Pound visited St. Elizabeths nearly every day for twelve years. Her husband's confinement forced her to live in the drab and run-down neighborhood surrounding the hospital. The rooms she rented, first at 10th Place, S.E. and then at Brothers Place, S.E., were small and bare, contained only the most functional necessities: bed, desk, chair, books. She seemed to exist only for her husband, one visitor remarked, and as a result suffered almost without respite.

Yet for all her selflessness she was terribly naïve; and Ezra was inordinately obstinate. He seemed to go out of his way to insult those who tried to help him most. His letters to MacLeish were full of rebukes and rebuffs:

July 30, 1956: "What the Hell do you read? Where has yr/ paideuma got to re 'Brain Washing'? Have you read Benton and Blackstone? How many years of anything are you willing to read at MY recommendation . . . ? I should have at least a little factual indication that your mind is opening to the possibilities of even yr/adored dunghill F.D.R. having erred a few points in his judgment both of the world situation and in his choice of associates."[36]

August 6, 1956: ". . . Wars are made to make DEBT and yr/old fuehrer's war was BLOODY successful. . . . Have you read testimony of army, navy and marines?? Can't make out what, if anything, you DO read."[37]

December 18, 1956: "Can I get yu to see that in 30 years you have NEVER mentioned to me ANY specific point on which you respect anyone's opinion. And when I call a louse a louse/a seller or giver of currency plates to the enemy/a cheater of the people re/price of gold, you never reply with anything specific. . . . In yr/great fog, come on, and name some SINGLE definition, some single buzzard among the mutts whom you have drifted among who will come clean on a PARTICULAR statement, or stand up against a particular accusation of error. . . ."[38]

He was less bitter in his correspondence with family—Mary and Boris de Rachewiltz—and close friends, such as Olivia Rossetti Agresti. Letters to his daughter and son-in-law touched on various subjects, ranging from Boris's participation on the editorial staff of Giuseppe Bottai's neo-Fascist publication, *ABC*, to drawn-out encyclicals against psychiatry and mental hospitals, drugs (marijuana and heroin: "POISON both of mind and body"), birth control, the Jews ("the jew is a disease"; "jewish control is the syphilis of any gentile nation"; "First great HOAX was substitution of kike god, as monopoly, for universal god"). He branched off into other areas: Graham Greene, Giuseppe Prezzolini, Catholicism, the Vatican Radio, the *Manifesto della raza*, Yeats, Dante, H. Dexter White, Joseph McCarthy, New Directions ("Nude Erections"), Westbrook Pegler, Talleyrand, Nicholas Murray Butler, Frobenius, Henry James, Egypt, H.D., Eleanor "OOozenfeld" ("who has carried vulgarity to the point of obscenity and has the mind of a lavatory attendant"), J. Edgar Hoover, Richard of Saint Victor, *The Cantos*.[39]

The Cantos saved him. The continuation of the masterwork was the real and most sustaining task of these years. *Section: Rock-Drill de los Cantares LXXXV-XCV* was published in 1955; *Thrones de los Cantares XCVI–CIX* came out in 1959. A tessellation of languages and civilizations and periods, both sequences carried on the tradition of the canticle songs as set forth in previous editions. For his efforts he received mixed reviews. His ear was sound, but he was frequently so obscure as to appear remote. Such had been the common consensus among critics since the appearance, in 1925, of his first volume of the epic (*A Draft of XVI Cantos*). Anticipating a similar reaction, Pound interrupts the first Canto of *Thrones* to remark on "this factor of difficulty and also that of choice":[40]

> If we never write anything save what is already understood, the field of understanding will never be extended. One demands the right, now and again, to write for a few people with special interests and whose curiosity reaches into greater detail.

Although it was not his intention, the presence of new work by Pound served also to remind people that one of America's foremost, if most forgotten poets, was still a prisoner on the public ward of a federal mental institution. In this sense, he was working harder than anyone to engineer his own release.

3

I can't work here. . . . The little and broken-up time that I get (with no privacy and constant interruption and distraction) makes impossible that consecutive quality of feeling so important to me. . . . My confusion is more important than a system that is a sop to mediocrity in being a mere limiting of the capacity of feeling and experience by a damning bourgeois regimentation. . . . This daily laceration and frustration of a creative impulse, carried on even a little while . . . can and surely will, with me I'm afraid, end with complete artistic impotence.
—Letter to Archibald MacLeish, August 1955[1]

I betrayed no one. You got that straight . . . it never occurred to me that a charge of treason could arise. It didn't arise until AFTER the collapse. The Brits ASKED Wodehouse to go off the air.[2] Boston judge ruled re/Best: no treason without intention. The army did not want me held . . . it is damned nonsense to say that either I or D.P. prefer me to stay in St. Eliz.
—Letter to Archibald MacLeish, August 1957[3]

Despite the fact that actual legal negotiations had ground to a halt by 1948, there were numerous attempts on the part of private individuals and groups to spring Pound from the asylum—or at least to draw public attention to his plight. Some of these efforts were less successful than others.

In the early 1950s, a number of public officials—Tom Clark, John Foster Dulles, George Stimpson, and Sam Rayburn—were contacted by Pound's backers. Not one of this well-connected foursome, however, was particularly interested in pursuing the matter, and it was quickly dropped. Senator Robert A. Taft and Ellen Borden Stevenson (Adlai's former wife) also entered the picture; both had suggestions to make, but neither could come up with a definitive plan.

Others, fortunately, were more interested in Pound's welfare. In 1953, an International Congress of Poetry, held in Venice, forwarded an official invitation to Pound, by way of the U.S. Embassy in Rome; the purpose of this good-will gesture was to demonstrate support for the poet. In 1954, Ernest Hemingway, having been awarded that year's Nobel Prize in literature, told the press in Rome: "I believe this would be a good year to release poets." He added that the Nobel Prize might well have been awarded to Pound rather than himself. The same year, José V. de Piña Martins, the Portuguese poet, broadcast an appeal for Pound's release over Vatican radio. His talk ("Ezra Pound—Prometheus Bound") was rebroadcast over the Italian radio and resulted in the publication of several articles and letters about the case in the Italian press. The *Paesa Sera* ran items by Carlo Scarfoglio and John Drummond, and Rapallo's *Il Mare* ran an entire series on the Imagist; one of the articles featured a letter from T. S. Eliot, hailing *il miglior fabbro* as "the greatest living master of English poetry."[4]

Nowhere, in fact, was there more interest in the Pound case than in Italy. This was due largely to the efforts of Mary and Boris de Rachewiltz, whose Tirolean residence served as something of a center for Poundian activity. Part of the work of the de Rachewiltz group, "Amici di Ezra Pound," included the distribution, among friends and inquirers, of clippings and offset or mimeographed copies of articles by and about *il poeta*. There were also appeals to the Italian government, including those made by the Chilean author Gabriela Mistral (Nobel Prize in literature, 1945) and Giovanni Papini (writer-poet-philosopher), to voice representations in Washington and to the ambassador in Rome, Clare Boothe Luce.

Mrs. Luce, a writer herself, became a favorite target of Italians backing Pound. Vanni Scheiwiller presented her with a petition in 1955, which included the names of Eugenio Montale, Alberto Moravia, and Salvatore Quasimodo. Another petition, drawn up by Diego Valeri, was delivered to the American Embassy in spring of 1956. It read:

> The undersigned Italian writers ardently appeal to the supreme political and judicial authorities of the United States for the restoration of liberty to their eminent colleague Ezra Pound, for ten years now confined to a criminal insane asylum, where he recently passed his seventieth birthday.
> The undersigned, some of whom were outspoken anti-Fascists and

suffered sentences at the hands of Fascism, though not entering into the political and legal merits of the question, would like to take this opportunity to express our conviction that Pound is "substantially" innocent of the accusations of high treason formulated against him at a time of struggle and kindled passion.

One can see in his conduct during the years of the war a case of madness akin to that of Hölderliń, Nerval or Dino Campana, a madness that, in his case as distinct from theirs, tragically entangled him in a lamentable, disproportionate adventure.

The undersigned, therefore, appeal to the enlightened comprehension and clemency of the American authorities for a benevolent re-examination of Pound's case and the withdrawal of the charges against this illustrious poet, whose cultural contribution to America and the entire world is so deserving of our gratitude; we express the hope that Pound, his liberty restored to him, may return to his Italy so loved by him, here to conclude his days in work-filled peace.

Among the subscribers of the Valeri petition were: Attilio Bertolucci, Enrico Pea, Vasco Pratolini, Mario Praz, Ignazio Silone, and Giuseppe Ungaretti.

For her part, Mrs. Luce took the Pound matter up with the State Department and twice, on trips home, discussed it with government officials. Although nothing came of her efforts, *Life* magazine, owned by the Ambassador's husband, Henry Luce, published an editorial (February 6, 1956) calling for the government to quash the indictment against Pound: "Pound's room at St. Elizabeths has been called 'a closet which contains a national skeleton.' There may be good arguments for keeping him there, but there are none for pretending he doesn't exist. The crimes of World War II have aged to the point of requital, parole or forgiveness. For this reason, if no other, the arguments for quashing the indictment against Ezra Pound should be publicly considered."

In England, meanwhile, two members of the Pound camp, Denis Goacher and Peter Whigham, both of whom had made the pilgrimage to St. Elizabeths, were active on behalf of the poet's release. Whigham wrote a brief account of Pound's life and work which was privately printed and distributed among London's literary set; Goacher wrote a foreword about Pound at St. Elizabeths for the Neville Spearman edition of *The Women of Trachis*. There were plans also for the publication of a number of Pound-recommended books—a selection of Blackstone's *Commentaries on the Laws of England*; Arthur Golding's translation of

Ovid's *Metamorphoses*; a new translation of Richard of Saint Victor's *Benjamin Minor; Selected Speeches* of the American statesman, John Randolph of Roanoke (1773–1833); and Gavin Douglas's translation of the *Aeneid*—but, ultimately, the series did not materialize.[5]

On the American front, Yale University was the site of a production, in 1955, of *The Women of Trachis*; sharing the bill with the Greek translation was a production of Eliot's *Sweeney Agonistes*. Between 1954 and 1956, the department of English at the University of California, Berkeley, sponsored *The Pound Newsletter*, edited by John Edwards and William Vasse. The material which the editors gathered for the *Newsletter* was later used for their *Annotated Index to the Cantos of Ezra Pound* (1959), a comprehensive guide to the first eighty-four *Cantos*. As in Italy, there were editorials and articles about Pound in a number of leading American periodicals. On April 1, 1957, an editor of *The New Republic* wrote "And yet we would like to see the government give this old man and this eminent poet his freedom—if not as an act of justice, then as an act of largesse." The September 1957 issue of *Esquire* contained a sympathetic study of the poet's case by Richard Rovere. And an editorial in *The Nation* (April 19, 1958) concluded with these words: "It will be a triumph of democracy if we set Pound free, not because he is a martyr, but because a sick and vicious old man—even if he were not the brilliant poet he is, with a luminous side that all but transcends his faults—has his rights too. In Italy he may yet write a few more beautiful pieces, and in that cracked but crystal mirror of his hold up to us once more the image of a civilization that too often drives its best creators into self-exile and political horror."

While not of major consequence so far as the outcome of the case was concerned, occasional expressions of this sort helped balance the effects of stories such as the Kasper affair, or the fury which arose among government officials over Dorothy Pound's unfortunate statement in writing, quoting her husband, that "the treason was in the White House, not in Rapallo."[6] There were other negative elements to combat. Karl Shapiro and Robert Graves, the leading proponents of an anti-Pound movement, took it upon themselves publicly to denounce their opponent at every given opportunity. Another public dissenter was Emanuel Celler, the New York Congressman and chairman of the House Committee on the Judiciary. Shortly before the poet's release, Celler held a press conference in which he told reporters: "I don't care how long Pound's been in there. Maybe we want to keep him in a little longer. . . . I can't understand how they'd let him out scot free. I can't conceive of that. Many of our men lost their lives as a result of his exhortations."[7]

An opposing point of view was provided by two politicians who also happened to write. On August 13, 1957, Senator Richard L. Neuberger of Oregon asked the Library of Congress to prepare an investigation of the entire Pound affair. One week later, on August 21, Representative Usher L. Burdick of North Dakota introduced House Resolution 403, which was referred to the Committee on Rules. The resolution read as follows:

> Whereas Ezra Pound has been incarcerated in Saint Elizabeths Hospital for the past twelve years on the assumption that he is insane; and
> Whereas many people visit him there and are convinced that he is not insane; Therefore be it
> Resolved, That the Committee on the Judiciary, acting as a whole or by subcommittee, is authorized and directed to conduct a full and complete investigation and study of the sanity of Ezra Pound, in order to determine whether there is justification for his continued incarceration in Saint Elizabeths Hospital.

The committee did not sit. Burdick referred the matter to the Legislative Reference Service of the Library of Congress, where the task of gathering material on Pound was turned over to a senior research assistant, H. A. Seiber, twenty-six years old.[8]

"The Medical, Legal, Literary and Political Status of Ezra (Loomis) Pound," also known as the Seiber Report, was delivered to Senator Neuberger and Representative Burdick several months later. A summarized version of the document was published in installments in the Congressional Record during the spring of 1958. Copies were reproduced by the Library of Congress for distribution among members of Congress. One copy went to Pound, who responded by sending Burdick a note: "I have always regarded package words as a pest. Notably the idiotic term 'anti-Semitism.' " Further: "It is impertinence to call me an amateur economist." Concerning the war years he wrote that he did "what I considered my duty in warning the U.S. against Roosevelt's hysteria." The letter concluded: "I seem to have been moved by emotion at some point of broadcasts, but component of error is to be expected in most human actions."[9]

Harry Meacham of Richmond, Virginia, president of the Poetry Society of Virginia, was another faithful Pound trooper. Through most of 1957 and 1958, Meacham waged an ambitious letter campaign on behalf of the poet, canvasing a sizable group of influential figures, among them Van Wyck Brooks, George Dillon, Norman Mailer, Westbrook Pegler, and Richard Wilbur. Others whose aid he attempted to enlist included the newspaperman James J. Kilpatrick, Jr., and Dag Hammarskjöld, Secretary-General of the United Nations. Both Kilpatrick and Hammarskjöld did what they could to help: Kilpatrick devoted several columns in the *Richmond News-Leader* to the injustices which Pound had suffered, and the Secretary-General campaigned for the poet with some hopeful results.

Hammarskjöld had actually been aware of the Pound problem long before he was contacted by Meacham. In a speech given at the Museum of Modern Art in New York, on October 19, 1954, he had cited Pound's verse:

> Modern art . . . makes us seers—seers like Ezra Pound when, in the first of his *Pisan Cantos*, he senses "the enormous tragedy of the dream in the peasant's bent shoulders." Seers—and explorers—these we must be if we are to prevail.

Later, Hammarskjöld took it upon himself to play a more direct role in the proceedings. At various intervals he talked over the Pound case with Henry Cabot Lodge, Francis O. Wilcox (Assistant Secretary of State), and Christian A. Herter, Jr. (Undersecretary of State). As a member of the Swedish Academy, he apparently discussed the possibility, with Swedish officials, of nominating Pound for a Nobel Prize, his hope being that such an award would help pave the way for Pound's release from St. Elizabeths. In November 1956, Hammarskjöld wrote to MacLeish that he had read his *New York Times* review of *Section: Rock Drill* with "high appreciation," adding, "You may know that—with the discretion imposed upon me by my office—I have been doing what I can in order to straighten out Pound's situation."[10]

Among the many artists, writers, and politicians who worked for Ezra Pound's release from "imprisonment-without-trial," none toiled harder or did more than Archibald MacLeish. Explaining his motivation to Ernest Hemingway, the statesman-poet-dramatist wrote (June 19, 1957): "I went down to see him [Pound] in December of '55. Second time I'd ever seen him. What I saw made me sick and I made up my mind I wouldn't rest till he got out. Not only for his sake but for the good name of the country: after ten years it was beginning to look like persecution and if he died there we'd never wash the stain out."[11]

And so, despite Pound's contemptuous correspondence and general resistance, MacLeish decided to dedicate himself to this singular task. In July 1956, he asked Senator J. William Fulbright if he would look into the situation. The Senator responded in the affirmative. Next, he wrote to Christian Herter, who had indicated to Hammarskjöld that he would be willing to exercise whatever influence he could in the matter. Herter reaffirmed his support. More difficult were MacLeish's dealings with Dr. Milton Eisenhower, brother of Dwight and president of Johns Hopkins University. The two were old friends but did not see eye to eye in regard to the Pound affair. In one exchange of letters between them, Dr. Eisenhower maintained that if Pound were released he could expect the charges against him to be pressed, adding that though he might be a good poet, this was immaterial. MacLeish, however, was not willing to surrender without a fight. Early in 1957, he wrote again to Dr. Eisenhower:

WIDENER W CAMBRIDGE 38
January 11 1957

Dear Milton:

I am still hard at work on the Ezra Pound matter about which I wrote you some time ago. After careful consultation with authorities at St. Elizabeths, including Dr. Overholser, I can say with confidence that it is the opinion of the responsible doctors that Pound is not now fit to stand trial and never will be. Under these circumstances the perpetuation of the legal charges against him seems to be irrelevant, not to put a stronger word to it. Robert Frost, T.S. Eliot and Ernest Hemingway are therefore writing the Attorney General suggesting that in view of his eleven years incarceration the nol prossing of the charges against Pound would be in order, not only in the interests of common humanity, but in the interest of the good name of the United States.

I know that you dissent from my view on the latter point. You wrote me, as you may recall, that it makes no difference whatever that Pound is a poet. In terms of logic this may be true but in terms of history and of civilization it is not. As you know better than I, nations are judged in the perspective of history by the way they treat their poets, philosophers, artists and teachers.

The reason for this present letter relates to this fact. I have the very best reason to believe that Pound is shortly to be awarded the Nobel Prize in Literature. I can think of nothing which would make this country look more ridiculous than to hold in an insane asylum, under criminal indictment, a recipient of the Nobel Prize in Literature. Everything our most virulent critics say about us would be justified by that single dramatic fact. If our action in so holding him could be justified in common sense we could perhaps shrug it off, but since in view of the medical testimony it cannot be justified we would look very silly indeed.

I trouble you with all this, not to try to convert you to my view but because I care deeply, as you do, about the repute of this republic, and because you are in a position to do something about it. I need not add that what I have told you about the Nobel Prize situation should be treated as confidential, except in so far as its repetition in confidence might help to bring about the desired action. By the desired action I refer solely, at this time, to the quashing of the charges, then remitting the whole problem of Pound's future to the medics who ought to dispose of it.

Forgive me for troubling you with all this again.

Affectionately
Archie[12]

Pound, of course, did not win the Nobel Prize in literature that year, or any other year, for that matter; nevertheless, a letter to the then Attorney General Herbert Brownell, Jr., was in the process of being prepared. MacLeish himself did not sign the document. Because he had held high office in the Roosevelt Administration, he realized that his own influence on the present Republican Administration would, by necessity, be limited. He was also aware of the influence a conservative "poet of the people" like Robert Frost might wield in such a battle. His immediate aim, therefore, was to mobilize the yeasty New Englander. Once assured of Frost's cooperation, he convinced Eliot to compose the letter. MacLeish edited it, then sent it around: Eliot appended his signature to it in London, Hemingway in Cuba, and Frost in Cambridge, Massachusetts. The final draft of the appeal was typed on the letterhead of the American Academy of Arts and Letters at the request of MacLeish, member and former president of the organization:

January 14, 1957

The Attorney General of the United States,
Washington
D.C.

Dear Sir,

We are writing to you about Ezra Pound who has been confined in St. Elizabeths Hospital in Washington for eleven years under indictment for treason.

Our interest in this matter is founded in part on our concern for Mr. Pound who is one of the most distinguished American writers of his generation, and in part on our concern for the country of our birth. As writers ourselves we cannot but be aware of the effect on writers and lovers of literature throughout the world of Pound's continued incarceration at a time when certain Nazis tried and convicted of the most heinous crimes, have been released and in many cases rehabilitated.

It is our understanding, based on inquiries directed to the medical personnel at St. Elizabeths Hospital, that Pound is now unfit for trial and, in the opinion of the doctors treating him, will continue to be unfit for trial. This opinion, we believe, has already been communicated to the Department of Justice. Under these circumstances the perpetuation of the charges against him seems to us unfortunate and, indeed, indefensible. It provides occasion for criticism of American justice not only at home but abroad and it seems to us, in and of itself, unworthy of the traditions of the Republic. Concerned, as we must be, with the judgments of posterity on this unhappy affair, we cannot but regret the failure of the Department thus far to take steps to nol pros the indictment and remit the case to the medical authorities for disposition on medical grounds.

May we add that this is a personal letter to you and that we have no intention at this time of making a public statement on this matter.

Could we be of service to you, a letter addressed to us in care of the American Academy of Arts and Letters at 633 West 155th Street, New York City, will have our immediate attention.[13]

Six weeks later an acknowledgment, from the office of the Attorney General, arrived at the Academy's offices in Manhattan; it was addressed to Robert Frost:

> February 28, 1957
> WASHINGTON, D.C.

Mr. Robert Frost
The American Academy of Arts and Letters
633 West 155 Street
New York, New York

Dear Mr. Frost:

This will acknowledge receipt of your recent letter, also signed by Ernest Hemingway and T.S. Eliot, regarding Ezra Pound who is confined in St. Elizabeths Hospital in Washington at the present time. I have asked that a review of the matter be made, and when it is completed I will communicate further with you.

> Very truly yours,
> Herbert Brownell, Jr.
> Attorney General[14]

The promised communication, dated April 10, 1957, came not from Brownell but from William P. Rogers, then acting as Deputy Attorney General. Rogers stated that he would be willing to meet with any or all of the signers of the original letter to discuss Pound's case. This was the break MacLeish had been waiting for. He sensed that Frost, and Frost alone, was the man best suited for the job at hand. But it was a question of directing the stubborn, eighty-three-year-old Frost, of manipulating him, and handling him with kid gloves and tact.

By the time the Rogers letter arrived, Frost was en route to England on a good-will tour, and to receive honorary degrees from both Oxford and Cambridge. MacLeish booked passage and followed after him. With T. S. Eliot also present, they conferred at the Hotel Connaught in London on a number of occasions during late May and early June. Upon his return to the States, MacLeish wrote to Frost, still in England, in care of Kathleen Morrison, director of the Bread Loaf Writers' Conference. He reminded Frost of the commitment he had made to the Pound campaign. On June 24, having returned home to Ripton, Vermont, Frost replied:

Dear ARCHIE

My purpose holds to help you get Ezra loose though I won't say my misgivings in the whole matter haven't been increased by my talks with Eliot lately, who knows more about Ezra than anybody else and what we can hope to do for his salvation. I should hate to see Ezra die ignominiously in that wretched place where he is for a crime which if proven couldn't have kept him all these years in prison. So you go ahead and make an appointment with the Department of Justice. I suppose we might be prepared to answer for Ezra's relative sanity and ability to get himself taken care of out in the world. Neither you nor I would want to take him into our family or even into our neighborhood. I shall be acting largely on your judgment. I can't bear that anyone's fate should hang too much on mine.

I am tied up here for the moment. I could be in Washington for any time on Wednesday July 17 or Friday the 19th after three o'clock or Saturday. But I should have thought that this time of year wouldn't find people in Washington and the affair might better wait until the Fall.

So much for business—bad business. We mustn't forget the good relations we have promised to have with each other this summer.

Ever yours—on either side of the Atlantic[15]

The meeting with Rogers took place late on Friday afternoon, July 19. MacLeish and Frost both attended; Eliot and Hemingway, at Mac-

Leish's request, had sent along individual letters, addressed to Frost, stating their views on the case. Frost brought the letters with him. When the meeting was over, MacLeish reported the results directly to Pound:

> 22 July 1957
> Conway [Mass.]

Dear Ezra:

Robert Frost and I went to see the boys at the Department of Justice last Friday. Hot as it was, Robert came all the way down from Ripton, Vermont.

We had with us letters from Tom Eliot and Ernest.

What the conversation boiled down to was about what we expected: though maybe a little more hopeful than we feared.

For the immediate future and so long as the [John] Kasper mess is boiling and stewing the Department will not move. I have never understood—and neither, incidentally, has your daughter Mary—how you got mixed up with that character.

Beyond that, though there are no commitments, the Department does not close the door provided somebody can come forward with a sensible plan for your future. The impression we got was that the future would have to be in the United States.

Robert has some ideas about a sensible plan which he would be glad to explore if you approve and which seems promising to me: a sound professional arrangement with your publishers which might work for you as it has for him over many years.

All this, you understand, is hypothetical as Hell. No commitments or near-commitments were made. But the door wasn't closed and we were left with the impression that once the Kasper stink has blown over they would be willing to consider proposals.

We ran into one thing you ought to know about. Somebody has spread the rumor at the Department of Justice (I heard it also in Italy) that you and your wife would really prefer to stay on at St. Elizabeths. If it is false, as I assume, your wife ought to make that clear to the Department. But if she does, ask her please not to quote me.

Did you ever get my note about our visit with that lovely Mary?

Yours faithfully, Archie[16]

During the spring, MacLeish and his wife had visited briefly with Mary de Rachewiltz in Italy; the Harvard-trained attorney had wanted to see for himself what housing arrangements could be worked out for Pound if he were allowed to return to his adopted land. As for MacLeish's allusion to a "professional arrangement with . . . publishers," New Directions now pledged to provide the poet with a guarantee of $300 per month for the duration of his life. It was not much perhaps, but with Dorothy's income from stocks and bonds, enough on which to live. Ultimately, however, the funds from New Directions were not necessary.

But with these details worked out, and Kasper safely behind bars, things began to happen. CBS Television's *The Last Word* had previously aired a program on Pound and *The Cantos*, narrated by David Daiches, which received a favorable response. The American Civil Liberties Union, represented by its executive director, Patrick M. Malin, forwarded letters supporting Pound to the Attorney General and the Secretary of the Department of Health, Education and Welfare. The Burdick Resolution, the Seiber Report, and the various articles and editorials about Pound which appeared in national magazines paved the way for a second visit by Frost to the Department of Justice to discuss the matter. The second Rogers–Frost encounter took place on October 23, 1957.

There were further developments. Christian Herter, still working on behalf of the poet and spurred on by MacLeish, wrote to Dr. Overholser at St. Elizabeths, inviting him to drop in someday "to discuss this difficult individual Ezra Pound." Dr. Gabriel Hauge, President Eisenhower's economic adviser (and brother-in-law of James Laughlin), discussed the matter with Sherman Adams, White House chief of staff, suggesting that the case be reviewed. On January 2, 1958, Attorney General Rogers (he had succeeded Brownell on November 8, 1957) wrote MacLeish: "I think the best thing to do is to discuss the matter with you when you are next in Washington. I am not sure whether it can be worked out or not, but I am certainly inclined in that direction, if it can be worked out from a legal standpoint. . . ."[17]

One final, illustrious scene: on February 27, Robert Frost attended an intimate luncheon at the White House. His tablemates that afternoon were Sherman Adams and William Rogers. In the evening, Frost was President Eisenhower's personal guest at an "informal, stag supper" which was served in the main White House dining room. The implication of these twin engagements can best be judged by the strict order of ensuing events. Five weeks after Frost's invitation to the White House, William Rogers sent out a smoke signal at a New York press conference. The report appeared in *The New York Times* of April 2: "Attorney General William P. Rogers disclosed . . . that Ezra Pound may escape trial and be allowed to go to Italy." The public responded well to the news, and freedom was suddenly a distinct possibility.

Now Sherman Adams approached President Eisenhower with a memo from the Department of Justice. The memo was duly initialed.[18] Within the week Frost was back in Washington for the briefest of meetings with Rogers. Frost said to the Attorney General: "I've dropped by to see what your mood is in regard to Ezra Pound." Rogers responded: "Our mood is your mood, Mr. Frost."[19]

The end was within sight.

The rest was mere formality. Pound's case had been taken over by Thurman Arnold, of the well-known Washington law firm of Arnold, Fortas and Porter. By coincidence, Arnold had been a student at Wabash College in Crawfordsville, Indiana, when Pound, not much his senior, was teaching there; by another coincidence, he had also been Julien Cornell's professor of law at Yale Law School.[20] On April 14, 1958, he filed a motion to dismiss the 1945 indictment, together with an affidavit by Dr. Winfred Overholser, a memorandum of points and authorities, and an appeal by Robert Frost. Appended to the latter were statements by John Dos Passos, Van Wyck Brooks, Marianne Moore, Ernest Hemingway, Carl Sandburg, W. H. Auden, T. S. Eliot, Robert Fitzgerald, Allen Tate, Dag Hammarskjöld, Richard Rovere, and Archibald MacLeish. Many of these declarations appeared in the correspondence section of *Esquire*, following Mr. Rovere's 1957 article about Pound in the same magazine. The remainder of the documents have been reproduced below; they represent the brunt of the final phase of the case.

UNITED STATES DISTRICT COURT
FOR THE DISTRICT OF COLUMBIA

UNITED STATES OF AMERICA
V.
EZRA POUND, Defendant

Criminal No. 76028

Motion to Dismiss Indictment

Comes now Ezra Pound, defendant, through his committee, Mrs. Dorothy Shakespear Pound, and moves that the indictment in the above-entitled proceeding be dismissed.

And for grounds of the said motion, he respectfully represents:

1. On November 26, 1945, defendant was indicted on charges of treason relating to certain radio broadcasts made by defendant in Italy during World War II. On November 27, 1945, he stood mute on arraign-

ment and a plea of not guilty to that indictment was entered by the Court. On December 4, 1945, defendant was admitted to Gallinger Hospital. On December 14, 1945, in pursuance of an appointment by this Court, Drs. Winfred Overholser, Marion R. King, Joseph L. Gilbert and Wendell Muncie submitted a joint written report to the Court that they had thoroughly examined the defendant on several occasions between December 4 and December 13, 1945, that it was their unanimous opinion that defendant was suffering from a paranoid state which rendered him mentally unfit to advise properly with counsel or to participate intelligently and reasonably in his own defense, and that he was insane and mentally unfit for trial. On January 18, 1946, the Court heard and granted a motion for a formal statutory inquisition to determine defendant's sanity. On February 13, 1946, the Court held such formal inquisition at which the jury, after hearing the evidence, report and conclusions of Drs. Overholser, King, Gilbert and Muncie, entered a formal verdict that the defendant was of unsound mind. Following that verdict, the defendant was committed to the custody of the United States and confined in Saint Elizabeths Hospital.

2. The defendant has remained in confinement at Saint Elizabeths Hospital since that time, where he has been the subject of constant and intense psychiatric tests, examinations, observation and study. As a result thereof, it is the opinion and conclusion of officials of Saint Elizabeths Hospital that defendant remains mentally unfit to advise properly with counsel or to participate intelligently and reasonably in his own defense and that he is insane and mentally unfit for trial, or to comprehend the nature of the charges against him.

3. Furthermore, it is the opinion and conclusion of these same officials that defendant's condition is permanent and incurable, that it cannot and will not respond to treatment and that trial on the charges against him will be forever impossible because of insanity.

4. Defendant is 72 years old. If the indictment against him is not dismissed he will die in Saint Elizabeths Hospital. He can never be brought to a state of mental competency or sanity sufficient to advise properly with counsel, to participate intelligently and reasonably in his own defense or to comprehend the nature of the charges against him. There can be no benefit to the United States in maintaining him indefinitely in custody as a public charge because that custody cannot contribute to his recovery and defendant's release would not prejudice the interests of the United States. The inevitable effect of failure to dismiss the indictment will be life imprisonment on account of alleged acts and events which can never be put to proof.

5. The primary alleged acts and events on which the indictment is based occurred prior to July 25, 1943. In the ensuing fifteen years memories have faded and direct evidence by the constitutionally-established minimum of two witnesses to each of the various alleged acts and events

have inevitably dissipated. In all probability, therefore, the United States lacks sufficient evidence to warrant a prosecution at this time.

6. Suitable arrangements for defendant's custody and care are otherwise available. In the event that the defendant is dismissed, Mrs. Dorothy Shakespear Pound, committee, proposes to apply for the delivery of the defendant from further confinement at Saint Elizabeths Hospital to her restraint and care with bond under such terms and conditions as will be appropriate to the public good and the best interests and peace of mind of the defendant in the remaining years of his life.

7. On the issues of fact thus presented, defendant respectfully requests a hearing.

WHEREFORE, Ezra Pound, defendant, by his committee, Mrs. Dorothy Shakespear Pound, respectfully moves that the indictment be dismissed.

Affidavit

DR. WINFRED OVERHOLSER, being first duly sworn, deposes and says:

1. I am the Superintendent of Saint Elizabeths Hospital, Washington, District of Columbia.

2. Ezra Pound was admitted to Gallinger Hospital, Washington, District of Columbia, on December 4, 1945. Between that date and December 13, 1945, I and Drs. Joseph L. Gilbert, Marion R. King and Wendell Muncie each examined Ezra Pound on several occasions, separately and together, pursuant to appointment by the Honorable Bolitha J. Laws, Chief Justice, United States District Court. On December 14, 1945, I and Drs. Gilbert, King and Muncie submitted our joint report to the Chief Justice that Ezra Pound was suffering from a paranoid state which rendered him unfit to advise properly with counsel or to participate intelligently and reasonably in his own defense, and that he was insane and mentally unfit for trial on the criminal charges then pending against him. A copy of this joint report is attached hereto as Exhibit A.

3. On February 13, 1946, I testified to like effect at a formal inquisition as to sanity in respect to Ezra Pound.

4. Pursuant to the determination and verdict of the jury at the aforesaid inquisition, that Ezra Pound was of unsound mind, he was committed to Saint Elizabeths Hospital.

5. I have on a large number of occasions, both alone and with other psychiatrists of the staff of Saint Elizabeths Hospital and others, intensively tested, examined, observed and studied Ezra Pound.

6. If called to testify on a hearing in respect to dismissal of the pending criminal indictment against Ezra Pound, I will testify and state under oath that Ezra Pound is, and since December 4, 1945, has been, suffering from a paranoid state which has rendered and now renders him unfit to advise properly with counsel or to participate intelligently and reasonably

in his own defense, and that he was and is, and has continuously been, insane and mentally unfit for trial.

7. Furthermore, if called to testify on a hearing, I will testify and state under oath that the condition of Ezra Pound as thus described is permanent and incurable, that it will not and has not responded to treatment, that further professional therapeutic attention under hospital conditions would be of no avail and produce no beneficial results and that he is permanently and incurably insane.

8. Furthermore, if called to testify on a hearing, I will testify and state under oath that there is no likelihood, and indeed in my considered judgment and opinion no possibility, that the indictment pending against Ezra Pound can ever be tried because of the permanent and incurable condition of insanity of Ezra Pound, and that Ezra Pound will die insane in Saint Elizabeths Hospital without trial of the charges against him if the indictment remains pending.

9. Finally, if called to testify on a hearing, I will testify and state under oath that in my opinion, from examination of Ezra Pound made in 1945, within two to three years of the crimes charged in the indictment, there is a strong probability that the commission of the crimes charged was the result of insanity, and I would therefore seriously doubt that prosecution could show criminal responsibility even if it were hypothetically assumed that Ezra Pound could regain sufficient sanity to be tried.

10. In the event that the indictment is dismissed, I will recommend the delivery of Ezra Pound from further confinement at Saint Elizabeths Hospital under suitable arrangements for his custody, care and restraint by his committee, Mrs. Dorothy Shakespear Pound. Further confinement can serve no therapeutic purpose. It would be a needless expense and burden upon the public facilities of the hospital. Ezra Pound is not a dangerous person and his release would not endanger the safety of other persons or the officers, the property, or other interests of the United States.

Memorandum of Points and Authorities
in Support of Motion to Dismiss

1. The motion to dismiss the indictment is properly addressed to the Court. The Court has inherent power to dismiss an indictment in circumstances where justice requires and where, as here, the United States will never be able to prosecute. *United States v. Pack*, 20 F.R.D. 209 (D. Del. 1957); *United States v. Janitz*, 161 F.2d 19 (3d Cir. 1947). In a case such as this where the defendant is insane and in federal custody the Court has a special responsibility and authority over the proceedings, since such a defendant during commitment stands in the position of a ward of the Court. *United States v. Morris*, 154 F. Supp. 695 (S.D. Cal. 1957).

2. The motion presents an appeal to the discretion of the Court. For this reason, we ask leave to lodge the attached Statement of Robert

Frost, who, along with many other poets and writers of distinction, has sought the release of Ezra Pound for the last several years. Although his statement does not speak to the legal issues raised, it is directly relevant to the serious considerations bearing upon this Court's exercise of its discretion.

Respectfully submitted,
THURMAN ARNOLD
WILLIAM D. ROGERS

Statement of Robert Frost

I am here to register my admiration for a government that can rouse in conscience to a case like this. Relief seems in sight for many of us besides the Ezra Pound in question and his faithful wife. He has countless admirers the world over who will rejoice in the news that he has hopes of freedom. I append a page or so of what they have been saying lately about him and his predicament. I myself speak as much in the general interest as in his. And I feel authorized to speak very specially for my friends Archibald MacLeish, Ernest Hemingway and T.S. Eliot. None of us can bear the disgrace of our letting Ezra Pound come to his end where he is. It would leave too woeful a story in American literature. He went very wrongheaded in his egotism, but he insists it was from patriotism—love of America. He has never admitted that he went over to the enemy any more than the writers at home who have despaired of the Republic. I hate such nonsense and can only listen to it as an evidence of mental disorder. But mental disorder is what we are considering. I rest the case on Dr. Overholser's pronouncement that Ezra Pound is not too dangerous to go free in his wife's care, and too insane ever to be tried—a very nice distinction.

Mr. Thurman Arnold admirably put this problem of a sick man being held too long in prison to see if he won't get well enough to be tried for a prison offense. There is probably legal precedent to help toward a solution of the problem. But I should think it would have to be reached more by magnanimity than by logic and it is chiefly on magnanimity I am counting. I can see how the Department of Justice would hesitate in the matter from fear of looking more just to a great poet than it would be to a mere nobody. The bigger the Department the longer it might have to take thinking things through.

The motion was heard in the District Court on April 18 by Chief Judge Bolitha Laws, who had presided at Pound's commitment to St. Elizabeths twelve years before. Present in the courtroom were Pound, his wife, and Omar, who at that time was a teacher at the Roxbury Latin School in Boston. Pound sat quietly at the back of the room, Dorothy and Omar at the counsel table with Arnold. Julien Cornell was also in attendance; he said nothing.

It was a brief and perfunctory proceeding. Mr. Arnold told the court that he represented not only Mrs. Pound (as Committee for Ezra Pound), but "the world community of poets and writers." The mainstay of his argument, as outlined in his motion and accompanying documents, was that unless the indictment against him were dismissed, the defendant would spend the rest of his life at St. Elizabeths, a virtual prisoner condemned for "alleged acts and events which could never be proved." A new element in Mr. Arnold's motion "was the probability that Pound had been insane at the time he made the broadcasts"; another was "the difficulty the government would face in producing witnesses for any future prosecution of the case."[21]

The Department of Justice, represented by United States Attorney Oliver Gasch, did not oppose the motion to dismiss the indictment against Pound. It was in the interest of justice and should be granted, Mr. Gasch told the court. When the order freeing Pound was handed down, Mrs. Pound rose from her seat, walked to the rear of the courtroom, and embraced her husband.

Order Dismissing Indictment

This cause came on for hearing on defendant's motion to dismiss the indictment and upon consideration of the affidavit of Dr. Winfred Overholser, the Superintendent of St. Elizabeths Hospital, and it appearing to the Court that the defendant is presently incompetent to stand trial and that there is no likelihood that this condition will in the foreseeable future improve, and it further appearing to the Court that there is available to the defense psychiatric testimony to the effect that there is a strong probability that the commission of the crimes charged was the result of insanity, and it appearing that the Government is not in a position to challenge this medical testimony, and it further appearing that the Government consents to the dismissal of this indictment, it is by the Court this 18th day of April, 1958,

ORDERED that the indictment by and the same is hereby dismissed.

Bolitha J. Laws
CHIEF JUDGE

Presented by
Thurman Arnold
William D. Rogers
COUNSEL FOR THE DEFENDANT
I consent
Oliver Gasch
UNITED STATES ATTORNEY

Although he was now free to leave the hospital, to visit friends, and to dine out, Pound continued to live at St. Elizabeths for several more weeks, having some dental work completed and slowly packing and moving out his books, papers, and other belongings. With Dorothy, he paid a brief visit to the offices of Arnold, Fortas and Porter. He wanted to thank them personally for their generosity; in addition to everything else, they had handled his case without charging a fee.

On April 29, Pound called on Representative Burdick at his home in Washington; H. A. Seiber was also present, together with reporters eager for news from the uncaged panther. Pound spoke with them for nearly an hour. "I've been making jokes about Jews all my life," he said. "Fifty years ago we had jokes about the Scots and the Irish and the Jews, and the best stories you got were from the Jews."[22] Asked about Robert Frost's efforts in his behalf, Pound replied: "He ain't been in much of a hurry." A week later the poet cleared the Frost air. Over tea, Harry Meacham read him an editorial in which it was stated that after forty years Frost had repaid Pound for his help in London. Pound smiled and said: "Frost's debt was paid when he published *North of Boston*."[23]

He was officially discharged from St. Elizabeths on May 7 into the custody of his wife. There was much red tape involved in obtaining passports, and it was the end of June before all details had been ironed out. While they were waiting, James Laughlin came to Washington to spend some time with Pound. One day, he, the poet, and Professor La Drière, in whose apartment Pound was staying, went to a downtown studio where, his voice in fine tone, the Great Bass made three one-hour recordings, a continuation of the Caedmon series begun earlier.

There were three visits to Virginia—Richmond, Jamestown, and Williamsburg—and daily jaunts about Washington, including a number of luncheons at the Aldo Café, a mecca for aspiring writers and artists. And then it was time to go. T. David Horton and his wife drove the Pounds to New York "in three stages" as Dorothy described their last weekend in America in a letter to Professor Giovanni Giovannini. They returned to Wyncote, to the house where the poet had grown up, and which was now occupied by the Gatter family, with whom Pound had been in correspondence since 1956. This was followed by two nights in Hopewell, New Jersey, at the summer residence of Alan C. Collins, president of Curtis Brown, Ltd., a literary agency whose London branch had handled Pound's work years before. From Hopewell they drove to

Rutherford to visit with William Carlos Williams. There they were joined by Winfield Townley Scott, a poet and long-time admirer of Ezra's. And Richard Avedon took photographs of the troubadour and the obstetrician together, arm-in-arm, as measure of a final farewell.

They went down to the ship the last day of June: Pound and his wife and young Marcella Spann. So the Great Bass, like Confucius leaving Lu or Ovid, Rome, was again an exile. The Italian liner *Cristoforo Colombo* was his vessel. They had a small, air-conditioned stateroom, with three bunks and several lounge chairs. Dressed in loose-fitting slacks, and with his shirt unbuttoned, Pound received friends who had come to see him off, among them the Italian Cultural Attaché and his wife. Michael Reck, of Canto 89, brought a potted ivy plant—"so Antaeus should not lose touch with the earth"[24]—and Robert MacGregor, managing director of New Directions, brought champagne, which was passed around. Ten days later on the sun deck of the liner in the harbor of Naples, Pound was photographed giving the Fascist salute. Interviewed, the man Eliot preferred to refer to as "neither sane, nor insane,"[25] saluted again and voiced the photo's lead caption: "All America," he told Italian *paparazzi*, "is an insane asylum."

Paradise

(1958–1972)

1

Ezra Pound returned to Italy bearing memories of an earlier arrival. In the 1920s he had stalked settings in quest of their "hallowed shades": Verona for Cavalcanti, Mantua for Sordello, Sulmano for Ovid, Rimini for Gemisto and Malatesta, Rome for Leopold and son. A place, he learned, has its own *virtû*. There was a deserted church in Rapallo he called "The Cat Church," and the feline scavengers helped him suppose it stood where once had stood a Roman temple (cats in *The Cantos* always precede divine visions).[1] A quiet corner in Ravenna was given over to Dante's tomb. The tomb and the courtly mermaids in Santa Maria dei Miracoli in Venice were ornamented and carved by the same Pietro Lombardo commemorated by Pound at Pisa. And at San Zeno (Verona), looming in the semidarkness, the coveted signed column, luminous in its detail: Pound saw it in 1911, the same year he visited the structurally influential Schifanoia frescoes in Ferrara and the unfinished Tempio Malatestiana in Rimini.

So Pound's personal destiny and tragedy were inextricably linked with Italy, and when he descended the gangplank in Genoa in 1958, having spent "one quarter of his working life in confinement,"[2] that was "the implication of an historical gesture."[3] Walter Savage Landor, a Pound favorite, had quit England for Tuscany, and his transmigration helped to bring about the literary demise of England. Landor died in Florence; and Browning died in Venice, Keats in Rome, Shelley off Leghorn.[4] Pound's transmigration from one locale to another—London to Paris to Rapallo to Washington—also terminated on Italian soil. The Mediterranean basin was home to him: it was here that he was determined to make his last-ditch stand.

Yet, for all his tempestuous will, time was running out on him; there was no use in denying it, no sense in attempting to shut it out. So he had returned to Italy to finish up *The Cantos*, to sew together the final patchwork of *Thrones de los Cantares XCVI–CIX* and to try and make cohere, before it became too difficult, the open-ended *Drafts and Fragments of Cantos CX–CXVII* and the drafts and fragments of still other unfinished canticle convergences. But there were other reasons for his coming back. Amidst the addled cosmography of a Cold War-splintered Italy, Pound hoped to locate a *paradiso terrestre*, something sacred and enduring, pure and benevolent. Instead, wrestling with self-doubt, he rediscovered what he already knew but had apparently overlooked: the Celestial City cannot be built on earth, nor can it be writ. "All the dark not in hell, or all the brightness in Paradiso,"[5] read a later letter. And in a last Canto (116): "But the record/the palimpsest—/a little light/in great darkness." Pound's version of Paradise, long in the making but fleetingly lived, was held whole in the "mind's space," indestructible as "the body is inside the soul."

That the body is inside the soul—
      the lifting and folding brightness
       the darkness shattered,
        the fragment.
         (Canto CXIII)

His destination was Castel Fontana, Schloss Brunnenburg, a twelfth-century castle in Tirolo, high over Merano, in the Italian Alps, where his daughter lived with her husband and two children. From his spacious room in the Roman stone tower he could see five castles; the Adige wound its way through the valley at his feet. Orchards and vineyards in full summer spread covered the nearby slopes. On the tower of the neighboring *Schloss* an inscription from Dante indicated that he, too, had once wandered these mountain paths. And inside the fortress, amid an extensive collection of Egyptian and African artifacts, Pound found wall space for his Gaudier-Brzeska pen-and-ink drawings; his vast archives of papers and books had been brought up from Rapallo; Gaudier's bust of Pound stood under a tree in the garden, facing east, so that the first rays of morning sun touched it.

Home finally, surrounded by family, he was full of bounce and ready for work and to entertain friends and neighbors. At a Brueghelesque feast to celebrate his daughter's birthday and his return to Italy he opened the dancing with an energetic polka ("The rhythm of a

Tirolean band gets you going").[6] A few days later, at a reception in his honor, he read from Canto 81, with its moving "Pull down thy vanity" passage. In good weather he read and wrote in a reclining chair in the garden, working over *The Cantos*, examining typescripts, rereading the priceless first editions of friends, re-examining and going once more through the yellowing notebooks of Ernest Fenollosa.

He took up carpentry again—made chairs, shelves, and a long, sturdy table. One day he climbed partway up the "Mut," the steep "weather mountain" that dominates the *Süd* Tirol, a choice location, he decided, for the construction of a marble temple with three columns; he was driven to a nearby quarry and the project was discussed at length, but in the end nothing more was done about it and it was forgotten. The poet saw to it, however, that nearly five hundred white grapevines were planted that fall in a section of the terraced castle vineyard. He also tried some horticultural experiments with the variety of maple tree which in some parts of New England yields maple syrup; his ideal was that everyone should be *"Bauernfähig,"* able to live off the land. At the same time he encouraged Mary with her translation of Cantos 98 and 99 into Italian and talked archaeology with his son-in-law, Prince Boris de Rachewiltz, out of which came the completion of the English edition of *Love Poems of Ancient Egypt* (1962), by Ezra Pound and Noel Stock.

Evenings at Brunnenburg were spent with Babbo reading aloud to the family—from his *Cantos* and his renderings of the *Classic Anthology, The Women of Trachis*, and the Confucian *Analects*; in addition, he recited poems from the *Confucius to Cummings* anthology he had prepared with Miss Spann, and for his grandchildren—Walter, aged eleven, and Patrizia, aged eight—the Joel Chandler Harris *Uncle Remus Tales*. Proud of his role as paterfamilias, he frequently took Walter and Patrizia into Merano to the horse races at the Hippodrome, where he bet, making a pool with friends; whenever he won, according to Charles Norman, he burst into loud laughter and sent the children to buy enormous ice-cream cones. That fall he was made a life-member of the racing club and began regularly to attend meetings of the business board, often full of schemes on how the club might expand its race-track facilities and thereby increase attendance.

On his seventy-third birthday, October 30, the local village authorities prepared, with the help of his daughter and Vanni Scheiwiller, Italian publisher of some fifteen of Pound's books, an exhibition ("a semi-centennial") of his early publications and other memorabilia. At the opening, Pound told those present that "every man has the right to have his ideas examined one at a time and not all confused one with the other."[7] Later, speaking in German for a radio interview to be beamed to Austria, he averred that "after the fogs of London and Paris he had found in Rapallo sunshine the possibility of renewing himself; it had been a good place for poetry, it was, in fact, the place where most of the Cantos were written. Now he hoped that Merano would revive him after his long sojourn in St. Elizabeths, and that here he would bring to an end his magnum opus."[8]

At last he had found a setting, a "perfect frame," as he described the turreted *Schloss* with its cobbled square courtyard and oversized wooden portals and gates. He wrote to friends that he felt good, by conservative estimate, for twenty more years. From his perch in the tower he continued to follow the world, perusing and clipping articles from a variety of newspapers and magazines: *Full Cry*; *Biblos*; *Gadfly*; *X, A Quarterly Review*; the *European*. If a particular article displeased him he scrawled *"maiale"*—pig—on it and laid it aside; if it appealed to him or contained the seed for a potential idea he wrote "save." Visitors to the castle, whether of political or literary persuasion, rarely departed without a bundle of clippings in hand and specific instructions on what needed doing next. Under his aegis William Cookson, an ambitious British university student, started *Agenda*, a literary journal bearing every sign of the poet's influence. When Sebastian Frobenius, grandson of Leo Frobenius, passed through Merano on his way to the Orient, Pound called a press conference, explained who the young man was and that he was going to do research in Japan. Frobenius took off with a long list of Pound's former Vou Club contacts to look up when he reached Tokyo. And Dallam Simpson, David Gordon, and Noel Stock, three of his more devout disciples, were houseguests at Brunnenburg during this period: Simpson and Gordon were performing secretarial duties for Pound, and Stock, on the strength of a Bollingen Foundation grant, had undertaken the monumental task of inventorying and cataloguing the poet's archives.

On September 1, 1958, the *Illustrazione Italiana* published Canto 98, with a copy of his daughter's translation and a prefatory essay by Pound dated Brunnenburg, July 22, in which he attacked "Endowments" ("the payola of 'endowments' is given freely to the concealers of truth") and his old nemesis, the groves of academe ("places where U.S.

history and economics are not taught, where imbecilities abound, and the works of John Adams, Van Buren, Alex del Mar, and Brooks Adams are not included in the curricula"). Played up by the news services, the article was subsequently spotted by someone in the American Embassy in Rome and forwarded to official Washington, with a batch of critical comments. Pound heard of the incident and responded by writing an inflammatory letter to Secretary of State Christian Herter:

14 September 1958

Dear Mr. Herter

I am informed that some subhuman ape in our embassy in Rome has stated that I have been making derogatory remarks about the U.S.

I have no means of verifying this statement, but may say in this connection that a certain Cose-schi has invited me to lecture or was suggesting that I do so, and that I have declined, as I needed three months' rest. I have also declined invitations to speak on Canada Radio, and am declining an invitation to speak on the British Radio.

I would point out, vide enclosure [reprint of *Illustrazione* introduction] that objection to the state of american universities, specifically for their neglect of U.S. History, does not constitute an attack on the U.S. but is rather a defense of what decency there is left in our country.

If some of the minor officials in your department consider the study of american history as aid and comfort to Moscow, that again displays a state of mind that might, or even should, arouse curiosity.[9]

Haunted by the same ghosts that had tormented him for years, he followed up his *Illustrazione* unleashing with a somewhat disjointed and confounding article, a rehash of views on by-now-familiar subjects—communism, anti-Semitism, Social Credit; "Ezra Pound to the Falsifiers" appeared in January 1959 in *Secolo d'Italia*, Rome:

Some think that I could interest myself in a socialist party. How is this possible, since Socialism is synonymous, archesynonymous, with imbecility?

I am accused of anti-semitism. Why do I respect Spinoza, esteem Montaigne as a writer, and endeavour to reestablish the fame of Alexander Del Mar who I think was a Jew. I have utter contempt for Marx and Freud. Marx lifted two intelligent chapters from English overseers of factories in that dismal island and buried them in a heap of confusionism. The work of Freud is a poison invented to counteract another poison concocted by that heretical scoundrel Calvin (the alias of Cauein, or Cohen, philo-usurer) who opposed a Vatican tied to Fugger.

Socialism is synonymous with imbecility because it wants to govern by multiplying bureaucracies, controlling and tyrannizing over all minor activities, and denying that the sovereign power of any type of state lies in the power to issue money.

Therefore I esteem C. H. Douglas, whose exact statements were betrayed and perverted by his so-called disciples.

Fascism had two merits in its opposition to Socialism.

As I see it, Mussolini followed Andrew Jackson in his opposition to the tyranny of state debts. He did not want Italy indebted to foreign individuals.

And Syndicalism was studied by those who favored elevating inferior classes.

I did not meet fascists who discussed Byzantine regulations recorded in the *Eparxiken Biblion*. But even in the United States of America, where each state has sovereign rights, there could be constitutionally established a representation in Congress of the professions, the arts, and labor.

Then, early in 1959, Pound's health began to deteriorate and with it his resolve to go on. For one thing, he could not catch his breath in the high Alpine air and was having a good deal of difficulty with his back and neck. Merano's winter and the inevitable hoarfrost that gripped the castle did not help much; nor did the messy tangle of a triad of women all trying to look after the Bard at once: Dorothy versus Mary versus Marcella. The details of daily living crowded in on him; he felt trapped. To add to his misery, he was forever reminded that not only had he been adjudged "incompetent" but he was in the custody of his wife, who, as "Committee for Ezra Pound," was legally in charge of all his money and property. The present procedure of having to account to her for each penny spent or saved was unnerving him. He became despondent and apathetic. "No use to myself or anyone," he wrote to Archibald MacLeish. Followed by: "One thing to have Europe fall on one's head. Another to be set in the ruins of same."[10]

By March 1959, Pound, his wife, and Marcella had been "irresistibly" drawn across the Italian peninsula to the Ligurian coast and Rapallo. They were staying at the Albergo Grande Italia e Lido, *"direttamente al mare,"* its stationery boasted. A month later they returned briefly to Brunnenburg so that D. G. Bridson, whose verse had been included in E.P.'s *Active Anthology* (1933) and who had visited him at St. Elizabeths in 1956, could film fourteen minutes' worth of the master for a BBC Third Programme. Back in Rapallo, the trio rented an apart-

ment on a renovated block in the center of town, not far from the sea.
The poet rallied and seemed somewhat improved, even took Dorothy and
Marcella on a short tour of Italian villages and cities, venturing, of all
places, to the site north of Pisa where the cage had been. The wire fence
still stood, but there was no sign of the camp; instead—a rose nursery,
"Rose Barni" on the sign facing the Via Aurelia, "Taishan" as imposing
as ever.[11]

From Pisa they went to Perugia and Assisi and then north to the
Lago di Garda. "Who can look on this blue and not believe?" Pound
had once mused, mirroring an asseveration he had made in *Guide to
Kulchur*: "I assert that the Gods exist." At Garda he truly did believe:
he saw gods float in the azure sky, reflect off the glass under water, the
form seen in a mirror. Within sight of this magic place, he asked Marcella Spann to marry him. At Garda he also remembered the voyage he
had made late in 1943 from Gais to Rapallo, passing around the south-
west shore of the lake, past Salò and what remained of the Republic: he
had thought then there was still hope.

He ought probably to have known better. Magic falters and fades,
passes out of things, romances and regimes alike. "Complications re/
Committee,"[12] he informed Hemingway, describing the present situation. Mention of divorce had only served to tighten Dorothy's hold over
him. "Pride, jealousy and possessiveness/ 3 pains of hell," he complained
in Canto 113, expressing publicly his private thoughts. But Dorothy
would have none of it—nor would Olga Rudge. And by October Miss
Spann had been bundled off for the States while the Pounds—Ezra and
Dorothy—were on their way back to Brunnenburg.

Soon the anguish began again. In Merano, he felt himself to be
misplaced, a prize anomaly, "like a whale out of water." Discouraged by
the turn of recent events and distressed by his present predicament, he
could no longer repress the tide of anger he felt toward his homeland. A
flurry of epistolary activity followed. He had already written to Brigit
Patmore: "Rosenstink, worst perjurer in Am/Hist/no lie to equal his
four-time swearing to uphold/const . . . complete betrayal."[13] He now
wrote to Archibald MacLeish: ". . . Curious as to how much of my 13
years due to what I said before P. Harbor while yr/adored dunghill FDR
had the U.S. illegally sinking boats of the axis powYERS."[14] And to
Harry Meacham: "When a murkn displays the inDEEpendence of living
outside the jurisdiction of the jewsfield gestapo, the british minions soak

him."[15] His letters, written in that invincible henchman's argot of his, found their way to the divers of the "Elizabethan" Ezuversity, were verifaxed and sent on. Mostly he crowed about plots, intrigues, conspiracies. America was filled with mysterious, implacable persecutors—daemons—the "usurai" whom he had castigated and was still castigating in *The Cantos*.

But often weariness crept even into his railing. All channels into which meaningful activity could flow had been blocked off. The field of action was so diminished that there seemed no purpose in anything. Hoping that a change of scenery would encourage him, his daughter accompanied him, early in December, by train, to Darmstadt, Germany, to see a production of his Sophoclean *Women of Trachis*, superbly translated by Eva Hesse; afterward he stood up on stage with the cast to great cheers and applause. The same play had been acclaimed in Berlin a few weeks earlier by the critic Kenneth Tynan. "The tragedy," he wrote, "comes across like thunder."

Back at Brunnenburg Pound, in better spirits, eagerly received visitors: Michael Reck, Albert Cook, Robert Lowell, Robert Fitzgerald. He read Ionesco's *Rhinoceros* and wrote a short appreciation of the play for a German periodical which ran a colloquium on Ionesco in 1960: "No one has the grace of the hippo's ear. As when emerging from the . . . deep she twirls it e're she falls asleep."[16] And Noel Stock had completed his difficult editing job of Pound's *Impact: Essays on Ignorance and the Decline of American Civilization*, a collection of articles and letters written, for the most part, during the late 1930s and early 1940s; Pound spent some of these days looking over and proofing the galleys.

While this work was in progress, he received a lengthy cablegram from "Elephant" (T. S. Eliot) in response to a recent letter in which Pound had expressed grave doubts about the quality of his own work. Eliot, according to Noel Stock, was full of praise; he told Pound not to worry, that he was one of the immortals, and that part of his work was sure to survive. Pound was relieved, and soon everyone in the castle was rereading Eliot's late plays (*The Confidential Clerk* and *The Elder Statesman*) as well as *After Strange Gods*,[17] the 1934 critical lament in which Pound's version of hell—Cantos 14 and 15—is berated as being "a Hell altogether without dignity." Years earlier, *il miglior fabbro* had panned the book in the *New English Weekly* for its lack of objectivity, but now he detected a new approach, which he summarized by adding a footnote to his own article on the "Immediate Need of Confucius" for the *Impact* collection: "Mr. Eliot's 'Primer of Heresy' (*After Strange Gods*) was not examined with sufficient care, nor did the present author chew on it sufficiently, especially in regard to the distinction between A Church, an orthodoxy, and a collection of intelligent observations by individual theologians, however brilliant. Eliot's use of Confucius in *The Rock* (section 5), is worth noting."

On January 18, 1960, Pound agreed to an interview with a reporter from the *New York Herald Tribune*. Exercising strong gentleness and a kind of gracious restraint he had not shown before, he told his interlocutor: "What mankind needs is an internal harmony which may balance the increase of brutality and desperation we are living through." His conversation ran the gamut. On space travel: "You cannot live in a Sputnik, and you cannot find your food in a Sputnik." On youth: "Young people today need more courage than any other generation in the past. But they can find their moral values in the beauty of nature." Asked about *The Cantos*, he spoke of the futility of casting an epic-ending paradise. He could not find the vision, the bold stroke that would bring his masterwork together. Mozart, Agassiz, and Linnaeus in the lush garden, "'neath overhanging air under sun-beat," represented only a partial solution to an apparently insurmountable problem. Finally, reminiscing, he said: "In the past I used strong language. I also made a number of blunders in my life. . . ." His biggest blunder, he said, had been one of omission: he had been unable to recognize benevolence when he saw it.

A week after his interview, Pound again left Tirolo. This time he was driven south via Milan to Rome, where he stayed with friends of the family, Ugo Dadone and Virginia Reeves, an American journalist, at the former's apartment on the Via Angelo Poliziano. Dadone, a retired military attaché and correspondent for the Angelo De Stefani Agency, was still full of a lusty, wartime spirit. Formerly a member of the Fascist party, he had become a sympathizer of the neo-Fascist movement, attending MSI (*Movimento Sociale Italiano*) functions and reporting their activities in the half-dozen or so reactionary journals which still proliferated in Italy. But political commerce, whether of right- or left-wing currency, no longer held for Pound the same fascination that it once had, and if he was sometimes seen in the company of such impenitent Black Shirts as Dadone, Camillo Pellizzi, Odon Por, Olivia Rossetti

Agresti, John Drummond, or Sir Oswald Mosley, it was because people of his own generation and background were the only ones with whom he could still converse. The rest, if we are to accept the first-hand accounts of visitors, was all mumbled monologue. That, and an .ultimate sally of letters to literary confreres.

He was anxious for one thing to make peace with MacLeish, whose efforts to get him released from St. Elizabeths he now saw with a clear eye.[18] "Forgive me for about 80% of the violent things I have said about some of your friends," he wrote "Archie," ". . . it is probably too late to retract 'em. . . . Violent language is an error. I did not get full of Agassiz. That might have saved me. Whether my errors can be useful to others, God knows."[19] A second letter followed: "I merely tried to get a few points across and get concrete answers to questions that NEED answers, i.e. universal or whatever. . . . I am broken by not being able to get any serious answers. . . . That ain't yr/fault, merely my exhaustion after years of struggle and I suppose yelling for help."[20] "Archie's" response, written some twelve years later, only four months before Pound's death, was sent by way of Harry Meacham: "Tell Ezra when next you write that I love him. He won't like it, but he has no choice."[21]

The summer–fall (1962) issue of The Paris Review contained a lengthy interview with Pound, conducted by Donald Hall in Rome during the first week of March 1960. In the course of their exchange the poet admitted that his return to Europe had been a disappointment. "The shock of no longer feeling oneself in the center of something is probably part of it," he ventured. And: "There are so many things which I, as an American, cannot say to a European with any hope of being understood." Unable to reorient himself to this "new" Italy, he began to miss the land he had left behind; he wanted to return to the States. "Developing nostalgia for early scenes,"[22] he wrote to Carl Gatter of Wyncote, and to a reporter for Newsweek (March 21, 1960), he said: "After a number of years abroad, foreigners begin to appear as unreal. Then you suddenly feel a hunger to go home again."

Dissuaded by close friends and family from making the trip, Pound felt an acute sense of disappointment. He traveled briefly to Tolentino for a Leopardi commemoration but his heart was not in it. He was baffled by the difficulty of daily responsibilities and was full of "regret" for much he had said and done, and for much he hadn't done. He worried about his "failure" to achieve what he had set out to do. He was oppressed by some sense of not having done what he should with his life. During a visit to Brunnenburg that summer, in need of rest, he was taken to Martinsbrunn, an all-purpose private clinic on the outskirts of Merano. Here he grew frail and thin, a shell of his former self:

> A blown husk that is finished
>> but the light sings eternal
> a pale flare over marshes
>> where the salt hay whispers to tide's change
>>> (Canto CXV)

The battle now was to maintain perception, not to surrender it, to push on, unending; but somehow the will was no longer there; the old man could not make it cohere, could not make it flow through.

A reporter appeared at his bedside. Pound did not stir. "Where are you living now?" the journalist asked him. "In hell," was Pound's reply. The journalist persisted, "Which hell?" And the poet, pressing his hands to his heart, mouthed the words, "Here, here."

2

Li Sao, Li Sao, for sorrow . . .

                        (Canto CXIII)

M'amour, m'amour
        what do I love and
             where are you?
That I lost my center
            fighting the world.
The dreams clash
          and are shattered—
and that I tried to make a paradiso
                 terrestre.
         (Notes from Canto CXVII et seq.)

The great silence descended the summer of 1961. Aphasia, abulia, cut off the flow. Pound simply stopped communicating with the world. It was an awesome silence, transcendent, "deep as the grave." It seemed to spring from the flesh, as though he had numbed the flesh. It was mystifying. A man who had once spilled words had succeeded in stilling his voice. Rumors circulated and crisscrossed. Had he discovered in silence a new language? A fulfillment?

When he did venture a remark, it was apt to cause a stir. At a gathering of scholars in Rimini in celebration of the d'Annunzio Centennial (1963), which he was attending with the Nobel laureate Salvatore Quasimodo, he was recognized and applauded until he rose. "Tempus loquendi, tempus tacendi," murmured the broken voice, quoting Ecclesiasticus, Jefferson, and the opening lines of Canto 31.[1] This dark and brooding silence at the end of his life was a reversal for Pound, but curiously it rhymed with the structure of his own major works. *The Cantos* drift into fragments, terminate pianissimo with the stillness of nature, the quiet of mountains and fields; *The Confucian Odes* close to the beat of soft drums and the description of a castle "high in the air and quiet"; *Mauberley* ends with a glazed, gazing face, *Propertius* on the Waters of the Damned.[2]

With the silence came a retreat from the written word as well. First *The Cantos* ground to a halt, then his correspondence. "I dodder and don't get the letters written,"[3] he wrote to Harry Meacham. "The plain fact," he added in another note, "is that my head just doesn't work."[4] That was while he was at Martinsbrunn late in 1960. But gradually he had regained enough strength to travel, and by the early spring of 1961 he was a guest in the Eternal City again and was staying with Ugo Dadone.

A brief revival accompanied his return to Rome. He began to come alive, to re-enact a scenario long since played out. In the glittering hours of the evening—supper at Crispi's, a tour among the byways of former days, ice cream at a café—Pound bounded along with the energetic gait of a much younger man. As before, he was champion of the proverbial Latin Quarter, monarch of his own fictional kingdom. He allowed himself to be courted by the pretentious *haut-monde*, the heralded literary set which he had denounced for most of his life, attending their roustabout galas and affairs, taking himself from one social gathering to another, from one sorrowful soirée to the next. He was made the fulcrum of a personality cult organized around him by those closest to him. With his floppy hat and coat, which he trailed like a cape, he was up and down the Via Veneto, turning up simply everywhere, like a bad penny, and always accompanied by his campy entourage.

On the other side of the fence stood the well-established and ostensibly well-intentioned Italian literati, the Ungarettis, Montales, and Pasolinis, who generally had a romantic affection for Pound and were glad to have him back in Italy. Their attempts to welcome him and make him feel at home, however, were often stymied by the poet's egregious followers and by some of his own unflattering remarks to the press. He was starting to rave again, preparing himself for the final outcry, which in turn must accompany the ultimate collapse and fall.

It was in the center of Rome, in the middle of the day. He was photographed at the head of a neo-Fascist, May Day parade, five hundred strong, a writhing column of *Missini* (MSI) goose-stepping their way up the Via del Corso from the Piazza di San Lorenzo in Lucina to the Piazza Venezia and the Vittoriana. They wore jack boots and black arm bands. They flaunted banners and shouted anti-Semitic slogans. They gave the Roman salute and displayed the swastika. They heaved rocks and bottles at the crowd, overturned cars, attacked bystanders. *Sinceritas? Chêng Ming? Decency in his conduct? Persistent awareness?*

The mind that had purified the language of the tribe and the body that had withstood the trials of the "gorilla cage" at Pisa and the snake pit in Washington now declined steadily.[5] The poet entered a clinic in Rome. From Rome he was transferred to the Villa Chiara, a rest home outside Rapallo, and in June 1961, he was taken to Merano and redeposited at Martinsbrunn. Discouragement was mingled with disdain for illness and all its dreadful apparatus. Pound was an aging relic, an old-fashioned agrarian populist who had outlived himself and the bulk of his generation.

Silence fell, and the pattern of his life underwent still another change. Summers were spent with Olga Rudge in the tiny hillside village of Sant' Ambrogio, with its vertiginous view of Rapallo on one side and Zoagli on the other. They lived in the same Casa 60, repainted and refurbished, where the Pounds and Miss Rudge had spent the last year of the war. The other months—January to June and September through December—they resided in Venice in the Hidden Nest. The proto-Odyssey had taken him back, out of Martinsbrunn *circa* May 1962, to where he began. Martinsbrunn specialized in general afflictions; his main trouble had been desiccation and refusal to eat food. And he wanted sea, sky, and sun and needed far more care than Dorothy Pound, at her age—nearly his—could give.

So he had allowed Olga Rudge to cart him off. But now the poet endured further vagaries of health. In the summer of 1962 he underwent surgery for prostate infection and less than a year later a second operation in the clinic at Rapallo. Afterward, he appeared to grow stronger, although he rarely spoke and seemed to have given up writing altogether. "Too much terrible anxiety loaded onto such a sensitivity," the Committee for Ezra Pound explained after his departure. For all his downheartedness, he nevertheless had made a full physical recovery. He could climb the long and steep *salita*, recently paved, from Rapallo on up to Sant' Ambrogio without a break in stride. And he could take the flats of Venice with ease. His peregrinations about the languorous city island took him from the Bridge of Sighs to the Accademia, from the Campo San Polo to the Doge's Palace. And quite often he still enjoyed a refreshing swim, periodically at the Lido, and in Rapallo off the sand-and-pebble Ligurian beaches.

In Venice there were other diversions as well: the opera, concerts, public lectures, art exhibits (notably the Biennale), and friends. The Ivanciches, Peter Russell, Joan Fitzgerald, Ugo Fasolo, Liselotte Höhs, Lotte Frumi, Giuseppe Santomaso, Count Vittorio Cini comprised the hub of the Venetian Vortex. It pleased the poet to take his friends on the rounds of local sites: the Giardini Publicanni (where on a plinth sits the stone bust of Richard Wagner); the Scuola degli Schiavone with its *quattrocento* Carpaccios; Peggy Guggenheim's walled-in loggia and treasure-laden museum. And at those times when he and Olga visited the San Marco area or the Fenice Theatre they took the opportunity to walk the maze past Santa Maria della Salute (the "Jewel Box") to the customs house and there took a *traghetto* across the Grand Canal. This chosen route reminded the poet of another compass-course age: Venice, 1908. In six decades he had, so to speak, come full circle.

He sometimes read or was read to: Confucius, Chaucer, Shakespeare, Sartre, Auden, Burroughs. He spent long hours in the Faustian dark at his desk in the third-story studio, sitting and staring into the dark, brooding on his past and how he might have altered it. More often than not, flames crackled in the fireplace; the Dolmetsch clavichord, a duplicate of the original which had been restrung for his grandson, leaned against a wall. From time to time, when the mood struck him, he read, and quite spiritedly, into a Grundig tape recorder: Shakespeare's "They that have power to hurt and will do none" and Christopher Smart's "I will remember my cat . . ."[6] Early one November morning, following his seventy-ninth birthday, he woke up the house with a startling outburst of

> Winter is icumen in,
> Lhude sing GOD-DAMN!!!

—and on that occasion, "with ferocious emphasis," there followed a long taping session of other pre-epic bits and pieces.[7]

All along, during all this, Pound worried needlessly about money, about not being able to earn enough to support himself. Following his 1958 return to Italy, both Archibald MacLeish and Ernest Hemingway sent him checks in generous amounts; Hemingway's for $1500 was intended as a response in kind to a note he had received from Pound: "Old man him be tired." Pound hand-canceled Hemingway's check and had it sunk in plexiglass to be used as a paper-weight souvenir. By this time the Great Bass had infiltrated the front ranks of the Establishment. His books, or at least some of them, were required reading at a number of American colleges and universities, and for the first time his royalties amounted to something more than a few pennies. This, coupled with Dorothy Pound's continued support and his own monthly Social Security pension, allowed him to live comfortably—although hardly in what one would call great luxury.

And then, slowly, honors came his way. In 1962, when *Poetry* celebrated its fiftieth anniversary, he received the Harriet Monroe Award of $500, and in September of the following year an award of $5000 from the Academy of American Poets. A humbled and some-times self-effacing Pound declared himself unworthy of his laurels. To Henry Rago, editor of *Poetry*, he described himself as "a minor satirist." And an interview (March 1963) with Grazia Livi for the Italian maga-zine *Epoca* surprised even his followers, who were convinced he had committed no moral wrongdoing:

> I have lived all my life believing that I knew something. And then a strange day came and I realized that I knew nothing, that I knew nothing at all. And so words have become empty of meaning. . . .
> It is something I have come to through suffering. Yes, through an experience of suffering. . . .
> I have come too late to a state of total uncertainty, where I am conscious only of doubt. . . .
> I do not work any more. I do nothing. I fall into lethargy, and I contemplate. . . .
> Everything that I touch, I spoil. I have blundered always.

Somewhere he had obviously gone astray. But where? What had been his "root error?"[8] Had he, like Mauberley, been wrong from the start, out of key with his time? He should never have quit America. He should never have gone back there. He should certainly never have buried himself in an idle Italian village whose most strident literary claim was that Nietzsche had begun (but not ended) his *Zarathustra* there. And, having buried himself in Rapallo, he should never have backed certain political horses as though they were the only ones running the race. Nor should the 1929 Crash and subsequent Depression have influenced him to the extent that they did, forcing him to relinquish one world in favor of a world much more base and cruel.

Gradually, lifelong friends passed away: Hemingway in 1961, Cummings in 1962, Williams in 1963. And then on January 4, 1965, T. S. Eliot succumbed. One month later Olga Rudge escorted Pound to England, by plane, for the memorial service at Westminster Abbey. Entering the Abbey by a special side door, to preserve his privacy, he paid his last respects to his *bon ami*.[9]

When it was over, Eliot's ashes went to East Coker; like Henry James before him, he had given up his American citizenship to become a British subject. Pound, who had retained his U.S. citizenship (renouncing it might have saved him), was a man without a country, hence a nonperson. White-haired, pale, with piercing eyes, he looked, said Stephen Spender, like he fit the role. He remained in London for two full days and conversed only with Valerie Eliot and Faber and Faber's Peter du Sautoy. From London he flew to Dublin and a brief visit with Mrs. William Butler Yeats, it being also the year of the Yeats centenary.

But Yeats was of another generation, another age—and of the "Men of 1914," the modernists who had worked so hard to resuscitate the English language, to save it from drowning in its own undertow, Pound remained the last. And of his own generation he remained among the last. "They were born within a six-year span," Hugh Kenner writes in *The Pound Era*: Joyce and Lewis, 1882; Williams, 1883; Pound, 1885; D. H. Lawrence, 1885; Hilda Doolittle, 1886; Marianne Moore, 1887; and T. S. Eliot, 1888. ("And Picasso, for that matter, 1881, and Stravinsky, 1882").[10] Of them all, Eliot, the royalist-classicist-Anglican, the poet who had once opted for Charles Maurras and the *Action Française*, but who had also written "Tradition and the Individual Talent" and the *Four Quartets*, was the one closest to Pound, the one whose friendship and praise he valued above the rest. Now, laying aside all religious and social considerations, and recalling instead their 1919 travels together through France, *il miglior fabbro* composed Possum's final and most fitting epitaph: it appeared in the winter 1966 Eliot memorial issue of *The Sewanee Review* and has been reprinted many times since:

> His was the true Dantescan voice—not honoured enough, and deserving more than I ever gave him. I had hoped to see him in Venice this year for the Dante commemoration at the Giorgio Cini Foundation—instead: Westminster Abbey. But, later, on his own hearth, a flame tended, a presence felt.
>
> Recollections? let some thesis-writer have the satisfaction of "discover-

ing" whether it was 1920 or '21 that I went from Excideuil to meet a rucksacked Eliot. Days of walking—conversation? literary? le papier Fayard was then the burning topic. Who is there now to share a joke with?

Am I to write "about" the poet Thomas Stearns Eliot? or my friend "the Possum"? Let him rest in peace. I can only repeat, but with the urgency of 50 years ago: READ HIM.

Pound back in Italy, summer 1958. With him are his son-in-law Boris de Rache-wiltz (to left of Pound), his daughter Mary (behind and to left of her husband), and grandchildren Patrizia and Walter. (*Wide World Photos.*)

Above: Dorothy and Ezra Pound at Schloss Brunnenburg, 1959. The prints are by Gaudier-Brzeska. (*Courtesy Harry Meacham.*)

Opposite: Oskar Kokoschka drawing Pound in the former's studio in Villeneuve, Switzerland, December 1963. (*Copyright by Horst Tappe.*)

Opposite, top: Pound in Venice, mid-1960s. (*Copyright by Horst Tappe.*)

Opposite, bottom: Pound visits James Joyce's grave in Zurich, 1967. (*Copyright by Horst Tappe.*)

Below: Pound in a Venice art gallery, circa 1967. (*Copyright by Horst Tappe.*)

Above: Il miglior fabbro with Stephen Spender at the Spoleto Festival, late 1960s. (*Copyright by Horst Tappe.*)

Opposite, top: Pound reading at the Spoleto Festival. (*Copyright by Horst Tappe.*)

Opposite, bottom: In 1969 Pound returned to the States. During his stay he revisited Hamilton College for the graduation ceremonies. (*Robert T. Chaffee. Courtesy the Burke Library, Hamilton and Kirkland Colleges.*)

Above: One of the last photos of Pound in his Venice workroom, 1971. (*Copyright by Horst Tappe.*)

Opposite and two pages following: Pound at his summer home in Sant' Ambrogio near the end of his life. (*Copyright by Lisetta Carmi.*)

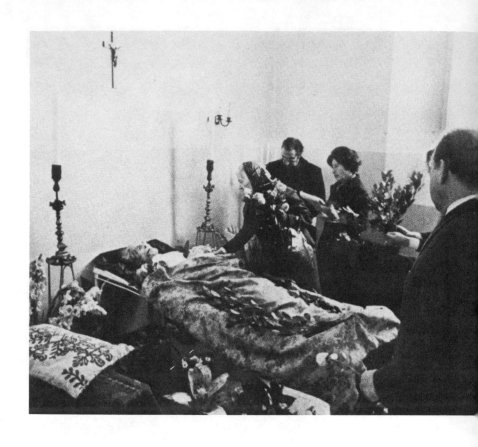

Olga Rudge, Pound's longtime companion, about to lay a bouquet of roses on Pound's body at Sts. John and Paul Hospital, Venice, November 1, 1972. (*Wide World Photos.*)

3

I have tried to write Paradise

Do not move
   Let the wind speak
      that is paradise.

Let the Gods forgive what I
    have made
Let those I love try to forgive
    what I have made.

                   (Canto 120)

During his last decade Pound was in and out of Swiss health clinics, continually searching for the "cure" which would restore his creative faculties. In January of 1964 he had gone to the Blue Cross Clinic in Basel to consult with a Dr. Walter Pöldinger, an Austrian geriatrician of some renown, whom Eva Hesse had recommended. He also paid a number of visits to the Montreux clinic ("La Prairie") of Paul Niehans, M.D., whose specialty was the injection of animal cells—mainly sheep —into the human blood stream. Three prolonged series of treatments with Niehans seem to have had little, if any, over-all effect on Pound.

July 1965 found him at Spoleto for the Gian Carlo Menotti Festival of Two Worlds, where his Villon opera *Le Testament* was performed as a ballet. "A waste of time," he afterward told intimates who were staying with him at the neighboring castle of Caresse Crosby. The opera had been composed to be sung in French always, with a minimum of accompanying stage choreography. Although it was warmly received by the critics, Pound was disappointed with this experimental version. He had experienced a similar reaction to a souped-up production of *The Winter's Tale* which he had seen performed by the Edinburgh Festival Company in Venice. "Ham and beatnik," he exploded on that occasion, rushing out of the theater before the first act was over.

It was at the 1965 Menotti Festival that Pound read, at a public reading, poems by Marianne Moore, Robert Lowell, and others, but none of his own; instead of mounting the stage, he read while seated in Menotti's box, with a microphone beside him, in a tremulous and weak voice which gained timbre and strength as he went along. As a protest against Pound's wartime activities, the Soviet poet Yevgeny Yevtushenko, who had also been invited to read, left the podium before Pound's arrival in the theater. A year later, the event repeated itself when the Russian poet Yevgeny Vinokurov followed suit. At the 1966 Festival, Pound was introduced by the English writer Patrick Creagh as "the most important single factor in modern English-language poetry," after which the visitant read, briefly, from *Hugh Selwyn Mauberley*, from Canto XIII ("If a man have not order within him/He can not spread order about him"), and from *Drafts and Fragments*:

> Time, space,
>> neither life nor death is the answer.
> And of man seeking good,
>> doing evil.
> In meiner Heimat
>> where the dead walked
>>> and the living were made of cardboard.
>>>> (Canto CXV)

His eightieth birthday was cause for celebration. Articles and tributes appeared in many newspapers, quarterlies, journals, and magazines in the United States, England, France, Germany, and Italy, and he was also the subject of a host of radio and television programs, including the Columbia Broadcasting System's *Camera Three* presentation of *In Search of Ezra Pound*, a three-part series written by Stephan Chodorov.[1] A number of commemorative books appeared, one of which was Noel Stock's *Ezra Pound: Perspectives*, with tributes by Marianne Moore, Hugh Kenner, A. Alvarez, Hugh McDiarmid, and other leading poets and writers. Pound himself celebrated with a trip to Paris, the first of three return visits in as many years. His host was Dominique de Roux, publisher of the French edition of *The Cantos* and editor of the two volumes on Pound in the *Cahiers de l'Herne* series.

At the rue Jacob home of Natalie Barney, his hostess for an afternoon, the grand old man of international poetry received friends, old and new, welcoming them with an amiable but wordless gaze. "I did not enter into silence," he told Dominique de Roux, "silence captured me." *L'amazone*, a name bestowed upon Miss Barney by the irrepressible Remy de Gourmont, walked with her guest through the wild English gardens surrounding her house; Pound spoke little. When informed about the new ceiling Marc Chagall had painted the year before for the Paris Opera House, he ventured a Balzacian obliquity: "They should have put it in Notre Dame." Later, *l'amazone* told newspapermen that she had found the poet "an eloquent listener."

On a tour of the city he had not seen in many years, Pound was driven by the Institut de France, the seat of the French Academy, the bastion of literary conservatism. As it was pointed out to him, Pound's face darkened and he looked the other way toward the Seine. He also reacted strongly, but in a positive fashion, to a production he saw of Samuel Beckett's *Fin de Partie* (*Endgame*) with its blind but spirited cripple, quintessential servant, old man confined to a trash bin (humanity as waste). "*C'était moi dans la poubelle*," he told James Laughlin. Later he was brought together with Beckett; the two ancient mariners had Joyce and Paris in common. They traded tales and reminiscences and forgot there was a time when they had not gotten along.

Active at times and encouraged by Olga Rudge ("She has an enormous courage"), Pound turned up suddenly in out-of-the-way places. He traveled by train and boat to Greece and remained there long enough to drink from the Grecian Castalia, the luminiferous spring near Delphi, high above the Corinthian Gulf. He traveled to Joyce's gravesite in Zurich to see the bronze statue of "jaunty Jim," rising out of the Irish-green turf, the gaze on the monument's face semi-pensive, a smile playing at the corners of the mouth. He made another tour of Italian towns and villages and posed for the camera of Vittorugo Contini for a book of photographs (*Spots and Dots*), published by Gianfranco Ivancich, brother of the Renata of Hemingway's *Across the River and into the Trees*. When *Spots and Dots* appeared, Pound attended a reception at Maniago, about eighty kilometers from Venice toward Trieste, and was persuaded to give a brief poetry reading for the benefit of those present, mostly students and university professors. On another occasion, Ivancich took Pound on a two-day cruise of the Adriatic to visit the Schloss Duino, near Trieste, the inspirational site of Rilke's *Duineser Elegien*. And in Paris again, where he had gone for the publication of the French translation of *ABC of Reading, How to Read*, and *The Spirit of Romance*, he was taken on a tour of the Salle Gaudier-Brzeska in the Musée de l'Art Moderne, a room full of vorticist sculpture and trenchant memories.

Late in October 1967, several days before Pound's eighty-second birthday, Allen Ginsberg arrived in Venice to pay the bard a week-long visit. Peter Russell and Michael Reck were also present at this historic encounter, and Reck took notes for an article he was preparing for *The Evergreen Review* (June 1968):

> One day in Venice recently, I saw an apparition that was real: a round face like an apprentice Santa Claus framed by an immense mane of flowing pitch-black hair and beard, its pink nose surrounded by equally black spectacles. From its neck dangled a great silver Buddhist medal. The apparition confronted another real one: a very thin aged face with a . . . silky fine wispy white . . . beard. Fixed staring eyes of a deep aquamarine, now losing their power, seemed to mirror a dreadful sadness.

Ginsberg had been confronted by this same enduring sadness a month earlier while spending a day with Pound at his Sant' Ambrogio home. They had eaten lunch together in the garden behind the house and had driven to Portofino to sit by the harborside, where the older poet maintained a deep and meditative silence. Now, in Venice, as Ginsberg recorded the week's events in a daily journal,[2] there was a warming-up process, a desire on Pound's part to communicate with his visitor. He listened to various records which Ginsberg had brought along—Bob Dylan, Donovan, The Beatles, Ali Akbar Khan—and to Ginsberg's own rabbinical chanting of Hare Krishna and Hari Om Namo Shivaye and Gopala Gopala Devaki Nandana Gopala mantras. They sipped wine together and Ginsberg spoke about American poetry, about Pound's influence on three generations of poets, from Crane and Williams to John Ashbery and himself.

Later, at a small local restaurant, Pound broke his sphinx-like silence to identify certain specific textual references from *The Cantos* which Ginsberg asked him about. The *Ras* of the Beat Vortex wanted to know the location of a few Venetian landmarks he had been unable to place, including San Giorgio dei Greci, where "in the font to the right as you enter/are all the gold domes of San Marco." Ginsberg had found no such reflection in the font; nor could he find "the soap-smooth stone posts where San Vio/meets il Canal Grande." And where was "Salviati"? In a slow, even voice, Pound answered these and other questions, giving precise information as to the whereabouts of each detail, while his auditor transcribed the words into a notebook for future reference.

Then the creator of *Howl* and *Kaddish* leaned over to Pound and said, "Your thoughts about specific perceptions and Williams' 'no ideas but in things' have been a great help to me and to many young poets. And the phrasing of your poems has been of concrete value for me as reference points for my own perceptions. Am I making sense?"

"Yes," Pound mumbled, "but my poems don't make sense."

Ginsberg and Reck assured the poet that his work made sense to them. "A lot of double talk," Pound snapped. He went on: "Bunting told me that there was too little presentation in *The Cantos* and too much reference, that I referred to things without presenting them." "And Bunting told *me*," Ginsberg countered, "that *The Cantos* are a model of economy in presentation of sensory phenomena, via words. . . . They are ground that we all can walk on."

"A mess," the old man persisted.

Ginsberg: "What, you or *The Cantos* or me?"

Pound: "My writing—stupidity and ignorance all the way through . . . stupidity and ignorance."

To which Reck said, "In your poetry you have an *ear*. That's the most important thing for writing poetry. So it's hard for you to write a bad line."

"It's hard for me to write at *all*."

Reck reminded Pound that he had influenced writers all over the world and cited Hemingway as *prima facie* evidence. Ginsberg joined in: "You have shown us the way. The more I read your poetry, the more convinced I am it is the best of its time. For the ear, Bill Williams told me in 1961—we were talking about prosody, and I'd asked him to explain your prosody to me—anyway, Williams said: 'Pound has a mystical ear.' Did he ever tell you that?"

"No," Pound retorted, "he never said that to me."

"Well, I'm reporting it to you now, seven years later, the judgment of the tender-eyed doctor."

Pound looked away, smiling, pleased. Ginsberg went on. He spoke again of Pound's overriding influence on twentieth-century verse. But the old man would have none of it. "The intention was bad," he said.

"That's the trouble—anything I've done has been an accident. Any good has been spoiled by my intentions, the preoccupation with irrelevant and stupid things." And then very slowly and clearly, he added, "But the worst mistake I made was that stupid, suburban prejudice of anti-Semitism. All along, that spoiled everything."

"Ah, it's lovely to hear you say that," Ginsberg responded. "Well no," he went on, "because anyone with any sense can see it as a humor, in that sense part of the drama. You manifest the process of thoughts, make a model of the consciousness. Anti-Semitism is your fuck-up, like not liking Buddhists, but it's part of the model and the great accomplishment was to make a working model of your mind. Nobody cares if it's Ezra Pound's mind but it's a mind like everybody's mind."

Pound nodded a little at the words, "Nobody cares if it's Ezra Pound's mind," but said nothing. He rose and retrieved his coat and cane. The party emerged from the restaurant and walked the short distance to the small house at Calle Querini 252. As they reached the front door, Ginsberg turned toward Pound: "I have told you what I came here to tell you. I also came here for your blessing. And now may I have it, sir?"

"Yes," Pound said, "for whatever it's worth."

"And more, and more," Ginsberg told him. "And I would also like your blessing for Sheri Martinelli, because it's worth a lot of happiness to her, now."

Pound looked at Ginsberg for a moment and then without speaking, smiled slightly and nodded.

Ginsberg had taken the master's hand and leaning over had kissed him, gracefully and naturally, on the right cheek. Pound appeared greatly moved. As he turned to walk into the house, he gazed a last time into the younger poet's eyes and said, "I should have been able to do better." Then he stepped across the threshold and was gone from sight.

On June 4, 1969, the poet and Miss Rudge flew to New York on a two-week visit. The trip, a last-minute decision, came as a surprise to almost. everyone, including his U.S. publisher, James Laughlin. The day after his arrival, Pound was a guest at the annual meeting of the Academy of American Poets in the board room of the New York Public Library. He sat in a large chair at one end of the room and paid rapt attention to the proceedings. The next day, Walter de Rachewiltz, now an undergraduate at Rutgers University, drove his grandparents to the Norfolk, Connecticut, home of Mr. Laughlin, and a few days later, on June 8, the entire group went up to Hamilton College, where Laughlin was to be awarded an honorary degree of Doctor of Letters. It was Pound's first visit to his old college since receiving his own honorary degree there in 1939.

Following lunch at the house of Austin Briggs, Jr., a professor of English, the poet donned cap and gown and joined the commencement exercises at the Sage Rink Hockey Arena, next to the tennis courts on which he had practically lived during his previous campus visit. The college had arranged for him to enter the building by a side entrance and to mount the platform after the others had assembled, to avoid two sets of steep stairs that would be used by the academic procession. Introduced by John Chandler, the president of Hamilton, Pound received a tumultuous standing ovation as the entire audience and platform party rose to its feet. He sat next to Laughlin on the platform, and, although he never actually spoke, he gladly shook hands with students and parents afterward and autographed copies of *Drafts and Fragments* for the library's extensive Ezra Pound collection.

Back in New York, Laughlin's wife gave them the keys to her apartment on Bank Street in Greenwich Village. Each day Miss Rudge mapped out a schedule that would entertain but not exhaust her companion. They returned to the New York Public Library, this time to the Berg Collection, to see the recently unearthed draft of Eliot's *Waste Land*, with its numerous pages of admonitions, queries, and cuts in Pound's bold scrawl, the original manuscript that Mrs. Valerie Eliot was preparing for publication. Another day, they went to an uptown gallery to view a Jean Arp exhibit. They dined with Mary Hemingway at the Voisin Restaurant and visited the flat of Robert Lowell and Elizabeth Hardwick. They walked over to West Ninth Street to see Marianne Moore, who was arthritic and confined to a wheelchair. Laughlin gave a number of informal dinner parties for Ezra and Olga at the Dorgene Restaurant, opposite the White Horse Tavern on Hudson Street. Lewis Freedman, a television producer, attended one; George Quasha, a young poet and university lecturer, attended another; and Frederick Morgan, editor-in-chief of *The Hudson Review*, appeared at still a third. On all three occasions Pound spoke very little. Quasha asked him what his impressions were of New York, and Pound responded: "Too much noise, too many people."[3]

The couple did a good deal of hiking around the Village area, past Patchin Place one morning and all the way east to the Brooklyn Bridge. They visited Little Italy and ate ice cream at a sidewalk restaurant. One outing took them to the publishing offices of New Directions at 333 Sixth Avenue. During the same week Walter de Rachewiltz drove them to Philadelphia to pay a call on the Heacock sisters, Priscilla and Esther, friends from Pound's early Pennsylvania days. The visit took place on June 15 at Stapely Hall, a Quaker retirement home in Germantown. Olga did most of the talking, and Walter took photographs. Before returning to New York, they visited the old Pound residence on Fernbrook Avenue in Wyncote. No one was at home that day; the car carrying Pound continued on its way. His thoughts turned now to another home, to Hailey, Territory of Idaho. He wanted to return to his birthplace, to savor it once more for all time. In the end, the trip was not made: instead, Venice.

The canal city was home to him. Here, in the last years, he would sometimes pose for hours hunched over a chessboard, as though contemplating the exigencies of the vorticist poem he had constructed about the game in 1914: "Red knights, brown bishops, bright queens/ Striking the board, falling in strong 'L's of colour." He enjoyed the long, drawn-out matches he played with Giorgio Manera, a Venetian lawyer half his age. He played not for the sport or the contest of it but for the game's ordered voids, the welcome, muted blocks of silence.

Silence was anthem to all the closing motions: a noh play at Palladio's theater; Vivaldi at Santa Maria del Carmelo; a Disney rendition of the *Festa del Redentore* (Feast of the Redeemer), fireworks in the sky and votive lights floating on the water. As always, he embraced visitors with gentleness and a strict rationing of words: Norman Mailer, Anthony Burgess, Cyril Connolly, Hugh McDiarmid, Isamu Noguchi, Peter du Sautoy, R. Buckminster Fuller. One initiate, Guy Davenport, found Pound, "silent, gracious, tormented, withdrawn, stubborn, tenacious of life."[4] The Bard had reinvented silence as a synthesis of form and format, a final and unlikely Taoist persona; it implied regret, repentance, withdrawal and a rejection of the modern world. "It was a great silence,"[5] vouchsafed Julian Beck; he and Judith Malina had come across the poet in Venice in June of 1965. With his flashing white hair and beard, and dark, deep, almost blind-looking eyes, he was a Tiresian prophet, a silent seer, Lear upon a corpsed stage.

And Dorothy Pound,[6] still a picture of Attic grace, lived half the year in Rapallo near Ezra, the other half in England near her son. Somehow she too had jumbled her life. By December 1970, "Pound's official widow" was able to write Harry Meacham: "I do not know where E.P. is. . . . I have not seen him in 18 months."[7] She was not complaining, merely relating a cold fact. She was too *Kensington*, said Agnes Bedford, to grumble. And on those occasions when she did meet with Ezra, he would rarely say a word. She blamed his saturninity on "the nightmare years" inside the house of bedlam: "Too much for anybody sane."[8] How far it had all come from where it had begun. Sitting in the same row as his wife at the theater in Rapallo, he studiedly ignored her presence. She managed to survive these years by rekindling ghosts. Memories sustained her; that, and pride: "I am 83, E. P. 84—nearly historical figures."[9] Three years after this narrative she was together with her husband for the last time (it was only the second time in four years their paths had crossed): "His voice so soft I can hardly make it out—plenty charm!"[10] It was the beginning of spring 1972.

So the Last Rower was closing doors.[11] Gradually he divested himself of life, allowed its raiments to fall away. The perpetual worry about having wasted himself continued to beset him. Silence was ultimately a form of atonement. Four consecutive days of interrogation by a journalist writing a portrait of the artist for the magazine section of *The New York Times* yielded less than half a page of notes; a *Life* magazine reporter fared no better. And a German television network, attempting to interview him, photographed him strolling through his garden in Sant' Ambrogio, immersed in thought, distant sea and sky stretched behind him to hazy infinity. Pound would not speak for the television. The camera swung nearer and nearer to the poet until only his face was seen, a white mask of cracks and crevices, framed by a ragged shock of hair and beard. Finally, for about fifteen seconds, all that could be seen was a single burning eye[12]—eye of one, who, like Dante, has transfixed his gaze upon Paradise. The vision lasts a moment and disappears, but the consciousness of the passion remains, and it is this passion which was mirrored in Pound's eyes. No Man, OU TIS, had at last, if only for an instant, found his way home.

Coda:
To the End

(1971-1972)

The Venetian bus, the *vaporetto*, a lumbering hulk of a ferry, slowly made its way across the canal. It was late May in Venice, 1971, a hazy morning of sirocco: cloud-filtered sunlight and a dry, sultry breeze. Ezra Pound's abode was located on a narrow walkway near one end of the sinuous Grand Canal, in the section of Venice called San Gregorio. Around the corner from the house, overlooking a small canal, was the Pensione Cici, where the poet often took his midday meal. Not far off, down a crosscurrent of winding *calles*, was Peggy Guggenheim's villa and art museum. And no more than a stone's heave away, across the Grand Canal, the plush lawn of the Gritti Palace Hotel.

My wish to meet Ezra Pound had been prompted by simple curiosity and admiration for his work. My curiosity was sharpened a week or two before the interview by a conversation I had with a well-informed literary critic, an Englishman, at a conference at Oxford on twentieth-century American and British poetry. When Pound's name came into the discussion, the critic grew loud and told me Pound was still, despite all rumors to the contrary, "a rabid supporter of fascism," whose greatest disappointment in life had been the fall of Mussolini. That, in any case, was one charge I was determined to judge for myself.

Arriving early at Calle Querini, I sat for a while at a nearby café and watched the gondolas glide smoothly by on the Giudecca. Then I knocked on Pound's door. Moments later from an open window peeped the head of a lady, who soon stood before me. Olga Rudge was petite and white-haired, with finely honed features; she struck me, in her middle seventies, as resilient and matter-of-fact. "Be careful," she warned, pointing to a brownish-white, foot-high slab of marble which rose menacingly from the doorway. "One of these days someone will trip and break his neck on it. I had it installed after the 1966 floods to keep out the *acqua alta*. The workmen who installed it thought I was mad." She pointed to her head. " 'The water seeps in from underneath,' they said. Well, from the looks of things, I was right."

I stepped over the slab and into the house. A bit cramped, it consisted of three snug rooms, each on a separate story, each with its own fireplace, and a minuscule kitchen-alcove area just off the entranceway. The room downstairs was bright yellow, with painted ocher columns and a shining glass star suspended on a thin wire from the high ceiling. Two dark armchairs, a monumental dark table, and twin mahogany bookcases with swinging glass doors were all the furniture in the room. The bookcases were amply stocked with the works of all those confreres—Yeats and Joyce and Eliot and Hemingway—that *il miglior fabbro* managed to inherit during the legendary early years when the question was where to go from Swinburne, and Pound with his triangular red Vandyke and flaming mop of hair seemed to be the only one with an answer.

Having seated me, Olga Rudge began to explain what I full well already knew: there was nobody more difficult to converse with than Ezra Pound. He answered no letters, accepted no phone calls, and at times resisted all attempts on the part of his interlocutors to draw him out. But one must not lose heart; his silence did not mean irreverence or indifference, she explained. On the contrary, he listened closely to everything, and was, despite his age, extremely interested in meeting young writers. "Ezra might seem detached and no longer interested, but he follows everything, nothing escapes him. Think of an automobile with its engine idling—it doesn't run but all its parts are moving."

With this introduction, Pound had suddenly come clambering down the stairs, a live wire of energy, bounding up to his visitor, taking the extended hand eagerly in both of his. He smiled slightly, beneath a thin white beard, eyes ablaze, skin starched and deeply lined. He said nothing but led the way back up the stairs, moving quickly, almost jerkily, to his room on the second floor.

The setting here was a scene from a Lillian Hellman play, the furniture handsome but a little worn. It was all inherited from another day: couch, chairs, a long bookcase ending in a desk. A marble-topped coffee table stood before the couch. A Greek vase sat on a shelf, wood carvings on the window sill. Artwork lent the room color: a recent portrait of Pound drawn by Kokoschka; a Max Ernst seashell painting in a leather-tied frame of four sticks of wood; the Bas Relief of Ixota; black-limned Wyndham Lewis sketches hanging against a far wall.

Silhouetted against a large bay window, shirt sleeves rolled up just beyond the wrist, the poet sat stiffly in his armchair facing the young interviewer; Olga Rudge sat in a high-backed wicker chair facing her friend.

Pound's companion and protector carried the brunt of the conversation, directed it toward the impending death of a dream: Venice, the besieged metropolis, was disintegrating, was slowly sinking into its own lagoon. Atlantis of the future, the lapping waters were devouring the land and the first stories of buildings. And what the dank and odorous canals didn't destroy, the smog-laden air did.

"Sounds like something out of Thomas Mann, doesn't it?" And then answering her own question, she quickly added, "Mann associated Venice with death, but when you think about it he associated *everything* with death—poor soul! he was obsessed with the idea of dying."

I asked Miss Rudge if she was familiar with the legend of Oscar Wilde riding the canals, on one of his visits to Venice, in a black gondola and claiming afterward that he had felt as if he had traveled through the filth-strewn sewers in his own coffin. Yes, well Wilde, she assured me, had a rather vivid imagination. Besides, Venice was really no different from any other city in Italy. If anything, the whole country was rotting away or was being wrecked by man. That was why there was so much violence in Italy. If a man's family has worked the land, has been peasant stock for a thousand years—for two thousand years—and you covered his land with asphalt, what could you expect? He goes crazy!

During all this, Pound watched us with piercing eyes, turning his head one way, then the other, as though following the progress of a tennis match, smiling gently whenever a particular volley took an interesting turn. And always he busied himself with his own hands and nails, rubbing the back of one gnarled root against the other, the joints swollen and rheumatic, the knuckles scraped raw. After about ten minutes he still had not uttered a word. There was a break in the conversation, and he said to me, sharply and quite audibly: "Where are you from?"

The formalities over with, I proceeded to question the poet about his work: "A few years ago you told Daniel Cory you had 'botched' *The Cantos.* Do you still believe that?"

Too soon: Pound ignored the question, turned back to his scarred hands, rubbing nervously. I asked more questions: more silence. I pulled back and waited. Then a flow, the voice parched but strong with a rough edge that corresponded to his visage, the words tumbling out in chunks:

"You ask about my London and Paris friends—Joyce, Hemingway, Brancusi, Eliot. When I was in Zurich in the winter of 1967 I saw Joyce's bare grave—Joyce's name with Nora's sat in a corner of the cemetery, the names nearly illegible on a stone hidden in the grass. . . .

"Hemingway has never disappointed me. . . .

"Brancusi seemed to me a saint . . . I said as much in *Guide to Kulchur.* . . . Le Musée de l'Art Moderne in Paris contains much of his work, but I would like to see his 'Table of Silence' in Rumania. . . .

"The last time I spoke with Eliot was at St. Elizabeths, about 1956, I think."

"Eliot had a lot to do with finally getting you out of St. Elizabeths, didn't he?"

"Indirectly, I suppose, as much as anyone. There was a paper to be signed. 'No use,' I told him. 'A travesty,' he said. It might have sprung me from the hole a lot sooner."

"Did Eliot's interest in drama have anything to do with your decision to translate *The Women of Trachis?*"

"The *Trachiniae* came from reading the [Fenollosa] noh plays for the new edition and the curiosity of wanting to see a Greek play performed within a new context."

"Didn't you once attempt a similar adaptation of the *Agamemnon* of Aeschylus?"

"Yes, long ago—I couldn't find the appropriate language . . . I gave it up."

"And *Electra*," said Olga Rudge, breaking into the conversation. "You began work on the Euripides play during the 'fifties."

Pound looked up but did not speak. Instead, he returned to his hands, skin wrinkled at the wrists and the back of the hand, an invisible tremor causing a stir of motion in his fingertips. An earnest but impassive expression began to mold the contours of his face. In the shadowed chamber, with sunlight spilling through the window, his profile looked heroic, looked craggy.

Olga's voice again, quietly breaking through, a buffer against the silence: "I promised to take Ezra to Rumania next summer."

"And this summer?" I asked.

"This summer, perhaps the Joyce Symposium in Trieste, and late in June we go to Spoleto for Signor Menotti's Festival of Two Worlds."

"You still manage to do a good deal of traveling," I suggested to Pound.

"No," he answered, "I haven't really done much traveling—in fact, I have stayed put for years at a time. I don't see that restlessness is necessary."

"For artists?"

"For anyone."

Following this brief exchange, Olga Rudge reminded me of the forthcoming publication of the original version of *The Waste Land*, Pound's most celebrated educational endeavor; published in facsimile, it would show just how heavy a hand *il miglior fabbro* had exercised in the final composition of the manuscript—on the whole, clearly, for the best. He had tightened the spring of the poem's power by eliminating prettiness.

Picking up on her lead, I asked *il poeta* if he knew what had happened to the manuscript, how it had been misplaced, and how he felt now that it had been recovered.

In the preface to the new edition, Pound remarks: "The more we know of Eliot, the better. I am thankful that the lost leaves have been unearthed. The occultation of *The Waste Land* manuscript (years of waste time, exasperating to its author) is pure Henry James."

But the brittle-boned figure before me had once again retired behind his impenetrable shield of reticence: he said nothing. The hands continued to work away at each other, and the eyes were quiet and far away. Then the lips began to move, searching for words which would not come.

Finally: "It is sad . . . very sad to look back."

September 1972: my second visit with Ezra Pound. A year and a summer have passed since our first encounter. And in the interim another controversy has flared up around the poet. This time the in-fighting was over the Emerson–Thoreau Medal awarded annually by the American Academy of Arts and Sciences "for outstanding contributions to the broad field of literature over the recipient's entire lifetime." A nominating committee—Leon Edel, Chairman; John Cheever; Lillian Hellman; James Laughlin; Harry Levin; Louis Martz; and Lewis Mumford[1]— had recommended that the octogenarian poet's towering influence on modern letters be recognized, that it was time to set aside his wartime activities, which they attributed wholly to mental illness. But nothing, with the exception of the writing of verse, had ever come easily to Pound; within a few weeks the opposition, led by Daniel Bell, the Harvard sociologist, contended that while Pound's literary contributions could not be challenged, his broadcasts for Mussolini during the war and the strident anti-Semitic texture of some of his Cantos made him a poor candidate for a humanistic award. It was the Bollingen Prize controversy all over again, a rekindling of that irresoluble debate: can a man's artistic achievement be separated from his morality and ideology? And if a moral yardstick is applied, whose morality is to be used?

The poet on trial again: it is as Leslie Fiedler describes it in *Waiting for the End*: "Each age must have its own, brand-new defendants, and the mass audience sitting in judgment in the middle of the twentieth century has tried and sentenced the poet once more, yet as if for the first time, in the person of Ezra Pound." Sitting in judgment, the *Staatsrat* or High Commission,[2] by a tally of 13 to 9, with two abstentions and two absentees, had voted against the committee's recommendation and against Pound. The verdict was official: Ezra Pound was not to join the ranks of the select—Robert Frost, T. S. Eliot, Katherine Anne Porter, Mark Van Doren, John Crowe Ransom, Hannah Arendt, and the other poets, novelists, and critics who had been chosen for the prize in the past; instead he was to remain forever outside the Kingdom of Art, a literary outcast, a permanent exile.

Then came the predictable aftermath—the approbations, accusations, denunciations, and denials, the same shower of pro-and-anti pronouncements that had followed the 1948 Bollingen Prize announcement:

Daniel Bell: "We have to distinguish between those who explore hate and those who approve hate. In short, one may appreciate the painful work of a man who has, at great personal cost, spent a season in hell; but it does not follow that one honors a man who advocates a way of life that makes the world hellish. Necessarily, one has to draw a distinction between the work and the man."

Irving Howe: "Pound wished none of us personal harm; his rantings against the Jews were utterly *abstract*, a phantasm of ideology that is a major dimension of their terribleness. . . . But the question of whether to honor Pound involves neither the granting nor the refusal of forgiveness. It involves something else: I do not believe that we can yet close the books of twentieth-century history, certainly not as long as any of us remains alive who can remember the days of the mass murder."

Martin Kilson: "As a Negro I am as outraged about anti-Negro intellectuals as a Jew about anti-Semitic ones but such outrage is not a matter of intellect but of politics, and in evaluating an intellectual's works I believe that short of the intellectual himself committing criminal or atrocious acts against humanity under the influence of his politics, his intellectual works should stand on their own."

Harry Levin: "The majority of the council, in overriding the recommendation, has attempted to rationalize its decision by repeated assertions that art cannot be isolated from morality. This is misleading, if not disingenuous, in its implication that Pound and his proponents were irresponsible aesthetes. There was never any disagreement over the principle involved. Members of the committee never questioned the assumption that aesthetics is grounded in ethics. Pound, like his master, Dante, is not only an artist but an impassioned moralist."

The Bollingen Prize committee, in 1949, resolved the Pound dilemma by separating the man from his work and giving the work the prize; the Council of the American Academy of Arts and Sciences, deciding twenty-three years later not to give the academy's Emerson–Thoreau Medal to Pound, did just the opposite. The endless philosophical debate seemed too remote, too abstract, for a poet of Pound's stature. It had nothing to do with him now as he lay on his back, lifeless, the classic Grecian head buoyed up by pillows, blue pajamas draped over his emaciated body. The haunting sapphirine eyes had clouded over. Hands were clenched to the bone. He chipped away with them at dead, eczematous skin. Like his adopted Venezia, he was wasting away.

An Arno Breker bust of Pound, which I had failed to notice before, stood at one end of the room atop a shelf. Breker had frozen the subject in old age, a robust old age, a distinct counterpoise to the man stretched out this day before me. The expression the sculptor had captured recreated the portrait of the persona who had been spotted mid-April 1971 inside the church of San Zanipolo at the funeral of Igor Stravinsky. He sat that morning at the rear of the large Gothic cathedral, attentive, poised, staring vibrantly at the black coffin, his ear trained on the strains of the composer's *Requiem Canticles*.

Absorbed in his own universe, the Great Bass seemed now not

aware of anyone else's presence in the room. Then, slowly, his focus shifted. He studied me. After a short while he said: "You're from New York, aren't you?" The conversation was resumed by him as if, indeed, it had never ceased, as if sixteen months hadn't actually passed, as if time itself had stood still.

He pulled himself, with some difficulty, to a half-sitting position. He stared at me openly and candidly. He moved his mouth as though to speak. And then he did speak, his emotion tearing loose in clots: "I hold no delusions. . . . What's done cannot be undone. . . . The error is all in the not done. . . . I was wrong. . . . Ninety-per-cent wrong. . . . I lost my head in a storm."

Olga Rudge, standing next to me, responded to his lament: "It's always because we love that we are rebellious; it takes a great deal of love to care what happens."

"Or hatred," Pound whispered.

Looking at him, seeing him before me like this, I felt strangely out of sync. I felt I had somehow traveled backward in time. I remembered reading some place a quotation by Jean Cocteau. He had called Pound "a rower on the river of the dead"—"un rameur sur le fleuve des morts." The Last Rower: it is the Ulysses image in its peculiarly American form—"that non-Homeric, romanticized figure out of Dante by way of Tennyson which so spectacularly haunts the imagination of Ezra Pound."[3]

Early-morning jaunts with Olga Rudge were still part of his day. He liked to walk along the Zattere, the promenade that runs parallel to the very blue Canale della Giudecca. Across the canal, shimmering dreamlike in the rippling water, the majestic churches and palaces of the Giudecca. Italians on their way to work often stopped and stared, or sometimes tipped their hats as the old gentleman moved along. But American tourists seldom recognized one of their best-known poets.

Once in the public eye—whether a restaurant, a café or simply a long, leisurely stroll—he would inevitably hide behind his veil of silence. It was at such moments that Miss Rudge took over, guiding the conversation, exercising charm, putting at ease whoever happened to be in their presence. If Pound resented his companion's overprotective demeanor he did not show it. When they entertained, they generally took their guests to Harry's Bar, Hemingway's old haunt, or Montin's, a *trattoria* on San Trovaso, frequented by artists and writers since the 1930s, when d'Annunzio made it his eating place. The young waiter at the San Trovaso restaurant was well acquainted with much of Pound's verse and seemed to know the old man's way. *"Volto sciolto, pensiero stretto,"* were the words he used to describe it—"An open countenance and closed thoughts."

Return to the occasion at hand, to the silence richer than almost any talk. I posed a question or two for the poet. Pound blinked: no response. But soon his parched lips began to move, sounds followed:

"It's very difficult for me to answer your questions. . . ."

One final exchange:

"Will you ever return to the United States?"

A quizzical smile, a long pause before answering:

"Anything is possible."

He passed away in Venice on November 1, 1972, two days after his eighty-seventh birthday, a few hours after being taken to Saints John and Paul Hospital, opposite the Colleoni Statue. He died peacefully in sleep.

In the last week of his life he saw a noh play and the Peter Brook production of *A Midsummer Night's Dream.* His last birthday party was full of joy: cake, champagne, neighboring children, friends. His conversation that day touched briefly on Jules Laforgue, Henri Michaux, and Marianne Moore. A number of months before his own death, he had lamented the passing of Miss Moore by reading her very beautiful and apt poem "What Are Years?" at a memorial service in Venice's Protestant Church. That was his last public reading. He read from his own work for a small gathering of friends inside the Hidden Nest two weeks before the end. And his last written words were very likely the few thoughts he had strung together as foreword to the Cookson-edited anthology published posthumously (Pound, *Selected Prose, 1909–1965*). The poet's statement ends:

> In sentences referring to groups or races 'they' should be used with great care.
> re USURY:
> I was out of focus, taking a symptom for a cause.
> The cause is AVARICE.

The funeral, on November 3, was more formality than rite. A simple and brief service, in the Palladium Basilica on the isle of San Gregorio, was without the customary black drapes, and there were none of the flowers for which Venetian funerals are known. The plain chestnut coffin stood before the altar in a shroud of Gregorian chant and Monteverdi; absolution was performed by a charcoal-robed Benedictine with aspergillum and censer (*te supplices exoramus pro anima famuli tui Ezra*).[4] No tributes came from either the Italian or American government. There were relatively few mourners. Neither Dorothy Pound nor Omar was present. Olga Rudge and Mary and Patrizia de Rachewiltz accompanied him on his last voyage.[5]

A poster printed by the "Gruppo di studio Ezra Pound" appeared the day after his death on what had become the neo-Fascist billboards of Milan—the granite and marble columns of Piazza San Biblia—loudly proclaiming in bold black print "Ezra Pound is dead," followed by several paragraphs in small print extolling the man found "guilty of having taken the Fascist side against the old, materialistic, usura-ridden world," and concluding with "Ezra Pound is born" in the same oversized black letters.[6] The controversy surrounding Pound had obviously not been resolved; he could not escape it even in death.

Following the service, four Venetian friends shouldered the coffin down the aisle, and then it was placed in a black-and-gold gondola and covered with wreaths. Chrysanthemums spilled yellow and white along the gondola's side, backed by long fronds of emerald palm. A bronze crucifix was affixed to the casket. The gondoliers pushed off from the landing stage and four of them, clad in black, guided the vessel out across the azure *laguna*, under bright sun, to the *campo santo* on the burial island of San Michele, not far from the plots of Sergei Diaghilev and Igor Stravinsky. Here, among exiles, surrounded by grass and trees, he was laid to rest. *In paradisum deducant te Angeli*, the priest sang, *in tuo adventu suscipiant te Martyres, et perducant te in civitatem sanctam Jerusalem.*[7]

Some weeks later a stone, designed by the American sculptress Joan Fitzgerald, was set in place at the head of the grave; in a delicate and solemn script it read simply:

EZRA POUND

Appendixes

Letters to Benito Mussolini

Nine letters from Ezra Pound to Benito Mussolini (FBI files, Federal Bureau of Investigation, Department of Justice, Washington, D.C.). Translated from the Italian by Robert Connolly, Director of the Paterno Library, Casa Italiana, Columbia University, New York City.

The following correspondence represents a partial selection of the fifty-odd pieces from Ezra Pound to Benito Mussolini which have been preserved as part of the FBI files. This selection (including the letters to Ciano and Mezzasoma) was seized by American officials in 1945 from Italian government files located at Milan, Rome, and Valdagno, Italy. The bulk of the material in the FBI files is uncatalogued, housed simply in large, plain folders, filed approximately by date. Pound's Italian, it should be noted, is often unwieldy and ungrammatical, at points all but indecipherable. When and where necessary, annotations of certain names and terms have been provided by the author.

*

> Via Marsala 12–5
> Rapallo
> 17 April
> Anno XI [1933]

HIS EXCELLENCY THE LEADER OF THE GOVERNMENT

Excellency and Duce

Enclosed with this letter I am sending Your Excellency the small book *ABC of Economics* and the manuscript of *Jefferson and/or Mussolini* written in February.

> With devoted homage,
> Ezra Pound

Attached to this note when it reached Mussolini was a memorandum from the Press Office of the Ministry of Foreign Affairs (signature illegible) which reads in part:

> The known American writer, Ezra Pound, has sent Your Excellency the enclosed book called *ABC of Economics* with an autograph dedicated to Your Excellency and the typewritten copy of *Jefferson and/or Mussolini*, recently written by the same Pound, but not yet published. . . . His books clearly demonstrate a friendly feeling for Fascism.

A 300-word review of the *Jefferson and/or Mussolini* manuscript was likewise attached. Written by an official in the Translation Section of the Press Office, it begins:

The author makes a comparison between the political and social conceptions and actions of Thomas Jefferson and those of Mussolini, recognizing that, owing to the different periods of time in which the two carried out their activities, the Duce is not at all inferior to the great President of the United States. Both are activated by their passion for construction, but owing to his purely Italian spirit, the Duce has a still greater passion for construction; in fact, no one can appreciate his contributions unless they begin by considering him a constructionist, an artist in the greater sense of the word.

*

> Via Marsala 12–5
> Rapallo
> 19 February
> Anno XII

Excellency and DUCE

The *Belvedere del Architettura* by Bardi, which I received yesterday, increases even more my admiration for all that has been accomplished. BUT, with the concept of "credit to the consumer," construction can be increased a *hundredfold*.

To give a house of the era to each and every Italian. With the concept of "negative interest" (stamp scrip), it will not be necessary to go into DEBT each time one wants to construct.

Everything that Your Excellency has done to mobilize the internal credit of the country has turned out magnificently. I don't think that it is a good idea, however, to stir up the people, by putting into their hands so soon the potential resources of the new economy.

BUT these two discoveries by the two geniuses, Gesell and Douglas, must not be ignored.

The bankers are afraid of "ras moneta," *Schwundgeld*, and many others do not understand that two kinds of money can exist simultaneously. Naturally, if there were only "ras moneta," "legitimate" profits, etc., might disappear; but as an auxiliary currency, the experiment has already been tried out.

Naturally, since the times of the Medicis, it has been known that a low interest [rate] is better for a country than a high one, but a "Negative" interest is that much more powerful. The tax falls on the money itself—on the money that does not produce, and not on the work.

Two faint glimmers of hope exist in the United States Senate. I haven't yet received the *Congressional Record* containing Cutting's speech (27 January), but it seems that he is beginning to see the light.

The London *Times* has also been forced to consider old Kitson as a possible contributor. (I don't know if they will publish his articles) . . . Every day a new book comes out, slipping past the conspiracy of the capitalist press, and revealing a bit here and there.

I do not speak of Senator Bankhead, because I don't believe that he understands things clearly, and I suppose that he was in some way intimidated by his "friends," after he spoke, last February.

Construction creates material CREDIT, and this must not be recorded as a "monetary debt."

I hope I have been clear; it is not easy to express oneself in a language not one's own.

With all good faith,
devotedly,
Ezra Pound

Pietra Maria Bardi, a popular Italian journalist, and the author of the *Belvedere dell' Architettura*, was also the founder of the Bardi Gallery of Art in Milan. The *Belvedere* is a lengthy treatise on Italian functional architecture, which goes to great lengths to extoll Mussolini's contributions in this particular area.

The January 27 speech of Senator Bronson Cutting of New Mexico appeared in that year's *Congressional Record* (73 Cong., 2 Sess., pp. 1475–76). Debating a Payment of Debts to Veterans amendment to the Gold Reserve Act of 1934, Cutting used the opportunity to present Congress with an argument which came very close to the argument put forward by Social Creditors in their bid for monetary reform. In part, he said:

> The place we want credit is in the hands of the consumer. I do not think it is necessary to argue that point at this time in the history of the United States. Three or four years ago people thought you were crazy when you talked about equating the purchasing power of the country with the productive power. Now everybody recognizes that, so far as speech is concerned. We talk about purchasing power, but we take little action about it.
>
> In my judgment the Government is going to have to finance the consumer as consumer—not primarily as a worker—and it is going to have to do it very soon. It can be done only through the establishment of some central government agency—call it a central bank or call it what you will—which will monopolize the credit system of the country for the benefit of the public and not for the benefit of the bankers. Such an agency must eventually absorb, at a greater or less rate of speed, the present Federal Reserve System. Our distributive system must be strengthened by the Government acting directly as an agent for the consumer.

And "old Kitson" is the monetary reformer Arthur Kitson. An important source for some of Pound's ideas on money, Kitson was the author of such economic studies as *The Money Question* (London, 1903) and *The Banker's Conspiracy* (London, 1933).

*

Via Marsala 12–5
Rapallo
15 April
Anno XII

Excellency and DUCE

I have received letters from America concerning the growing interest of the Administration for the ideas of Douglas. I have already written to the Chief of the Press Office, that Senator Cutting has spoken most clearly (27 January in the Senate).

Cutting writes me, "I am afraid they (the Administration) don't want to ask themselves a question to which the answer is so obvious."

Ass/to Sec. writes me from the Treasury Dept. that Sec. Morgenthau has asked him to write to me "che apprezzano i miei espressioni."

(your views appreciated and ALL the problems you touched upon are having the thoughtful attention of the Administration.)

I had written with regard to the basis of Douglasite "cultural heritage as the basis of VALUES," etc., "lack of non-static purchasing power," etc.

(Their letter could be a lump of sugar to pacify the undersigned baby— but I am almost certain that Douglas is winning over opinions and votes.)

Meanwhile, I am enclosing a note received this morning. Perhaps it is too condensed to be clear.

VIVA SABAUDIA
Ezra Pound

The third paragraph of this letter ("Ass/to Sec.") including the parenthetical sentence which follows it, was originally written in English; it is copied verbatim.

The "note" referred to, which Pound appended to his mailing, is a three-page circular by A. L. Gibson, British Social Creditor; it is entitled *The Social Credit Proposals of Major C. H. Douglas*, and a subheading of topics discussed lists as subject matter the following: 1. Open the National Credit Office; 2. Apply the Just Price; and 3. Issue the National Dividend.

A hand-written comment by Pound appears on the third page of the circular, following the "Issue of the National Dividend" section; it reads: "Against misery. Not necessarily against that which Delcroix believes is saintly poverty."

Sabaudia, whose existence the correspondent so heartily celebrates, was a newly constructed urban center, located approximately forty miles south of Rome in the southern tier of the Pontin region, on the Lake of Sabaudia. Completed early in 1934, Sabaudia comprised a total area of 144.3 square kilometers, and had a stable population of 1800. Today, it is used as a summer resort by vacationing, heat-weary Romans.

This particular letter, incidentally, was forwarded to Mussolini via the office of Count Galeazzo Ciano, to whom Pound wrote: "I respectfully request that the enclosed be transmitted to the Head of the Government." An administrator in Ciano's office, attaching a memorandum to the letter for Ciano's benefit, notes that Pound's Italian is "incomprehensible," and adds: "One thing that is clear is that the author is mentally unbalanced."

*

Via Marsala 12–5
Rapallo
25 May
Anno XII

Excellency and DUCE

With my respects I enclose this souvenir of a neglected chapter of American economic history.

Paper currency = a note against "merchandise and lumber." In practice it was [considered] a "certificate of work done," when my grandfather was laying the foundation for a city in the wilderness, before the arrival of the bank monopolies.

It is clear that the paper money was GOOD, that is, from the worn condition of the bill. It is obvious that the system worked.

Primitive money—that is, the man who issued the money owned the merchandise. Naturally, the bankers were jealous and opposed to this primitive form, just as today they are opposed to the creative force of the state.

I don't know if McNair Wilson's book, *The Promise to Pay*, is known in Rome. It is clear but a bit long.

With all my faith,
Ezra Pound

The "souvenir" which Pound enclosed with his letter, and of which he writes, was a sample of the scrip which his grandfather, Thaddeus Coleman Pound, issued while administering the Union Lumbering Company, Chippewa Falls, Wisconsin.

R. McNair Wilson, heart specialist, war correspondent, medical correspondent for the London *Times*, and an economic historian was also an avid correspondent of Pound's. Wilson's *Mind of Napoleon* had been an important source book for the poet, and he boosted Wilson's book, *The Promise to Pay*, wherever and whenever he could.

*

Via Marsala 12–5
Rapallo
1 June
Anno XII

Excellency and DUCE

I do not know if the Press Office receives the *New English Weekly* regularly, but the note on page 148 regarding the Senators present at the dinner for C. H. Douglas mentions the following:

Democrats	*Republicans*
Black (Alabama)	Borah (Idaho)
Bone (Washington)	Frazier (N. Dakota)
Clark (Missouri)	La Follette (Wisconsin)
George (Georgia)	Nye (N. Dakota)

Farm/Labour

Shipstead (Minnesota)
Thomas (Utah or Oklahoma—I'm not sure which)
Wagner (New York. Lives in New York City)
Wheeler (Montana)

The supper was given by Cutting (Senator from New Mexico), Rainey, Speaker of the House, and other representatives. It is apparent that interest exists among Western agriculturalists, and it is clear that these economic ideas are no longer considered "poetic oddities." Here, too, we see clearly their desire to free themselves from the hold of the usurers.

With all my faith,
Ezra Pound

The note in the *New English Weekly* of May 31, 1934 (vol. v, no. 7) to which Pound refers reads as follows:

. . . On April 22 Major Douglas and Father Coughlin, whose personal following exceeds that of any Hollywood queen, and whose weekly broadcasts are now based upon Social Credit, conferred together in Washington for several hours. Next day Major Douglas returned to New York by air to deliver his lecture in the New School for Social Research, after which he again went to Washington. On Wednesday he was the guest at a luncheon at the Brookings Institute [*sic*], and in the evening he was guest of honour at a supper given by Senator Cutting. A list of the forty-four people present would furnish a striking testimony to the upward spread of interest in Social Credit in the United States: they included Senators Black, Bone, Borah, Clark, Frazier, George, La Follette, Norris, Nye, Shipstead, Thomas, Wagner, and Wheeler; Representatives Speaker Rainey, Busby, Dies, Goldsborough, Lewis, Kvale, Patman, and Steagall; Administration officials Chapman, Collier, Peek, and Hopkins, and publicists Gardner Jackson and Farmer Murphy. On the following day Major Douglas was back in New York to broadcast over station WJZ and NBC network.

*

Via Marsala 12–5
Rapallo
August 2
Anno XII

Excellency and Duce

You have done it again, in the midst of a personal tragedy, and even the god-damn frogs have to admit it.

But the laundry girl can't get married, because there is little work. She has been "fidanzata" for 2 years. This is the very best type of working class, clean, steady; she began carrying the basket as a child, when I first came here ten years ago. And this is a concrete argument for the study of SOCIAL credit, or for the new economics, Gesell, principle of negative interest. You can't kill usury but it is possible, È POSSIBLE, to start the COUNTER-PROCESS.

I have just written a critique of J. P. Warburg's book (*Money Muddle*), astute banker's pathology. Need to him means: the need to go on banking. Anything which isn't deposited in the bank does NOT fit into his frame of reference. He was perhaps responsible for the great bank reform, healthy and prudent, proposed and carried out in America. BUT he has a psychology of the profession DEFORMED by the profession. And the sophisms, the double entendres, even the word *money* is used in a duplicate sense, that is, metal, legal paper WITH bank-money and then on the other page, excluding bank-money, and he is so clever that he deceives even himself.

Everything that Italy DOES, she does well. Division of labor/human/good, good/and the economists (most of them don't understand the need for acting humanely) but the economic facts, the money question, and the *nature of money* remain.

With all my faith,
Ezra Pound

The first two paragraphs and the first sentence of the third paragraph of the above letter were written to Mussolini in English; the rest of the letter was written in Italian.

The critique of Warburg's book, *The Money Muddle*, was to appear as "A Banker's Elegy" in *Time and Tide*, XV, 32 (August 11, 1934).

*

Via Marsala 12–5
Rapallo
22 December
Anno XIV

Duce! Duce!

Many enemies, much honor.

I want to see all USURERS among the enemies of Italy. But, DUCE! the system of TAXES is a pernicious remnant of the past, a corpse, which must be buried along with the Bomb King and Franz Joseph. Inasmuch as the STATE furnishes a MEASURE of exchange, the state works. The State has a right to demand compensation for its work. And this compensation is fundamentally DIFFERENT from a tax.

Inasmuch as the banknote of the STATE exists, the state works and furnishes the MEASURE and has the right to a compensation (revenue stamps, stamps for stamp scrip, invented by Avigliano, and by Gesell) of a maximum of 1% per month. The savage uses one tool, whereas the civilized man uses a hundred of them.

A means of EXCHANGE.

Another for savings.

All the expenditures of the State must be paid for in prescribable money. All services, everything which lasts for a day and must be done over again the next day, must be paid for in a transient currency.

Your Excellency has already indicated as much by saying: I BECOME INFURIATED WHENEVER THEY TELL ME THAT WORK IS A BLESSING. In place of certain durable products, certificates of stock can be issued; that is, the usual state bank notes, which are now used for all merchandise and services.

In place of SAVINGS 5% state notes can be used, just as they are used today. All this would eliminate a great deal of "red tape" and all the complications and problems of cancellation of credit, etc.

VIVIA L'ITALIA
Ezra Pound
jure italico

A carbon copy of this letter was found in the FBI files; the original was located recently in the *Archivio Storico dei Ministero Affari Esteri* (Historical Archive of the Ministry of Foreign Affairs) in Rome and appeared in an article, *"Ezra Pound e il fascismo"*, by Niccolò Zapponi (*Storia Contemporanea*. Bologna, Italy, September 1973).

The "Bomb King" ("King Bomba") was Ferdinand II (1810–59), Monarch of the Two Sicilies; his ruthless and ferocious repressiveness earned him his strange sobriquet.

Avigliano, although mentioned in passing by Pound in *Oro e Lavoro* (*Gold and Work*), is more difficult to trace. A possible candidate is a Francesco Avigliano, who wrote a book entitled *L'enigma sociale* (Milan: 1926, 1928, 1936), published by the Dante Society.

*

Via Marsala 12–5
Rapallo
15 May
Anno XV

A tax is not a share

A nation need not and
should not pay rent for
its own credit

TO THE LEADER OF THE GOVERNMENT

Excellency and Duce

Availing myself of the invitation proffered by His Excellency Polverelli four years ago, I am sending Your Excellency a copy of the GLOBE, which has finally published my article on the EMPIRE. The article was written last September, but its publication was delayed because of preparations for a large mailing.

It is not a political magazine. I am their European correspondent, but I cannot vouch for the opinions of the other writers. I can only assure Your Excellency that I shall send news in good faith concerning Italy.

They write me from the Office: Prejudice is much against Nazi and Fascism.

Pressure is not exerted on *Globe* by commercial advertisers, and thus there is at least a certain amount of freedom. But no director of a magazine having a large circulation can ignore the opinions of his readers.

The danger of poisoning from England exists in America. The two share a common language and certain customs. . . .

This is a fragment of a longer letter, the second half of which has not yet turned up.

His Excellency Gaetano Polverelli succeeded Alessandro Pavolini as Minister of Popular Culture on February 5, 1943. Prior to this, Polverelli had been head of Mussolini's Press Office (1932–33) and was Undersecretary of the Ministry of Popular Culture until his appointment as Minister. The invitation in question was a letter Polverelli had sent to Pound in response to the latter's epistle of February 8, 1933; on that occasion, Polverelli suggested to Pound that any articles deemed important enough to be seen by the Duce be sent to Mussolini directly. The article itself ("Europe–MCMXXVI: Reflections Written on the Eve of a New Era") appeared in *Globe*, I, 1 (May 1937).

In the above letter the awkward phrase "Prejudice is much against Nazi and Fascism" was written by Pound in English just as it appears.

*

POUND   October 28—XXI

Service Note

REPORT TO IL DUCE

I say "Report to Il Duce" because this material has to do with various offices (Finance, Foreign Affairs), although it is herein presented as an instrument of propaganda.

A spontaneous Communist movement does not now exist in England. The few intelligent and sincere Communists in England are Communists not because they are pro-Bolshevik, but because of their anger against usury and against the usurious system.

All (I say all) the heads of the Communist Party and all of their important seconds, as far back as 1938, were known to have been salaried agents of Moscow and were assigned to do industrial espionage work.

But for a long time now there have been various movements for an economic and monetary reform which, from the times of H. George and the Single Tax, Distributionists, Social Creditors, followers of S. Ambrose and of Lancelot Andrewes in the Christian and Catholic tradition, opposed usury, etc.

Among these the most important is the Green Shirt Party or "Social Credit" group (Major C. H. Douglas). The meeting between Douglas and Mosley was arranged by this writer, and from the day on which the meeting took place, Mosley was taken more seriously, that is his name almost completely disappeared from the press and the silent treatment was carried on against him as it was carried on against Douglas from 1917 up until the time of his party's victory in Alberta, a province of 600,000 inhabitants, toward 1935.

In Alberta Social Credit picked up from Gesell the mechanism of free or prescribed money but applied it in an exaggerated and incompetent manner. Taxes of 2% a week, that is 104% a year, were paid instead of 12% a year as was levied by Wörgl. (And with systems which did not guarantee the adherence of the markets.)

In New Zealand, in Texas, etc., notable groups of these various reformers exist and any official mention on the part of the Fascist Republican Government which would induce these reformers to believe that serious revolution is about to take place in Italy would enhance the prestige of the Republic.

The announcement that a reform, a real monetary reform, will be put into effect for the benefit of the Italian people, would also help. We can count on a rather strong resistance on the part of the mercantile industrialists, liberals, Italian usurers, to impede the implementation of any serious reform in this field which is not imposed by the higher authorities.

LIAISON

Refer to Offices of Communications and Interior

The proposal for an autobus from Spezia to Salò via Genoa, Tortona, Piacenza, and Cremona, is designed to give the Republic a new backbone.

Liguria is now completely cut off from all means of communication. Even before, one had to take three trains to get from Rapallo to Brescia. Now a person must spend the night in Genoa in order to reach Milan from Rapallo.

The Ligurians are keen mercantile industrialists and sons of smugglers. The Ligurian coast is living proof of the love of God against the smugglers. It seems that "Mazzinian" in many cases means "Mason."

But to give the impression that the new Government actually exists, an improvement of communications in addition to a direct route would help. It would be wonderful to be able to improve the conditions which have existed since September 8th.

PRESS

As a result of the appointment of the present Secretary of the Party to the post of director of *Il Messagero* the prevailing conditions of this past month should improve. The new director will help to change the typographical setup of several papers.

The Italian rotogravure maintains a format of the Sketch, Sphere Type Anglo-plutocratic. USSR EN CONSTRUZION has a format more adaptable to the republican era. It is useless for the *Corriere della Sera* to maintain traces of its infamous past. "Tempo" was always a putrid black newspaper.

Ezra Pound

This 1943 "Service Note" to Mussolini was one of several such communiqués which Pound sent to Il Duce at Salò.

Concerning Douglas, Social Credit, and Alberta, Canada: the situation was not exactly as Pound would have it. It is true that William Aberhart and his Social Credit party were elected into office in Alberta in 1935, but Social Credit, as a monetary system, was never actually implemented with any degree of success. It is as Gorham Munson has described it in *Aladdin's Lamp* (New York: 1945, p. 207): "All Aberhart was permitted to accomplish was a kind of provincial "new deal," some amelioration of the lot of the debtor. He was not allowed to take the smallest step in installing Social Credit, and therefore the widespread notion that Social Credit was tried and failed in Alberta is erroneous; what failed was the bungling attempt to introduce Social Credit."

It was Alessandro Pavolini who gave up his government post to become the director of *Il Messagero*, a position he later relinquished to become party secretary of the Italian Social Republic.

APPENDIX II
Letters to Galeazzo Ciano

Four letters from Ezra Pound to Count Galeazzo Ciano (FBI files, Federal Bureau of Investigation, Department of Justice, Washington, D.C.). Translated from the Italian, except as noted, by Robert Connolly.

These letters from Ezra Pound to Count Galeazzo Ciano, Mussolini's son-in-law, were written in 1934, at which time Ciano was Minister of Italian Press and Propaganda. In June 1936, he was appointed Minister of Foreign Affairs, a post he held until February 1943, when he was made Ambassador to the Holy See. In July, he joined the dissident members of the Fascist Grand Council who forced Mussolini's resignation. Interned in Germany, he was delivered by the Germans to the Italian Fascists at Verona, tried by them for treason, and executed by a firing squad on January 11, 1944.

*

> Via Marsala 12–5
> Rapallo
> 3 March
> Anno XII

Excellency,

I received news yesterday that The Central Office of the Conservative Party (London) is beginning to wake up, and that all the officers have received a circular ordering them to study the economics of C. H. Douglas in its derived form called "Nationalist Economics."

Douglas is the economist of whom I spoke last year when I had the privilege of meeting the Leader of the Government. Because I was in a great rush I am afraid I might have spoken in a confused manner.

Douglas's starting point is: "Every factory, every industry (under the present system) produces 'prices' more rapidly than it distributes purchasing power."

. . . .

I received news from America that some senators are preparing a bill based on the Douglas principle. Details are not yet available.

. . . .

In truth, it seems to me that the lira is not based on gold but is at the discretion of His Excellency, the Leader of the Government, and is therefore no longer in the hands of the bankers; but I am uncertain if this point is to be made public.

                                    With expressions of high respect,
                                    Ezra Pound

The above letter to Ciano was originally written in Italian. Following its receipt, Ciano notified Pound that he should feel free to write to him directly in English, which the poet apparently did.

*

                                    Via Marsala 12–5
                                    Rapallo
                                    16 March
                                    Anno XII

S. E. Conte Galeazzo Ciano
Capo dell Ufficio Stampa del Capo del Governo

I thank Your Excellency for the invitation to write in English (or American) and hope you realize my "lingua materna" is NOT the language of diplomacy.

I have just had news that the Rothermere [news] papers hold stock in various airplane works and that the attempt to boost "aviation shares" etc. etc. . . . [is as] one wd. expect, but as the news is now spread, and seems unlikely to be contradicted, it rather puts an edge on my statement in review of Goad's *Corporate State*, forwarded a few weeks ago.

It will be nearly impossible to print fair and just news about Italy in honest papers in England or America if Rothermere is allowed to creep under the Fascist aegis.

The *Corriere* (I think) declared months ago that there was no fascism save Italian Fascism, but that view will not be spread by the Rothermere papers.

I don't want to bother you with stale news of things you already know. But I will go into detail any time you like, IF I happen to have any detail.

I wrote before that although I have had five books published last year, and five due this year, my book on the DUCE [*Jefferson and/or Mussolini*] simply does NOT get printed.

As I think it as good as any prose I have written I can't put this down to prejudice against me, but as [a] sign of unwillingness to receive what I believe a fair and just account of Italy, and of the constructive nature of Italian Fascism.

The anti-Fascist doctrinaires are hopeless. The honest men are often far from the centre of power. I cannot find anyone in England who understands Europe, though an increasing number of Englishmen are "on to" Rothermere, Niemeyer, Bark, Herb. Lawrence, Vickers, the Bank of Eng.

When I say Englishmen, I mean the honest ones, the damned rascals understand international rascality, all right enough.

So long as these people are trusted as you wd. trust cobras, I have nothing to say. But it is pleasant to know that both Rother/ and Beaver got swatted at the recent London Elections.

IF you have need of an honest party in England, I believe the GREEN

SHIRTS are that. And I am sending you a marked copy of *New Democracy*, which may shed a little light on the matter.

Whatever the superficial differences, the details of local procedure, this is the constructive party, and the party that is worth having for a friend. People one can meet and not have to wash one's hands after touching. That does NOT in the least mean they will at once understand the last ten years of Italian history or that they will be able to see over the differences in terminology, ideology, etc.

But they wd. not be trying to pick your pocket or sell guns to Italy and France on the same day, or dress up as Fascists in order to commit all the crimes in the calendar.

I may frequently want to get a rock-drill in order to make Orage or Douglas SEE something, but I swear they are both honest, that you can't buy 'em, that you can't get 'em to say "yes" when they mean "no". I have seen the movement when there weren't more than six of us. If there were not bed rock truth in it, I don't see how it could have lasted from 1917 or '18, when Orage chucked his Guild Socialism, in order to propagate Douglas' ideas.

It is an Economics with ETHICS underneath it, and that takes count of man being human, and of his wanting art and letters.

They are English (or Scotch) and I don't think they understand anything South of the Alps, or possibly South of the Channel, but they are not "antistorico." You can't tell Douglas that a peasant in the Abruzz' and a London Bank clerk are not likely to have the same outlook in "dicto millesimo," the same month and year. Nevertheless, I am convinced that they are your best English allies, for 1940, if not for ANNO XII.

Goad's *Corporate State* is a reference to Harold E. Goad's *The Making of the Corporate State, A Study of Fascist Development*, a pro-Fascist retrospective dealing partially with "Democracy in Italy." The book was published in 1932 by Christophers of London.

The Viscount Harold Rothermere, whose newspapers supposedly "held stock" in various "airplane works," was chief proprietor of the *Daily Mail*, the *Daily Mirror*, and the *London Evening News*.

Sir Otto Niemeyer was a director of the Bank of England and a member of the Finance Committee of the League of Nations; His Excellency Peter Bark, a Russian-born nobleman, was managing director of the Anglo-International Bank Ltd.; Sir Herbert Lawrence was chairman of Vickers Ltd., one of the largest of the British industrial conglomerates, and a member of the Royal commission on Coal Industry; Sir Douglas Vickers was chairman of the board of Vickers Ltd. from 1917 to 1926 and president of the firm from 1926 to 1938.

*

Via Marsala 12–5
Rapallo
27 May
Anno XII

To: Conte Ciano

I don't know whether the DUCE shd/be bothered with these gnat bites.

And I can not judge the timing, but I wish he could make some *economic* declaration that would be absolutely clear.

The Pope [Pius XI] has done fairly well in denouncing international finance. But it isn't ENOUGH. Roosevelt wobbles hither and yon.

Even a broadcast of leading questions re/economics might be useful.

Faithfully,
Ezra Pound

*

Via Marsala 12–5
Rapallo
7 October
Anno XII

S. E. Il Conte Galeazzo Ciano
Sottosegretario di Stato
Roma

My Dear Conte Ciano

I think the best plan will be for me to nail down the editor of *Esquire* [Arnold Gingrich] and make perfectly sure that he is ready to print what I send him. After which I will come down to Rome and one of Yr/assistants can help me pick out the photos.

I am sending my last book [*Make It New*] to the Capo del Governo in yr. care, as indication that I am not yet buried. The english-american printing and book trade may be able to delay my book on "J. and/or M." but they can not censor my prefaces.

I enclose a list of questions which I am sending to professional economists and trained seals, in an attempt to break down camouflage. You will I hope agree that men who cannot or dare not answer these questions are not fit to teach economics in Universities.

Stato civile/DEATHS: Scarcity economics died in Milan yesterday at 4:14 p.m. no mourners in attendance. No flowers.

Photographs of the funeral/a few of the port of Zara, with that damn island in the front yard/etc. *might* be useful, also a couple of the "opere della regime."

P.M. Baldi has a good eye for photos/if he is working with the department. But one never knows what he is doing.

Very faithfully yours,
Ezra Pound

If you have an absolute "knock out" of Zara/something showing the situation of the Yugoslav fórt in harbour/and Italian stone work in Zara/I could send that at once in connection with a mss/I shipped to the U.S. ten days ago. I do NOT know whether the mss/will be printed and cannot guarantee the publication of photos with it.

I cán't be *sure* an edtr/in Chicago will *want* to say Wilson was drunk at Versailles, and that the treaty makers didn't know M. meant metres and not miles re/that channel.

According to a letter which Pound wrote September 23, 1935, to Alessandro Chiavolini, Mussolini's private secretary, the poet had written to Gingrich about the possibility of publishing an interview with the Duce in

Esquire. "*Esquire*," the Chiavolini letter reads, ". . . is still silent. It has published many of my articles and it has run polemics by Upton Sinclair and the reactionary George Sokolsky. The editor refuses to commit himself . . . but like any good writer or historian, I would like to have about ten interviews with the Duce, although I fully understand the enormity of such a request in these times." The piece which Pound proposed was never commissioned.

The list of questions to which Pound refers and which he enclosed with this mailing was that infamous list of eight queries he concocted and printed under the heading "Volitionist Economics." Copies were sent to a wide spectrum of correspondents, the purpose being to compile a cross-section survey of economic thought.

"Scarcity economics died in Milan yesterday at 4:14 p.m." is a reference to a speech given by Mussolini on October 6 in Milan. A letter written by Pound to T. S. Eliot in the fall of 1934 (later included in the preface to the American edition of *Jefferson and/or Mussolini*) reads in part:

> On Oct. 6th of the year current (anno XII) between 4 p.m. and 4:30 Mussolini speaking very clearly four or five words at a time, with a pause, quite a long pause, between phrases, to let it sink in, told 40 million Italians together with auditors in the U.S.A. and the Argentine that the problem of production was solved, and that they could now turn their minds to distribution. . . . The more one examines the Milan Speech the more one is reminded of Brancusi, the stone blocks from which no error emerges, from whatever angle one looks at them.

APPENDIX III
Letters to Fernando Mezzasoma

Seven letters from Ezra Pound to Fernando Mezzasoma (FBI files, Federal Bureau of Investigation, Department of Justice, Washington, D.C.). Translated from the Italian by Robert Connolly.

The following are excerpts from seven letters written by Ezra Pound to Fernando Mezzasoma, Minister of Popular Culture for the Republican Government at Salò. The letters were all written in 1944.

*

Via Marsala 12–5
Rapallo
January 16
Anno XXII

The Minister of Popular Culture

Excellency:

The note on this morning's "Radio Journal" is useful for internal purposes but worthless as a response to London's criticism of our radio propaganda. You people refuse to learn from the events which have occupied most of England and America for the past twenty years. . . . I am fed up. Anyone involved in Italy's propaganda broadcasts should at least be acquainted with the cast of mind of those who live in England and the United States and be able to judge their response to our broadcasts.

Perhaps I'm wasting my time, but I am anxious to help. Personally, I am quite satisfied with the provisions of the 13th, but I know what the response of the intelligentsia will be in England and the United States. . . . Socialization of production involves bureaucracy which in turn means increased stupidity and inactivity. I do not necessarily refer to the provisions of the 13th, but to the effect these provisions will inevitably have on the Anglo-American mind. . . .

For the past twenty years ignorance has been created, fomented, and spread by the putrid Italian-Jewified plutocratic press. And well-intentioned youth are still not well enough informed. . . . We are wasting time. In twenty years the Ministry has never really controlled its own printing press. A few bureaucrats have run the entire show. When ordered to print profit-making works they have sent them to large publishing houses, ignoring the smaller houses who genuinely want to help foster Italian culture. . . .

"Journalists are all crazy," a renowned statesman told me not long ago. The Anglo-American journalists are certainly crazy because they believe the pack of lies which go under the guise of "inside dope." This pack of lies differ from those printed by the dirty slaves of usury. In reality, the newsmen don't always believe these lies, but they are convinced that their reading public does. In England the public wants to believe them; in Jewified America the individual is shrewd enough not to have to swallow this nonsense. . . .

That's enough for this morning. I will mail this tomorrow by registered mail. Please send me a line or two to assure me you have read it. . . .

*

Via Marsala 12–5
Rapallo
January 23
Anno XXII

Minister of Popular Culture

Excellency:

Thank you for your letters of the 17th and 19th. Pettinato finds my notes "interesting." After several weeks' delay, they suggested that he publish the articles in English. I give him permission to translate my Ligurian-Yankee into Piemontese. Rivoire, on the other hand, has "followed me . . . on the *Meridiano*." He finds my articles interesting and original and writes "that he will soon publish at least one of them. . . ."

Nothing will get done until I or Nicoletti or some one who understands the meaning of this war has been granted the use of a printing press.

The material left with Nicoletti six weeks ago has not been printed yet. . . . Another editor wants articles on irrelevant subjects. But we are at war now.

. . . It took me twenty years to consolidate the material approved by Sammartano for radio broadcasts.

My Introductory Textbook (copy enclosed), contains material which, according to the chief librarian of American History in the Library of Congress, cannot be found in any other book in the USA.

An article on money came out fifteen days ago, but I hesitate to say where because one of those mysterious counter-orders to which we have become so accustomed, might prevent publication of a second article.

The ignorance of newspaper publishers and government officials is a great deterrent. They are not even aware that a monetary problem exists in Italy. The very mention of the word "money" strikes terror in their hearts. . . . The peasants in this country are being poisoned by the Jewish air; they desire a new Government. . . .

*

Via Marsala 12–5
Rapallo
February 27
Anno XXII

Minister of Popular Culture

Excellency:

In reference to your recent letter: I do not believe a simple formula can save the world. It is a question of dynamics. The Germans are strong because they believe they can create a new order . . . they believe that they can establish a just peace for a thousand years to come. With the exception of the local Republicans, the people here in Rapallo are empty-headed. They think of nothing but deceiving their neighbors. And the Republicans here bicker with their families and among themselves.

The forty-five days created much ill-will. The older people are disgusted (and justly so) because of the many betrayals which occurred. . . .

The Fascist regime is only as good as its propaganda. . . . Italy is full of people who do not know what Fascism means. They see only the riots and the strict regimentation of the system. . . . There is obviously a great need for an immediate exchange of ideas. . . .

*

Via Marsala 12–5
Rapallo
March 31
Anno XXII

F. Mezzasoma

Dear Minister:

Until recently, England was the main target of our radio propaganda campaign. But now it appears that the Empire is committing suicide and losing India. She must begin to consider the stupidity of her government. . . .

You have never answered my question regarding radio broadcasts within this country. Some of the music played over the air these days . . . is enough to make one sick. If this isn't deliberate sabotage, then what is it? . . . Station

EIAR is full of treachery. Some of this music is putrid and banal and should be eliminated.

We have seen that London continues to flood the night air, from 2:30 to 4:00 a.m., presumably for the benefit of the JEWnited States. (I am writing this at 4:00 a.m.) It would thus be advisable to make at least half a dozen speeches and have them transmitted, as we used to, at 2:30, 3:30, 4:30, and 5:30 in the morning; if you have transmitters powerful enough to reach America, that is. It is not advisable to attempt to transmit a full hour-long program (as we did from Rome) because not enough good material is available. The record library in Rome has already been completely depleted. But we could broadcast for ten minutes every hour and repeat each broadcast a number of times.

The purpose of these broadcasts seems obvious to me: "London lies" (and is well aware of her lies).

"Do not believe the lies broadcast by B.B.C."

My own voice should probably be used for this project. The rest of the broadcasts can be made by others.

Sammartano promised to write to me but has been mysteriously silent for the past four days. . . .

I do not know if the Ministry is taking steps to reveal to the public the exact nature of the Moscow Administration. This must be done; something must also be done with the daily newspapers which are still in the hands of the reactionaries, anti-Fascists, anti-social-republicans. . . . I would very much like to find a publication where a serious group of Fascist Republicans can collaborate—that is, work together with mutual understanding and respect. . . .

*

Via Marsala 12–5
Rapallo
September 14
Anno XXII

My dear Minister:

You will have to excuse me if I write to you occasionally about matters not directly under your jurisdiction. . . . In Rapallo the main plaza has been devastated by bombs, although several of the arches dating back to the fourteenth century were undamaged. It now seems that "the genius" of Genoa has ordered them torn down, probably with good intentions, but . . .

The Riviera has already lost much and we do not want the plaza at Rapallo to be among the treasures lost. These old arches resisted the bombing raid and several of them are works of art.

There is one arch in particular with a side panel which was conserved and restored with loving care by the late Luigi Monti, a friend of d'Annunzio . . . which served as a memorial to him and as a remembrance of the reawakening of ceramics (Ars Umbra).

Perhaps you can put this letter in the hands of someone who can halt the destruction. The city is so completely abandoned that I don't know who recognizes me these days.

Finally, if someone were willing they would also do well to bring a little cement and calcimine to help the people in these mountains make cisterns so that they can go on a bit longer. The main problem in these hills is the lack of water; the evacuees (myself included) drink up what little there is left. . . .

*

Via Marsala 12–5
Rapallo
November 13
Anno XXII

F. Mezzasoma

My dear Minister:

I do not know if the enclosed Cantos [72 and 73] are useful in any way. No doubt they are too crude for the refined and too complex for the simple-minded.

Here in Rapallo, three of us have come up with a second manifesto, but G. Soldato, who presently resides in Alessandria, thinks it is all a waste of time. He is an active propagandist. Perhaps he has a point. . . .

I'm not sure if I ought to proceed with the manifesto or if these points wouldn't be better incorporated in some other publication. In any event, I am sending you a rough draft.

Pettinato and Farinacci are wasting their time working with party politics. . . .

I do not know who represents the Central Italian peasants. . . . The abuse heaped upon these people has done much to alienate their good will. . . . The government has done nothing to eliminate the tubercular germs from milk . . . but I don't believe that pasteurization would be popular here.

Do not abandon the periphery!

*

Via Marsala 12–5
Rapallo
December 28
Anno XXII

Precisely, My Dear Minister:

. . . Our Tigullian nucleus has disintegrated. . . . Ignorance abounds. . . . Of all the cursed Protestant sects (Jewified ones), the Quakers are the least Jewified for they do not sing. They have no hymns. . . . I believe the Quakers are the only ones who do not meow in church. . . .

The Italian newspapers are not very useful. . . . In Italy, people south of Rome read newspapers which are never even seen in the north. . . .

We should have a mimeograph machine in Rapallo. There is one which belonged to a Scotchman by the name of [John] Drummond who used to publish a philo-Fascist bulletin. . . . With proper authorization, I could try to locate the equipment. I would take responsibility toward Drummond who was a sort of disciple of mine.

For twenty years now, the Italians have ignored the anti-usury movements of other countries and have refused to help them. . . . The agreement between Mosley and the Social Creditors arose out of the knowledge that Fascism was the only movement capable of upholding monetary justice. . . .

After two intelligent articles, *Il Secolo XIX* of Genoa published one that was completely incomprehensible. We do not necessarily have to be followers of Gesell, but the author who ignores him is either ignorant and does not deserve his salary, or is a coward who doesn't dare face what Gesell stood for. We must remember that Mussolini and Gesell both preferred Proudhon to Marx. . . .

Ambiguous journalism creates distrust. The Republic can afford to tell the truth. We have nothing to hide.

I was distressed to read that some of those who betrayed Italy are now returning to power. The monopolists betrayed Fascism; they were ready to sell the country down the river. . . . Other points of interest: 1. The Americans are beasts but they are not cowards. . . . They must not be allowed to destroy Europe. . . . 2. I was greatly irritated by a recent radio broadcast in which the commentator was seemingly ignorant of Douglas's economic views. In Western Canada, where the Social Credit movement is strong, they had enough sense to rebel. They realize that usury is sin. . . .

APPENDIX IV
Brief Concerning Bail

Memorandum of law on application for bail, submitted November 27, 1945, to the United States District Court for the District of Columbia.

UNITED STATES DISTRICT COURT
DISTRICT OF COLUMBIA

UNITED STATES OF AMERICA
—against—
EZRA POUND   Defendant.

This memorandum is submitted in support of the defendant's application for admission to bail pending trial on the indictment and is confined to a discussion of the law bearing upon the application, the facts being set forth in a separate affidavit of defendant's counsel, Julien Cornell.

THE INDICTMENT

The defendant was indicted at a criminal term held July 1943, of the District Court of the United States for the District of Columbia, upon presentation of the Grand Jury of the District charging him with having committed the crime of treason in violation of Section 1 of the United States Criminal Code, by the transmission of certain broadcasts over a radio station at Rome, Italy, in which it is alleged that he, being a United States citizen, and owing allegiance to the United States, adhered and gave aid and counsel to an enemy state, namely, the Kingdom of Italy. The defendant having not yet been furnished with a copy of the indictment, and the full text not being available to counsel, the indictment is not here set forth.

The defendant's counsel is informed and believes that a superseding indictment has been, or will soon be requested by the Department of Justice alleging the same crime and on substantially the same grounds.

CONSTITUTIONAL PROVISIONS

The crime of treason is the only crime which, because of its importance in Colonial times, was defined in the Constitution of the United States.

"Treason against the United States, shall consist only in levying War against them, or in adhering to their Enemies, giving them Aid and Comfort. No Person shall be convicted of Treason unless on the Testimony of two Witnesses to the same covert Act, or on Confession in open Court," (U.S. Constitution, Art. 3, Sec. 3.)

STATUTORY PROVISIONS

The definition of the crime of treason is also contained in the Criminal Code in language derived from the constitutional provision.

"(*Criminal Code, section 1.*) *Treason.* Whoever, owing allegiance to the United States, levies war against them or adheres to their enemies, giving them aid and comfort within the United States or elsewhere, is guilty of treason." (R.S. Sec. 5331; Mar. 4, 1909, c. 321, Sec. 1, 35 Stat. 1088.) (18 U.S. Code, Sec. 1.)

The punishment for treason is specified in Sec. 2 of the Criminal Code.

"Whoever is convicted of treason shall suffer death; or, at the discretion of the court, shall be imprisoned not less than five years and fined not less than $10,000. to be levied on and collected out of any or all of his property, real and personal, of which he was the owner at the time of committing such treason, any sale or conveyance to the contrary notwithstanding; and every person so convicted of treason shall, moreover, be incapable of holding any office under the United States." (R.S. Sec. 5332; Mar. 4, 1909, c. 321, Sec. 2, 35 Stat. 1088.) (18 U.S.C. Sec. 2.)

The laws of the United States have always contained certain procedural safeguards on behalf of a defendant accused of treason, which are derived from the Act of April 30, 1790, 1 Stat. 119 and include the following:

"*Copy of indictment and list of jurors and witnesses for prisoner.* When any person is indicted of treason, a copy of the indictment and a list of the jury, and of the witnesses to be produced on the trial for proving the indictment, stating the place of abode of each juror and witness, shall be delivered to him at least three entire days before he is tried for the same. When any person is indicted of any other capital offense, such copy of the indictment and list of the jurors and witnesses shall be delivered to him at least two entire days before the trial." (R.S. Sec. 1033.) (18 U.S.C. Sec. 562.)

"*Counsel and witnesses for persons indicted for capital crimes.* Every person who is indicted of treason or other capital crime, shall be allowed to make his full defense by counsel learned in the law; and the court before which he is tried, or some judge thereof, shall immediately, upon his request, assign to him such counsel, not exceeding two, as he may desire, and they shall have free access to him at all reasonable hours. He shall be allowed, in his defense, to make any proof that he can produce by lawful witnesses, and shall have the like process of the court to compel his witnesses to appear at his trial, as is

usually granted to compel witnesses to appear on behalf of the prosecution."
(R.S. Sec. 1034). (18 U.S.C. Sec. 563.)

A still further safeguard was added by the Act of June 8, 1872, 17 Stat.
282, now contained in Sec. 287 of the Judicial Code.

> "*Challenges*. When the offense charged is treason or a capital offense, the
> defendant shall be entitled to twenty and the United States to six peremptory
> challenges. On the trial of any other felony, the defendant shall be entitled to
> ten and the United States to six peremptory challenges;" (28 U.S.C. Sec. 423.)

If the defendant should stand mute, or refuse to plead or answer upon his
arraignment, it is provided by statute that the court shall enter a plea of not
guilty on his behalf.

> "*Standing mute*. When any person indicted for any offense against the
> United States, whether capital or otherwise, upon his arraignment stands
> mute, or refuses to plead or answer thereto, it shall be the duty of the court
> to enter the plea of not guilty on his behalf, in the same manner as if he had
> pleaded not guilty thereto." (R.S. Sec. 1032) (18 U.S.C. Sec. 564.)

Admission to bail is expressly permitted by statute in all capital offenses.
(The crime of treason is a capital offense—Criminal Code Sec. 2 supra.)

> "Bail may be admitted upon all arrests in criminal cases where the punish-
> ment may be death; but in such cases it shall be taken only by the Supreme
> Court or a circuit court,* or by a justice of the Supreme Court, a circuit judge,
> or a judge of a district court, who shall exercise their discretion therein, having
> regard to the nature and circumstance of the offense, and of the evidence, and
> to the usages of law." (R.S. Sec. 1016) (18 U.S.C. Sec. 597.)

> *NOTE: The term "Circuit Court" is contained in the section as originally
> enacted and now applies to the district courts under Sec. 291 of the Act of
> March 3, 1911 (36 Stat. 1167) which abolished the Circuit Courts and trans-
> ferred their powers and duties to the district courts.

ARGUMENT
A DEFENDANT ACCUSED OF TREASON MAY BE ADMITTED TO BAIL WHILE AWAITING TRIAL WITHIN THE DISCRETION OF THE COURT.

As expressly provided in the statute set forth in full above, "bail may be
admitted upon all arrests in criminal cases where the punishment may be
death" and bail may be taken by a district court or by a judge thereof "who
shall exercise their discretion therein, having regard to the nature and circumstances of the offense and of the evidence, and to the usages of law." (18
U.S.C. Sec. 597, as made applicable to district courts by Act of March 3,
1911, 36 Stat. 1167.)

As provided by Sec. 2 of the Criminal Code, 18 U.S.C. Sec. 2, punishment
for treason may be death or a fine and imprisonment at the discretion of the
court. These statutes taken together expressly provide, therefore, that a defendant arrested on a charge of treason may be admitted to bail while
awaiting trial, and that such bail may be taken by a district court or judge
thereof, in his discretion, having regard to (1) the nature and circumstances
of the offense, (2) the evidence against the defendant, and (3) usages of
law. Discretion with regard to the granting of bail exists only in capital cases,
as in all other cases the allowance of bail is mandatory. (18 U.S.C. 597.)

The crime of treason is so rare in our recent history that there is little precedent in the way of usage by which the court may be guided. Defendant's counsel has not had an opportunity to examine all the cases involving treason in recent years, to determine whether bail has been sought or permitted in any of them. The only treason case which has reached the United States Supreme Court in modern times is *Cramer v. U.S.*, 325 U.S. 1. Although the opinions do not shed any light on the matter of bail, they may prove helpful as containing the only authoritative discussion of the crime, as well as a learned review of its history in English and American law.

It was established very early in the history of the United States that the crime of treason is bailable under the statutes. In the case of *U.S. v. Hamilton*, 3 Dallas 17 (1795), the United States Supreme Court issued a writ of habeas corpus on the petition of a prisoner who had been arrested on the warrant of a district judge, charged with the crime of high treason, in that he aided insurrectionists by attending their meetings. The prisoner had been committed to jail without any hearing and he not only requested that he be properly arraigned, but also that he be admitted to bail. Despite the fact that the man was accused not merely of propaganda, but of actual aid to a rebellious group within the United States, the Supreme Court directed that he be admitted to bail until the trial and fixed the bail in the sum of $4000. with two sureties for $2000. each. In another capital case, this one involving the crime of piracy, Hon. Bushrod Washington, Associate Justice of the Supreme Court, sitting in the Circuit Court for the District of Pennsylvania, admitted the defendant to bail. *U.S. v. Jones*, Fed. Cas. No. 15496, (1813).

In the latter case, Justice Washington in admitting the defendant to bail in the sum of $10,000. stated that he granted bail because the defendant was ill and continued imprisonment would be harmful to him, although there was no immediate or certain danger that he would die if not released.

> "As to Jones, it is proved by the physician who has attended him since February, in jail, that his health is bad, his complaint pulmonary, and that, in his opinion, confinement during the summer might so far increase his disorder as to render it ultimately dangerous. The humanity of our laws, not less than the feelings of the court, favor the liberation of a prisoner upon bail, under such circumstances. It is not necessary, in our view of the subject, that the danger which may arise from his confinement should be either immediate or certain. If, in the opinion of a skilful physician, the nature of his disorder is such that confinement must be injurious, and may be fatal, we think he ought to be bailed."

If Justice Washington had no compunctions about applying rules of humanity to a man accused of piracy, and suffering only from a physical ailment, this court has ample precedent for admitting to bail Ezra Pound, who has been charged with a crime hardly more heinous than piracy, and not only appears to be insane at the present time, as a result of previous imprisonment, but may very likely be rendered permanently insane, and may lose his life, if imprisonment continues.

Respectfully submitted,

JULIEN CORNELL
Attorney for Defendant

APPENDIX V

Transcript of Final Hearing

On April 14, 1958, a motion was filed in the United States District Court for the District of Columbia for dismissal of the thirteen-year-old indictment against Ezra Pound. On April 18, in the same court, the indictment against Pound was dismissed.

*

UNITED STATES

vs.   Criminal No. 76028

EZRA POUND

The above-entitled matter came on for hearing in the United States District Court for the District of Columbia at 10:30 o'clock in the forenoon of Friday, April 18, 1958,

BEFORE:

HONORABLE BOLITHA J. LAWS, Chief Judge of the United States District Court for the District of Columbia, there being the following

APPEARANCES:

OLIVER GASCH, ESQUIRE, United States Attorney, on behalf of the United States;

MESSRS. ARNOLD, FORTAS & PORTER BY THURMAN ARNOLD, ESQUIRE,

MESSRS. TAYLOR, GUSTIN & HARRIS BY ROBERT W. FURNISS, JR., ESQUIRE, and

JULIEN CORNELL, ESQUIRE, all on behalf of the Defendant.

The following proceedings and transactions were then had:

PROCEEDINGS AND TRANSACTIONS

THE DEPUTY CLERK: Case of the United States vs. Ezra Pound.

MR. ARNOLD: May it please the Court, I appear on behalf of Mrs. Pound, committee of Ezra Pound, and through her I appear on behalf of Ezra Pound, and also at the request of—an almost unanimous request of leading writers and poets in the United States and in England.

Robert Frost asks leave to file a statement and he had hoped to be here but it was set yesterday and he had a lecture and he couldn't come.

So much for that.

THE COURT: Judge Arnold, is Mr. Pound present?

MR. ARNOLD: I suppose so.

THE COURT: That is all right.

MR. ARNOLD: Now, as to the case, this is a motion to dismiss an indictment. We have handed in a memorandum of points and authorities of cases, with which your Honor is familiar, which I think makes it clear that, in the discretion of the Court and in the interest of justice, you have the power to dismiss that indictment.

I have not been officially informed as to the position the Government will take but I think the cases give you discretion to dismiss the indictment clearly in the interest of justice.

If the indictment is dismissed, and the purpose of the dismissal of the indictment is to obtain the release of Ezra Pound, he expects to go to Italy after he is released and will apply for a passport.

Our position is that there are only two reasons for the incarceration of the person who has been adjudged too insane to be tried. The first is that he may be cured and face trial. The second is that he might be a danger to himself or to persons and property.

We have attached the affidavit of Doctor Overholser to the effect that he could never be cured and, second, to the effect that he is not a danger to persons and property. So I think both of those two reasons disappear.

And, indeed, I believe that under those circumstances on habeas corpus it would be unconstitutional to hold him longer however justified his first commitment was. I do not think it necessary to raise the constitutional point. It will not be if this motion is granted.

Now, Mr. Pound is here in court. Ezra Pound is here in court. The Court has, no doubt, read the affidavit of Doctor Overholser. He is here in court in case the Court wishes to question him under oath on the matters charged in the affidavit. Unless the Court requests I will not put him on the stand because the affidavit is clear and what we would get would merely be the technical terms for the mental illness of Doctor Pound and I personally, unless the Court wants Doctor Overholser, am just simply telling the Court that he is here for questioning.

And that, your Honor, in simple terms is the case we present to you unless your Honor desires to ask me any questions.

THE COURT: I think not. Mr. Gasch?

MR. GASCH: May it please the Court, I have studied the affidavit of Doctor Overholser. I have conferred with him and I am satisfied of the incompetency of the defendant to stand trial.

I am advised that there is no present prospect of an improvement in that condition, so that we cannot say that in the foreseeable future the defendant would be competent to stand trial.

In view of that circumstance, I do not oppose and, in fact, consent to Mr. Arnold's motion. I believe the motion is filed in the interest of justice and that it should be granted.

THE COURT: Mr. Gasch, I have read this affidavit and I would like to ask you: Have you any evidence whatever to the contrary of the facts set forth by Doctor Overholser?

MR. GASCH: No, sir, I have not.

THE COURT: Then, in particular, I would like to ask you about this statement made in the ninth paragraph, that there is a strong probability that the commission of the crimes charged was the result of insanity and that "I would, therefore, seriously doubt the prosecution could show criminal responsibility even if it were hypothetically assumed that Ezra Pound could regain sufficient sanity to be tried."

Have you any evidence to refute that statement or anything to the contrary?

MR. GASCH: No, sir, I have not. In our consideration of this matter I felt that the first hurdle, present incompetency of the defendant to stand trial, was such a barrier to proceeding that I did not endeavor to check into the second question or barrier which, obviously, does confront us in view of Doctor Overholser's affidavit.

And I might mention to you, your Honor—

THE COURT: Well, did you want an opportunity to do that?

MR. GASCH: Your Honor, in view of the fact that it would be incumbent upon the Government to go back into a period of twelve or fourteen years ago and to attempt to seek psychiatric testimony as to this causal connection, I think, based on my experience with other cases wherein we do not have that time interval, it would be virtually impossible for us to get the type of evidence that we would need in this case even if there was a showing of competency, which there is not.

THE COURT: I understand. Your position is then that you consent to the dismissal?

MR. GASCH: Yes, your Honor.

THE COURT: All right. Would you like to say anything further?

MR. ARNOLD: No, your Honor.

THE COURT: Well, the sole question presently before the Court is whether the criminal case against Mr. Pound shall be dismissed. The United States Attorney states he has no objection—on the contrary, he consents.

Now, the Court has considered the affidavit of Doctor Overholser, the Superintendent of St. Elizabeths Hospital where the defendant has been confined for more than twelve years.

It appears, this affidavit indicates, that throughout all of this time, as well as at present, the defendant has been mentally ill to such an extent that he has not been able and is not now able to stand trial, and the affidavit also indicates there is no likelihood that at any future time he would be able to stand trial.

And then, as has been read to the District Attorney, the further statement is made that there is a strong probability that the commission of the criminal acts charged against the defendant was a result of his mental illness.

The Court construes the acquiescence of the District Attorney in the dismissal of the indictment and his consent to it as constituting, in effect, a joining in the motion of the defendant to dismiss the criminal case against him and, under these circumstances, the Court orders the dismissal of the criminal charges against the defendant.

An order to that effect will be entered.

Will you prepare an order to present to the Court?

MR. ARNOLD: Yes.

THE COURT: All right, gentlemen. I think that concludes the hearing.

(Thereupon the instant hearing was concluded.)

Notes

PREFACE

1. The author is indebted to William M. Chace, who suggested the phrase "unencumbered sensibility" and several others in the preface during a meeting with the author in January 1974.

SETTINGS (1885–1939)

1.

1. Patricia Hutchins, *Ezra Pound's Kensington* (London: Faber & Faber, 1965), p. 25.
2. D. D. Paige, ed., *The Letters of Ezra Pound, 1907–1941* (New York: Harcourt, Brace & Company, 1950), p. 72 (hereinafter referred to as *Letters*).
3. Noel Stock, *Poet in Exile: Ezra Pound* (Manchester: Manchester University Press, 1964), p. 211.
4. *Letters*, p. 322.
5. Noel Stock, *The Life of Ezra Pound* (New York: Pantheon Books, 1970), p. 1.
6. *Ibid.*, 1–2.
7. "Indiscretions, or *Une Revue de Deux Mondes*" in *Pavannes and Divigations* (New York: New Directions, 1958), p. 50.
8. Donald Hall, "Interview with Ezra Pound," *The Paris Review*, 28 (Summer–Fall 1962): 40.
9. *Ibid.*
10. Michael Reck, *Ezra Pound: A Close-Up* (New York: McGraw-Hill, 1967), p. 6.
11. *Ibid.*
12. A portion of the aborted dissertation was published as an essay, "The Quality of Lope de Vega" in *The Spirit of Romance* (1910).
13. Hugh Kenner, *Bucky: A Guided Tour of Buckminster Fuller* (New York: Morrow, 1973), p. 83.
14. *Ibid.* See also Kenner, *The Pound Era* (Berkeley and Los Angeles: University of California Press, 1971), p. 556.

15. August 1907, Ezra Pound archives, D. D. Paige transcripts: The Beinecke Rare Book and Manuscript Library, Yale University, New Haven (hereinafter referred to as Paige transcripts).
16. October 1907, Paige transcripts.
17. See *Letters*, p. 5, *n*.
18. Paige transcripts.
19. Jeannette Lander, *Ezra Pound* (New York: Frederick Ungar, 1971), pp. 21–22.

2.

1. I am indebted to Noel Stock, *The Life of Ezra Pound*, pp. 45, 50–51, for phrases and thoughts contained in this paragraph.
2. The framework of this and the following paragraph is taken from A. Alvarez, "The Wretched Poet Who Lived in the House of Bedlam," *Saturday Review*, July 18, 1970, p. 28.
3. *Letters*, p. 8.
4. A. Wade, ed., *The Letters of W. B. Yeats* (London: Hart Davis, 1954), p. 543.
5. Information concerning Pound's early days in London is compiled from the following sources: William Van O'Connor, *Ezra Pound* (Minneapolis: University of Minnesota Press, 1963), p. 9; Charles Norman, *The Case of Ezra Pound* (New York: Funk & Wagnalls, 1968), pp. 19–20; Reck, *Ezra Pound: A Close-up*, p. 14.
6. Letter to Harriet Monroe (January 1915), *Letters*, p. 49; see Mark Van Doren's preface to *The Letters of Ezra Pound*, p. vii, for commentary on this letter.
7. Samuel Hynes, *Edwardian Occasions* (New York: Oxford University Press, 1972), p. 126.
8. *Ibid.*, 125.
9. *Ibid.*, 124.
10. Herbert N. Schneidau, *Ezra Pound: The Image and the Real* (Baton Rouge: Louisiana State University Press, 1969), p. 12.
11. Paige transcripts.
12. Schneidau, *Ezra Pound*, p. 12.
13. Information concerning Pound's literary relationship to Yeats as set forth in this and preceding paragraphs is compiled from the following sources: F. R. Leavis, "Pound in his Letters," reprinted in J. P. Sullivan, ed., *Ezra Pound* (London: Penguin, 1970), pp. 217–22; Richard Ellmann, "Ez and Old Billyum" in Eva Hesse, ed., *New Approaches to Ezra Pound* (Berkeley and Los Angeles: University of California Press, 1969), p. 63; Richard Ellmann, *Yeats: The Man and the Masks* (New York: Macmillan, 1948), p. 212; *Letters*, p. 25; O'Connor, *Ezra Pound*, p. 10.
14. Ellmann, *Yeats: The Man and the Masks*, p. 213.
15. Ezra Pound and Ernest Fenollosa, *The Classic Noh Theatre of Japan* (New York: New Directions, 1959), p. 4.
16. Forrest Read, ed., *Pound/Joyce: The Letters of Ezra Pound to James Joyce* (New York: New Directions, 1965), p. 4.

3.

1. Kenner, *The Pound Era*, p. 174.
2. *Ibid.*
3. *Letters*, p. 11.

4. Alvarez, "The Wretched Poet Who Lived in the House of Bedlam," p. 27.
5. I am indebted to the following works for information regarding *Blast* and vorticism as contained in these paragraphs: Reck, *Ezra Pound: A Close-Up*, p. 26; Richard Mayne, "Wyndham Lewis," *Encounter*, vol. XXXVIII, 2 (February 1972): 47; Henry Regnery, "Eliot, Pound and Lewis: A Creative Friendship," *Modern Age*, vol. 16, 2 (Spring 1972): 147.
6. The futurists tended to glorify war, the vorticists did not; for the latter, war was merely "a symptom of the real disease." Moreover, the futurists were determined to obliterate all of past history, whereas the vorticists wanted to uphold the "real" traditions, the traditions amid which great artists and true innovators "always" worked. Basically conservative, and not revolutionary, vorticism's savage rage was "reserved exclusively for the men in the street, the mob, and the meretricious artists serving them" (William M. Chace, *The Political Identities of Ezra Pound and T. S. Eliot* [Stanford University Press, 1973], p. 11). A more explicit discussion of the differences between the two movements is to be found in Ezra Pound's *Gaudier-Brzeska: A Memoir* (1916).
7. The chosen term, "futurism," was announced to the world in an impassioned manifesto published on the front page of the Paris newspaper, *Le Figaro*, February 20, 1909.
8. Clark Emery, *Ideas into Action: A Study of Pound's Cantos* (Coral Gables: University of Miami Press, 1958), p. 72.
9. "Vorticism," Fortnightly Review, vol. XCVI (N.S.), 573 (September 1, 1914): 461–71.
10. Regnery, "Eliot, Pound and Lewis: A Creative Friendship," p. 147.
11. Mayne, "Wynham Lewis," p. 47.
12. Regnery, "Eliot, Pound and Lewis: A Creative Friendship," p. 147.

4.

1. *Letters*, p. 48.
2. Paige transcripts.
3. *Letters*, p. 14.
4. Lawrance Thompson, ed., *Selected Letters of Robert Frost* (New York: Holt, Rinehart & Winston, 1964), p. 71.
5. *Ibid.*, 75.
6. *Ibid.*, 84.
7. *Ibid.*, 96.
8. *Ibid.*, 98.
9. The material in these paragraphs regarding the Pound-Joyce relationship is based primarily on Reck, *Ezra Pound: A Close-Up*, pp. 31–32.
10. Kenner, *The Pound Era*, p. 274.
11. *Poetry* Magazine Papers, 1912–36: Special Collections, The University of Chicago Library, Chicago.
12. *Letters*, p. 40.
13. Regnery, "Eliot, Pound and Lewis: A Creative Friendship," 150.
14. Letter to John Quinn, January 25, 1919: Manuscript Division, New York Public Library, New York.

5.

1. I am indebted to Michael Reck, *Ezra Pound: A Close-Up*, pp. 34 and 102, for the direction and flow of my opening thoughts.
2. For information in this section I consulted the following texts: Norman, *The*

Case of Ezra Pound, p. 24; Read, *Pound/Joyce*, p. 150; Kenner, *The Pound Era*, p. 302.

3. Letter to John Drummond (May 1934), *Letters*, p. 259.
4. The clearest, most concise explanation of the "A + B theorem" can be found in Kenner's *The Pound Era*, p. 307: "Costs comprise (A) salaries, wages, and dividends, which flow into the economy as purchasing power, and (B) plant and bank charges which do not; and 'A will not purchase A + B.'" The Douglas hypothesis that money distributed by production will not buy the product (total cost *always* exceeds total purchasing power) means that there is a perpetual shortage of money. This shortage must be made up by creating money. The money is created as interest-bearing debt.
5. Alastair Hamilton, *The Appeal of Fascism* (New York: Avon, 1971), p. 322.
6. *Ibid.*
7. See Norman, *The Case of Ezra Pound*, p. 24, and A. R. Orage, Commentary to C. H. Douglas, *Credit-Power and Democracy* (London: Cecil Palmer, 1921).
8. Hamilton, *The Appeal of Fascism*, p. 323.
9. "In Explanation," *Little Review*, vol. 4 (August 1918): 5–9.
10. Frederick J. Hoffman, *The Twenties* (New York: The Free Press, 1965), p. 24.
11. *Ibid.*, 26.
12. *Ibid.*
13. *Letters*, p. 145.
14. Read, *Pound/Joyce*, p. 150.
15. Reck, *Ezra Pound: A Close-Up*, p. 39.
16. *Letters*, p. 128; the phraseology in this paragraph is largely Reck's, *Ezra Pound: A Close-Up*, p. 39.
17. *Letters*, p. 239.
18. Sister Bernetta Quinn, O.S.F., *Ezra Pound: An Introduction to the Poetry* (New York: Columbia University Press, 1972), p. 110.
19. Reck, *Ezra Pound: A Close-Up*, p. 160.
20. Letter to Iris Barry (July 1916), *Letters*, p. 90.
21. Letter to the Editor of the *English Journal* (January 1931), in *Letters*, p. 231.
22. Ezra Pound, *Selected Poems*, edited and with an Introduction by T. S. Eliot (London: Faber & Faber, 1928).

6.

1. Read, *Pound/Joyce*, p. 187.
2. *Ibid.*
3. "The Island of Paris: A Letter," *The Dial*, vol. LXIX, 4 (October 1920): 407–408.
4. Reck, *Ezra Pound: A Close-Up*, p. 42.
5. Harold M. Hurwitz, "Hemingway's Tutor, Ezra Pound," *Modern Fiction Studies*, vol. XVII, 4 (Winter 1971–72): 470.
6. *Selected Essays of Ezra Pound*, edited and with an Introduction by T. S. Eliot (London: Faber & Faber, 1954), p. xii.
7. Material regarding Pound's relationship to Hemingway in this and following paragraphs is from Hurwitz, "Hemingway's Tutor," pp. 469–82.
8. T. S. Eliot, *The Waste Land*, A Facsimile and Transcript of the Original Drafts, Including the Annotations of Ezra Pound, Edited by Valerie Eliot (New York: Harcourt Brace Jovanovich, 1971).
9. Regnery, "Eliot, Pound and Lewis: A Creative Friendship," p. 151.

7.

1. Norman, *The Case of Ezra Pound*, p. 26.
2. *Ibid.*
3. Letter to Mrs. Boyd Trego (March 1925), Paige transcripts.
4. "Cavalcanti" from *The Literary Essays of Ezra Pound* (Norfolk: New Directions, 1954), p. 152.
5. Hugh Kenner, "The Magic of Place," *Italian Quarterly*, vol. 16, 64 (Spring 1973): 6.
6. *Ibid.*
7. Norman, *The Case of Ezra Pound*, pp. 27–28.
8. Kenner, *The Pound Era*, p. 388.
9. Letter to Olga Rudge (April 8, 1926), Paige transcripts.
10. *Poetry* Magazine Papers, 1912–36: The University of Chicago Library.
11. The detail about Pound's letters, postcards, etc., is from Norman, *The Case of Ezra Pound*, p. 29. Information concerning Pound's proposed meeting with Mussolini is from Niccolò Zapponi, "Ezra Pound e il fascismo," *Storia Contemporanea*, vol. IV, 3 (September 1973): 452.
12. Zapponi, "Ezra Pound e il fascismo," p. 452.
13. Pound's eighteen-point program appeared in *Il Meridiano di Roma* on December 1, 1940, under the title, "Di un sistema economico." It reappeared in 1944 in the Pound collection *Orientamenti* (Orientations), Venice, Casa Editrice Delle Edizioni Populari, an edition which was later seized by the Federal Bureau of Investigation.
14. *Jefferson and/or Mussolini* (New York: Liveright, 1936), pp. 17–18.
15. *Ibid.*, 73.
16. Norman, *The Case of Ezra Pound*, p. 29.
17. The Woodrow Wilson Papers, Library of Congress, Washington, D.C. The letter from Pound to President Wilson is undated but is stamped "Washington, D.C. Received and acknowledged March 29, 1913." It reads:

    To the President of the United States: Your Excellency: I petition that the tariff on books be removed, or that it at least be removed from all the books of which there is no edition printed in America. The burden of this latter tax falls chiefly upon scholars who can little afford it and acts rather as a preventive of importation than as a producer of revenue. Naturally the books are usually belles lettres and serious work which does not much profit the publisher. Also, the American firms which import these books, and to whom they are usually sold at a great reduction, are apt to charge ridiculous prices to the American buyer and to make the tariff an excuse. Thus I have known a 6 shilling English book to be sold in the United States @ 10 shillings although the American firm had bought it @ 3/6. The extreme case is reached when a man like Dr. Rennert [Professor of English literature, University of Pennsylvania] has to pay for importing his own work on Lope de Vega.
    Yours Faithfully, Ezra Pound
18. Papers of President Franklin D. Roosevelt, P.P.F. 98, Franklin D. Roosevelt Library, Hyde Park, N.Y.
19. Stock, *Poet in Exile*, p. 212.
20. The article "My Five Husbands" by "Stella Breen" (the pen-name of George Steele Seymour) was printed in no. 2 (Autumn 1927): 87–111. It is of a type that one would expect today to find in a "confessions" magazine.
21. Read, *Pound/Joyce*, p. 254.
22. *Ibid.*

23. William Butler Yeats, Preface to *The King of the Great Clock Tower* (Dublin: The Cuala Press, 1934).
24. Richard Ellmann, ed., *Letters of James Joyce*, vol. III (New York: The Viking Press, 1960), p. 311.
25. Stuart Gilbert, ed., *Letters of James Joyce*, vol. I (New York: The Viking Press, reissue, 1966), p. 381.
26. Stock, *The Life of Ezra Pound*, p. 334.

8.

1. Paige transcripts.
2. William Butler Yeats, "A Packet for Ezra Pound," published as introduction to *A Vision* (New York: Macmillan, 1937).
3. Hall, "Interview with Ezra Pound," p. 23.
4. I have drawn upon the following sources for data concerning *The Cantos* in this and the previous paragraph: Reck, *Ezra Pound: A Close-Up*, p. 189; Gilbert Highet, *The Classical Tradition* (New York: Oxford University Press reissue, 1970), p. 503; Eva Hesse, "Books Behind the Cantos (Part One: Cantos I–XXX)," *Paideuma*, vol. 1, 2 (Fall-Winter 1972): 140–42.
5. Alvarez, "The Wretched Poet," p. 29.
6. Michael Wood, "Ezra Pound," *New York Review of Books*, February 8, 1973, p. 10.

9.

1. Lander, *Ezra Pound*, p. 83.
2. Stock, *The Life of Ezra Pound*, p. 325.
3. *Ibid.*
4. *Ibid.*
5. *Ibid.*, 326.
6. Ezra Pound, *Impact: Essays on Ignorance and the Decline of American Civilization*, edited and with an introduction by Noel Stock (Chicago: Regnery, 1960), p. 270.
7. Stock, *Poet in Exile*, p. 153.
8. Earle Davis, *Vision Fugitive: Ezra Pound and Economics* (Lawrence, Kansas: The University of Kansas Press, 1968), p. 110.
9. Paige transcripts.
10. *Ibid.*
11. *Ibid.*
12. Alvarez, "The Wretched Poet," p. 27.

10.

1. David Reid and Mark Turner, "Interview with Hugh Kenner," *Occident*, vol. VII, new series (1973/4), pp. 19–48.
2. Stock, *The Life of Ezra Pound*, p. 337.
3. Chace, *The Political Identities of Ezra Pound and T. S. Eliot*, p. 31.
4. Stock, *Poet in Exile*, p. 156.
5. ———, *The Life of Ezra Pound*, p. 324.
6. Mary de Rachewiltz, *Discretions* (Boston: Little, Brown, 1971), p. 100.
7. Erika Ostrovsky, *Voyeur Voyant: A Portrait of Louis-Ferdinand Céline* (New York: Random House, 1971), p. 275.
8. Stock, *The Life of Ezra Pound*, p. 357.

INFERNO (1939–1945)

1.

1. Pound's mother-in-law, Olivia Shakespear, a widow for some years, died in London in October 1938. In December Pound went to London, on behalf of his wife, to settle matters connected with the estate and to see Omar. He had not seen the boy since 1930 and was not to see him again until 1947.
2. Guy Davenport, "Ezra Pound: 1885–1972," *Arion* [new series], vol. I, 1 (1973): 188–96. Particulars in this excellent article provided the framework for the paragraph in question.
3. According to an FBI special investigatory report on Pound prepared during May 1943—and available from the Department of Justice, Washington, D.C. —there is reason to believe that the poet's 1939 American junket was financed by the Italian Fascist government. The report states (p. 18): "James Laughlin advised [Federal agents] that when Pound came to the United States in 1939 he saw Pound on numerous occasions and recalled that Pound had had his fare to the United States paid by the Italian government. . . . When asked if Pound had definitely told him that the Italian government had paid his fare, Laughlin could not recall that this ever happened, but stated that he knew that Pound had no money and therefore it was impossible for Pound to come to the United States in any other manner." It is conceivable, on the other hand, that Laughlin was not aware, even in 1943, of the 1938 death of Olivia Shakespear and of Dorothy's subsequent inheritance of considerable funds.
4. Stock, *The Life of Ezra Pound*, p. 360.
5. Norman, *The Case of Ezra Pound*, p. 39.
6. *Ibid.*, 36–37.
7. Charles Norman, *Ezra Pound* (New York: Macmillan, 1968), p. 360.
8. Information in this paragraph is taken from Norman, *The Case of Ezra Pound*, p. 39, and T. S. Matthews, *Great Tom* (New York: Harper & Row, 1973), p. 176.
9. Stock, *The Life of Ezra Pound*, pp. 363–64.
10. John C. Thirwall, ed., *The Selected Letters of William Carlos Williams* (New York: New Directions, 1957), p. 184.
11. Stock, *The Life of Ezra Pound*, p. 363.
12. *Ibid.*, 363–64.
13. FBI special investigatory report, p. 18.
14. Norman, *Ezra Pound*, p. 371.
15. ———, *The Case of Ezra Pound*, p. 41.
16. *Ibid.*
17. Norman, *Ezra Pound*, p. 369.
18. Stock, *The Life of Ezra Pound*, p. 365.
19. *Ibid.*

2.

1. *Letters*, pp. 342–43.
2. Lander, *Ezra Pound*, p. 90.
3. *Letters*, p. 374.
4. Stock, *The Life of Ezra Pound*, p. 376.
5. *Ibid.*
6. *Ibid.*, 377.
7. *Ibid.*

8. February 1, 1940, *Letters*, p. 336.
9. Stock, *The Life of Ezra Pound*, p. 377.
10. November 4, 1939, Paige transcripts.
11. Stock, *The Life of Ezra Pound*, p. 378.
12. *Ibid.*, 377.
13. *Ibid.*, 381.
14. *Ibid.*, 383–84.
15. Pound-Por correspondence, Pound archives (Beinecke), permission: Aditi Nath Sarkar.
16. Harry M. Meacham, *The Caged Panther: Ezra Pound at St. Elizabeths* (New York: Twayne, 1967), p. 110.
17. The letter in question and information concerning Pound's initial dealings with the Italian Fascist government have been derived in part from Zapponi, "Ezra Pound e il fascismo," pp. 423–79.
18. Robert A. Corrigan, "Ezra Pound and the Italian Ministry for Popular Culture," *Journal of Popular Culture*, vol. 5, 4 (Spring 1972): 772–73.
19. Zapponi, "Ezra Pound e il fascismo," p. 454.
20. *Ibid.*, 461.
21. Ezra Pound general correspondence files, Federal Bureau of Investigation (Department of Justice), Washington, D.C.
22. Copies of the tapes of the broadcasts cited in this section are available both at the United States National Archives and the Library of Congress, Washington, D.C.
23. In May 1945 the FBI confiscated Pound's original radio scripts, copies of which were housed at the Italian Ministry of Popular Culture, 56 Via Veneto, Rome. It was these scripts, and not those which the FCC had transcribed, which the Department of Justice prepared to use in court. But even the original scripts do not solve all of the textual problems, for Pound often ad-libbed, writing one thing and saying another.
24. H. A. Seiber, "The Medical, Legal, Literary and Political Status of Ezra Weston (Loomis) Pound (1885–   )—Selected Facts and Comments," Senior Specialists Division, the Library of Congress Legislative Reference Service, March 31, 1958, Revised April 14, 1958. *Congressional Record—Appendix*, April 29, 1958, pp. A3895-A3901.
25. FBI special investigatory report, p. 37.
26. Another alternative is offered by James Laughlin. Olga Rudge apparently told him in 1964 that the reason they could not leave Italy was that the consular official would not put a visa in daughter Mary's U.S. passport, which had expired, and they all, Mrs. Pound included, agreed not to leave Mary behind in Italy.
27. Norman, *The Case of Ezra Pound*, p. 8.
28. Reynolds and Eleanor Packard, *Balcony Empire: Fascist Italy at War* (New York: Oxford University Press, 1942), pp. 250–51.
29. Pound files, FBI, vol. 10, p. 35.
30. *Ibid.*, vol. 13, p. 31.
31. *Ibid.*, vol. 10, pp. 32–33.
32. Felice Chilanti, *Ezra Pound fra i Sediziosi degli Anni Quaranta* (Milan: All'Insegna del Pesce D'Oro, 1972), p. 18.
33. From Canto 74.
34. Mary de Rachewiltz, *Discretions*, p. 173.
35. Norman, *The Case of Ezra Pound*, p. 55.

3.

1. William Carlos Williams, *Autobiography* (New York: Random House, 1948), pp. 316–19.
2. FBI special investigatory report, p. 17.
3. The Adjutant General's Office, Department of the Army, Washington, D.C.
4. Now Section 2381, Title 18, United States Code.
5. Norman, *The Case of Ezra Pound*, p. 63.
6. Stock, *The Life of Ezra Pound*, p. 393.
7. *Ibid.*, 400; subsequent material dealing with Pound and the Salò Republic is also based in part on facts supplied by Stock in *The Life of Ezra Pound*, pp. 400–402.
8. Goedel was arrested by the Allied command in 1945, at which time, interviewed by federal agents, he denounced Pound and, according to FBI files, offered to testify against the poet in a court of law. Here is a prime example of Pound's tendency to misjudge people.
9. For material contained in this and the preceding paragraph see Stock, *The Life of Ezra Pound*, pp. 401–402, and Meacham, *The Caged Panther*, pp. 26–27.
10. Pound general correspondence files, FBI.
11. *Ibid.*
12. *Ibid.*
13. *Ibid.*
14. All three of the aforementioned reports are from the FBI Ezra Pound general correspondence files.
15. Stock, *The Life of Ezra Pound*, pp. 403–404.
16. Mary de Rachewiltz, *Discretions*, p. 197.
17. Hall, "Interview with Ezra Pound," p. 51.
18. The same line appears in a Pound letter to Mezzasoma (March 11, 1944): Pound general correspondence files, FBI.
19. Pound files, FBI, vol. 11, pp. 68–71.
20. Pound general correspondence files, FBI.
21. They did, however, appear in print separately in the Fascist newspaper *Marina Repubblicana*. Lines 9 through 35 of Canto LXXII, omitting line 18, appeared in the issue of January 15, 1945; Canto LXXIII was published in its entirety on February 1, 1945.
22. Letter to the author from Mary de Rachewiltz, February 2, 1974.
23. Mary de Rachewiltz, *Discretions*, p. 195.
24. Stock, *The Life of Ezra Pound*, p. 406.
25. Information in this paragraph is from Kenner, *The Pound Era*, p. 470.
26. *Ibid.*; two additional facts are noteworthy: Homer Pound passed away early in 1942; Isabel Pound died at Gais on February 9, 1948.

4.

1. Kenner, *The Pound Era*, p. 587.
2. Mary de Rachewiltz, *Discretions*, pp. 242–43.
3. Pound files, FBI, vol. 12, p. 9.
4. *Ibid.*, vol. 14, p. 23.
5. Interview by Edd Johnson, Philadelphia *Record*–Chicago *Sun*, May 9, 1945.
6. Robert L. Allen, "The Cage," *Esquire*, February 1958; reprinted in William Van O'Connor and Edward Stone, eds., *A Casebook on Ezra Pound* (New York: Thomas Y. Crowell, 1959), pp. 33–38. In addition to the factual information provided by Allen and the others acknowledged in footnotes, the

author used these sources to fill out the present section: David W. Evans, "Ezra Pound as Prison Poet," *The University of Kansas City Review*, Spring 1957; reprinted in Walter Sutton, ed., *Ezra Pound: Twentieth Century Views* (Englewood Cliffs, N.J.: Prentice-Hall, 1963), pp. 80–86; Wood, "Ezra Pound," p. 10; Chace, *The Political Identities of Ezra Pound and T. S. Eliot*, p. 92; Stock, *The Life of Ezra Pound*, pp. 415–16; Kenner, *The Pound Era*, p. 462; Norman, *Ezra Pound*, p. 397.

7. Stock, *The Life of Ezra Pound*, p. 409.
8. Chace, *The Political Identities of Ezra Pound and T. S. Eliot*, p. 93.
9. David Park Williams, "The Background of *The Pisan Cantos*," *Poetry*, January 1949; reprinted in O'Connor and Stone, eds., *A Casebook on Ezra Pound*, pp. 39–43.
10. Wood, "Ezra Pound," p. 10.
11. Stock, *The Life of Ezra Pound*, p. 409.
12. *Ibid.*, 411.
13. *The Paris Review*, 28 (Summer–Fall 1962): 17.
14. Stock, *The Life of Ezra Pound*, p. 416.
15. Norman, *The Case of Ezra Pound*, p. 76.
16. Julien Cornell, *The Trial of Ezra Pound* (New York: John Day, 1966), p. 13.

PURGATORY (1945–1958)

1.

1. Davenport, "Ezra Pound: 1885–1972," p. 190, served as inspiration for my opening thoughts; so too did Wood, "Ezra Pound," p. 8.
2. Julien Cornell, *The Trial of Ezra Pound*, pp. 16–22.
3. See Stock, *The Life of Ezra Pound*, p. 418, for information concerning this and several other points in the present section.
4. Cornell, *The Trial of Ezra Pound*, pp. 71–75.
5. Kenner, *The Pound Era*, p. 495.
6. Charles Olson Papers, Wilbur Cross Library, University of Connecticut, Storrs.
7. *Ibid.*
8. Stock, *The Life of Ezra Pound*, p. 419.

2.

1. Ezra Pound archives, Beinecke Library, Yale University.
2. Reck, *Ezra Pound: A Close-Up*, p. 75.
3. May 10 or 11, 1947, Pound archives (Beinecke).
4. February 20, 1946, Pound archives (Beinecke).
5. Cornell, *The Trial of Ezra Pound*, p. 41.
6. Wood, "Ezra Pound," p. 8.
7. Cornell, *The Trial of Ezra Pound*, pp. 51–52.
8. *Ibid.*, 54.
9. Norman, *The Case of Ezra Pound*, p. x.
10. Cornell, *The Trial of Ezra Pound*, p. 66.
11. *Ibid.*, 67.
12. Norman, *Ezra Pound*, p. 442.
13. Cornell, *The Trial of Ezra Pound*, pp. 110–11.
14. *Ibid.*
15. Reck, *Ezra Pound: A Close-Up*, p. 84.
16. Norman, *Ezra Pound*, p. 440.

17. Eustace Mullins, *This Difficult Individual, Ezra Pound* (New York: Fleet, 1961), pp. 307–308.
18. Reck, *Ezra Pound: A Close-Up*, p. 88.
19. *Ibid.*, 90.
20. March 12, 1946, Pound archives (Beinecke).
21. March 28, 1946, Pound archives (Beinecke).
22. August 8, 1946, Pound archives (Beinecke).
23. William Carlos Williams Collection, Lockwood Memorial Library, State University of New York at Buffalo.
24. E. E. Cummings Collection, Houghton Library, Harvard University, Cambridge.
25. August 12, 1946, Pound archives (Beinecke).
26. Jackson Mac Low Private Collection, Bronx, N.Y.
27. Reck, *Ezra Pound: A Close-Up*, p. 79.
28. William Fleming, "The Melbourne Vortex," *Paideuma*, vol. 3, 3 (Winter 1974): 326.
29. Letter to the author from Sheri Martinelli, May 31, 1973.
30. Norman, *Ezra Pound*, p. 450.
31. The quotation in question and the information concerning John Kasper which follows is principally from Norman, *Ezra Pound*, pp. 452–53.
32. The quotation from Pound's circular and information concerning the Square Dollar Series and other of Kasper and Horton's publishing ventures is from Stock, *The Life of Ezra Pound*, pp. 430–31.
33. Mullins, *This Difficult Individual, Ezra Pound*, pp. 286–87.
34. Mary de Rachewiltz, *Discretions*, p. 288.
35. Kenner, *The Pound Era*, p. 588.
36. Archibald MacLeish files, Special holdings and collections, Library of Congress, Washington, D.C.
37. *Ibid.*
38. *Ibid.*
39. Berg Collection, New York Public Library.
40. Sister Bernetta Quinn, *Ezra Pound: An Introduction to the Poetry*, p. 149.

3.

1. MacLeish files, Library of Congress.
2. In 1941, having been a German prisoner of war, the English-born P. G. Wodehouse agreed to do five broadcasts for the Columbia Broadcasting System in Berlin. Believing that the broadcasts were intended solely for the United States and that this was a time when humor was needed, he made light of his experiences in the internment camps. The Nazis recorded the talks and then exploited them heavily, beaming them to Britain, where it was immediately assumed that Mr. Wodehouse had become a collaborator. The reaction was violent, but, in December 1944, Anthony Eden, then Foreign Secretary, exonerated Mr. Wodehouse completely in a speech before Parliament and said that there was "no question of a trial and no question of a charge." On January 1, 1975, Wodehouse was named Knight Commander of the Order of the British Empire (K.B.E.) by the Queen of England.
3. MacLeish files, Library of Congress.
4. Material concerning efforts to free Pound cited in this and following passages is contained in Stock, *The Life of Ezra Pound*, pp. 437–39.
5. *Ibid.*, 442.
6. Norman, *The Case of Ezra Pound*, p. x.
7. Seiber Report, Library of Congress, p. 1.

8. Norman, *The Case of Ezra Pound*, p. 189.
9. *Ibid.*
10. Meacham, *The Caged Panther*, p. 116.
11. MacLeish files, Library of Congress.
12. Meacham, *The Caged Panther*, pp. 117–18.
13. *Ibid.*, 118–19.
14. Thompson, *Selected Letters of Robert Frost*, p. 563.
15. *Ibid.*, 569.
16. *Ibid.*, 570–71.
17. Meacham, *The Caged Panther*, p. 124.
18. Telephone interview with Sherman Adams, February 13, 1973.
19. Meacham, *The Caged Panther*, p. 124.
20. Norman, *The Case of Ezra Pound*, pp. 190–91.
21. *Ibid.*, 191.
22. *Ibid.*, 199.
23. Meacham, *The Caged Panther*, p. 132.
24. Reck, *Ezra Pound: A Close-Up*, p. 134.
25. Meacham, *The Caged Panther*, p. 113.

PARADISE (1958–1972)

1.

1. Kenner, "The Magic of Place: Ezra Pound," p. 9, addresses itself to "hallowed shades," Italian cities and their ghosts, *virtù*, as well as divine visions. Dante's tomb and Pietro Lombardo's mermaids are dealt with by Kenner in *The Pound Era*, p. 342.
2. ———, *The Pound Era*, p. 536.
3. ———, "The Magic of Place: Ezra Pound," p. 5.
4. *Ibid.*
5. Letter to John Sullivan (June 18, 1959), Humanities Research Center, University of Texas, Austin.
6. Stock, *The Life of Ezra Pound*, p. 450.
7. Norman, *Ezra Pound*, p. 462.
8. *Ibid.*
9. Meacham, *The Caged Panther*, p. 166.
10. MacLeish files, Library of Congress: re "Committee for Ezra Pound"; see Stock, *The Life of Ezra Pound*, p. 454.
11. Information contained in this paragraph appears in Norman, *Ezra Pound*, p. 464; Meacham, *The Caged Panther*, p. 182; and Kenner, *The Pound Era*, p. 547.
12. Stock, *The Life of Ezra Pound*, p. 454.
13. December 28, 1958, Humanities Research Center.
14. September 5, 1959, Archibald MacLeish file, Library of Congress.
15. Meacham, *The Caged Panther*, p. 173.
16. "Hommage à Ionesco," *Rhinozeros* Munich [I] (1960): 12–13.
17. This book, based on Eliot's Page-Barbour Foundation lectures at the University of Virginia, 1932, was issued in one edition only, with printings in both London and New York (*After Strange Gods: A Primer of Modern Heresy*, New York: Harcourt, Brace, 1934). His strictures on theology ("The society that we desire . . . reasons of race and religion combine to make any large number of free-thinking Jews undesirable") started a hue and cry of "anti-Semitism!" which has never been stilled. Eliot's detractors have cited

"Burbank with a Baedeker: Bleistein with a Cigar" ("The rats are underneath the piles./The jew is underneath the lot.") and other poems as added fuel for their fire.

18. MacLeish summed up his reactions to the immediate outcome of the case in a letter to Ernest Hemingway (September 30, 1958); the letter is part of the Ernest Hemingway Collection in the possession of Carlos Baker, Princeton University, Princeton, N.J.:

"Someday we ought to catch up on the Ez business. It still has me puzzled. Last January I shifted from the Attorney General to the State Department and talked to Chris Herter who agreed to intervene (which he did) but who told me that one thing was certain: Ez couldn't go back to Italy. So he did. I think Frost gets a large part of the credit. The old boy despised Ez for personal reasons but once he got started nothing could stop him and I think Rogers finally gave up out of sheer exhaustion. I haven't seen Frost since. Anyway, as you know, Ez hasn't changed none. If anything his letters are more abusive than previous which was plenty."

19. Meacham, *The Caged Panther*, p. 183.
20. MacLeish files, Library of Congress.
21. Harry Meacham Papers, Alderman Library, University of Virginia, Charlottesville.
22. February 1960, Carl Gatter Collection, Philadelphia Free Library, Philadelphia.

2.

1. Davenport, "Ezra Pound: 1885–1972," p. 195.
2. *Ibid.*, 190.
3. Meacham, *The Caged Panther*, p. 192.
4. *Ibid.*, 189.
5. *Ibid.*, 190.
6. Kenner, *The Pound Era*, p. 560.
7. ———, "E.P. Remembered," *Paideuma*, vol. 2, 3 (Winter 1973): 490.
8. Hugh Kenner ponders Pound pondering his past in *The Pound Era*, p. 556.
9. Reck, *Ezra Pound: A Close-Up*, p. 142.
10. Eliot's ashes and the expiration of Pound's generation are the substance of Kenner's *The Pound Era*, p. 551; Yeats's centenary is taken up on p. 553.

3.

1. Stock, *The Life of Ezra Pound*, p. 457.
2. Quotations in this section are taken from Allen Ginsberg's "Encounters with Ezra Pound," *City Lights Anthology* (1974): 9–21.
3. My chief source for information concerning these aspects of the 1968 New York expedition is Noel Stock, *The Life of Ezra Pound*, pp. 458–60.
4. Letter from Guy Davenport to the author, March 5, 1973.
5. Letter from Julian Beck to the author, October 3, 1973.
6. D.P., as she was known affectionately to her friends, passed away December 8, 1973, thirteen months after her husband's death.
7. Meacham Papers, Alderman Library.
8. *Ibid.*
9. *Ibid.*
10. *Ibid.*
11. Kenner, *The Pound Era*, p. 560.
12. Reck, *Ezra Pound: A Close-Up*, p. 144.

CODA: TO THE END (1971–1972)

1. Of these members, Lillian Hellman did not vote, and Lewis Mumford was opposed to Pound's nomination, writing Edel: "Why not give it to Henry Miller?"
2. The Emerson-Thoreau committee meeting at which Pound was nominated was held on January 18, 1972. The council meeting at which the nomination was rejected took place April 19, 1972. The members present at the second and decisive meeting were: Thomas Adams, David Apter, Daniel Bell, Konrad Bloch, Nicolaas Bloembergen, Morton Bloomfield, Harvey Brooks, Bernard Davis, Richard Douglas, Jacob Fine, Paul Freund, Eli Goldston, Stephen Graubard, William Jencks, Wassily Leontief, Jean Mayer, Agnes Mongan, Talcott Parsons, Alexander Rich, Walter O. Roberts, Cyril Smith, Krister Stendahl, Arthur Sutherland, and Walter Whitehill. Of the approximately 2100 Fellows of the Academy, the following members resigned as a result of the controversy: Jerome Lettvin, O. B. Hardison, Brooks Atkinson, Malcolm Cowley, and Allen Tate; Hugh Kenner refused to accept election.
3. Leslie Fiedler, "Caliban or Hamlet: A Study in Literary Anthropology," published in *Unfinished Business* (New York: Stein & Day, 1972), pp. 93–103.
4. Davenport, "Ezra Pound: 1885–1972," p. 188.
5. Omar Pound, accompanied by Peter du Sautoy, took the first available flight from London to Venice but was unable to arrive in time for the ceremonies, which were held during the morning hours; Ezra Pound's son-in-law and grandson also arrived too late from the United States; and Dorothy Pound was too old and frail to undertake the long journey from her home in England.
6. Aldo Tagliaferri, "Ezra Pound's *Jefferson and/or Mussolini,*" *Italian Quarterly,* vol. 16, 64 (Spring 1973): 115.
7. Davenport, "Ezra Pound: 1885–1972," p. 188.

AUTHOR'S NOTE

Translations of documents and letters from Italian into English in the main body of this work are by Robert Connolly and myself.

I would like to reiterate my indebtedness to the following authors from whose works I drew considerable material concerning the facts surrounding Ezra Pound's life, particularly in the "Settings" and "Paradise" sections of my book: Hugh Kenner, Harry Meacham, Charles Norman, Michael Reck, and Noel Stock.

Donald Hall's "Interview with Ezra Pound" also provided me with certain invaluable commentaries for these sections.

Additionally: the remark in "Paradise" about Pound's marriage proposal to Marcella Spann comes from a letter I received from Eva Hesse.

The note in "Coda: To the End" about d'Annunzio's discovery of the San Trovaso restaurant where Pound frequently took his meals is from Reck's *Ezra Pound: A Close-Up.* As supplement to the "Coda" I consulted the following: Cyril Connolly, *The Evening Colonnade* (New York: Harcourt, Brace, 1975); Gianfranco Ivancich, ed., *Spots and Dots: Ezra Pound in Italy* (Venice, Italy: privately printed, 1970); Alan Levy, "Ezra Pound's Voice of Silence," *The New York Times Magazine,* January 9, 1972.   —C.D.H.

Index

357

358 | INDEX